THE CITY PAROCHIAL FOUNDATION
1891–1991

The
City Parochial Foundation
1891–1991

A Trust for the Poor of London

Victor Belcher

Scolar Press

Published by
SCOLAR PRESS
Gower House
Croft Road
Aldershot
Hants GU11 3HR
England

Gower Publishing Company
Old Post Road
Brookfield
Vermont 05036
USA

British Library Cataloguing in Publication Data
Belcher, Victor
The City Parochial Foundation 1891–1991: a trust for the poor of London.
1. London (England). Charities. History
I. Title
362.58094212

ISBN 0–85967–879–2

Phototypeset by Intype, London
Printed in Great Britain at the University Press, Cambridge

Contents

Abbreviations

COS	Charity Organisation Society
CPF	City Parochial Foundation
DNB	*Dictionary of National Biography*
FWA	Family Welfare Association
HYELM	Hostels for Youthful Employees of Limited Means
GLC	Greater London Council
ILEA	Inner London Education Authority
LCC	London County Council
MBW	Metropolitan Board of Works
Minutes	Minutes of the Central Governing Body of the Foundation. The references in the Notes are to the volume and page numbers.
NACRO	National Association for the Care and Resettlement of Offenders
PP	*Parliamentary Papers*
PRO	Public Record Office
TEB	Technical Education Board
WVS	Women's Voluntary Service

Chairman's Foreword

Few who attended the inauspicious and very brief first meeting of the Trustees of the City Parochial Foundation on 21 April 1891 would have dared to anticipate the value and importance the Foundation was to assume for the poor of London during the next 100 years. Few probably were fully aware of just what had gone into setting up the Foundation. For all in any way involved or interested in the Foundation, this fascinating account provides many penetrating insights into one piece of social history and the complexity of philanthropy in operation.

All was not plain sailing. The Clerk and trustees had great difficulty in persuading the parishes to disgorge the legal documents establishing ownership of the properties which produced the money. It was some time before the Foundation was in command of all its assets. In addition, very little money was available in the early days for those who could properly be described as poor. By virtue of the recommendations of the Charity Commissioners, reinforced by the views of some early powerful trustees, the greater part of the income was assigned to the new polytechnics, which left little scope for other grant-making.

The Foundation eventually became and has since remained a significant grant-making Trust in respect both of its income and of its wider influence. This is undoubtedly a great tribute to the trustees and staff who have served in the past. They have left a fine tradition of service and of insight to those responsible for managing its affairs in the centenary year. From the outset trustees, often very busy in other walks of life, have given generously of their time and expertise, and, together with remarkable staff commitment and energy, have ensured the Foundation's growth and abiding concern for the poor of London.

As the history unfolds it is clear that there were significant trustees and Clerks who played a powerful role in the determination of grant-making policy; some, notably the Clerks, influenced the wider development of social policy.

From time to time over the earlier years, the trustees have wondered whether and in what form there would continue to be a significant role for the philanthropic work of the Foundation. Were they to see the number of applications received and grants made at the end of these 100 years, all their doubts would be dispelled. They might well be surprised and saddened to see poverty, deprivation and disadvantage still so evident amid the general affluence of late twentieth-century London. They would, however, take a just pride in their management of the endowments which, despite the enormous difficulties created by the Second World War, have proved to be of such long-term value, thus enabling considerable help to be given to many thousands of people.

One of the wisest and most helpful decisions the original trustees made was to insist upon full and printed minutes of proceedings; this has clearly been a bonus for the author. Full though the minutes are and copious the supporting records, they still however leave tantalizing questions for those of us looking back on those earlier years of the Foundation. The early focus of the Foundation seemed clearly to be on the 'deserving' poor. No organization working in the field of addictions was funded for the first sixty years. In having this emphasis were the trustees simply reflecting the views of their times, or were there discussions which led to such distinct policies being adopted? Were trustees more cautious and less inclined to take risks? Were there charitable bodies who were dissuaded from applying? Did Rachel McMillan, working with the poorest children in London before the First World War, ever know of the Foundation or make approaches to it? What was the nature and extent of the voluntary sector in the first half of the twentieth century? The historian indicates answers to some of these questions, and for some we can only speculate. It is clear that as the body of trustees changes over time, so do the perceptions of need and consequently the policies adopted. The early 'capture' of the Foundation by the educational establishment and its subsequent release from this constriction shows only too well the influence of the trustees upon its corporate policies.

In 1991 we try so to manage the Foundation that its resources continue to grow. We also try to support work on behalf of the poor of London, amongst whom are included migrants and refugee groups as well as disadvantaged people from many different ethnic minority communities.

Any bi-centennial history will ask questions about our policies and priorities, and wonder about some of the paths we have taken. To be Chairman at the Foundation's first Centenary has been a great privilege. Trustees and staff alike, whilst most conscious and respectful of the legacy of our predecessors, continually strive with considerable thought and energy to adjust our philanthropy to new demands and opportunities. All is done, on the evidence since 1891, in an atmosphere that is truly friendly and enjoyable.

The challenge remains as great as ever. But so, too, is the satisfaction and privilege of serving, and above all the conviction that the poor in London benefit. For they must remain at the forefront of all we do.

John Smallwood
Chairman

Author's Preface

'The Trustees, rightly or wrongly, hide their light under a bushel. They like to do good by stealth.' These words were used by Donald Allen (later Sir Donald Allen), the long-serving Clerk of the Foundation in his evidence before the Nathan Committee on the law and practice relating to charitable trusts in 1951. There was an element of self-effacement in such a statement, but the sentiments expressed would be largely inconceivable today. Of course, even in Allen's day, the Foundation was by no means unknown in the world of philanthropy. Beveridge had referred to it in his influential *Voluntary Action*, published in 1948. Allen himself was a member of the Nathan Committee and in 1951, largely at the behest of the Committee, produced a brief history of the Foundation. It had a limited distribution, however, chiefly among those organizations which already came into contact with the Foundation in the normal course of events. David Owen's monumental and excellent *English Philanthropy 1660–1960*, published in 1965, devoted the best part of a chapter to the Foundation, but its circulation was generally confined to the academic community.

Over the past decade the Foundation's trustees have taken several steps to try to promote a greater awareness of its work, and the decision to celebrate its Centenary in a variety of ways should be seen as part of that process. It was in this spirit that the trustees asked me, as a historian who was not connected with the Foundation, to write a Centenary history which would be both a record of its activities and a critical evaluation of its effectiveness in aiding the poor of the

metropolis. Whether the work succeeds in these aims is for the reader
to judge.

This book is concerned with three main aspects of the Foundation's
history: the composition of the body of trustees charged with carrying
out the Trust which was established in 1891, and the administrative
structures which have been devised to perform that work; the management of the Foundation's endowment, which consists principally of
land and buildings; and the grants made from the income of its Central
Fund which constitutes the core of its activities. The City Church
Fund, which is the other major fund in the Foundation's charge, is
dealt with in less detail, because the trustees' role in connection with
this fund is largely a passive one; they look after its resources but
have virtually no say in how the income is spent. Therefore, no attempt
has been made to give any details of the grants which are made by
other bodies out of its income, except where the trustees have expressed
concern or raised issues of policy in connection with those grants.
Likewise, the short history of the Trust for London, which was established after the abolition of the Greater London Council as a separate
entity but with the Foundation as its trustee, is not covered, although
some of the effects of its existence on the Foundation's own work are
discussed.

The main source for this study has been the very comprehensive
minutes of the Foundation's Central Governing Body. Although called
such, they are, in fact, hardly minutes at all, but consist of detailed
reports on virtually every item of business that came before the Central
Governing Body and the committees of the Foundation, together with
a record of the decisions taken on the basis of those reports. They
constitute a model of record keeping and are for the historian a mine
of information, indeed almost an embarrassment of riches. Where
necessary the minutes have been supplemented by reference to the
files of the Foundation, and to external records, particularly those of
the Royal Commissions and Parliamentary Committees which were
either directly concerned with the establishment and subsequent work
of the Foundation or examined its activities *inter alia* as part of a more
general inquiry. All sources are cited in the Notes at the end of each
chapter.

Several people have assisted with the preparation of this history in
a number of ways. I would particularly like to acknowledge the assistance of those trustees and former trustees who have read the manuscript at various stages and have made many constructive comments,
especially John Smallwood, the Chairman, Lady Marre, the Vice-
Chairman, Dr David Avery, the Venerable George Cassidy, Professor
Gerald Manners, in large measure, and Dr Ronald Tress, who,
although no longer a trustee, has given freely of his time and made

many valuable suggestions. Members of the Foundation's staff have been most obliging in meeting my many requests for documents and other facilities. I would particularly like to single out the Clerk, Timothy Cook, who has been an ever-helpful presence in supplying information and ideas, and encouragement and exhortation. Other members of his staff who have been very helpful are Tony Price, who provided several useful comments on the chapters dealing with the estate and has assisted with the compilation of Appendix C, and Alison Harker, who made a number of observations on the later chapters dealing with grants. The former Clerk, Bryan Woods, gave much useful information and advice on numerous occasions. Of the Foundation's professional advisers, Bill Killick gave me the benefit of his vast experience and intimate knowledge of the Foundation's estate and set me right on a number of technical points, and Mark Farrer and Raymond Cooper provided many perceptive insights which went beyond the narrowly legal. I would also like to thank Professor F. M. L. Thompson for his constant encouragement and belief that the obstacles that always seem to occur when embarking on a work of this kind can be overcome. Finally, I would especially like to thank my wife and family for their patience and forbearance during the writing of this book. Without their co-operation it could never have been completed.

While acknowledging most gratefully the considerable assistance which has been given by these and other persons not specifically mentioned, I must stress that any mistakes are entirely my responsibility and that the views expressed are my own.

London
July 1991

Introduction

Charity occupied a very important place in Victorian life. A society which believed implicitly in the virtues of *laissez-faire* recognized that there were going to be those who fell by the wayside, either through accident, illness, disability or sheer bad luck, and charity existed to ensure that they were properly assisted in their distress. Conversely, however, it was not there to help those who had fallen on hard times as a result of their own improvidence or fecklessness. For them there were the harsh realities of the poor law and the rigours of the work-house test. Above all, useful and beneficent as charity could be, it was not to be allowed to threaten the social order by providing sustenance for a large and dangerous underclass, whose very existence was seen as a menace to the smooth running of the body politic.

These ambivalent feelings dominated late-Victorian thinking, the dilemmas they posed made all the more acute by the sheer scale of the resources that charitable bodies could command. No one has tried to quantify the funds that were available to all the charitable agencies in London in the second half of the nineteenth century, a task, indeed, that may not be possible, but there have been attempts to provide some rough estimates. The 1861 edition of Sampson Low's *The Charities of London* referred to 640 charitable institutions operating in the metropolis with an aggregate income of £2.5 million, but there were many that he left out and his figure was undoubtedly on the low side. Nevertheless, as a base figure it is indicative. (To put this figure into perspective, it should be recalled that £2.5 million in 1861 is very approximately equivalent to £100 million in 1990.) Some estimates put

1

the sum as high as £7 million, but perhaps more striking than the actual figures are comparisons with other forms of expenditure. The amount that was spent on charity in London was certainly very much higher than the official expenditure on poor relief, and, as *The Times* pointed out in 1885, was higher than the revenues of the governments of Denmark, Portugal, Sweden, Switzerland, and the Persian Empire.[1]

That such an outpouring of charity was matched by need was little doubted. Although the extent of poverty in the metropolis was not to become fully apparent until the last two decades of the century, and especially after the publication from the late 1880s of the results of Charles Booth's great survey, in which he classified nearly one-third of the population as living in various degrees of poverty, there was ample evidence beforehand. The signs of distress were only too apparent, especially in certain parts of London at certain times. In the 1860s a combination of trade depression, the decline of traditional industries and severe winters created conditions in the East End which touched the conscience, and aroused the unease, of Londoners who had benefited from the prevailing economic system. As a result, they gave freely to local relief organizations, soup kitchens and the Mansion House Relief Fund which was opened at times of greatest adversity. This last came to symbolize both the liberality of those who contributed to charity and the indiscriminate manner in which that charity was distributed. There were many voices raised in warning that by failing to distinguish between the deserving and undeserving poor, those who administered such relief were contributing to the pauperization of its recipients and swelling the ranks of the dangerous substratum of the idle, casual and criminal poor.[2]

It was also in the 1860s that public attention first began to be drawn to the parochial charities of the City of London, as a result of investigations by the staff of the Charity Commission which led to statements in Parliament and discussions among charity reformers, culminating, at the end of the decade, in some strategically placed letters in *The Times*. The myriad of small trusts, well over a thousand in number, which made up the charitable endowments of the City parishes together provided a very sizeable income, which by 1865 already stood at over £65,000 (equivalent to between £2.5 million and £3 million at 1990 prices). Moreover, most of the endowments consisted of property in the City with a rapidly rising value as the City was being transformed into a vast business and commercial centre, at the same time as the remaining poor were being driven out to surrounding districts by the very same process of change.

On the one hand, reformers were genuinely determined that these charity funds, which had been intended for the poor where the poor no longer existed, should be put to the use of the poorer classes elsewhere in the metropolis. On the other hand, imbued with the philosophy of their age, they were equally worried about the possibly harmful effects of so much largesse being dispensed at the whim of parish trustees with little investigation into the real need or moral condition of the recipients. Their concern was as much with the widespread distribution of doles in money and in kind as it was with the misuse of charity fund for 'love feasts' or wine in the vestry. It is against the background of this uncomfortable duality that the origins of the City Parochial Foundation should be seen.

The story that unfolds is of the achievement of the reform of the parochial charities in spite of the innate conservatism and obstructionism of City interests. It was, indeed, the only major reform of the City that succeeded, out of the many that were attempted in the second half of the nineteenth century, and owed much to the perseverance of one man, James Bryce. But the strength of the opposition meant that some temporizing was necessary, and the City of London Parochial Charities Act of 1883 which established the Foundation, signal accomplishment as it may have been, was a less than perfect instrument.

The Charity Commissioners, who were given the task under the Act of drawing up a scheme to provide the framework for the operations of the new Foundation, were, of course, also men of their age, and a number of events which occurred while they were going about their assignment made it seem to them even more necessary to ensure that the income from the amalgamated endowments should be spent on the deserving and not the undeserving poor. In particular, they focused on the attributes of self-help and the desire for improvement which were thought to be among the most important of the characteristics which distinguished the two groups. The particular manifestation of these virtues on which they alighted as an excellent use for a substantial proportion of the available funds was technical education for the working classes on the model of the Polytechnic in Regent Street which had been founded by Quintin Hogg.

Thus, when the Foundation began its work in 1891, to the constraints of the Act of 1883 were added others imposed by the Charity Commissioners in the Central Scheme which was to govern its operations. The subsequent history of the Foundation is of an initial acceptance of those limitations by its trustees, many of whom, of course, fully shared the dominant ideas and outlook of the time, and of a conscientious attempt to carry out the objectives which had been preordained. As the endowment prospered, however, and it became possible to devote more resources to other ways of aiding the poor, so those additional activities came to assume an increasing importance, and the restrictions on the trustees' discretion came to seem irksome.

This was particularly the case in the 1930s, when the economic malaise once more heightened the awareness of the grinding burden of poverty.

Following the devastating interruption of the Second World War, the struggle to obtain relatively unfettered freedom of action was resumed, and this objective was at last achieved in the 1960s, although by then such had been the rise in the Foundation's income and the effects of inflation that the mandatory demands on its funds had become little more than symbolic. Those who ran the Foundation's affairs at the time were naturally no more free of the predilections of their age than their late-Victorian predecessors had been, and the priorities they chose reflected current preoccupations. It is, for instance, instructive to note how very gradual was the breakdown of the concept that a distinction should be drawn between the deserving and undeserving poor. The ways in which priorities changed is, perhaps, one of the more revealing aspects of the history of the Foundation's grant-making in more recent decades.

In this, as in other matters, of course, the Foundation did not operate in a vacuum. Its policies were formulated and decisions were taken against the background of changes in the concepts of welfare and developments in social policy. Conceived at a time when the regimen of the poor law may well have been at its harshest, the Foundation's work has spanned the periods of Liberal social reforms up to the First World War; the subsequent retrenchment and depression, when the state was forced to intervene in further areas of social welfare; the emergence after the Second World War of the Welfare State and its seemingly inevitable upward and onward progression, when questions were being asked whether there was any longer a significant place for charity and voluntary action; and the sudden arrest of that progress and, some would say, the retreat from the high point of public welfare provision. The history of the Foundation has to be seen in the general context of these developments which had such a profound influence on its activities. And, finally, over the whole period of a hundred years, the question that has constantly to be borne in mind is how far did the Foundation succeed in its appointed task of benefiting 'the poorer inhabitants of the Metropolis'?

NOTES

1. *The Times*, 9 Jan. 1885, 9: Kathleen Woodroofe, *From Charity to Social Work in England and the United States* (1962), 23, 26–7: David Owen, *English Philanthropy 1660–1960* (1965), 169–70, 469, 476–8: Gareth Stedman Jones, *Outcast London: A Study of the Relationship between Classes in Victorian Society* (1984 edn.), 244–5.
2. Woodroofe, op. cit., 6–14: Jones, op. cit., 241–61: M. E. Rose, 'The Crisis of Poor Relief in England, 1860–1890' in *The Emergence of the Welfare State in Britain and Germany 1850–1950*, ed. W. J. Mommsen (1981), 50–70.

Part I
The origins of the Foundation

1 The agitation for reform

The small parish of St Mildred, Bread Street, lay a short distance to the south-east of St Paul's Cathedral. In the mid-1860s its income from various endowed charities amounted to about £800 per annum. Accounts submitted to the Charity Commissioners which covered the financial years 1866–7 and 1867–8 show that out of a total of some £1,600 over the two years, £189 was spent on the salaries of the vestry clerk, parish clerk, organist and pew opener, £35 on clothing for the church's choristers, £60 on donations to the curate, £518 in payment of the poor rate assessed on the parish by the City of London Union, and no less than £241 on 'Breakfast and dinner on Ascension-day, audit dinner and refreshment after vestries and visiting parish estates and cab hire'. Donations to the ward school amounted to £21 and gifts to the poor only £81, or 5 per cent of the charitable income. Even this degree of beneficence created difficulties, for by that date there were only two inhabited houses in the whole parish, the remaining area being largely taken up with offices and warehouses, and no resident poor. So attempts had to be made to seek out poor persons elsewhere who had had some connection with the parish in the past. It is small wonder that so much of the surplus seems to have been swallowed up in administrative expenses.[1]

This information, which was cited as an example of the state of affairs of many parishes within the ancient square mile of the City of London, was contained in a long letter to *The Times* in June 1869 signed 'Civis'. The identity of 'Civis' is unknown, but the information at least may have been provided by Thomas Hare, one of the inspec-

9

tors of charities, who would certainly have been in a position to know all the facts. In 1853 Hare had been appointed as one of its first inspectors by the new permanent Board of Charity Commissioners established under the Charitable Trusts Act of that year. He was then a 47-year-old barrister, whose 'Reports in Chancery' were acknowledged as an essential part of every barrister's library. In later life he was to become best known as the author of a system of proportional representation, but his immediate task as an inspector for the Charity Commission was to investigate the myriad of parochial charities in the City of London. This he did with the 'untiring industry and clearness of intellectual vision' which impressed all those who came into contact with him. In 1872 he was appointed an assistant commissioner with a seat on the Board, a post he held until his retirement in 1887.[2]

Hare's detailed reports on the parochial charities were submitted to the Board between 1854 and 1860. When they were eventually published as an appendix to the report of the Royal Commission on the City Parochial Charities in 1880, together with some additional reports compiled by Hare himself to bring matters up to date, they occupied over 350 pages of small print.[3] They provided the essential bedrock of fact to back up the reformers' claims. From the start, however, Hare, who was a keen proponent of the reform of both charity administration and charity law, used his reports as a vehicle for impressing on the Board the unsatisfactory nature of the situation which he found in many parishes and the need for fundamental change. As early as May 1856 he wrote in his report on one parish: 'It is impossible, however, not to observe that so great a change has taken place in the population of these and other City parishes that the original objects and need of the endowments have in many cases wholly ceased, and that the application of the City charities generally ought in justice to be the subject of an extensive legislative revision.'[4] In reporting at the same time on another parish (that of St Mildred, Bread Street, which was later to face public exposure) he thought that 'it might be necessary for the Board to consider whether there are any means of restraining such an improper application of the fund, or whether the trustees might be regarded as irresponsible'.[5]

When he had finished his main body of reports in 1860 Hare submitted some 'Observations' to the Board. In these he remarked on the extensive social and economic change taking place in the City as it became less a place of residence and more a district of offices and warehouses, which 'drives the poorer classes to distances more and more remote or compresses them within narrow and unwholesome spaces'. He thought that as a matter of principle 'charitable endowments are the patrimony of the poor and necessitous, and that, in applying them for their benefit, every succeeding generation must deal with the subject . . . according to the best of its knowledge and judgement' and that the situation called for 'the introduction of principles of administration which have not hitherto been applied, if these charitable estates are to be rendered of any real benefit to the poorer classes.' He advocated parliamentary action to establish a Board for the consolidated management of the charity estates and the use of the proceeds for better housing for the poor. He ended with a rhapsodical vision of a new era of civic improvement in which the use of the parochial charities for this purpose would act as a stimulus for private developers to follow suit.[6]

Hare's official reports and comments were, of course, confidential to the Charity Commission, but his was a profound influence behind the scenes. He spoke publicly on the need for the reform of charity law and administration, especially at meetings of the Social Science Association (or, to give its full name, the National Association for the Promotion of Social Science), which had been founded in 1857 and which became a forum for the exchange of views of those concerned with charity reform.[7] The Charity Commissioners themselves, constrained by inadequate powers under the existing legislation, could, or would, do little. Occasionally they were asked to devise schemes for individual charities or parishes, but it was a long and cumbersome process, in which the agreement of existing trustees had to be obtained. Finally, doubtless prompted by their indefatigable inspector, the Commissioners gave the mildest of hints that all was not well in their annual report for 1863. They referred to the increase in value of certain endowments, especially in and around London, 'resulting in some instances, especially in charities applicable within the City of London, in a disproportion of the endowments to the purposes or objects of the foundations, which may well deserve at no distant period the interposition of the legislature to regulate their application.'[8]

The Commissioners cited as evidence the digest of charities in London and Westminster which they had been able to prepare, largely on the basis of Hare's investigations, and received valuable support in 1865 when Bishop Tait (then Bishop of London, later Archbishop of Canterbury, and one of the most respected churchmen of the century) moved in the House of Lords for the publication of the digest. He called the attention of the House to the increase in funds at the same time as the population was decreasing, and said that large amounts of money were not being put to proper use. He supported a proposal that parochial funds should be used for the promotion of middle-class education, and suggested that the area which benefited from the charities should be extended over the whole of the metropolis. 'Certainly,' he said, 'the present state of things was anomalous.'[9] The Bishop's intervention was significant because of his authority within the Established Church. Thereafter it can be said that, in general, the clergy were in favour of reform, even if they frequently found themselves at loggerheads with their own vestrymen over the matter.

One of the movements to which the Bishop had alluded had as its objective the establishment of schools for the children of the middle class where they could obtain practical training for jobs in industry and commerce. A leading figure in this early manifestation of the technical education movement was the Reverend William Rogers, rector of St Botolph, Bishopsgate, who was later to be both a member of the Royal Commission on the parochial charities and one of the first trustees of the City Parochial Foundation. As Rogers himself described it, 'my longing eyes were fixed on the parochial charities of the City. . . . Why, with the consent of those who administered them, should they not be turned to wiser and worthier ends, and, as one, what better direction could be indicated than the promotion of education.' He called a meeting at the Mansion House late in 1865 but 'the trustees of the parochial charities were conspicuous by their absence'. 'We very soon found that nothing was to be reckoned upon from the trustees of the parochial charities,' he rather dolefully added, and the Charity Commissioners were powerless to divert funds. Nevertheless, he persisted and the Corporation for Middle Class Education, as his movement became, did succeed in founding a school. He even managed to obtain donations from two City parishes, but this was a rare exception to the general rule.[10]

Armed with the support of the Bishop of London the Commissioners made a bolder pronouncement in their report for 1865. 'The Digest of the parochial charities of the city of London,' they averred, 'exhibits the great disproportion which the endowments have in many cases acquired to the objects of their foundation, and the results of our extended inquiry, which has been prosecuted by our inspectors, under our direction, into the circumstances of these charities has been to show that disproportion only in stronger relief.' They reiterated that the funds which were not serving their original objects needed reapportionment and implied that the only effective way to do this was through the passage of new legislation in Parliament.[11] This sense of purpose was assisted by the appointment of Arthur Hobhouse (later knighted and eventually ennobled as Lord Hobhouse) as a Charity Commissioner in 1866. Hobhouse, a barrister with an astute legal brain and liberal instincts, was a keen proponent of reform and contributed frequently to meetings of the Social Science Association. Although he moved on from the Charity Commission in 1869 when he became one of the first Commissioners to be appointed under the Endowed Schools Act of that year, he retained a close interest and involvement in all matters concerning charities and was an influential figure when reform of the parochial charity system finally became a practical possibility.[12]

The active vestrymen of the parishes and the trustees of the charities, usually one and the same persons, were by now girding themselves for battle, but as yet the impulse for reform was confined to a small circle. A major breakthrough came in June 1869, however, when *The Times* printed a long letter on the subject from Sir Charles Trevelyan and accompanied it with a leading article.[13] Trevelyan, who was the father of the historian Sir George Otto Trevelyan and grandfather of George Macaulay Trevelyan, had pursued a distinguished but not uncontroversial career in the home and Indian civil service. In the former he was instrumental in introducing the system of competitive public examinations for entrants, and in the latter he rose to be Governor of Madras.[14] On his return to England from India in 1865 he had enthusiastically adopted a number of good causes, of which charity reform was one. He had addressed meetings of the Social Science Association and was one of the founders, in 1869, of the Charity Organisation Society (now the Family Welfare Association), which attempted to bring order out of the chaos of conflicting charitable agencies and charity jurisdictions.[15]

In his letter to *The Times* Trevelyan remarked on the vast changes taking place in the City of London as it was being 'converted into an exchange or counting-house for the metropolis'. As the poor were being driven out to surrounding districts, so the income of charities had increased through the rise in property values. He asked how the founders of the charities might react if they had the opportunity to inquire how their intentions had been fulfilled. 'Then would come out the shameful, the almost incredible fact that the City parochial charities, which were consecrated to the poor, have in the great majority of cases been misappropriated to the benefit of the rich.' He cited a number of the worst abuses and referred to the scheme of the Reverend William Rogers for using charitable funds for educational purposes, an application which under certain circumstances was specifically allowed for charities, where their original objectives had failed, in W. E. Forster's Endowed Schools Act. 'But any mode of getting rid of these charitable funds', he thundered, 'is better than the pervading demoralization of the sinecure rector, the full blown church officials, and the show paupers at 60*l.* a year each.' *The Times* praised Trevelyan for drawing attention to the abuses of the City parochial charities, which 'furnish a striking instance of the evil that results from adherence to the letter of Founders' wills on the one hand, and disregard of their spirit on the other'. It castigated Parliament for not having acted already and supported the idea of using surplus funds for the purposes of education.

Later in the same month *The Times* published the letter from 'Civis' referred to above, and early in 1870 it provided space for two more letters from Trevelyan, the first of which it once again backed up with a leading article. Trevelyan's views, which he developed further in these letters, were later expounded in depth in an address to the Social Science Association in 1871 which was printed as a pamphlet.[16] He considered the parochial system to be now quite moribund. 'It has died of atrophy. The corpse is still fair to outward view, but the worms are busy within.' Under the doctrine of *cy près* once the original object of a charity had 'failed' the funds could be applied to analogous uses, and as it was becoming increasingly difficult to use charity income in accordance with the wishes of the founders he advocated a much more widespread application of this doctrine. He stressed particularly the claims of education, especially technical education in which London was considered to be deficient in comparison with many continental cities. More controversially, he proposed that the various charity estates should be sold to the highest bidders and the proceeds invested in government stock. In view of the rise then taking place in the value of property in the City, which was one of the major factors making reform seem so pressing, this was a remarkably short-sighted recommendation. But, using arguments which have a familiar ring today, Trevelyan opposed all forms of corporate ownership and thought that property should remain in private hands. By selling off the charity estates, he reasoned, the number of small proprietors would be increased and property ownership would be extended down the social scale. *The Times* declared that 'the parochial condition of the City of London amounted to a national scandal which ought no longer to be endured' and approved of the sale of charity estates.

The eager espousal of Sir Charles Trevelyan's cause by *The Times* may not have been entirely related to the merits of his case. The newspaper had become a bitter critic of the outmoded and anachronistic government of the City of London and doubtless saw the exposure of the manifest abuses of the parochial charities as yet another stick with which to beat the beleaguered City Corporation.[17] The issue of the City's parochial charities touched on a number of wider concerns in the mid-Victorian period, of which the state of local government in the metropolis was one. Municipal reform was one of the clarion calls of the age and the exclusion of London from the Municipal Corporations Act of 1835 only made the case for imposing some order on the multitude of local jurisdictions seem more pressing. The City of London with its time-hallowed institutions of the Court of Aldermen, Court of Common Council and Court of Common Hall, its elaborate ritual, its richly endowed livery companies, and its privileges and customs protected by numerous charters of venerable antiquity, was

the single greatest obstacle to the rationalization of London government. A Royal Commission was appointed in 1853 to inquire into the
affairs of the Corporation and for a dozen years or so from 1856 bills
to reform the Corporation were introduced in practically every session
of Parliament. All were defeated or withdrawn. The City had a most
effective parliamentary bill agency, and its merchants and tradesmen
used all their power and influence, and the lavish wining and dining
which they had brought to a fine art (symbolized by the famed turtle
soup), to win over enough supporters to thwart their opponents at
every turn.[18] As W. A. Robson put it with characteristic understate-
ment, 'It is not necessary to suggest that these festive occasions were
deliberately devised to curry favour in high places in order to appreciate the subtle result of their cumulative effect over a very long span
of years.' Robson, one of the great scholars of London local government, was a trenchant critic of the City Corporation, but even he had
to admit to a grudging admiration of its achievement in resisting
change. 'The record of the City Corporation in delaying, obstructing
or defeating legislation aimed at the reform of London government
between 1835 and 1880', he wrote, 'was one of unbroken success from
their point of view.'[19]

In this light, the fact that it took until the last decade of the century
for Hare's official harrying and Trevelyan's public anger to produce
any practical results is not surprising. What is more remarkable is
that a radical reorganization of the City parochial charities proved
possible at all. It might be presumed that giving up charitable endowments which they were finding it increasingly difficult to put to any
useful purpose would have been a small sacrifice for the City's rulers
to make, but the vestrymen and charity trustees were the selfsame
merchants and tradesmen, and their lawyers, who formed the core of
the City's resistance to change. They clung tenaciously to their privileges and property of all kinds with the attitude that what the City
had been given, the City would retain.

Of all its units of administration the City's parochial structure
seemed the most archaic and irrelevant to the realities of nineteenth-
century life. There was even some doubt about how many parishes
there were within the ancient square mile. The Royal Commission on
the parochial charities seemed uncertain whether the number was 108,
109 or 110,[20] and the City Parochial Charities Act listed 112. In fact,
there was some reason for this confusion as a few minor amalgamations
were taking place at about this time, but the basic structure – and
numbers – had remained virtually unchanged for some seven centuries.
William Fitzstephen, writing in about 1180, said that there were 126
parish churches in a slightly wider area, and it now seems clear that
the network of small parishes dated back to at least the mid thirteenth

century and probably to the end of the twelfth.[21] The phenomenon of such a profusion of parishes was unique in western Europe, the result of a desire to worship in small congregations; 'the tiny parish church was almost as intimate as the house church of the Roman Empire in times of persecution'.[22] It was also a reflection of the wealth of London in the eleventh and twelfth centuries, at a time when it was normal and natural to dedicate much of that wealth to church building and other religious uses. So established did this parish structure become that it survived the Great Fire of London in 1666 when the majority of the medieval churches were destroyed and a large number of them were never rebuilt. Thus, by the nineteenth century the situation whereby a number of parishes had united for ecclesiastical purposes but remained separate for civil (and charitable) functions made an already outdated system seem even more absurd.

Nearly all of these parishes, from the tiniest to the moderately large ones on the City's outskirts, had a number of charitable endowments. Hare's reports record some 1,400 individual charities spread over 106 parishes; in one parish alone, St Sepulchre, there were over a hundred, and in another, St Giles, Cripplegate (the most populous of all the parishes), 83.[23] Many of the charities were of considerable antiquity, a large number having been founded in the Tudor and early Stuart period when a combination of piety, fear, habit, the wish for social esteem, social responsibility and just plain altruism led to an almost prodigal display of liberality on the part of the merchant elite of London. W. K. Jordan has calculated that in the period 1480 to 1660 the 'almost incomprehensibly large total' of £1,889,000 was given in charitable benefactions in London and Middlesex, of which nearly 80 per cent was provided by residents of the City.[24] Moreover, the great bulk of this wealth, some 82 per cent, was invested as endowments, the income from which was to be available for specified uses in perpetuity. In Jordan's words, 'The great endowments vested by these men were most prudently arranged, their trusts were shrewdly invested by knowledgeable and responsible feoffees, and they were strategically disposed in such wise as to accomplish the purposes on which the donors had long reflected.'[25] In the light of the subsequent debate over the objects to which the charities should be put, it is interesting to note the results of his careful study of those original purposes. One-third of the charitable funds were invested for poor relief in one form or another, and a further 13 per cent in benefactions which assisted the poor, such as the founding of almshouses. Nearly 30 per cent, however, was given for education by the founding of grammar schools, the expansion of universities or the provision of fellowships and scholarships. 'These merchants believed in the virtues of education with an almost fanatical intensity, for a variety of reasons to which they gave eloquent testimony in the phrasing of their great bequests.' Less than 20 per cent, however, was dedicated to religious purposes, of which about half was for church-building. One further comment of Jordan's is perhaps worth repeating. In noting that most of the large donors had the needs of the whole city in mind, he added that 'the most impressive fact about London donors of our period is that they were in no sense parochial.'[26]

Some of the more bizarre purposes of charities cited by the reformers suggest that not all the original donors had bestowed the careful thought on their benefactions that Jordan suggests, but, in any case, it was inevitable that many of the objects of centuries ago would now be quite unrealizable. At the same time the value of the charities was rising at a prodigious rate. Already in 1865 the returns showed their annual income, at about £65,000, to be double the admittedly inaccurate returns of forty years earlier. By 1876 the figure had risen to just about £100,000 and showed every sign of continuing to increase.[27] The same factors which led to this rise in income, however, were making it increasingly difficult to fulfil the objects of the charities' founders, for the City was undergoing a vast physical and social transformation which caused property values to soar as it drove many erstwhile residents, including the remaining poor, to surrounding parts of the metropolis.

In 1851 the population of the City of London reached a peak (since the first official census of 1801) of over 131,000. By 1861 it had declined to 114,000, in 1871 to 76,000, in 1881 to 50,000, and by the end of the century to 27,000.[28] The exodus which lay behind these statistics was the result of a huge programme of rebuilding and adaptation which had as profound an effect on the appearance of the City as it did on the lives of its inhabitants. The architectural historian, Sir John Summerson, has said that in the 1860s 'London was more excavated, more cut about, more rebuilt and more extended than at any time in its previous history.'[29] This was indeed the decade of the greatest demographic change, when the City lost a third of its population, but the process had begun much earlier and, ironically, was certainly underway at the time when its highest population was recorded, in 1851. As insurance company headquarters, banks, office buildings and warehouses proliferated, so residential buildings were demolished or converted. On top of this, huge public buildings like the General Post Office swallowed up whole quarters, while a series of 'improvements' in the form of new thoroughfares and street widenings cleared up pockets of low-rent housing, and the extension of railways to new termini within the City led to wholesale demolitions in their path.[30] As development companies bought up sites, rents rose and those lower income earners whose homes had not already been destroyed were forced to leave. They migrated to the East End or south of the Thames, or, frequently, to the nearby areas of Clerkenwell or Finsbury, where ramshackle additions to tenement buildings or new structures in courts and open spaces exacerbated already overcrowded conditions, and created the festering slums which were eventually to so disturb the Victorian conscience and lead to the appointment of the Royal Commission on the Housing of the Working Classes in 1884.

There was an innate selfishness in the City's attitude to these changes, as it steadfastly refused to acknowledge that it was becoming an island of burgeoning wealth surrounded by the poor and dispossessed, many of whom had been pushed out of its own bounds and for whom it no longer accepted any responsibility. It was the sharpness of this contrast, growing almost by the day, which eventually became irrefutable and made real reform in this one small area more or less inevitable.

The dramatic transformation of the City from a place of work and residence to the scene more familiar at the present time, full of bustle and activity by day and practically deserted by night, was the single most important factor behind the movement for the reform of the parochial charities. The recalcitrance of most of the charities' trustees in refusing to recognize that their obligations extended beyond the narrowly parochial gave added urgency to the reformers' endeavours. Also present, however, was that other current of concern which lay behind the Victorian impulse for reform, namely, the belief that the indiscriminate relief of poverty could be positively harmful, and that a clear distinction should be drawn between the deserving and undeserving poor. In so far as the parochial trustees in their sometimes desperate search for recipients of the funds at their disposal did not inquire too closely whether there was real need, they were thought to be countenancing abuses of the system of charity. Such feelings inevitably had their effect on the kind of proposals that were put forward for the alternative use of the charity funds.

The attempt to co-ordinate the activities of the various bodies giving charitable relief, which lay behind the foundation of the Charity Organisation Society, was in large part motivated by the desire that assistance should be confined to the deserving.[31] Sir Charles Trevelyan was closely involved with the COS and these ideas played some part in his thinking, but they were a more dominant element in the reasoning of his brother-in-law, Andrew Johnston, the Liberal MP for South Essex, whom Trevelyan enlisted in aid of his cause.[32] Johnston promoted a bill in Parliament early in 1870 at the height of the public attention caused by his more famous relative's letters to *The Times*. The bill 'to provide for the better arrangement of Parishes within the ancient Walls of the City of London, and for the better Management of the Parochial Charities and Trust Funds' was essentially Trevelyan's own and contained some of the features which were later adopted in subsequent legislation. It made the mistake, however, of trying to do two things at once – to rearrange the parish structure and reduce the number of churches, and to resolve the problem of how best to utilize the parochial charities. It provided for the establishment of an administrative Royal Commission combining the powers of the Ecclesiastical and Charity Commissions. Ecclesiastical and charitable endowments were to be vested in the Commission which had power to sell them and, after compensation of existing interests, invest the proceeds in the public funds. The investments were to be classified as 'The City of London Churches Fund' and 'The City of London Charitable Trusts Fund', and the Commission was to prepare and lay before Parliament schemes for the application of the funds. The City was to be re-apportioned into fewer parishes and the surplus of the churches' fund was to be used for the erection of new churches or the better endowment of existing ones elsewhere in the metropolis. Surplus charitable funds were to be devoted 'to the extension and improvement of education within the metropolis, and to the promotion, by such means as the Commissioners may judge best, of the well being of the poorer inhabitants of the metropolis'.[33]

As soon as the bill was published alarm bells sounded in the City. A meeting of the clergy at Sion College addressed by Trevelyan and Johnston was generally receptive to the proposals, but in this as in so many other things the clergy did not carry their vestrymen with them.[34] There were mutterings of secularization of the church and 'revolutionary' tendencies. The City's efficient parliamentary machine clicked into gear and when the bill was introduced into the House of Commons in March 1870 it was adjudged to be a private bill, sent to the examiners of petitions for private bills and disappeared without trace. Johnston had no chance to even speak on the bill. Later, at the meeting of the Social Science Association addressed by Trevelyan, he rather wistfully stated that he now favoured separating the ecclesiastical from the lay charities and concentrating on the latter because he despaired of any real reform of the former.[35]

Johnston did speak twice in the House of Commons on charity matters in 1870 and 1871 and took the opportunity to draw attention to the state of affairs in the City, where, he declared, 'the waste, improvidence, and misappropriation which had been discovered were such as this House would hardly believe.'[36] On the second occasion he moved a resolution opposing the exemption of endowed charities from income tax on the grounds that these charities were subject to so many abuses that they did positive harm. In the City, charity funds were spent 'in dinners, in relief of rates (in other words, into the pockets of the rich merchants), and in an elaborate system of pauperizing'.[37] By the last he meant the indiscriminate distribution of doles, which he regarded as a more heinous offence than the appropriation of funds for audit dinners or vestry entertainments.

The ease with which their parliamentary initiative had been stifled set back the reformers' cause. Hobhouse remarked that up to that point he had thought that they had won the argument and merely needed to devise the machinery of reform, but 'the events of the last few months had convinced him that they were still in the missionary stage of the contest'.[38] It has been said of the 1870s that they 'were not fruitful years for metropolitan municipal reform'.[39] In the early part of the decade the Liberals were in power, but Gladstone had many pressing problems to deal with, and local London issues were not given a high priority. The return of the Conservatives in 1874 promised a longer respite for the Corporation.

The issue was not allowed to fade from public view, however. A popular novelist, William Gilbert, published two books attacking the City in 1873 and 1877,[40] in which he dwelt at length on the abuses of the parochial charities. He referred to Trevelyan's letters and *The Times* leaders, which he regarded as 'the proximate cause of the movement which has taken root'.[41] Of more consequence was Joseph Firth's weighty tome on *Municipal London* which appeared in 1876.[42] Firth, who was becoming the acknowledged leader of the municipal radicals, only touched on the parochial charities in his wide-ranging analysis of the government of the City and its ills, but he gave the basic statistics and cited Trevelyan's letters.[43]

When the preparation of another return of the charities' income in 1876 showed that this had increased by 50 per cent in a little over a decade, the Charity Commissioners themselves returned to the fray. Their annual report for 1876, which was published early in 1877, spelt out the catalogue of abuses more clearly than before and gave as an example one (unnamed) parish where the charities brought in £800 per annum, but the population only numbered 46, of whom but four or five slept in the parish and none was poor. (This parish was, in fact, the selfsame St Mildred, Bread Street, whose trustees must have been growing thoroughly weary of such a constant battering.) The report pointed out that it would be a cumbersome and time-consuming process for the Commissioners to apply schemes as each locality had to be treated separately, and they urged Parliament to apply a solution.[44]

In April 1877 the Hon. John Charles Dundas, a Liberal MP who had not previously been noted for his interest in London matters, drew the attention of Disraeli's Home Secretary, R. A. Cross, to this paragraph of the report and asked whether the government would initiate an inquiry or legislation. Cross merely replied that he was in communication with the Commissioners.[45] Three weeks later Henry Fawcett, MP for Hackney, whose constituency would almost certainly stand to gain from a widening of the area to which the charities could be applied, asked Cross what steps he was going to take. Cross was uncertain but 'it was quite clear that matters could not be left as they now were'.[46] Fawcett returned to the attack in July but Cross prevaricated, stating that he hoped to avoid legislation and would confer with the parochial authorities.[47]

Matters now had to await another parliamentary session, but in May 1878 W. H. James, Radical Liberal MP for Gateshead and a known scourge of the City Corporation,[48] moved a resolution calling on the government to introduce legislation to carry into effect the recommendations of the Commissioners' report. He spoke at length on the subject and said that he would press his motion to a division unless the government announced some positive action 'instead of putting off and temporizing with the subject'. Cross produced evidence that there was a growing demand from within the City for a Royal Commission, including from one of its MPs, and said that the government now agreed that such an inquiry should be held. On hearing this James withdrew his motion.[49]

There had indeed been a flurry of activity in the City, much of it orchestrated by Edwin Freshfield, a solicitor whose clients included Lloyd's and the Bank of England.[50] Freshfield, who was a church-warden of St Margaret's, Lothbury, and a trustee of charities there and in other parishes, was an eloquent and responsible advocate of the case for leaving control in local hands. He had been one of the few to respond to William Rogers' appeal for funds to establish a school for the children of clerks and tradesmen, devising a scheme for utilizing the considerable income of one of the charities of St Margaret's for this purpose.[51] He was also largely responsible for the texts of a series of memorials which were sent to the Home Secretary in 1878 drawing his attention to the present situation of the parochial charities whereby, 'owing to the great increase in the value of property, the altered habits of the people, and the consequent diminution in the number of residents within the City, particularly of the poorer class, a large portion of the funds of these charities cannot be applied to the purposes, by any possibility, specified by their donors.' The memorials recommended the appointment of a Royal Commission to provide a scheme or schemes for the application of the charity funds, 'provided that in all cases, so far as is practicable, the present trustees may be continued in the administration of their trusts.' Early in July Freshfield called a meeting of the churchwardens of several parishes which passed a resolution not to oppose the appointment of a Commission but calling for the income of the charities to remain in the hands of existing trustees who were to be given extended powers 'under the sanction and supervision of a fixed Commission'.[52]

As one of its first trustees, Edwin Freshfield was subsequently to give invaluable service to the City Parochial Foundation for over ten years. Although a staunch defender of the rights of the present trustees to continue to have a major say in how the charity funds were spent, he nevertheless was fully aware that a thorough revision of the parochial charity system was necessary. He was doubtless not alone in this, but from their subsequent behaviour many others probably regarded the appointment of a Commission as a convenient deflection of the pressure for reform. After all, other Commissions on the City had not been conspicuously successful in bringing about change, and one chosen by a Conservative government was not likely to have a strong radical emphasis.

Meanwhile, in Parliament throughout the summer of 1878 Henry Fawcett continued to harry Cross, and the long-awaited Royal Commission was appointed on 10 August 1878.[53]

NOTES

1. *The Times*, 30 June 1869, 11.
2. *DNB*: *The Times*, 7 May 1891, 5: *PP*, 1854, XIX, *First Report of the Charity Commissioners for England and Wales*: David Owen, *English Philanthropy 1660–1960* (1965), 203–4.
3. *PP*, 1880, XX, *Report of the Royal Commission appointed to Inquire into the Condition and Administration of the Parochial Charities in the City of London*, Appendix III, 367–734. (The Appendices of the Report were paginated separately; the page references given here and below are to the manuscript page numbers in the copy in the Official Publications Library of the British Library.)
4. Ibid., 577.
5. Ibid., 660.
6. Ibid., 371–3.
7. Owen, op. cit., 204, 321, 326–7.
8. *PP*, 1864, XVIII, *Eleventh Report of the Charity Commissioners*, 5.
9. *Hansard*, 3rd ser., CLXXX, 705–7.
10. *Reminiscences of William Rogers Rector of St Botolph Bishopsgate*, compiled by R. H. Hadden (1888), 158–70.
11. *PP*, 1866, XXIII, *Thirteenth Report of the Charity Commissioners*, 3–4.
12. L. T. Hobhouse and J. L. Hammond, *Lord Hobhouse A Memoir* (1905), 19, 52–3.
13. *The Times*, 17 June 1869, 8–9, 10.
14. *DNB*.
15. Owen, op. cit., 323: Charles Loch Mowat, *The Charity Organisation Society 1869–1913: Its Ideas and Work* (1961), 19, 45–6.
16. *The Times*, 26 Jan. 1870, 7, 9; 4 Feb. 1870, 4: Sir Charles Trevelyan, *The City Parochial Endowments* (1871).
17. I. G. Doolittle, *The City of London and its Livery Companies* (1982), 38, 43, 58–9.

18. Ibid., 21–135: David Owen, *The Government of Victorian London 1855–1889: The Metropolitan Board of Works, the Vestries and the City Corporation* (1982), 226–59.
19. William A. Robson, *The Government and Misgovernment of London* (1939), 41, 76.
20. *Royal Comm. on Parochial Charities*, 5, 17–28.
21. Christopher N. L. Brooke, *London 800–1216: The Shaping of a City* (1975), 121–49.
22. Ibid., 126.
23. *Royal Comm. on Parochial Charities*, 713–34.
24. W. K. Jordan, *The Charities of London 1480–1660: The Aspirations and Achievements of the Urban Society* (1960), 20.
25. Ibid., 26, 65.
26. Ibid., 21–2, 33, 206.
27. *Royal Comm. on Parochial Charities*, 17–28.
28. Censuses of 1851–1901.
29. John Summerson, *The London Building World of the Eighteen-Sixties* (1973), 7.
30. John Summerson, 'The Victorian Rebuilding of the City of London' in *The London Journal*, 3 (1977), 163–85.
31. A. F. Young and E. T. Ashton, *British Social Work in the Nineteenth Century* (1956), 91, 93–4: Mowat, op. cit., 114–44.
32. *Who Was Who 1916–1928: Who's Who of British Members of Parliament, I, 1832–1885*, ed. Michael Stenton (1976).
33. Trevelyan, op. cit., 9: *Royal Comm. on Parochial Charities*, q. 7822.
34. *The Times*, 7 April 1870, 4; 8 April 1870, 12.
35. Trevelyan, op. cit., 16.
36. *Hansard*, 3rd ser., CCIII, 369–70.
37. Ibid., CCV, 1509.
38. Trevelyan, op. cit., 17.
39. Owen, *The Government of Victorian London*, 255.
40. William Gilbert, *Contrasts* (1873); *The City, An Inquiry into the Corporation, its Livery Companies, and the Administration of their Charities and Endowments* (1877).
41. Gilbert, *The City*, 60.
42. Joseph F. B. Firth, *Municipal London; or, London Government as it is, and London under a Municipal Council* (1876).
43. Ibid., 529–30.
44. *PP*, 1877, XXVI, *Twenty-Fourth Report of the Charity Commissioners*, 5–6.
45. *Hansard*, 3rd ser., CCXXXIII, 1665–6.
46. Ibid., CCXXXIV, 858.
47. Ibid., CCXXXV, 594–5.
48. Doolittle, op. cit., 93, 94, 95.
49. *Hansard*, CCXXXIX, 1694–1704.
50. Judy Slinn, *A History of Freshfields* (1984), 119, 128–9.
51. *Reminiscences of William Rogers*, 170: *PP*, 1882, XII, *Report from the Select Committee on Parochial Charities (London) Bill and London Parochial Charities Bill*, q. 963.
52. *PP*, 1878, LX, *Copy of certain Memorials addressed to the Secretary of State for the Home Department calling attention to the Condition and Administration of the Parochial Charities in the City of London: PP*, 1882, XII, *Report from the Select Committee, ut supra*, qq. 1005–12.
53. *Hansard*, CCXLI, 327, 1244, 1852.

2   The Royal Commission of 1878–80

The chairman of the Royal Commission 'appointed to Inquire into the Condition and Administration of the Parochial Charities in the City of London' was the Lord Privy Seal, the Duke of Northumberland. There were six other members of the Commission – two churchmen, Robert Gregory, canon of St Paul's Cathedral, and William Rogers, prebendary of St Paul's and rector of St Botolph, Bishopsgate; two Conservative MPs, George Cubitt and Albert Pell; a Liberal MP and lawyer, Farrer Herschell; and a prominent City merchant and banker, Henry Hucks Gibbs.

Algernon George Percy, sixth Duke of Northumberland, had recently been appointed Lord Privy Seal by Lord Beaconsfield (Benjamin Disraeli). He had served in the House of Commons as a Conservative MP for 13 years before succeeding to the Dukedom in 1869. Since then he had taken an active part in promoting the welfare of the people of the Tyneside area, supporting schools and hospitals and donating land for parks and open spaces. A steadfast supporter of the Church of England, he was patron of 27 livings and had sought to extend the influence of the Church throughout his domains.[1] He had presided over the annual congress of the Social Science Association in Newcastle in 1870, although his presidential address was not exactly suffused with liberal sentiment, and he was also at one time chairman of the council of the Charity Organisation Society.[2] He was a conscientious chairman of the Royal Commission, missing only four sessions.

Robert Gregory, who had been appointed a canon of St Paul's by Disraeli in 1868, was of the High Church party in religion and a Tory in politics. As vicar of St Mary-the-Less in Lambeth for over twenty years he had contributed much to the social life of the parish, revitalizing schools, founding a school of art and instituting a number of improvements. For Gregory, however, all these activities had to be centred on the Church. He was a determined opponent of board schools, and although he served on the London School Board from 1873 to 1876 it was as a critical voice, trying to limit the damage which he thought the Board was doing to the voluntary school system. For several years he was the treasurer of the National Society, or to give it its longer title, the National Society for Promoting the Education of the Poor in the Principles of the Established Church. Gregory's great achievement, however, was the restoration of St Paul's Cathedral to its former glory, both as a building, for he was responsible for several embellishments to the interior, and as a place of worship. In 1891 he was appointed Dean of St Paul's, a position he held until shortly before his death in 1911.[3] He was the only member of the Commission to attend all its meetings and took the chair when the Duke of Northumberland was absent. Not surprisingly, he was a staunch defender of the right of the Church to retain the income from those charities which were of an ecclesiastical nature. He was later to serve as one of the City Parochial Foundation's initial trustees for over ten years.

Gregory's fellow cleric on the Commission, William Rogers, was of a different persuasion. It would probably not be an exaggeration to describe him as a social reformer first and a churchman second. He was given the sobriquet of 'Hang Theology' Rogers because of his lack of concern with doctrinal matters, and one critic said of him, 'He may be an atheist but he is a gentleman.' Gregory, himself, in his autobiography stressed his differences with Rogers over the parochial charities, and remarked that Rogers had once said, 'Your ideas and mine, Gregory, differ fundamentally. I believe in flannel petticoats and you believe in the Church Catechism.'[4] Rogers was particularly interested in educational reform and had sat on the Royal Commission on Education in 1858. As rector of St Botolph, Bishopsgate, he had devoted much of his energies to establishing schools for the children of clerks and shopkeepers; his work in this respect, leading to the formation of the Corporation for Middle Class Education, has already been mentioned in Chapter 1. As a governor of Alleyn's charity in Dulwich he also helped to reconstitute Dulwich College and its associated schools.[5] Rogers was a constructive member of the Commission, missing only two of its sessions. He was later to play a major part in the foundation of the Bishopsgate Institute and was a trustee of the City Parochial Foundation for the first six years of its existence.

George Cubitt, later Baron Ashcombe, was the son of the speculative builder Thomas Cubitt. He sat in the House of Commons as a Conservative MP for Surrey West from 1860 to 1885 and then for Epsom from 1885 to 1892. He was the second Church Estates Commissioner from 1874 to 1879 and may have been appointed to the Commission for this reason. In 1880 he was made a Privy Councillor.[6] His role on the Commission was not a particularly forceful one, but he attended regularly and was absent on only three occasions.

Albert Pell was Conservative MP for South Leicestershire from 1868 to 1885 but, according to James Bryce, who admired him greatly, he was 'no more of a party man than his sense of party loyalty required. His political opinions might be described as half tory, half radical.' He had served as a poor law guardian in his native parish in Northamptonshire since 1853 and was an acknowledged authority on the poor law. He was opposed to the system of outdoor relief, virtually securing its abolition in his own district, and was fiercely critical of doles and those forms of charity which he considered an encouragement to indigence. As a nominated guardian for St George-in-the-East in Tower Hamlets, where he owned house property, his views were well known in the capital, but where there was a genuine need he was among the first to recognize it and pressed strongly for a more effective use of the parochial charities. Bryce described him as 'a true friend of the poor'.[7] Pell missed some meetings of the Commission when he was away in the United States and Canada in June 1879 as an assistant commissioner to the Duke of Richmond's Royal Commission on Agriculture, but his was a dominant influence on the charities Commission and in the subsequent moves which led to the establishment of the Foundation.

As a busy barrister, Farrer Herschell had to miss several sessions of the Commission. He was a Liberal MP for Durham from 1874 to 1885, and on the return of Gladstone to power in May 1880 he was appointed Solicitor-General and knighted. In 1886 he was elevated to the position of Lord Chancellor with the title of Baron Herschell. His position in the government was of assistance in the struggle to put the recommendations of the Commission into legislative form. Herschell was a member of the council of the Social Science Association and his liberalism was described as 'a matter of profound conviction'.[8]

Henry Hucks Gibbs, who essentially represented the City's interests on the Commission, was head of the merchant house of Antony Gibbs & Sons. He was also prominent in the banking community, a director of the Bank of England from 1853 to 1901 and Governor of the Bank from 1875 to 1877. He had served on the Royal Commission on the Stock Exchange in 1877–8. A leading member of the Conservative Party in the City, Gibbs was briefly one of the City's MPs in 1891–2. He was also active in the affairs of the Church and was vice-president of the Bishop of St Alban's Fund for extending church work in east London. Described as 'a staunch, outspoken Churchman and Tory', he yet had many and varied interests. An expert on currency matters, he was also a philologist who contributed to the compilation of the Oxford English Dictionary, a Spanish scholar, and a bibliophile.[9] He was the third member of the Royal Commission to become a trustee of the City Parochial Foundation, from 1891 to 1893, although he never actually attended a meeting. In 1896 he was created Baron Aldenham.

The Commission has been described as 'not one of the century's more distinguished inquiries'.[10] Certainly it did not attract a great deal of attention either when it was sitting or afterwards, and its members did not include anyone with the requisite reforming zeal to catch the public eye. On balance it was a conservative Commission which was unlikely to advocate radical solutions. Nevertheless, it was assiduous in carrying out its duties. It digested a great body of evidence and met in 28 sessions between 19 November 1878 and 21 November 1879, calling 231 witnesses, mostly rectors, churchwardens, vestry clerks, trustees of the charities, and a number of individual experts. The information it collected together, when presented to the public in 1880, provided irrefutable evidence of maladministration stretching over decades. If its recommendations were thought by many critics to be too timid, its deliberations did in the end result in legislation and a substantial measure of reform, which is more than can be said for many another nineteenth-century commission.

Its members had the inestimable advantage of being able to read Hare's detailed reports on the charities, which they duly acknowledged in their report, and of having available detailed statistics which they also published. These must have convinced even the doubters among them of the need for remedial measures. The overall figures of declining population and increasing value of the endowments provided a sharp enough contrast, but the examples of some individual parishes, in addition to those which had already achieved notoriety, made an even deeper impression. In several parishes the income seemed totally disproportionate to need. St Michael, Cornhill, which covered some four acres and had a total population of 254 (by the now outdated 1871 census), none of them paupers, enjoyed an annual income of nearly £3,000 from its charities. St Martin Orgar, with a population of 212 and no paupers, had £2,273 at its disposal, but had at least applied to the Charity Commissioners for a scheme for better use of its income. St Lawrence Jewry, population 214, had an income of £2,592, and St Edmund King and Martyr, a three-acre parish with only 153 inhabitants, had to contrive ways of spending over £2,000 per annum in charitable ends. There were many other examples. St

Michael-le-Querne, a tiny parish only one and a half acres in extent and with a resident population of no more than 71, and an income of £1,164 which had doubled since 1865, displayed such flagrant abuses that it came under the stricture of the Commission on a number of counts. There were many such instances of a rapid and substantial increase in the value of charity estates, as at All Hallows, Lombard Street, where the rental of a number of houses in Gracechurch Street had risen from £482 per annum in 1854 to £1,200, but nothing could match the startling transformation in St Peter-le-Poer, where one estate which had produced merely £60 per annum as late as 1873 now brought in an annual income of £1,450.[11]

As the questioning of witnesses proceeded the Commission concentrated on certain issues. Despite Hare's insistent probings, it had not been possible to obtain accurate information from every parish. Several claimed that they had an absolute right to do as they liked with their charity income – 'as the parish pleases', as it was expressed in the case of St Margaret Pattens – and there was some hostility to the Commission.[12] The authorities of St Mary Aldermanbury declined to appear.[13] In a number of instances title deeds had conveniently been lost or had perished in the Great Fire of 1666 and the property concerned had been appropriated for general parish uses. Some parishes refused to submit returns of their property to the Charity Commissioners as 'they consider they have the right to use them irresponsibly for what they consider to be the good of the parish',[14] and in many others the methods of accounting were woefully deficient. The rector of St Vedast, Foster Lane, the Reverend Thomas Pelham Dale, thought that the audit of the accounts of his parish was 'quite illusory'. The churchwarden kept the charity income in his own account and on one occasion on being asked to produce it he had had to borrow the money.[15] It was not unusual for vestry clerks to keep charity funds in their personal accounts, and at least one had misappropriated the funds and had been declared bankrupt.[16]

It soon became obvious that in very many cases the original objectives of the donors could not be carried out. For the most part this was because of a decline in the numbers of the resident poor – 'we have no poor' was a constant refrain of the parish representatives[17] – but there were other purposes which were becoming equally incapable of realization. The virtual collapse of the apprenticeship system in the City meant that the trustees of several gifts which had been left for apprenticing youths to a trade had great difficulty in carrying out their trusts, and this prompted a debate in the Commission on what other educational ends would be appropriate uses for such funds.[18]

Some parishes literally did not know what to do with their income from charities and merely let it accumulate,[19] but most found ways of spending the money which the Commission clearly regarded in many instances as an abuse of trust. One of the most common practices was to use it to pay the salaries of the vestry clerk and other parish officials. Sir Henry Peek, a baronet and MP, was asked to give evidence as one of the richest ratepayers in the parish of St Mary-at-Hill and said of his parish that 'the surveyors, the vestry clerks and a great many other people really look upon the parish estate as a fair source of income; their fathers before them looked upon it in the same light, and their grandfathers too.'[20] The parish had paid a grant of £200 per annum to the rector out of its 'very large funds', but Peek had complained to the Charity Commissioners, who had decreed that this was a misappropriation of funds. St Edmund King and Martyr was a very small parish with a very large income which spent considerable sums of money on church officers, including superannuated ones, prompting the incredulous question from Albert Pell, 'You have an organist afflicted with a paralytic stroke, to whom you pay 110*l.*, and you have got a verger, who is confined to his bed, to whom you give 76*l.* a year?'[21]

Several parishes – some twenty-five were cited in evidence – used the income to help defray the poor rate levied on their ratepayers. At least one of the members of the Commission, Canon Gregory, thought that this was a perfectly legitimate use of funds for which no other uses had been specified,[22] but most of the others thought that this practice in effect merely subsidized the wealthy ratepayers. As the Duke of Northumberland put it to one vestry clerk, 'It seems to me that the relief of the poor should be called the relief of the rich, because the rich pay the rate, do not they?'[23] Some witnesses who tried to defend the practice faced some hostile questioning, but the representatives of St Antholin were at least straightforward enough to say that they applied the money in this way 'for want of a better purpose'.[24]

Few things aroused the concern of the members of the Commission more than the handing out of doles in money and kind. The words of Sir Henry Peek fell on receptive ears when he said that 'People used to come into St Mary at Hill and the adjoining parishes, just precisely as they now go hop-picking into Kent in the autumn, and when they got all the doles they could they went away, and we saw no more of them till the doles came round again.'[25] The rector of St Michael Queenhithe explained how he had attempted to do away with small doles on Christmas Eve and reserve the money for cases of sickness or distress, but had met with resistance from his parishioners who thought of the gifts as their right. 'I think it principally went in plum pudding,' he added.[26] Another vicar thought that the giving of doles at set times 'begets a number of set applications from greedy applicants',[27] while at All Hallows, Barking, the distribution of money on New Year's Day 'did not lead to the sobriety of the district'.[28] To compound matters the recipients were often chosen indiscriminately. One overseer said, rather puzzlingly, 'it is very difficult to know exactly who they are, except in one or two instances', and at St Swithun as recipients died 'others turn up in their place'.[29] What exercised the Commission was the thought that doles could act as a magnet to a pauper class and that parish relief might in many instances be unknowingly duplicated by outdoor relief from the City of London Union.[30] A number of the more forward-looking parishes, aware of these criticisms, had begun to replace doles with a carefully administered system of pensions.[31]

There were undoubtedly more flagrant abuses, however. A favourite use of charity funds was to provide wine in the vestry for meetings or for consumption after (and sometimes before) services. At St Vedast, Foster Lane, a bottle was made available to the sexton every Sunday, apparently for his own use.[32] The authorities of St Sepulchre at least spread their largesse around by giving custom to eight wine merchants. Faced with intense questioning, they claimed in mitigation that some wine was given to the poor at times of sickness, but received little sympathy for what was contemptuously described as 'a dole of wine'.[33] Audit dinners, Easter feasts, a day's excursion in the country followed by a dinner for the churchwardens and their friends were all cited as time-hallowed practices, but the example which most caught the commissioners' attention, and subsequently the public's imagination, was the 'love feast' at Richmond enjoyed by the ratepayers of St Clement Eastcheap. Originally a sum of five shillings had been left some four hundred years ago for this means of reconciling disputing parties, but now the day's revelry cost about £60 to £70.[34]

The most bizarre misuse of charity funds occurred at St Michael-le-Querne and St Vedast, Foster Lane. Both parishes, which were united for ecclesiastical purposes, contributed money towards the prosecution of their rector, the Reverend Thomas Pelham Dale. An ostensible reason for this action was that he had questioned the way in which the parish trusts were being managed, but there were more fundamental issues involved, including doctrinal differences.[35] James Bryce later remarked in the House of Commons that 'Perhaps they looked on this as what the lawyers called a *cy près* application of the funds bequeathed for the combustion of heretics.'[36]

Some parishes, whatever the origin of their charitable income, thought that it should be used first and foremost for the maintenance of the parish church and its services, and virtually all insisted that charities of an ecclesiastical nature should be restricted to purposes connected with the church.[37] The result was that sums of money were still being set aside for lectures or sermons to congregations that had all but disappeared, and in many parishes the funds for repairing and maintaining the fabric of the church were 'far beyond the amount required'.[38] Even such a resolute defender of the principle that charities set up for religious objects should be used only for ecclesiastical ends as Canon Gregory hinted through his questions that he would support a move to utilize such funds for the upkeep of churches in poor neighbourhoods within ten miles of the City.[39]

The picture was not entirely one of misappropriation and irresponsibility, however. Some charities were already being administered according to schemes which had been approved by the Charity Commissioners or the Court of Chancery, and several parishes had applied for further schemes, but obtaining approval was an 'extremely slow' business. St Martin Orgar had submitted a scheme to the Charity Commissioners in 1871 and 'there it has remained', while St Andrew Undershaft had been waiting eight years for its proposals to be ratified.[40] Despairing of official solutions, many authorities devised their own means of assisting charitable bodies. St Alban, Wood Street, supported the Metropolitan Dispensary and the Charity Organisation Society. The latter was also favoured by St Augustine, where, the rector rather diffidently explained, 'As we had this very large annual income, and no positive claims upon it under the terms of the bequest, we thought ourselves at liberty to give some moderate assistance to charities of general public utility.'[41]

The Commission concluded its investigations by examining independently a number of expert witnesses. Sir Charles Trevelyan described his efforts to expose the state of affairs some ten years earlier and repeated his views of that time, including his advocacy of private ownership. He wanted to see the building of new churches and the improvement of existing ones, and suggested several uses for secular charity funds, including provision for the old and infirm, the building of provident dispensaries, and technical education, remarking that 'apprenticeship answers to what is now called technical education'. From their questions to him, the members of the Commission were already forming an opinion that some of the larger parishes on the edge of the City might have to be treated separately, and Trevelyan thought there was a case for making such a distinction.[42]

Sir Henry Peek also thought that there could be no better use for charity funds than advancing education, but he favoured 'providing schools for the class above the poor'.[43]

Sir Seymour Fitzgerald, the Chief Charity Commissioner, believed that the Charity Commission could be the instrument of reform 'without having additional machinery', but that its role was basically one of overall control and that administration should be handled locally. He also spoke strongly against doles which he thought were 'productive of the most unmitigated evil'.[44] Robert Hedley, one of the inspectors of the Local Government Board, also attacked doles and thought that the ways in which the income from the City charities was presently being spent tended to encourage pauperism.[45]

Of all the witnesses, the influential Sir Arthur Hobhouse pressed for the most fundamental changes. He recommended the formation of a new body to administer all of the parochial charities of the City and apply their benefits to the wider metropolitan area. The creation of such a body in the face of what was certain to be strong opposition from existing trustees would be 'a question of political power', and an Act of Parliament would be needed to spell out the objects to which the funds should be applied. Even though he was a former Charity Commissioner himself, Hobhouse thought that the Charity Commission should have only a limited role in this process.[46]

The City Solicitor, T. J. Nelson, predictably took a different view. He favoured a local solution, leaving existing trusts alone where the original purposes were still valid, and adopting the *cy près* doctrine to find alternative uses where objects had failed. He did, however, think that there might be a surplus which could be used to create a general fund.[47] On the day of the final sitting Edwin Freshfield led a deputation of churchwardens to make much the same points. He, too, did not object to the setting up of a central body to administer any surplus funds but thought that all the parishes should be represented on it. It fell to Freshfield to have the very last word as he remarked, somewhat philosophically, 'Whenever we get a glimpse of social history it is deeply interesting.'[48]

The Commission took a further four months to compile its report, which was issued in March 1880. After reviewing the demographic and social changes which had taken place in the City and summarizing the evidence presented to the Commission, the report concluded that the present administration of the charities 'is not calculated to be productive of the full benefits which ought to accrue to the class for whose advantages these charities were originally founded', that the intentions of the founders could not in general be carried out and that it was impossible to put into effect a satisfactory rearrangement of the charities under the existing system. As the law as it was presently constituted could not provide an adequate remedy, the report accepted that new legislation was necessary.[49]

At this point, however, in the eyes of many of those who had eagerly awaited its publication, the report seriously weakened its case when it stated that 'as long as these [charities] can, in accordance with the letter and the spirit of the bequests, be employed for the purposes contemplated by the founders, there would seem to be no sufficient reason for depriving their present administrators, subject always to strict supervision, of the right of dealing with these funds, provided that no injury to the general interests of Society, as at present understood, results from such dealing.' Where it was impossible to fulfil the original trusts the state was justified in stepping in to prescribe new objects suited to the wants of the present time, and where the sums available had increased out of all proportion to the founders' expectations, there was a case for central control of the surplus thus created.[50]

The report advocated the establishment of an 'Executive Commission' consisting of three persons, one of whom was to be a member of the staff of the Charity Commission, to examine the deeds and charters of the charities and their mode of administration. The charities were to be classified as ecclesiastical or 'eleemosynary' – a favourite term of the members of the Commission which in their usage meant, in effect, secular. The surplus funds of the religious charities should be handed over to the Ecclesiastical Commissioners (the forerunners of the modern Church Commissioners) for the building and repair of churches and to satisfy the spiritual needs of poorer parishes in the metropolitan area. In dealing with the secular charities, the new commission was to determine which funds could remain in the hands of the existing trustees and hand over the residue to a specially constituted board made up of 15 members chosen by ballot from representatives of the City parishes, two members from the Common Council of the City, two from the Metropolitan Asylums Board, two from the Metropolitan Board of Works (the weak governing body of the metropolis outside the City) and four co-opted members, with a paid chairman and secretary to be appointed by the Home Secretary.[51] In the proposals for the creation of such a board, which probably owed much to the suggestion of Sir Arthur Hobhouse, can be seen the first steps towards the eventual establishment of the City Parochial Foundation.

The board was to have the duty of framing new schemes for 'obsolete' charities and the application of surplus funds. It was to try to promote the general benefit of the inhabitants of the metropolis, for example, by using funds to provide open spaces or build lodging houses. It should, however, keep in mind as far as possible the intentions of the founders of charities, by, for instance, using bequests for apprenticeships 'in the promotion of industrial education in the institutions created for this purpose'. While the board was to have wide discretion, its schemes had to be approved by the Charity Commissioners, who were to inherit the powers of the temporary executive commission when it was wound up.[52]

Finally the report reiterated that the members of the Commission had been motivated by the 'desire to effect the union of these charities . . . with as little disturbance of existing ideas and interests as is consistent with the effective discharge of the duty imposed upon us'. It was signed by all seven members, but Rogers, Herschell and Pell expressed written reservations. Rogers did not agree that charities which had come to be applied to religious ends, though not originally intended for such purposes, should continue to be devoted to ecclesiastical uses. Herschell shared this view and also wanted the new board to have far more discretion and not be subject to the final control of the Charity Commissioners. Pell agreed with this point and spelt out some of the ways in which the surplus charity funds could be used for the benefit of the poor in the metropolis. He supported the establishment of self-help organizations like provident institutions and favoured the acquisition and preservation of open spaces in poorer neighbourhoods. He also thought that the report had not been emphatic enough in condemning the application of funds 'to the provision of articles of first necessity, such as food, clothing, and fuel, the distribution of which has proved universally mischievous'.[53]

The appearance of the report was not greeted with any great enthusiasm. *The Times*, reviewing the report in a leading article on the eve of publication, remarked, 'The Commission is by no means a revolutionary body, nor will its recommendations startle the public by any dangerous innovations in the accepted mode of dealing with funds appropriated to charitable uses.' It disliked the proposed new administrative board as yet another authority in a metropolis which already had a multiplicity of such bodies, and thought that in any case it was unbalanced by having too many representatives of the City on it.[54] The Reverend R. H. Hadden, who was William Rogers's curate at St Botolph, Bishopsgate, wrote an article for *The Nineteenth Century*, the influential periodical edited by James Knowles. Hadden was later to be a much-embattled vicar of St Botolph, Aldgate, and later still a trustee of the City Parochial Foundation. At this time, however, he worked closely with Rogers and his views probably reflected those of his rector, even thought they were critical of the Commission's recommendations. 'That they were ever intended to be carried out – at any rate, that they were ever considered likely to be carried out – is hard to think,' he wrote. Furthermore he found in the report a 'tenderness of compassion' to existing interests which was unwarranted. In particular he condemned the proposed administrative body as 'a packed Board'. The solution was for Parliament to lay down the broad principles and set up a strong board representative of the whole metropolis to carry them out.[55] *The Times*, too, thought that it was 'abundantly clear that some mode of re-organization is urgently needed'. There was a confident expectation that something would soon be done.

NOTES

1. *The Times*, 3 Jan. 1899, 6.
2. *Transactions of the National Association for the Promotion of Social Science* (1871), 1–23: Charles Loch Mowat, *The Charity Organisation Society 1869–1913: Its Ideas and Work* (1961), 45.
3. *DNB*: *Robert Gregory 1819–1911 Being the Autobiography of Robert Gregory, D. D., Dean of St Paul's*, ed. W. H. Hutton (1912).
4. *Autobiography of Robert Gregory*, 123 and n.
5. *DNB*: *Reminiscences of William Rogers Rector of St Botolph Bishopsgate*, compiled by R. H. Hadden (1888), *passim*.
6. *Who's Who of British Members of Parliament, II, 1886–1918*, ed. Michael Stenton and Stephen Lees (1978).
7. *DNB*: *The Reminiscences of Albert Pell Sometime MP for South Leicestershire*, ed. Thomas Mackay (1908), esp. xlii–xliv.
8. *DNB*.
9. *DNB*: *The Complete Peerage*, ed. G. E. C., *sub* Aldenham.
10. David Owen, *English Philanthropy 1660–1960* (1965), 281.
11. *PP*, 1880, XX, *Report of the Royal Commission on Parochial Charities*, pp. 5, 6, 17–28.
12. Ibid., p. 6 and Minutes of Evidence, qq. 1471, 5350, 5459.
13. Ibid., qq. 6815–19.
14. Ibid., qq. 4035–9.
15. Ibid., qq. 1317–20.
16. Ibid., qq. 735, 748, 1801–2.
17. Ibid., qq. 3494, 3958, 7566.
18. Ibid., qq. 646–8, 6190, 6261.
19. Ibid., qq. 2553–4, 6500–1, 7566.
20. Ibid., q. 7570.
21. Ibid., qq. 5090–5101.
22. *Autobiography of Robert Gregory*, 122–3.
23. *Royal Comm. on Parochial Charities*, q. 4075.
24. Ibid., qq. 362, 527–36, 1474, 1480–2, 1489–1511, 4703–65.
25. Ibid., q. 7566.
26. Ibid., q. 6009.
27. Ibid., q. 5537.
28. Ibid., q. 26.
29. Ibid., qq. 1801–2, 7401.
30. Ibid., qq. 7856–7969.
31. Ibid., qq. 728, 3196.
32. Ibid., qq. 324, 326, 1273–88, 1477–8, 1536.
33. Ibid., qq. 2489–2528.
34. Ibid., qq. 324, 326, 548–61, 803–6, 1483, 1536, 4742–4, 5470, 7264–8.
35. Ibid., qq. 1207–10, 1952–66, 2003–4.
36. *Hansard*, 3rd ser., CCLXI, 1295.
37. *Royal Comm. on Parochial Charities*, qq. 916, 1097, 1852–6.
38. Ibid., p. 8, qq. 6500–1.
39. Ibid., q. 7592.
40. Ibid., qq. 794–6, 2077, 3272, 5736–60, 6190.
41. Ibid., qq. 3496–501, 3957.
42. Ibid., qq. 7820–48.
43. Ibid., qq. 7566–80.
44. Ibid., qq. 7613, 7649, 7692–4.

45. Ibid., qq. 7856–69.
46. Ibid., qq. 7751–811.
47. Ibid., qq. 8089–153.
48. Ibid., qq. 8156–237.
49. Ibid., pp. 9–10.
50. Ibid., p. 10.
51. Ibid., pp. 10–11.
52. Ibid., p. 11.
53. Ibid., pp. 13–15.
54. *The Times*, 23 March 1880, 9.
55. Reverend R. H. Hadden, 'The City Parochial Charities' in *The Nineteenth Century*, IX (Jan.–June 1881), 324–37.

3　The passing of the Act

The return of a Liberal government in the general election of 1880 held out the prospect of early legislation on the City charities following the publication of the Commission's report. Gladstone's second administration soon had other preoccupations, however, and these were at times to lead to a near paralysis of government. Initially, the concern was with foreign affairs and the admission of Charles Bradlaugh, who, as an atheist, refused to take the oath, but very quickly Irish affairs came to dominate the whole business of Parliament. It was not just that bills relating to Ireland took up an inordinate amount of parliamentary time, but that practically all legislation, no matter what subject it dealt with, came to acquire an Irish dimension. The small Irish contingent in the House of Commons, brilliantly led by Charles Stewart Parnell, believed that one way in which they could progress towards Home Rule was by keeping the Irish question continually in the forefront of the public mind in England. They, therefore, used every device they could to delay and disrupt government business, particularly the tactic of interminably prolonging debates which we would now call filibustering but which was known at the time as 'obstruction'. Both contemporary observers and later historians have remarked how the preoccupation with Ireland diverted attention from domestic issues in general and social problems in particular in the early 1880s.[1]

Sir William Harcourt, the Home Secretary, to whom Gladstone was content to leave matters of social policy, was sympathetic with the wish to settle the minor but persistent problem of the City charities, but the possibility of devoting any government time to it came to seem increasingly remote. It was thus left to a backbencher, James Bryce, newly elected as MP for Tower Hamlets and unversed in the intricacies of parliamentary procedure, to introduce legislation and steer it through a fractious House of Commons. That he managed to do so after three years' endeavours was a tribute to his remarkable skill and perseverance. In that Parliament it was impossible for a private member to secure the enactment of a bill which was even in the slightest degree contentious without a good deal of temporizing and manoeuvring behind the scenes. The City of London Parochial Charities Act of 1883, while it did not satisfy all the aspirations of those who had been battling long and hard for reform, was nevertheless a very considerable achievement.

James Bryce (1838–1922), lawyer, scholar, politician and statesman, was one of the outstanding men of his time. After an Oxford education he entered Lincoln's Inn in 1862 and was called to the Bar in 1867. A Fellow of Oriel College, Oxford, from 1862, he was appointed Regius Professor of Civil Law at the university in 1870. But it was as a historian that he was best known in the academic world. His masterly study of the Holy Roman Empire was written while he was still in his twenties, and his analysis of the American political system, *The American Commonwealth*, published in 1888, was accepted as a standard work on the subject on both sides of the Atlantic. He also played a material part in the founding of the *English Historical Review* in 1886, and towards the end of his life in 1921 produced another classic in *Modern Democracies*. Altogether he received degrees from thirty-one universities, of which fifteen were in the United States. He entered Parliament as Liberal MP for Tower Hamlets in 1880 and, changing constituencies to South Aberdeen in 1885, remained in the House of Commons until 1906. During that period he held several ministerial positions, including Under Secretary for Foreign Affairs, Chancellor of the Duchy of Lancaster, President of the Board of Trade and, briefly, Chief Secretary for Ireland. From 1907 to 1913 he was a much admired Ambassador to Washington, and on his return to England he was raised to the peerage as Viscount Bryce. During the First World War he did much to promote the idea of the League of Nations. As a Liberal reformer he was interested in educational questions and had been employed as an assistant commissioner on the Schools Inquiry Commission in 1865–6. Later, as President of the Board of Trade, he presided in 1894–5 over the Royal Commission on Secondary Education, known as the Bryce Commission, which was instrumental in establishing the modern state system of secondary education.[2]

It was this man of many talents who first raised the matter of the Royal Commission's report on the City charities in the House of

Commons when in May 1880, having barely taken the oath as a new MP, he asked when copies were likely to be distributed to members.[3] He returned to the charge, this time with Firth's support, in the late summer by asking questions about the Government's intentions; Harcourt replied that it would be considering the matter in the parliamentary recess.[4]

Bryce, however, uneasy at the delay and fearful that the Government would never be able to fit legislation into its overcrowded timetable, decided to introduce a private member's bill in the next session. As MP for Tower Hamlets he was naturally concerned at the waste of resources which might be applied to his own impoverished constituency, but of equal importance as a motivating factor was his association with Sir Arthur Hobhouse, whose influential critique, *The Dead Hand*, consisting of several of his speeches on the need for charity reform, including references to the City parochial charities, was published in 1880. There was a close affinity between these two instinctive liberal reformers, and Bryce later acknowledged the assistance Hobhouse had given him in framing the City of London Parochial Charities Act; 'he gave me invaluable help both in suggesting the provisions needed and in revising the drafts of the Bill,' he remarked.[5] Hobhouse may well have been responsible for many of the salient features of the Act, but Bryce's role should not be underestimated, and his performances in support of his bill, both on the floor of the House and in Select Committee, received much praise.

Bryce's bill received its first reading in January 1881 and was eventually enacted into law in August 1883 after some amendment and much travail. The bill originally began with a long preamble, itself the cause of dissention, describing the changes which had taken place in the City and how, in consequence, a great part of the income of the parochial charities was 'now unapplied, or wasted, or misapplied'. In contrast there were many parts of London in which funds were needed for the religious, educational, moral and social needs of persons employed in the City but no longer residing there, and, moreover, there was a large surplus from the charities' income which could be used to satisfy the similar needs of the poorer inhabitants of the greater metropolis. Therefore, 'after making due compensation for all vested interests', it was necessary to provide for the better application and management of the charities 'so as to render them more generally beneficial to the poorer classes of London and its suburbs'.[6]

Up to three commissioners were to be appointed to inquire into the charities and classify their property as ecclesiastical or general, in accordance with the objects of the charities, as recommended in the report of the Royal Commission. Where charities had mixed objects the commissioners were to determine how much of the property should

be deemed to be for ecclesiastical purposes and how much for general.
They were also to draw up a list of all persons who could legitimately
claim to continue to receive payments from the endowments and provide the opportunity for others with vested interests to claim compensation. They were then to devise a scheme or schemes for the future
application and management of the charity property and endowments,
and the most important clauses of the bill laid down the principles to
be adopted in framing these schemes.

Crucially, the parishes were to be divided into two schedules for
this purpose. The first contained the eight most populous parishes
(reduced to five in the Act) and the second the remainder. Why such
a distinction was made so early in the life of the bill and eventually
encapsulated in the Act has frequently puzzled those who have had
to administer the Act. Bryce explained to the Select Committee considering his bill that he was attempting to adopt the principle
expressed in the Royal Commission's report that wherever possible
the administration of the charities should be left in the hands of
existing trustees. The most practicable way of doing this, he considered, was to distinguish between the largest and most populous
parishes on the fringe of the City, 'where there is reason to think that
the charity funds can be properly and fittingly spent on local charitable
purposes', and the rest.[7] Indeed, the parishes which he originally
placed in this category – St Giles, Cripplegate; St Botolph, Aldgate;
St Botolph, Bishopsgate; St Bride, Fleet Street; St Andrew, Holborn;
St Botolph, Aldersgate; St Sepulchre; and St Bartholomew-the-Great
– contained over half the City's population and over a third of its
charitable income. The Royal Commission's report had come down
firmly in favour of not disturbing existing interests wherever possible.
Bryce may have anticipated – correctly in the event – that he would
be criticized for not adhering closely enough to the recommendations
of the report, and have wished to show that on this point at least he
was trying to follow its spirit.

Under the terms of the bill, the appointed commissioners were still
to be empowered to produce schemes for the parishes in the first
schedule, but they were to retain those uses of charitable funds which
could be demonstrated to be still legitimate, and otherwise provide for
objects which were beneficial to the inhabitants of each parish or to
persons who worked there. In addition, existing bodies of trustees
could be joined together or new ones established. For the parishes in
the second schedule, however, a new governing body was to be set up
to administer their charities, and after allowing for the retention of
those purposes which were still useful to the residents of the parishes,
the benefits were to be applied throughout the metropolis, which was

defined as the Metropolitan Police District and the City and Liberties of London.

The objects which the executive commissioners were to promote were generally the same for the parishes in both schedules. The ecclesiastical charities were to be applied to such current ecclesiastical uses that were still considered to be beneficial, and, in the case of the larger parishes in the first schedule, to whatever other purposes the commissioners deemed 'most conducive to the spiritual benefit of the inhabitants of the said parish'. Out of the income of the second, larger group of parishes, however, a surplus fund was to be made available to the Ecclesiastical Commissioners to be applied in the more populous districts of the wider metropolis towards the erection and maintenance of new churches and the endowment of new benefices, the maintenance of the fabric of existing churches or better endowment of existing benefices, and generally to the extension of the spiritual teachings of the Church of England.

The common objects which the commissioners were to have in mind in framing schemes for the secular charities of both groups of parishes were the promotion and improvement of the education of the poor; the establishment and maintenance of libraries; preserving, providing and maintaining open spaces, recreation grounds or drill grounds; the promotion and extension of provident institutions; and generally contributing to the physical, moral and social improvement of the poorer inhabitants. The main differences were that in the parishes in the first schedule these benefits were to be confined to those who lived or worked in the parishes, while for the charities of the parishes in the second schedule they could be extended to anywhere in the metropolis. For the latter group also the educational aims were further defined as being achieved by means of exhibitions, technical instruction, secondary education and art education, or otherwise as decreed by the commissioners, and in addition to libraries, the establishment and maintenance of museums or art collections were to be valid objects.

The schemes when finalized were to be approved by the Committee of the Council on Education, and there were extensive provisions for submitting objections. The expenses of the complex procedure of drawing up and validating the schemes were to be repaid out of income available from the charities. No scheme was to apply to a charity established within the last 50 years unless the existing trustees of that charity consented. Another provision of an avowedly liberal bill was that in making educational arrangements as much regard was to be given to the needs of girls as of boys.

Finally, a crucial and inevitably contentious element of the bill was the composition of the new governing body. Under the original terms of the bill this was to consist of seventeen persons, five nominated by the Crown, five by the London School Board, two by the Corporation of London, two by the Metropolitan Asylums Board, and three co-opted by the remainder. Once established, the new body was to have considerable discretion in how it applied the income available to it, subject always to the terms of the schemes which were to be devised by the executive commissioners.

The named supporters of Bryce's bill were Walter James, already known for his radical interventions on London matters, and two other Liberals, Arthur Cohen and Horace Davey. The bill's first reading in January 1881 was a purely formal matter, but it was not an auspicious time to introduce the measure. Later in the same month George Cubitt, mindful perhaps that there was little likelihood of Bryce succeeding, asked Harcourt if the government intended to introduce its own legislation. Harcourt's observation to Cubitt that he had left out 'should the state of public business permit' provoked laughter all round.[8] What the Home Secretary was alluding to was that Parliament was in the grip of yet another bout of Irish obstruction, as the Parnellites registered their unremitting opposition to further coercive legislation for Ireland which the government was attempting to introduce in that session.[9]

Nevertheless, on 31 March Bryce was able to move that the bill should be referred to the examiners to determine whether it was a public or private bill in accordance with parliamentary practice, while pointing out that this procedure meant that there would be little opportunity for it to proceed further in that session.[10] Surprisingly, a decision was quickly taken that it could be classed as a public bill and the second reading was scheduled for the end of May.

At once the City began to mobilize its opposition. On 29 April Freshfield summoned a meeting at the Cannon Street Hotel of churchwardens and other interested parties (but significantly not the clergy), which passed a resolution to oppose the bill. A committee was set up, to be chaired by Freshfield, to counter Bryce's proposals by formulating measures of its own including alternative legislation if necessary.[11]

The bill's supporters were by no means idle themselves. In May Bryce addressed a meeting of the Charity Organisation Society at the Westminster Palace Hotel, and a more general meeting at the Foresters' Hall, Clerkenwell, consisting of members of various clubs, societies and working men's associations which stood to benefit from the measure. Hobhouse, Trevelyan, who described himself as 'an old labourer in this cause', Firth, Walter James and James Beal were present at the latter meeting.[12]

The debate on the second reading took place on 25 May. Bryce made a powerful speech, which had a considerable impact on the House, recounting the background to the bill and explaining its provisions. Harcourt spoke in favour, commenting that 'he was sorry that the government were unable, from causes which the House well understood to take up the subject themselves; but it was some consolation for them to know that it was in such competent hands', and promised that the government would do all it could to further the bill's progress. Pell, who had added his name to the movers of the bill in a useful gesture of cross-bench support, said that it was a moderate measure and warned its opponents that if they defeated it they could be faced with something very much worse. Nevertheless the City's MPs and their supporters succeeded in talking out the bill and it ran out of parliamentary time.[13]

The issue was now, however, firmly on the parliamentary agenda and Bryce made it clear that he would reintroduce his bill in the next session. He still hoped to effect a compromise with his opponents, but instead they spent the summer drafting their own legislation. They even tried to finance their opposition out of charity income, but were prevented from doing so by the Charity Commissioners.[14]

Both bills were introduced early in the next session in 1882. Bryce's was now called the Parochial Charities (London) Bill and the City bill was confusingly called the London Parochial Charities Bill. The most important change in Bryce's measure (to which Sir Henry Peek now added his name) was that the parishes of St Batholomew-the-Great, St Botolph, Aldersgate, and St Sepulchre were dropped from the first schedule, leaving only the five largest parishes to enjoy the benefits of their charitable income entirely within their own boundaries. This was hardly calculated to placate the City or guarantee the bill an easy passage. On the other hand, the composition of the new governing body was changed, in greater deference to the City's interests, to consist of five members nominated by the Crown, three by the City Corporation, two by the London School Board, two by the Metropolitan Asylums Board, one by Sion College, one by the churchwardens, and three co-opted members. The establishment and maintenance of convalescent hospitals in the metropolis was also added to the objects to be considered in utilizing the funds of the general charities.[15]

The aims of the City bill were to ensure that the benefits of the charities were applied firstly to the residents of the individual parishes, secondly to the inhabitants of the City in general, and thirdly, and only in the case of a surplus, to the poor of the metropolis, and that existing trusts should be left alone wherever possible. It called for five commissioners to be appointed instead of three, two by the Crown, one by the City Corporation and two by the present trustees of the charities. The new governing body to administer the surplus funds would consist of 50 members, of whom 29 were to be elected in the

City wards from among present trustees and six were to be nominated by the City Corporation. Among the objects of charity funds which were thought particularly worth singling out were the provision of pensions for professional men, merchants and tradesmen living in reduced circumstances. In an important additional clause the bill wanted not only charities which had been established within the last 50 years to be left alone but also any schemes for other charities which had been approved within that time. This would have removed another large slice of charitable income from the control of the governing body.[16]

Both bills were given a second reading in February 1882. Sir Farrer Herschell, now Solicitor-General, said that in general the government backed Bryce's bill, but that it differed in some respects from the report of the Royal Commission and that he could not pledge support for all its details.[17] A Select Committee was then appointed to consider both bills, which, because of Gladstone's large majority in the House, was heavily weighted in favour of the Liberal reformers. The chairman was George John Shaw-Lefevre, a barrister and bencher of the Inner Temple, who had held several ministerial offices and was currently Gladstone's First Commissioner of Works and a Privy Councillor. He was also a founder and the first chairman of the Commons Preservation Society. Other members besides Bryce himself included J. F. B. Firth, Walter James and Horace Davey. From the Royal Commission, however, only George Cubitt was chosen.

The deliberations of the Select Committee were indeed far from being a tame rerun of the sessions of the Royal Commission. With its inbuilt bias in favour of Bryce's bill the Committee gave the City's representatives a rather torrid time. These were principally Robert Pearce, a solicitor who had acted as secretary to the churchwardens' committee, and Edwin Freshfield. Both were questioned closely, not only about some of the anomalies which had troubled the Royal Commission, but also about how representative the City's opposition really was, why it generally excluded the clergy, and how far it protected the vested interests of the narrow social stratum from which the existing trustees were drawn. At one point the intensity of Bryce's questioning of Freshfield led to a quarrel with the latter's few supporters on the Committee and the room had to be cleared.[18]

Other witnesses included John Baggallay, a 'Manchester merchant', who was one of the trustees of the estates of St Mary Aldermary, a parish which had refused to give evidence before the Royal Commission. Predictably his evidence now was unconsciously damning.[19] Albert Pell was also summoned, as was Sir Seymour Fitzgerald, the Chief Charity Commissioner. The latter strongly supported Bryce's bill, but thought that the Charity Commissioners were equipped to do the work of the special commissioners to be appointed under the terms of the bill. If the job was to be done in three or four years he would need another commissioner and three or four extra inspectors or assistant commissioners, but he could manage without any additional staff if the enquiry was allowed to take 'any reasonable time', whatever that might have meant. He was opposed to the special treatment of the five most populous parishes, but, significantly in the event, he was also suspicious of the power to be given to the new governing body, preferring to see a number of such bodies rather than one all-embracing one.[20]

The Reverend W. H. Milman, the honorary secretary of Sion College, gave valuable endorsement to Bryce's bill on behalf of the City clergy. Among the questions which Bryce asked him was whether he would consider it a proper use of charity funds to provide for the repair and maintenance of churches of architectural and historic interest. He had previously asked Albert Pell whether he would support the application of funds for the maintenance of any 'historical building', and received a favourable reply in both cases.[21] Bryce was one of the original committee members of the Society for the Protection of Ancient Buildings, which had been founded some five years earlier, but this was still an early date for such considerations to receive any prominence and their expression now was doubtless the result of Bryce's personal interests. He was subsequently to incorporate them in the Act.

Bryce provided a long personal memorandum for the Select Committee's consideration. It was, not surprisingly, a moving and well-written document. He defined the main aim of his bill as helping 'the humbler classes of the population, by aiding them in their self-respect, and by assisting to provide them with means of intellectual and moral improvement and social recreation, such as neither the State nor private liberality has sufficiently supplied'. That population was no longer to be found merely in the City parishes, for 'the representatives and successors of the busy crowd that filled them three centuries ago are to be sought, not in the caretakers who sleep at the top of a huge pile of offices, or the two or three pauper families to be found here and there in some corner, tempted to it, perhaps, by the doles which the parish charities provide, but in the vast labouring population all round the ancient City, which works for it, which is the substratum, so to speak, of the wealthy and business classes who own its property and conduct its commerce.'[22]

There was never any doubt that the Committee would endorse Bryce's bill, but it proposed several amendments. In deference to the susceptibilities of the City, the preamble was much curtailed and the description of charity funds as being 'unapplied, or wasted, or misapplied' was omitted. (Freshfield had threatened to 'take every consti-tutional means in my power to oppose the Bill' if these words had remained.[23]) The Charity Commissioners, augmented temporarily by up to two additional commissioners and more staff, were to take on the role of executive commissioners in making inquiries and formulating schemes. This change, which Bryce voted for in committee, was con-sidered to be sensible because it removed the expense and difficulty of creating a new bureaucracy to implement the Act, but it meant that a pre-existing organization with its own conceptual framework was called on to devise the systems through which the charities were to be administered rather than entrusting the work to a new body with fresh ideas. Clauses added by the Select Committee provided for payment by the new governing body of capital or annual sums to the trustees of existing institutions, or, in the case of open spaces, to the Metropolitan Board of Works or other local authorities to which such open spaces may have been conveyed, and for the creation of new bodies of trustees to which capital or annual sums could be paid. Finally, the proposed composition of the governing body was substan-tially altered by the Committee to a membership of nineteen, five of whom were to be nominated by the Crown, four by the Corporation of London, and the remainder as determined by the Charity Com-missioners in the scheme which they were to draw up.[24]

The bill left Committee in late May 1882 but once again parliamen-tary time was in short supply, for much the same reasons as in the previous year. On 6 May, in Phoenix Park, Dublin, the new Chief Secretary for Ireland, Lord Frederick Cavendish, and the Under Sec-retary, T. H. Burke, had been assassinated, and amidst the inevitable anti-Irish backlash the government had introduced a harsh coercion bill which the Irish contingent of MPs resisted to the utmost. The result was a fresh bout of obstructionism, and debate on one clause alone of the coercion bill occupied the whole of a 28-hour sitting.[25] There was little opportunity to discuss non-Irish matters in that summer of 1882.

But if Bryce's bill commanded relatively little attention in Parlia-ment there was a flurry of activity outside. Another meeting of the City's churchwardens was held at the Cannon Street Hotel in June, and the mood was a truculent one. Freshfield said that as far as all but the five largest parishes were concerned, 'the bill seemed to be practically one of complete confiscation', and Alderman Cotton, one of the City's MPs, announced that he was moving a resolution that the bill so departed from the recommendations of the Royal Com-mission that it should not be allowed to proceed. One vestry clerk claimed that the bill was merely part of the general attack on the City Corporation. 'The City Guilds and the City Charities', he intoned, 'are, as it were, the outworks, the forts connected with the Corporation, which is the citadel at which they are aiming.' In no mood to heed warnings that it had better accept this bill or face a more drastic one, the meeting resolved to endorse Cotton's action.[26]

Bryce tried to seek a compromise, and if contemporary reports of the negotiations are accurate he was prepared to concede a very great deal to see his bill pass into law. He accepted that the division of charity funds into ecclesiastical and general should remain sacrosanct and that firm priority was to be given to City parishes in the distribution of ecclesiastical funds. When funds were allocated to the parishes they were to be administered by trustees chosen by the parishes, and only when the whole or a major part of the income ceased to be so applied was management to pass to the new governing body. In addition Bryce undertook to try to change the composition of the governing body so that five members would be nominated by the trustees and two or three by the City Corporation, thus doubling the City's guaranteed representation.[27]

These concessions, however, failed to save the bill. An intractable final difficulty occurred when Lyulph Stanley, the Liberal MP for Oldham, announced that he was going to move an amendment merging the surplus ecclesiastical funds with the general funds. This was regarded as a wholesale threat to the ecclesiastical endowments, and the session ended before an agreement could be reached. There was a strong and truculent Nonconformist element in the House of Commons which had suddenly woken up to the advantageous position given to the Established Church in Bryce's bill, and which now threatened to wreck the whole measure as a consequence. It was the City, however, which lost out by this added delay, because Bryce's negotiations with its representatives had been conducted without prejudice to future action and Bryce found that he did not have to compromise to the same degree in the next session.[28]

The bill which Bryce introduced into the House of Commons in February 1883, although technically a new bill, was virtually identical with that which had emerged from the Select Committee in the previous year. In moving the second reading in May Bryce appealed to the House to let such an important measure of reform go through and particularly entreated his Nonconformist friends not to allow their abstract principles to stand in the way of supporting it. Once more, however, the churchwardens, vestry clerks and trustees in the City bestirred themselves into action to oppose the measure.[29]

The bill was referred to a Select Committee which Shaw-Lefevre again chaired and in which the only substantial change from the Committee of 1882 was the addition of Lyulph Stanley. The Committee's deliberations were naturally much briefer, but it did recommend some additional amendments, most of them concessions to City interests. The maintenance of the fabric and services of parish churches within the City was made the first call on ecclesiastical funds, and the benefits of the general charities of the larger parishes in the first schedule were extended to all the resident and working population of those parishes rather than just to the poor, although the promotion of working men's and women's institutes was added as a legitimate application of their funds. Additionally, the expenses 'reasonably or properly incurred' by the existing trustees in their appearances before the Select Committees were to be repayable. In an equally important bid to placate the Nonconformists a new clause stipulated that membership of any Church was not to be made a condition of benefiting from the general charity funds. Finally, the maintenance of the fabric and monuments of any City churches 'of architectural or historic interest' was made a specific object of the ecclesiastical charities.[30]

The bill returned to the House for the report stage in late July 1883. This was a relatively quiescent period as far as Parnellite activity was concerned,[31] but there were other hurdles to overcome and the passage of the bill was by no means a foregone conclusion. The City interests felt that, with a House of Commons which was fundamentally hostile to their position, they had obtained as much in the way of concessions as they could expect, and they tempered their opposition. They were doubtless also concerned at the development of a new opposition to Bryce and the threat this posed to themselves. The latest criticism came from among the ranks of the reformers themselves and, taking up the discontent which had surfaced at a late stage in the proceedings of 1882, focused on the favoured position of the Established Church under the terms of the bill. Lyulph Stanley alluded to 'a sop of £30,000 a-year given to the Church of England to buy them off' in reference to the surplus ecclesiastical funds being given to the Ecclesiastical Commissioners, and moved an amendment to allow the Charity Commissioners to apply obsolete and useless ecclesiastical endowments to general purposes. This was defeated, as was an amendment by Alfred Illingworth, a Liberal who favoured disestablishment, that the two new members of the Charity Commission to be appointed should not belong to the Church of England. Another amendment to appoint a Roman Catholic as one of the new commissioners was given short shrift, but a motion by Firth to omit the provision that surplus ecclesiastical funds could be used for building new churches in the metropolis was only narrowly defeated by six votes.[32]

Shaw-Lefevre played an important part in steering the bill through these debates and it received its third reading at shortly after four o'clock in the morning of 31 July. Even then a concession on the timetabling of future legislation had to be made to the Irish after an intervention by Captain O'Shea. Illingworth complained that the bill had always seemed to be debated between 2 a.m. and 4 a.m.[33]

Bryce was immediately subjected to fierce criticism in the correspondence columns of *The Times* and in some other sections of the press for the largesse shown to the ecclesiastical authorities in his measure. He would privately probably have acknowledged that there was much substance to the criticism, but he replied publicly that while he would have preferred to see ecclesiastical funds used for non-denominational purposes, it had to be admitted that they had originally been intended for the use of the Church and that any attempt to disendow the Church in the City of London would not have passed the Commons let alone the Lords. Nevertheless, there were those who thought that 'the remedy provided by this Bill is worse than the disease'.[34]

The intemperate nature of much of this criticism may have had some effect, however, for when the bill was debated in the House of Lords, the Bishop of Rochester, no less, successfully moved an amendment on the same lines as Firth's that the erection and maintenance of new churches should be removed as one of the objects for which surplus ecclesiastical funds could be used, and that the encouragement of theological instruction should be substituted. This was an eminently sensible change, for it was becoming patently obvious that too many new churches had already been erected in the metropolis for the religious needs of its population. Other Lords' amendments showed a deference to existing interests. A new clause urged the Charity Commissioners in framing any scheme to retain the management of endowments by existing bodies of trustees, if necessary altered or strengthened, if that seemed to the public advantage. The Lords also increased the size of the new governing body to twenty-one and required four of the members to be appointed by the Charity Commissioners to be chosen in the first instance from among existing trustees. They also extended the legitimate expenses of the trustees to include any charges which they had incurred in connection with the Act or the similar bills in the sessions of 1881 and 1882.[35]

The City of London Parochial Charities Act received the royal assent on 20 August 1883. Shortly afterwards a long article in *The Times* praised the measure as 'the first instalment of London's municipal reform' and congratulated both Bryce and the government for consistently giving him what support it could. It doubted the wisdom of dealing separately with the five largest parishes in view of the rapid demographic changes taking place in the City, and acknowledged the criticism that the proper balance might not have been struck between ecclesiastical and secular interests in disposing of charity funds. However, it thought that parliamentary approval could not have been obtained for a bill diverting funds set up for religious purposes to lay uses, and remarked that, 'as Mr Bryce recently stated, it is necessary to keep in view the attainable as well as the desirable.' Much would depend on how the Charity Commissioners performed their duties under the Act, and here *The Times* had to admit that the Commission was 'a very unpopular body . . . with charity reformers'.[36] Indeed those involved in the world of philanthropy could be excused certain mixed emotions on the passage of Bryce's Act. Their joy at the splendid achievement of such a measure of reform was tempered with apprehension at how the Charity Commissioners would set about their task of translating the principles of the Act into a workable scheme.

NOTES

1. Helen Merrell Lynd, *England in the Eighteen-Eighties: Towards a Social Basis for Freedom* (1945), 140.
2. *DNB*: H. A. L. Fisher, *James Bryce (Viscount Bryce of Dechmont, OM)* (1927).
3. *Hansard*, 3rd ser., CCLII, 432–3.
4. Ibid., CCLIV, 1938; CCLVI, 1045.
5. L. T. Hobhouse and J. L. Hammond, *Lord Hobhouse A Memoir* (1905), 52–3.
6. *PP*, 1881, III, *London City (Parochial Charities) Bill*.
7. *PP*, 1882, XII, *Report from the Select Committee on Parochial Charities (London) Bill and London Parochial Charities Bill*, Bryce's memorandum.
8. *Hansard*, CCLVII, 719: *The Charity Record and Philanthropic News*, 26 Jan. 1881, 27.
9. F. S. L. Lyons, *Charles Stewart Parnell* (1977), 144–5.
10. *Hansard*, CCLX, 341–3: *The Times*, 1 April 1881, 7.
11. *The Times*, 5 May 1881, 10: *Select Committee on Parochial Charities*, qq. 1024ff.
12. *The Times*, 12 May 1881, 11; 25 May 1881, 7; 2 June 1881, 4.
13. *Hansard*, CCLXI, 1291–1302: *The Charity Record*, 2 June 1881, 184.
14. *Charity Record*, 7 July 1881, 232: *Select Committee on Parochial Charities*, qq. 395–431, 534–43.
15. *PP*, 1882, V, *Parochial Charities (London) Bill*.
16. *Select Committee on Parochial Charities*, qq. 44–56: *Charity Record*, 1 Sept. 1881, 292–4.
17. *Hansard*, CCLXVI, 1203–4: *The Times*, 21 Feb. 1882, 9.
18. *Select Committee on Parochial Charities*, qq. 3–2082: *Charity Record*, 6 April 1882, 115–19, 121–3.
19. *Select Committee on Parochial Charities*, qq. 746–954.
20. Ibid., qq. 2434–2695.
21. Ibid., qq. 2385, 2950–5.
22. Ibid., qq. 269–75.
23. Ibid., q. 1076.
24. *PP*, 1882, V, *Parochial Charities (London) Bill* [*as amended by the Select Committee*].
25. Lyons, op. cit., 211, 225.
26. *Charity Record*, 29 June 1882, 217–19.
27. Ibid., 7 Sept. 1882, 292.
28. Ibid., 29 June, 17 Aug., 7 Sept. 1882, 217–19, 279, 292.
29. Ibid., 17 May, 7 June 1883, 158, 184–5: *The Times*, 3 May 1883, 8.
30. *PP*, 1883, VIII, *Parochial Charities (London) Bill* [*as amended in Select Committee*].
31. Lyons, op. cit., 238.

32. *Hansard*, CCLXXXII, 683–7, 869–84: *The Times*, 28 July 1883, 9; 30 July 1883, 8: *Charity Record*, 2 Aug. 1883, 250.
33. *Hansard*, CCLXXXII, 1095–1104: *The Times*, 1 Aug. 1883, 7.
34. *The Times*, 2 Aug. 1883, 5; 4 Aug. 1883, 8; 6 Aug. 1883, 10: *Charity Record*, 16 Aug. 1883, 266–8.
35. *PP*, 1883, VIII, *Lords Amendments to the Parochial Charities (London) Bill.*
36. *The Times*, 1 Sept. 1883, 7.

4 The Charity Commission and the Central Scheme

The modern Charity Commission only dates as a permanent body from 1853. Its creation owed much to the earlier reforming zeal of Henry Brougham and his belief that the myriad of endowed charities, many of which no longer served a useful purpose, could be used to finance a vastly expanded system of education. As a result of Brougham's promptings, commissioners were appointed to inquire into charitable trusts. Initially their investigations were confined to charities with educational objects, but eventually virtually all charities were subjected to scrutiny. The inquiry took place over some twenty years, mainly in the 1820s and 1830s, and led to calls for the appointment of a permanent board of commissioners with supervisory powers over charitable endowments. Eventually, Parliament acceded to these requests when the Charitable Trusts Act of 1853 established the Charity Commission on just such a permanent footing.[1]

The origins of the Commission in a scheme for educational reform had a considerable influence on its early policies, and the emphasis on education was reinforced when, in 1874, it took over the work of the Endowed Schools Commissioners appointed under the Endowed Schools Act of 1869.[2] As a result, the Charity Commission was increasingly regarded as a body which wanted to see virtually all charity funds put to educational ends. Moreover, because it advocated a system of competitive scholarships and favoured more specialized, post-elementary training, it was criticized for assisting the middle classes at the expense of the poor.[3] It incurred the opprobrium of leading reformers, and Lord Shaftesbury was quoted in the *Charity Record* as saying that he would not have given his labours so readily to charity 'if he had thought the money subscribed would be placed in the hands of the Charity Commissioners'.[4] The *Charity Record*, an influential organ of philanthropic opinion in the 1880s, was continually inveighing against the Commissioners as 'a body of men who are devoted to high-class education'.[5]

To some extent the Commissioners brought criticism on themselves by their obsessively secretive, bureaucratic nature. In fact, the Commission had only limited authority and was chronically understaffed, and yet attracted to its service a number of highly talented individuals, both as Commissioners and as inspectors and assistant commissioners on its staff. The task of reducing the thousand or so City parochial charities to an orderly system so that the 1883 Act could be put into operation was a daunting one, even though the groundwork had been laid in Hare's reports and the subsequent inquiries of the Royal Commission. All those who claimed vested interests either as pensioners or as recipients of grants, salaries or other payments had to be identified and their claims assessed, endowments had to be checked for their date of origin and other factors to determine whether they came under the terms of the Act, and schemes had to be promulgated not only to embrace the bulk of the charities of the multiplicity of small parishes but also for the larger individual parishes named in the first schedule of the Act and for any new institutions or bodies which might be set up. The men chosen to undertake this task were fully up to the calibre of earlier servants of the Commission like Thomas Hare.

The new Commissioners appointed under the 1883 Act were Sir Francis Richard Sandford and James Anstie. For the past fourteen years Sandford had been Secretary to the Committee of the Privy Council on Education, as the Education Department was officially termed. As such he had been the head of the educational establishment in Whitehall and had been the civil servant principally responsible for carrying out Forster's Education Act of 1870. His appointment must have seemed an ideal one to the Commission, with its bias towards education, but whether the circumstances were not entirely to Sandford's liking or for whatever reason, he appears to have played little part in the deliberations of the Commission and left after a year to take up the post of Under Secretary for Scotland.[6] Sandford was replaced as a Commissioner, but all of the work in connection with the City charities at board level seems to have fallen to the lot of James Anstie, the second appointee. Anstie was a QC and an examiner at the University of London, but more importantly in the eyes of those who greeted his appointment with surprise and acclaim, he was a Nonconformist. Indeed, Gladstone made no secret of the fact that his choice of Anstie was in response to pressure from his Nonconformist supporters. It was an inspired appointment. Anstie took up the work with great zeal, and the Reverend R. H. Hadden, who was subsequently a trustee of the City Parochial Foundation, in praising his 'marvellous foresight and singularly unobtrusive energy', said that London was in his debt.[7]

Anstie was fortunate in the choice of the new assistant commissioners who were to help him in his task. They were Henry H. Cunynghame and Edward Bond, both barristers and equally distinguished in their separate ways. Cunynghame had a highly varied career as 'a soldier and a barrister . . . an artist and a capable scientist with a number of inventions to his name', whose obituarist 'doubted whether any important official position has ever been held by an odder or, in some ways, a more remarkable personality.'[8] After a brief period in the army and a short and relatively unsuccessful time at the bar, he had been appointed to a special commission to inquire into the administration of British Guiana. As a result he had come to the attention of Sir George Young, one of the Charity Commissioners appointed under the Endowed Schools Act, who recommended him to the Commission.[9] After a highly successful spell with the Charity Commission he served on other commissions and was chairman of the Royal Commission on Mines in 1906. He was an Under Secretary in the Home Office for many years and was knighted in 1908.

Edward Bond was a Hampstead resident who, as a young barrister, had assisted Octavia Hill in her battle to try to save the fields of Swiss Cottage from the builder. He could even claim the singular distinction of having been engaged, very briefly, to that redoubtable lady.[10] He was a member of the London School Board but resigned to take up his post of assistant commissioner. When his work with the Commission was finished he stood unsuccessfully for Parliament, but was later both a Moderate member of the London County Council, where he was briefly chairman of the Technical Education Board, and a Conservative MP. It was said of him, however, that he seldom spoke in the House and confined himself to measures of practical reform. To these he devoted much of his time and, among other positions, he was chairman of the East End Dwellings Company.[11] He was also a trustee of the City Parochial Foundation from 1895 to 1907 and from 1909 to 1920.

Anstie, Cunynghame and Bond eventually formed themselves into a separate section of the Charity Commission, and among the officials assigned to assist them was Howard Batten, who was later to be the first permanent Clerk of the Foundation.[12] At times they also called on the services of other Commissioners and staff, especially in later years when there was some urgency about completing their task.

The work of this small group was for several years conducted well out of the public gaze and would doubtless have continued that way if outside events – and pressures – had not forced the Commission's hand. The first successful bid for a slice of the parochial charity cake in advance of the Commissioners' own share-out surprisingly did not come from a body of educational reformers but from the open spaces movement. Concern at overcrowding and the density of urban development had deep roots, but it was not until the rapid expansion of cities in the nineteenth century that this became an object of reforming zeal. As with many movements during the age of reform the motives were mixed.

The concept of 'lungs for the metropolis' first surfaced in 1829 during a parliamentary debate on the estate bill of Sir Thomas Maryon Wilson, which was thought, erroneously in the event, to pose a threat to Hampstead Heath. In the same debate other speakers managed to link the recreative value of the Heath and the frustration of Sir Thomas's building plans with the need to combat the growing revolutionary menace posed by the rapid expansion of London, a nebulous idea which was perhaps never entirely far away from much of Victorian philanthropy.[13] And when, in the following decade, there were demands for just such a lung in the East End, where the fields were being swallowed up by working-class housing, one of the factors behind the public agitation which eventually led to the formation of Victoria Park was the fear of disease and pestilence taking root in such overcrowded districts and spreading across London.[14] The notion that large open spaces, particularly on the commanding heights like Hampstead, were advantageous to the general health of London because they provided sources of fresh air, was frequently cited by the open-space enthusiasts as a reason for supporting their cause.[15] That there was also a strong element of altruism in the desire to ameliorate the conditions of life of the working class, however, cannot be doubted.

The movement gained fresh impetus in the mid-1860s from the simultaneous threat to a number of large commons on the edge of London, including Hampstead Heath, Wimbledon Common and, although not strictly a common, Epping Forest. The result was the formation in 1865 of the Commons Preservation Society, of which George Shaw-Lefevre was the first, long-serving chairman. The society became extremely influential and attracted many distinguished members, including James Bryce, who acted as chairman for a time when Shaw-Lefevre was occupied with official business.[16]

Hampstead Heath proper was preserved for public use when it was purchased by the Metropolitan Board of Works in 1871. The involvement of the Charity Commissioners and the funds of the parochial charities came about in the next decade when it was perceived that there was a threat to develop the lands immediately to the east of the

Heath, namely East Park on the Maryon Wilson estate and Parliament Hill Fields belonging to the Earl of Mansfield. Local opposition soon attracted metropolitan support and a Heath Extension Committee was formed with no less a person than the Duke of Westminster as president. Shaw-Lefevre was chairman of the executive committee and Baroness Burdett-Coutts and Octavia Hill were among the members. Initial attempts in 1885 by this high-powered committee to persuade the MBW to undertake the entire cost of purchase, estimated at £300,000, failed, and Shaw-Lefevre set about devising another solution.

Shaw-Lefevre had, of course, recently been chairman of the Select Committee on the City parochial charities bill and it is hardly surprising that his thoughts turned to the funds of the City charities which were then in a kind of limbo; he would also have been in close touch with Bryce, who was then actively involved in the Commons Preservation Society and may have helped to put the idea in his mind. His solution was to draw up an enabling bill which empowered, but did not compel, the vestries of Hampstead and St Pancras to provide £50,000, the Charity Commissioners £50,000 out of the City parochial funds, and the MBW the rest. Despite the predictable opposition of the City Corporation to this use of the City charity funds, more on principle than in disagreement with the actual use to which the money was to be put, Shaw-Lefevre's Act was passed in 1886.[17] Thereafter, the Charity Commissioners were in no doubt that they had a clear obligation to provide £50,000 and, after some hesitation, the vestries complied, but the MBW prevaricated. Eventually, the Board agreed to provide half the total purchase money if the outstanding balance of about £50,000 could be raised by private subscription. This was achieved, and, after some interminable legal wrangling about when the Charity Commission could actually pay out its share, the MBW completed the purchase in 1889, and the 260 acres generally known as Parliament Hill Fields were added to Hampstead Heath.[18] (Significantly, Bryce's Act specifically allowed the funds of the City parochial charities to be used towards the purchase of open spaces which were conveyed to the MBW or other local authorities.[19])

This was, however, by no means an end to the matter as far as open spaces were concerned. Flushed with their success over Parliament Hill Fields, the open-space enthusiasts wanted more of the City charity funds to be used for the purchase of parks and recreation grounds. In December 1887 a 'large and influential deputation' from the Commons Preservation Society, the Kyrle Society and the Metropolitan Public Gardens Association presented a memorial to the Charity Commissioners calling for just such a use of the funds at their disposal. Octavia Hill was a member of the delegation and her somewhat hagiographic early biographer described the memorial, which is a very comprehensive and impressive document, as 'largely her work', but Bryce was also present and other strong personalities were doubtless involved.[20] What they had specifically in mind besides Parliament Hill was Clissold Park in Stoke Newington and the Lawn, Henry Fawcett's old home in Lambeth, which had come on to the market. Eventually both were preserved by Acts of Parliament and the Charity Commissioners contributed £47,500 to the purchase of Clissold Park and £12,500 to the acquisition of Vauxhall Park, as the Lawn was renamed. In addition, before the City Parochial Foundation was established, they were prevailed upon to contribute a further £51,000 towards other open spaces, namely Avondale Park, North Kensington, £2,000, Royal Victoria Gardens, North Woolwich, £10,000, Brockwell Park, £25,000, ground in East Ham, £2,000, and for the enlargement of Peckham Rye, £12,000, making £161,000 in all.[21]

Such a sum was a large proportion of the accumulated capital of the City charities, or, as it was sometimes expressed, a heavy charge on income, and while the preservation of open spaces was specified as a worthy object under the 1883 Act it was by no means the only one. Concerned at the way in which the funds of which they were the temporary guardians were being hijacked for this single purpose, the Commissioners cast around for other ways in which the money could be utilized. Not surprisingly, they thought in terms of education and focused on what was considered at the time to be a crucial gap in educational provision – the dearth of opportunities for young people just starting out in employment to obtain any further general and technical training. The City had already taken one initiative towards the expansion of technical education when a number of livery companies, partly in response to mounting criticism of their affluence and privileged position, banded together with the City Corporation to found the City and Guilds of London Institute which was incorporated in 1880.[22] It was a logical step to contemplate the use of the City parochial funds for similar ends.

That the Charity Commissioners were put in the position of having to make such choices at an early stage, rather than being allowed to pursue their labours at their own pace and eventually arrive at a dispassionate assessment of the needs which could be satisfied by the City parochial funds, had much to do with apprehensions about the state of the nation in the 1880s and the feeling that time was not entirely on the side of the governing classes. The first factor was the so-called 'great depression'. Whether it is strictly correct historically to talk in terms of such a phenomenon, by the mid-1880s there was certainly perceived to be a depression and, moreover, one of long enough standing for a Royal Commission to be appointed to inquire into its nature and causes. Contemporaries were concerned at the declining rate of growth, the worsening terms of trade, and the increasing effectiveness of foreign competition, which many held to be the result of superior scientific and technical training. In 1881 yet another Royal Commission had been set up on the subject of technical instruction with the aim in part of seeing what could be learnt from Continental practice. One of its recommendations had been that ancient endowments should be applied to secondary and technical education.[23]

Additionally, at the very time that the Commissioners began their work, the publication in 1883 of the anonymous tract, *The Bitter Cry of Outcast London*, created equal measures of guilt and alarm at the living conditions it portrayed, soon to be reinforced by a growing concern at the rebelliousness, both organized and disorganized, of the lower classes. Events like the serious rioting of February 1886, in which looting took place in St James's and Mayfair, and the violence of 'Bloody Sunday' in Trafalgar Square in the following year spread apprehension of a greater terror to come, and gave added urgency to the search for palliatives.[24] Such considerations were, as we have seen, by no means absent from the open-spaces movement. In his history of Hampstead, Professor Thompson has remarked that 'In the eighties the dedicated minority of open-space enthusiasts was caught up in a much wider movement of upper-class concern for the plight of the urban working classes mingled with a fear of their capacity for violence.'[25]

There was, however, a much more direct relationship in the case of technical education. On the one hand, technical education was safe in class terms; it was unlikely to give artisans ideas above their station. On the other hand, it could make them more productive and efficient and give them greater pride in their labours, and, the cynical might add, occupy their time. C. T. Millis, who was Principal of the Borough Polytechnic for 30 years, wrote a perceptive little study of technical education over sixty years ago in which he observed that there were two forces at work behind the technical education movement: 'one a feeling of political and social unrest on the part of workmen, and the other a desire for self-improvement and for raising the status of their trade.'[26]

Given that technical education was one of the preoccupations of the times and that the Commissioners already possessed a tendency to favour the use of charitable endowments for educational purposes, it was perhaps predictable that they would wish to see the funds of the City charities applied to this end. What could not have been predicted was the precise form which this took, namely the large-scale and rapid expansion of the polytechnic movement associated with the name of Quintin Hogg. The impetus came from Henry Cunynghame. The consequences were considerable. On the one hand the importance of

the Commissioners' actions to the development of the London polytechnics can hardly be overstressed; they were the essential catalyst
for growth. Conversely the City Parochial Foundation was saddled for
over sixty years with an obligation to the polytechnics which, however
worthy in itself, imposed a severe restriction on the Foundation's
freedom to determine its own policies and priorities.

The event which seems to have done most to influence the Commissioners' thinking was a visit which Cunynghame paid to the Regent
Street Polytechnic. In July 1886 he had been directed by the Commission to attend the Congress on Technical Education in Bordeaux.
After the Congress he visited Paris to study the provision of education
for the working classes with particular emphasis on technical instruction, and on his return produced a typically thorough report which he
submitted in January 1887.[27] He was then asked to study institutions in
London and some provincial centres devoted to similar ends. As Quintin Hogg's daughter described it:

> In the course of his investigations Mr. Cunynghame visited the Polytechnic. No
> one knew his reasons for coming; he was merely a stranger who asked to be shown
> the place, and Mr. Mitchell [the secretary] took him all over it, unconscious that
> he was 'entertaining an angel unawares'. Mr. Cunynghame was immensely struck
> with all he saw, brought other members of the Commission to investigate it also,
> and reported very strongly in favour of some of the money being spent in establish-
> ing or endowing similar conditions [*sic*].[28]

Cunynghame was also in no doubt about the importance of the
occasion, or, despite a certain modesty, his own part in events:

> In saying all this I do not wish to appropriate more than my due. Quintin Hogg
> gave the idea and invitation, the Charity Commissioners took it up and threw into
> it the whole weight of their influence and experience, some of the City Companies
> stripped themselves bare to find the money to help – but the suggestion to institute
> Polytechnics was mine. The printed reports furnished by the Commissioners show
> this and I am not going to forgo the satisfaction and pleasure of thinking of the
> share I took in their splendid work.[29]

The Polytechnic which so impressed Cunynghame and his colleagues
was the remarkable achievement of a remarkable man. The Eton-
educated son of the brilliant barrister and politician, and sometime
chairman of the East India Company, Sir James Weir Hogg, Quintin
Hogg had a strong sense of Christian mission which had led him in
the 1860s to found a ragged school in Of Alley (now York Place) near
Charing Cross. Forced by success to move to larger premises in Castle
Street (now Shelton Street) near Covent Garden, he decided in 1871
to add an evening institute, which was the essential origin of the
Polytechnic. In 1878 the much-expanded institute moved to Long
Acre, where the combination of educational work, especially in techni-

cal subjects, and recreation, which became the hallmark of the polytechnic movement, was first developed. Within a few years the premises in Long Acre had once more become inadequate, and in 1882
the institution moved to Regent Street, where the Royal Polytechnic
Institution, which had been founded there in 1838 as a venue for
lectures and exhibitions in the industrial arts, had been forced to close
down. The name, derived from the Ecole Polytechnique founded in
Paris in 1795, was ideally suited to Quintin Hogg's establishment, but
its adoption thereafter as the name of the institute was the purely
fortuitous result of the availability of the building. As Sidney Webb
put it, 'The title springs from a mere local accident of no significance.'[30]
However, the opportunity was quickly taken to develop further the
scheme of technical education which the very name seemed to
encourage.[31]

Cunynghame's official report to the Commissioners on the results
of his investigations was dated December 1887.[32] In it he cited the
Polytechnic as 'a model' of the kind of institution which combined
education with the facilities of a club for boys over 15, and suggested
that 'if it is desired to benefit the great mass of artizans and the poorer
classes generally, the cheapest and most effectual plan would be to
provide for institutions which should combine healthy recreation with
instruction designed chiefly for evening work, but also having day
sides to be also assisted by scholarships of small value', that is, on
the lines of the Polytechnic. He advocated setting up a limited number
of large institutions rather than several small ones, and added an
appendix containing proposals and a plan for a model polytechnic
which would cost about £70,000 to build and equip and could operate
on an endowment of £5,000 per annum. He even suggested possible
venues.[33]

Even before his long and detailed report was officially submitted,
Cunynghame had convinced the Commissioners of the virtues of his
ideas, and they had begun to prepare the ground for appropriating a
substantial proportion of the City parochial funds to put them into
practice. By October 1887 the Commissioners had finished their initial
task of preparing statements containing details of the charities which
came under the terms of the Act. Over the past twelve months they
had published statements relating to the larger parishes in the first
schedule of the Act, and on 1 October they formally published a
further 51 statements for the parishes in the second schedule. The
occasion was marked by a long article in *The Times* which was
unsigned, but which was clearly based on information supplied from
within the Commission, in effect on what we would term today a press
release. In the article it was estimated that the residual income which
would be available from the parishes in the second schedule was likely

to be about £37,000 per annum for ecclesiastical ends and some £57,000 for general charity purposes. Already many demands were being made on this income. The article referred specifically to the open spaces movement, for which £100,000 had already been promised by that date, and the campaign for free libraries. However, it considered that the best way in which the objects of the Act could be carried out was by founding 'working men's and women's institutes', adapted to both intellectual and recreative needs, in which there would be, *inter alia*, classes in technical instruction, evening classes, libraries and gymnasia, on the model of the Regent Street Polytechnic.[34]

The article mentioned another institution which, in its opinion, was being conducted on the right principles. This was the Beaumont Institute, or People's Palace, in the East End, which Cunynghame and the Commissioners believed was tailor-made for spreading the educational experiment of the Polytechnic further afield. The institute owed its origins to an earlier charitable bequest to found a philosophical institution in Mile End. For years this institution had teetered on the edge of failure before being rescued by a bizarre combination of circumstances in the early 1880s. The unlikely stimulus was the publication in 1882 of Walter Besant's novel *All Sorts and Conditions of Men* in which he envisaged the establishment of a 'Palace of Delight' which would become an intellectual and social centre for the East End. This in turn galvanized local activity which aimed to transform the institute into just such a 'palace'. The Charity Commissioners appointed new trustees and issued a scheme to erect new premises on land which belonged to the Drapers' Company. The Company itself became heavily involved in providing funds for a technical school and an annual endowment. Cunynghame took credit for the latter, having, by his account, promised an equivalent amount out of the City parochial funds. A new building, the Queen's Hall, was opened by Queen Victoria in 1887, and under the energetic direction of Sir Edmund Hay Currie the People's Palace prospered as an ideal polytechnic-like institution, even if its finances became increasingly disordered.[35]

With east London at least partially taken care of, and the needs of central and west London catered for by the Regent Street Polytechnic, the next priority was to stimulate local movements in other districts to campaign for the establishment of similar institutions. Committees of influential persons were formed in south London, north London and the area of Pimlico, Chelsea and Fulham. Such a degree of organization savoured strongly of orchestration from Gwydyr House (the Whitehall headquarters of the Charity Commission), a supposition later confirmed, in fact, by Millis.[36] The way in which the Commission worked is indicated by an event which occurred at a conference on technical education which was held in December 1887 at the Royal

Victoria Hall (Emma Cons's temperance music hall, the forerunner of the Old Vic, which had its educative and social side). In the course of the proceedings, a representative of the Charity Commission announced that funds from the City parochial charities were now available for the endowment of institutions of popular education and recreation. Caroline Martineau, the second Principal of Morley College, later recalled how some of those present 'listened incredulously' to what was being said.[37]

South London led the way, largely because the movement there was energetically directed by Evan Spicer (later Sir Evan Spicer), a leading Congregationalist who was subsequently Chairman of the London County Council and for over forty years a trustee of the Foundation. In January 1888 a deputation waited on the Commissioners to appeal for funds to found a polytechnic in the vicinity of the Elephant and Castle and, not surprisingly, received a very sympathetic hearing. Anstie indicated that if money for such a purpose could be raised locally the Commissioners would be likely to match it pound for pound.[38] The response was overwhelming and within a short time a target of £150,000 had been set to enable three such institutions to be built south of the Thames. The committee even organized a very well-attended meeting at the Mansion House in July at which the Prime Minister, the Marquess of Salisbury, was present to support the resolution, 'That this meeting, being convinced of the urgent need in this country of technical and commercial education, approves of the scheme for the establishment in South London of polytechnic institutes.'[39]

During the first half of 1888 several deputations called on Gwydyr House. Some sought funds for free libraries or public wash-houses, but Anstie, who received them all, steadfastly refused to be diverted from his main objective. Those that advocated founding polytechnics were carefully steered in the right direction, away from narrowly parochial establishments to ones catering for whole districts which, Anstie thought, should cost at least £100,000 to build and furnish. The south-west was well advanced with the promise of a site in Chelsea from Earl Cadogan, but north London suffered from factionalism and divided objectives. Anstie was impatient and told yet another deputation from there that 'he was extremely sorry to find that the movement in north London was so backward, as the Commissioners were very much embarrassed already by the lapse of time.'[40]

In April 1888 the Commissioners issued their annual report for 1887. It was the first to contain more than a perfunctory mention of their work in connection with the City charities, and referred both to the funds earmarked for open spaces and the move to establish institutions like the Regent Street Polytechnic and the People's Palace throughout the metropolis, to which a large proportion of the surplus charity funds might be devoted. When *The Times* covered the report it quoted the section on the City parochial charities at length.[41]

By the time of the next annual report, released early in 1889, the Commissioners could expound at length on the remarkable progress they had made.[42] The formulation of a scheme had been delayed by a number of appeals against the statements of charity property, but these had enabled the Commissioners 'to watch the progress of existing experiments' and had provided 'an opportunity for the formation of public opinion, and the development of public interest and effort'. In south London the target of £150,000 had been reached and the Commissioners wanted to place on record their 'sense of the energy and ability by which the South London movement has, under the chairmanship of Mr. Evan Spicer, been characterized, and the important assistance which it has given us in our attempt to utilize the surplus of the City Parochial Funds for the benefit of the poorer classes.' Plans were already well advanced for the establishment of polytechnics, either by building new premises or adapting existing ones, at New Cross (where the Goldsmiths' Company had already offered assistance), Borough Road, Battersea, Chelsea and Clerkenwell (where the Marquess of Northampton had offered to provide a site). In addition there was every possibility that similar institutions would be established elsewhere in north London. The Commissioners had also identified some smaller ventures like the Royal Victoria Hall, which were deserving of assistance and might become satellites to the new polytechnics. As a measure of the respectability which had been conferred on the movement to establish polytechnics, the Prince of Wales had agreed to accept the presidency of both the south and north London committees.

The report stressed the Commissioners' view that while such institutes should also provide for wholesome recreation and general education, their main purpose was technical instruction. It also carried an exposition of the reasons which had led the Commissioners to embrace this cause so whole-heartedly:

> The existence of a fund which must by law be applied to the benefit of the poorer classes, and which may properly be applied to educational purposes, presents an opportunity not only for promoting, in a general way, the spread of sound knowledge amongst the people at large, but for advancing, in particular, the technical and industrial skill and knowledge of the great body of artizans and labourers.

So convinced, indeed, were the Commissioners of the rectitude of their chosen solution that they announced that the composition of the body of trustees who were to administer the funds would be determined with this work in mind.

In addition to producing a scheme for the multitude of parishes in the second schedule of the Act, Anstie and his colleagues had to decide how the funds of the charities of the parishes in the first schedule were to be utilized for the benefit of the inhabitants of those parishes. They were able to report a good deal of progress in this direction as well. At first they had thought of establishing polytechnics in some of the parishes, but had quickly realized that in areas which were still subject to depopulation there was no way in which such institutions could be sustained and they would be the subject of justifiable criticism. Instead, guided it seems by local initiatives, they had settled for institutes of a different kind which would provide substantial libraries, reading rooms and rooms for lectures and meetings. In this way they could also satisfy the statutory obligation to cater for those who lived or worked in the City and appease the demands of the free library movement. They proposed that the main institutes should be built in Bishopsgate and Cripplegate, to serve the eastern and western halves of the City respectively. Because these institutes were designed to meet more than merely parochial needs, it was always envisaged that they would have to be subsidized from the main body of funds.

In St Bride, Fleet Street, there were plans to found a similar institute, again with considerable local backing. Fleet Street had been the centre of the printing industry for centuries, and there was a strong desire that the institute there should focus on the needs of operatives in that industry. Thus, from the start it was given a slightly different form and made more provision for technical instruction than the Bishopsgate and Cripplegate Institutes. Of the two remaining parishes in the first schedule, St Andrew, Holborn, lay mostly outside the City and was largely bereft of charitable funds which came under the Act, while St Botolph, Aldgate (although there was no mention of this in the report) still had much of the flavour of the old corrupt City parish and was staunchly resistant to change. There the Reverend R. H. Hadden, as a new reforming rector, had to be protected by bodyguards at vestry meetings, and any attempt to put the very substantial charity funds of the parish to good use were met with cries of 'education is the parent of juvenile crime' and 'this technical education fad is all rubbish'. Eventually the Commissioners created a new body called the Aldgate Freedom Foundation with a number of carefully defined aims, and also established a technical institute out of the old Sir John Cass charity and other educational trusts.[43]

The draft Central Scheme (as it was officially called) covering the 107 parishes in the second schedule of the 1883 Act was finally published on 31 August 1889.[44] It was inevitably a long and complex document although many of its provisions were already well known. The gist of the scheme, which, with later amendments and additions, governed the operations of the Foundation until 1989, was that the funds of the charities which were covered by the Act were to be amalgamated into a Central Fund for the non-ecclesiastical charities and a City Church Fund for the remainder. Out of the capital of both funds (consisting of stocks and accumulated cash balances) a sum of £40,000 was to be set aside, in the proportion of three-fifths from the Central Fund and two-fifths from the City Church Fund (corresponding to the estimated size of the respective incomes of each fund), to pay for the expenses of carrying out the Act. This sum included £3,669 to reimburse the existing trustees of the charities for their costs. Out of the remaining capital of the Central Fund £149,000 had been appropriated for the acquisition of open spaces (to which £12,000 was added for an extension to Peckham Rye when the scheme was finalized) and slightly over £150,000 for various institutions. Of the latter sum, £40,000 each was allotted to the Bishopsgate and Cripplegate Institutes, then in an advanced stage of planning, and over £50,000 to a proposed City Polytechnic which was to be formed from an amalgamation of the new Northampton Institute to be built on land promised by the Marquess of Northampton, and the already established Birkbeck Institute and City of London College. The Regent Street Polytechnic was to receive a little over £10,000 for improvements and a contribution to maintenance costs, the People's Palace £6,750 and the Royal Victoria Hall £6,000.

The main calls on the capital of the City Church Fund were the sums considered necessary for the restoration and repair of a number of the City churches, estimated to amount in all to £43,000. In determining what grants they should give, the Commissioners had relied on assessments by Ewan Christian, the surveyor to the Ecclesiastical Commissioners,[45] and had elected to assist 31 churches in all with sums ranging from a few hundred pounds to £8,000 for St Bartholomew-the-Great. A clause was inserted, however, that other churches, not specifically named, could also be assisted if the Commissioners received reports satisfying them that there was such a need.

The Commissioners' latest estimate was that the annual income available to the Central Fund would be about £50,000, and the scheme specified a number of payments which were to be made out of that income. Precedence was given to the compensation of vested interests and the continuance of payments to existing pensioners and recipients of aid whose claims were considered to be legitimate. The scheme named over 350 persons who came into these categories, with details of the amounts they were to receive, but indicated that this was not necessarily an exclusive list, and placed an upper limit of £7,500 on the money that could be applied to these purposes. In addition £500 could be spent annually on 'pensions or occasional or temporary grants in case of emergency to poor persons' who had been living or working in any of the parishes for not less than five years. The investigation of any claims and even the distribution of the money, it was suggested, could usefully be delegated to the Charity Organisation Society.

Annual payments were also to be made to various institutions which had recently been established or were about to be established (as detailed on page 121). In addition the Commissioners could require annual sums not exceeding £5,000 in total to be paid to any polytechnics or similar institutions which might be established in the future for the benefit of the poorer classes. In all, including this last sum, some £28,000 out of the annual income of the Central Fund was directed to be spent on present and future institutions of a predominantly educational kind.

If preliminary calculations were correct, after the deduction of pensions and grants of all kinds, the initial residue of the Central Fund would be about £14,000 per annum. Some analysts of the scheme, however, considered that the capital sums should also be regarded as charges on income at the prevailing rate of interest and, after deducting these, concluded that only some £4,000 would be available to the Foundation for general charitable uses. Whatever income was left to the Central Fund was directed to be spent in one or more of six ways, five of which were educational. Annual grants to institutions could be increased, examinations could be held for students at such institutes or elsewhere and certificates and prizes given, scholarships could be awarded, and, in conjunction with other bodies, diplomas 'for proficiency in technical or mercantile skill and knowledge' could be granted. Almost grudgingly, it seemed, the scheme also allowed the residue to be applied to any of the other purposes named in the Act 'for the benefit of the poorer classes of the Metropolis' and cited specifically the provision and maintenance of open spaces, recreation grounds or drill grounds.

The annual income of the City Church Fund was estimated to be about £35,000. Out of this approximately £5,500 was to be spent in continuing payments to the rectors and other clergy of the City parishes during their tenure of office. A total of £16,000 was also to be paid to the ministers and churchwardens of the parishes, as set out in detail in a long schedule, for the compensation of some vested interests and for the maintenance of the fabric and services of their churches. There was a proviso that if the sums allotted for these latter purposes did not prove sufficient the Charity Commissioners could order an increase. To assist them in making the potentially contentious decision of how much was to be allocated to each parish, the Commissioners wisely relied on the advice of a special committee which had been appointed for this purpose by the Bishop of London, consisting of the Bishop of Bedford, the Archdeacon of London, Henry Hucks

Gibbs, Edwin Freshfield, the Reverend Robert Gregory and Sir John Jennings.[46] In addition to these sums, 10 per cent of the amount allocated from the capital account for the restoration and repair of churches (estimated to be £43,000 at the time of the scheme) was to be repaid annually to the capital account. Any surplus income was to be paid over to the Ecclesiastical Commissioners for use elsewhere in the metropolis.

The scheme also contained a clause that when the difficult task of determining exactly how much charity property was applicable to general uses and how much to ecclesiastical purposes had been completed, the governing body would have the option of applying to the Charity Commissioners for the establishment of a separate body to manage the City Church Fund.

According to the terminology of the scheme the Central Fund and the City Church Fund were together to constitute the City Parochial Foundation, a name which was not used in the 1883 Act and which may indicate that the Charity Commissioners were consciously or unconsciously arrogating to themselves a particularly positive role in its establishment. The trustees who were to administer the Foundation were to be known collectively as the Central Governing Body. According to the Act, however, this body was to be called 'the Trustees of the London Parochial Charities' and was to be a body corporate with perpetual succession and a common seal. This is the reason why the City Parochial Foundation had the subsidiary name of the Trustees of the London Parochial Charities, the latter being, strictly speaking, the legal name of its governing body.

The Act decreed that the Central Governing Body, as it was now to be known, was to consist of 21 persons, five of whom were to be nominated by the Crown and four by the Corporation of London. How the remaining places were to be filled was left to the Charity Commissioners, provided that four of the twelve were allotted in the first instance to existing trustees of the charities. By their draft scheme the Commissioners proposed that two members would be nominated by the London County Council, two each by the University of London, University College and King's College, two by the Ecclesiastical Commissioners, and one each by the governors of the Bishopsgate and Cripplegate Foundations, the four last being chosen from among existing trustees.

Each member was to hold office for six years but was eligible for re-election, and a rota was devised to ensure that there would be elections for at least a third of the places every two years. At least six ordinary meetings were to be held during a year, plus any number of special meetings, and the quorum for meetings was fixed at seven. A Chairman was to be elected annually. Provision was made for the formation of committees consisting of not less than seven members, of whom three would constitute a quorum. One such committee, a Pension Committee, was required to be set up by the scheme, and its membership was to include the nominees of the Ecclesiastical Commissioners and of the Bishopsgate and Cripplegate Foundations, that is, at least initially all former trustees of the parochial charities.

An office could be built or acquired for the conduct of the Foundation's business and £6,000 was to be made available out of the Central Fund capital account for this purpose if required. A Clerk was to be appointed and such other officers 'as shall be necessary', and the costs of administration were to be divided between the Central Fund and the City Church Fund in proportion to their respective incomes.

When the draft scheme was published what was patently obvious to all who read it was how much of the capital and income of the parochial charities had already been appropriated to various uses by the Charity Commissioners, and how little discretion in the expenditure of the funds then available had been left to the Central Governing Body. When the final financial statement was issued a few years later this became even clearer. The total stock and cash balances which were transferred to the Central Fund capital account amounted to a little over £410,000, of which some £340,000 had already been promised in payments or was required to meet costs, leaving only about £70,000 for additional lump-sum payments which the governing body might wish to make or for investment to swell the modest residual income. The City Church Fund fared better. Of its accumulated capital of about £170,000, £111,000 was left after payments.[47] Even these amounts remaining were not immediately available to the Foundation, however. The scheme stipulated that all the personal property belonging to the various charities (stocks and shares and cash balances) was to be vested in the Official Trustees of Charitable Funds and all real property in the Official Trustee of Charity Lands. This was not an unusual provision in schemes formulated by the Charity Commissioners, but in this instance they felt that they had to explain their action, claiming that it relieved the governing body of an administrative burden and removed some of the friction which might have been encountered in transferring funds.[48] It meant, however, that a case had to be made out when the Foundation wanted to obtain some of its funds from the Official Trustees. If it was not quite going cap-in-hand, it often seemed that way, especially in the early years.

Having spent an inordinate amount of time in producing their draft scheme, the Commissioners initially allowed only two months for comment, but, after strong protest, agreed to extend the time limit to the end of 1889. On the whole the scheme was not very favourably

received. *The Times* carried a long article from 'a Correspondent' criticizing the extent to which the Commissioners themselves had determined
what was to be done with the charity funds, and asking 'why should
the accident that two or three nominees of the Government – some of
them not even permanent officials – are imbued with a particular view
determine the application of a valuable property for years to come?'
He thought that polytechnics were still experimental and that it was
imprudent to place such a heavy reliance on them, and extolled instead
the virtues of open spaces, for which he cited support from Bryce,
Hobhouse and Octavia Hill. The Central Governing Body as constituted by the scheme was unrepresentative and had too many members
from institutes of higher education. 'The Commissioners have determined that the substance of these funds shall swell the long list of
educational endowments, and have constituted a Board which will
finish their work and apply the funds in the way they desire.' Too
much money was being allocated to the repair and restoration of City
churches, which, he thought, would lead to over-restoration of the
kind deplored by 'William Morris and his friends', and the £16,000
set aside annually to maintain churches and services which no one
attends was 'so singular a waste of resources'. The scheme should be
altered so that more discretion would be left to a governing body
'really representative of London'.[49]

The *Charity Record*, no friend of the Charity Commission, took much
the same line, castigating the proposals as 'most unfair to the people
of London'. It, too, particularly criticized the composition of the governing body. 'The Charity Commissioners are at their old game, and
the proposed constitution of the central governing body, brings out
clearly the fact that the Gwydyr House authorities desire to apply as
much as they can of these charity funds for educational purposes.'[50]

The formal objections submitted to the Charity Commission, many
of which were published as a House of Commons paper by order of
James Bryce, tended to echo these views.[51] Bryce, himself, while pol-
itely remarking that the scheme was 'satisfactory in the main', offered
a number of suggestions for improvement. He was certain that had
the London County Council been in existence at the time of the Act,
it would have been given ample representation on the governing body,
and thought that it should have at least five nominees at the expense
of those from educational bodies and the Bishopsgate and Cripplegate
Foundations. He questioned the large grants to these two institutes
and to the City Polytechnic, arguing that under the spirit of his Act
the charity funds in the five large parishes which had been singled
out should have been sufficient to meet the needs of the City. While
not doubting the value of technical education, he pointed out that
under the Technical Instruction Act of that very year this was now

an object to which local rates could be applied (an argument also employed in an article on the scheme in the journal of the Charity Organisation Society[52]), and wondered if the heavy concentration on this use meant that the charity funds were 'not quite sufficiently directed to the needs of the very poorest classes'. In general, he thought that there was a 'tendency for benefactions intended for the very poor to fall into the hands of a somewhat higher class'. His main criticism, however, was that the Commissioners had exercised far too much control over the governing body and had left it with far too little income to apply 'to such purposes as the changing circumstances of the future might from time to time suggest'. 'The experience of charitable foundations,' he wrote, 'shows that elasticity, and the power of introducing variations easily, are absolutely essential to the utility of endowments.'

The recently formed London County Council submitted a long and cogent criticism in the form of a report from its Corporate Property, Charities and Endowments Committee, which was signed by Lord Hobhouse (as he had by then become) as the committee's chairman. The report strongly opposed the use of such a large proportion of the funds for the Bishopsgate and Cripplegate Institutes, and considered that there was too great a concentration on polytechnics, which were new and untested; in particular it remained to be seen how far they would be used by the poorer inhabitants of the metropolis. Other objects were suggested for consideration, principally more open spaces, but also the provision of baths, wash-houses, provident institutions, convalescent hospitals, smaller lending libraries, public meeting rooms and improved dwellings. More importantly, however, greater discretion should be left to the governing body, on the grounds that 'it is more prudent to trust the gradual working of the judgment of competent men, drawn from various walks of life, and working through considerable spaces of time, and to let them mould the uses of the funds under the guidance of events, than to settle the whole at once into a new fixed system, according to the judgment of a single office, however ably it may be manned.' The most trenchant criticism, however, was reserved for the ecclesiastical provisions, which, in so far as they gave substantial sums to City churches, served to 'perpetuate a great deal of the existing excess and waste'. The report, however, acknowledged that the main fault here lay with the 1883 Act. Finally, and predictably, the Council wanted more places on the governing body – six now and two more later in place of those nominated by the Ecclesiastical Commissioners when the ecclesiastical property had been separated from the general – and also urged that there should be four nominees from the School Board for London.

The Metropolitan Public Gardens Association, the Kyrle Society

and the Commons Preservation Society jointly made a long submission. Naturally, their chief aim was to press for a greater proportion
of the funds to be spent on open spaces, but they also made many of
the same criticisms as the LCC and Bryce, perhaps not surprisingly
as Bryce was one of the signatories for the Commons Preservation
Society. They questioned whether polytechnics benefited the very poor,
wanted less to be spent on libraries in the City, and called for more
authority over the funds to be left to the Foundation, greater elasticity
and a more representative governing body. The metropolitan vestries
and district boards, taking their cue from a model objection circulated
by Hampstead Vestry, also thought that the money left to the governing body was inadequate and its powers too constrained. They wanted
free libraries in the wider metropolis rather than in the City, local
technical institutes, more representation for the LCC and the London
School Board on the governing body and a greater proportion of the
funds of the ecclesiastical charities left to the Ecclesiastical Commissioners. The Kensington Vestry even went so far as to castigate
the draft scheme as 'immature, and insufficiently considered'.[53] A
number of political clubs, mainly Liberal and Radical Associations,
sent in statements criticizing the amount to be spent on City churches;
even the City of London Liberal Association resolved 'That, in the
opinion of this Committee, the sums allocated by the Scheme to ecclesiastical purposes are excessive and wasteful.' The clubs also called for
more representation on the governing body for the LCC and the
London School Board.[54]

The City authorities naturally took a somewhat different view. Meetings were held in various parishes and a series of objections was lodged
with a common theme. A lead was provided by the parish of St
Sepulchre, which, not unreasonably aggrieved at having been relegated
from the first division of large parishes during the passage of Bryce's
bill, had appointed a special committee in 1883 to consider how it
should respond to the Act.[55] The main points made by the parish
vestries, and supported in a separate objection by the City Corporation, were that the scheme had ignored those trusts which still
had a legitimate object and had appropriated for the purposes of
education 'the funds devoted by their founders to the relief of the aged
poor', that the number of pensioners and other recipients of grants
did not cover all those inhabitants or their employees who were in
need, that the sum of £500 set aside for the temporary relief of distress
was inadequate, and that no provision was made to meet the ordinary
costs of parish administration. They questioned whether the Commissioners had not exceeded their powers in dealing so comprehensively with ecclesiastical charities, and considered that the amounts
allocated for the restoration and repair of churches and the mainten-

ance of their fabric and services were inadequate. They agreed with other critics that insufficient funds had been left at the disposal of the Central Governing Body and wanted the six educational representatives on the body to be replaced by nominees of the parishes.[56]

The vestry clerks met separately and, besides bemoaning their lot at having been virtually ignored in the compensation of vested interests, were petulantly aggrieved that ministers should have a say in how the money allocated for the maintenance of their churches should be spent as 'sometimes rectors are inclined to go faster in the way of "improvements" than the churchwardens would approve'.[57] A number of the City livery companies passed resolutions regretting their lack of representation on the governing body, and suggesting that they would be satisfied if a nominee could be appointed by the City and Guilds Institute. With this request the Commissioners were readily and happily able to comply.[58] The City and Guilds Institute itself was anxious that the new polytechnics might compete with its own provision of technical education, but was mollified by being given a representative on the Central Governing Body.

There was little overt support for the Commissioners' scheme. Somewhat surprisingly, *The Times* carried a leading article which expressed contrary views to those of its own correspondent a little earlier. With particular reference to the LCC's objections, it generally favoured the scheme and approved of the setting up of polytechnics, stressing the pump-priming aspects of the contributions from the parochial charity funds, and adding that if these contributions were stopped other money which had been promised would be held back. It counselled against further delay and thought that there was no guarantee that the LCC would do a better job.[59] A little later an amazing letter appeared in *The Times* from Robert Pearce, the clerk to the Cripplegate vestry and the solicitor who, with Edwin Freshfield, had orchestrated the City's opposition to Bryce's bill. Now he praised the Commissioners and virtually every aspect of the scheme, although he thought that there should be greater representation on the governing body for the LCC and the London School Board.[60] The Commissioners might well have been wary of Greeks bearing gifts, but Pearce was being tipped as a possible Clerk of the Foundation[61] and there may have been an element of self-serving in his seeming volte-face.

The weight of opinion, however, was set firmly against certain aspects of the draft scheme, but although some of the objectors suggested other ways in which the money might be spent, the principles behind their reasoning were not so very different from those of the Commissioners. Direct charity was invariably eschewed. As the LCC put it, in almost its only words of grudging praise for the scheme, 'it is wiser to aim at elevating the mental level and social capacity of the

mass, and not to attempt the direct alleviation of individual misery.'
Only the backward-looking City parishes and the Charity Organisation
Society, which somewhat ambiguously questioned 'whether the charities could be used for relief purposes in such a way as to promote the
better administration of relief',[62] referred to the possibility that the
funds could be used for the relief of poverty in the eleemosynary spirit
in which a good many of the original endowments had been framed.

In fact, the Commissioners were merely exemplifying in a rather
extreme form ideas about social policy which almost all their critics
also embraced. Central to these was that abhorrence of 'doles', of
indiscriminate giving, which, it was widely thought, swelled the ranks
of an indigent, pauper class. Moreover, in the troubled times of the
1880s, the existence of this 'residuum', as it was frequently called by
contemporaries, seemed to pose a severe threat to social order. The
Charity Commissioners, and those appointed to assist them, were
lawyers to a man, members of that 'new professional gentry' which
has been identified as dominating urban attitudes towards the poor in
late-Victorian England.[63] This social group looked upon philanthropy
as a potent weapon in the attempt to reduce the body politic to order,
and to misuse charitable funds was a cardinal sin. The Commissioners
may have feared, perhaps even unconsciously, that, however carefully
the trustees of the amalgamated charities were chosen, there was no
guarantee that they would not perpetuate some of the worst features
of the present administration of those charities. The result would be an
unforgivable, even dangerous, waste of scarce resources. Polytechnics,
properly constituted, on the other hand, could hardly be faulted. They
promoted the intellectual, moral and spiritual improvement of the
working classes, they could aspire to be centres of civilization, 'people's
palaces', in their neighbourhoods, and, just as importantly, they
required a positive effort of will on the part of those who participated
in their benefits. They fostered those very qualities of self-help and
independence which distinguished the deserving from the undeserving
poor.

Convinced of the wisdom of their proposals, the Commissioners were
not about to be deflected from their chosen course. They replied at
length to the various criticisms of their scheme, sometimes not without
a hint of exasperation, especially at the LCC, whose report, they noted,
had been passed 'by little more than an even vote', but in the end
they virtually ignored the objections, and the only change of any
substance made to the scheme was in the composition of the Central
Governing Body. The number of nominees from the University of
London, University College and King's College was reduced to one
each, and of their replacements two were assigned to the LCC (making
four in all, the same representation as the City Corporation) and one

to the City and Guilds of London Institute. In addition it was stipulated that if and when the City Church Fund was completely separated from the Central Fund and given its own governing body, the two nominees of the Ecclesiastical Commissioners would be replaced by members chosen by the London School Board. The Central Scheme, as amended, was submitted to the Committee of the Council on Education on 1 February 1890 and approved by them on 29 April. It was then laid before Parliament.[64]

Even at this late hour the City vestries would not give up their opposition. Led by St Sepulchre and backed by the City Corporation, they petitioned Parliament and sent deputations to the City's MPs and any other Members who would listen. Sir Robert Fowler moved an address against the scheme but received so little support that he did not press the matter to a division. The St Sepulchre committee acknowledged defeat, even though 'no stone has been left unturned to secure to their grand old Parish those legacies and gifts, which they have striven so hard to preserve'.[65] The Central Scheme received the approval of the Queen in Council on 23 February 1891.

NOTES

1. David Owen, *English Philanthropy 1660–1960* (1965), 182–208.
2. Ibid., 261.
3. Ibid., 264–8.
4. *Charity Record*, 19 May 1881 (quoted in Owen, op. cit., 307).
5. *Charity Record*, 4 Aug. 1887, 249.
6. *Post Office Directory*, 1885, 1886: *DNB*.
7. Joseph Foster, *Men-at-the-Bar* (1885): *The Times*, 5 Jan. 1884, 5: A. G. B. Atkinson, *St Botolph Aldgate: The Story of a City Parish* (1898), 221 (chapter written by R. H. Hadden).
8. C. H. Dudley Ward and C. B. Spencer, *The Unconventional Civil Servant: Sir Henry H. Cunynghame* (1938), 10: *The Times*, 6 May 1935, 14.
9. Ward and Spencer, op. cit., 177–8.
10. E. Moberly Bell, *Octavia Hill* (1942), 143–4, 156–8: Gillian Darley, *Octavia Hill: A Life* (1990), 175–8, 188–90.
11. *Who's Who of British Members of Parliament, II, 1886–1918*, ed. Michael Stenton and Stephen Lees (1978): *Who Was Who 1916–1928*: *The Times*, 20 Aug. 1920, 13.
12. *Post Office Directory*.
13. F. M. L. Thompson, *Hampstead: Building a Borough, 1650–1964* (1974), 144–5.
14. Charles Paulsen, *Victoria Park: A Study in the History of East London* (1976), 1–2, 15–16.
15. Thompson, op. cit., 326.
16. G. Shaw-Lefevre, *English Commons and Forests* (1894), 27–46: Owen, op. cit., 492–6.
17. *The Times*, 17 Sept. 1886, 7; 21 Sept. 1886, 4; 13 Nov. 1886, 9.
18. Shaw-Lefevre, op. cit., 47–58: Thompson, op. cit., 324–34.
19. 46 & 47 Vict., c. 36, public and general, clause 16.

20. *The Times*, 17 Dec. 1887, 16: Bell, op. cit., 222–3: the text of the memorial and accompanying letter is printed in *PP*, 1890, LV, *Return of . . . certain Objections and Suggestions received by the Charity Commissioners . . . and of certain Memoranda and Reports prepared by the Charity Commissioners . . .*, 43–59.
21. CPF, Central Scheme, schedule II, part I.
22. C. T. Millis, *Technical Education: Its Development and Aims* (1925), 53–72: *Survey of London*, XXVIII, *The Museums Area of South Kensington and Westminster* (1975), 238–42.
23. Helen Merrell Lynd, *England in the Eighteen-Eighties: Toward a Social Basis for Freedom* (1945), 113–32, 357–9, 371: S. B. Saul, *The Myth of the Great Depression, 1873–1896* (1985 ed.): Stephen F. Cotgrove, *Technical Education and Social Change* (1958), 19–23: S. John Teague, *The City University: A History* (1980), 23.
24. *The Bitter Cry of Outcast London* (1883, reprinted 1970, ed. Anthony S. Wohl): Gareth Stedman Jones, *Outcast London: A Study in the Relationship Between Classes in Victorian Society* (1984 ed.), 290–6: Lynd, op. cit., 282–3: Bentley B. Gilbert, *The Evolution of National Insurance in Great Britain: The Origins of the Welfare State* (1966), 32–6.
25. Thompson, op. cit., 325.
26. Millis, op. cit., 6: Cotgrove, op. cit., 16–18.
27. *Return of . . . certain Objections, ut supra*, 72–112.
28. Ethel M. Wood, *The Polytechnic and its Founder Quintin Hogg* (1932 ed.), 135.
29. Quoted in Ward and Spencer, op. cit., 180–1.
30. Sidney Webb, *London Education* (1904), 135.
31. Wood, op. cit., 93.
32. *Return of . . . certain Objections, ut supra*, 112–216.
33. Ibid., 125–34.
34. *The Times*, 3 Oct. 1887, 4.
35. *Return of . . . certain Objections, ut supra*, 166–7: Ward and Spencer, op. cit., 182–7: Owen, op. cit., 293.
36. Millis, op. cit., 81.
37. Cited in Denis Richards, *Offspring of the Vic: A History of Morley College* (1958), 80–1.
38. *The Times*, 17 Jan. 1888, 8.
39. Millis, op. cit., 81.
40. *The Times*, 20 Jan. 1888, 7; 12 March 1888, 4; 28 March 1888, 12; 2 May 1888, 16; 29 May 1888, 5; 1 June 1888, 10; 26 July 1888, 6; 27 July 1888, 11.
41. *PP*, 1888, XXXIV, *Thirty-Fifth Report of the Charity Commissioners for England and Wales*: *The Times*, 21 April 1888, 6.
42. *PP*, 1889, XXVIII, *Thirty-Sixth Report of the Charity Commissioners*.
43. Atkinson, op. cit., 208–38 (chapter written by Hadden): Owen, op. cit., 294.
44. *PP*, 1890, XXVI, *Thirty-Seventh Report of the Charity Commissioners*: *The Times*, 26 Sept. 1889, 13: *Charity Record*, 3 Oct. 1889, 309–10.
45. *PP*, 1889, XXVIII, *Thirty-Sixth Report of the Charity Commissioners*.
46. Ibid.: *Robert Gregory 1819–1911 Being the Autobiography of Robert Gregory, D.D., Dean of St Paul's*, ed. W. H. Hutton (1912), 124–5.
47. *PP*, 1894, XXVIII, *Forty-First Report of the Charity Commissioners*.
48. *PP*, 1892, XXVII, *Thirty-Ninth Report of the Charity Commissioners*.
49. *The Times*, 26 Sept. 1889, 13.
50. *Charity Record*, 3 Oct. 1889, 313.
51. *Return of . . . certain Objections, ut supra* (in which all the objections cited are to be found except those for which a separate source is given).
52. *The Charity Organisation Review*, V (1889), 455.

53. Charity Commissioners, file 205629A/83.
54. Ibid., file 205629A/82.
55. Guildhall Library, MS. 7230.
56. Ibid., 144–53.
57. *The Times*, 19 Oct. 1889, 11.
58. Charity Commissioners, file 205629A/77.
59. *The Times*, 9 Dec. 1889, 9.
60. Ibid., 20 Dec. 1889, 10.
61. *Charity Record*, 16 April 1891, 131.
62. *Charity Organisation Review*, V (1889), 456.
63. Stedman Jones, op. cit., 240, 269–70.
64. *PP*, 1890–1, XXVI, *Thirty-Eighth Report of the Charity Commissioners*.
65. Guildhall Library, MS. 7230, 187–286.

Part II

The Foundation 1891–1939:
The dominance of the polytechnics

5 Trustees and administration

The Foundation had what could be described as a hesitant start. The members of the Central Governing Body nominated by the various bodies specified in the Central Scheme gathered together for their first meeting on 21 April 1891 at the Mansion House in the City, which was made available by Joseph Savory, the incumbent Lord Mayor of London and one of the City Corporation's nominees. However, on finding that the University of London had failed to make a nomination, those present decided that the Central Governing Body was not yet properly constituted and adjourned the meeting to 1 May.[1] It may be that they had only been called together to satisfy the requirement of the Central Scheme that the first meeting should be held within two months of the date of the scheme (23 February 1891), but if so, the attendance of fifteen trustees was remarkably high.

The University of London soon chose its nominee. He was Sir Philip Magnus, the Secretary and Organizing Director of the City and Guilds of London Institute, who had been a member of the Royal Commission on Technical Education and was acknowledged as one of the country's foremost experts on the subject. As the Charity Commissioners had intended, the representatives of education in general, and technical education in particular, formed a strong contingent on the Central Governing Body, led by Magnus, Quintin Hogg (nominated by the Crown), Evan Spicer (nominated by the London County Council) and Sir Owen Roberts (the nominee of King's College, who had played a major part in the establishment of the City and Guilds Institute and had recently been knighted for his services to technical education).

79

City influences, however, predominated. Not only were there four nominees of the City Corporation, but several of the other trustees had close connections with the City. Under the terms of the Central Scheme, the first two nominees of the Ecclesiastical Commissioners and those of the Bishopsgate and Cripplegate Foundations had to be chosen from among the trustees of the City parochial charities at the time of the passing of the 1883 Act; while the appointees of the Crown included the Dean of St Paul's and Charles James Drummond, the Secretary of the London Society of Compositors, who could be said to represent the interests of one of the most important of the City's trades. In addition, Sir Owen Roberts, besides his educational accomplishments, was Clerk of the Clothworkers' Company.[2] This preponderance of City interests does not appear to have worked to the Foundation's disadvantage; on the contrary, it may have helped to dissipate more easily and quickly the initial hostility to the Foundation on the part of those who looked on it as a body which had confiscated funds that rightly belonged to the City parishes.

The presence of three trustees who had served on the Royal Commission of 1878–80 was doubtless intended to provide continuity. Two of them, Robert Gregory, the Dean of St Paul's, and William Rogers, the rector of St Botolph, Bishopsgate, also provided a solid core of ecclesiastical influence. The third, Henry Hucks Gibbs, in fact never attended a meeting and was disqualified in 1893 for non-attendance. An element of continuity of a different kind was also provided by the presence of Edwin Freshfield as a nominee of the Ecclesiastical Commissioners. Freshfield, as we have seen, represented the best and most responsible kind of parochial trustee, who had readily admitted that reform was necessary, but vigorously defended the retention of local control, and had orchestrated opposition to Bryce's bill.

When the trustees convened again on 1 May 1891 their first task was to elect a Chairman for the year. Perhaps not surprisingly their choice fell on their host, the Lord Mayor, Joseph Savory. But what was perhaps thought of as a short-term arrangement proved in the event to be remarkably long lasting, for Savory remained Chairman (re-elected annually) until his resignation from the Central Governing Body on the grounds of ill-health in 1920. He was an excellent and punctilious Chairman who brought to the Foundation considerable business acumen – acquired in the family business as a goldsmith and silversmith – and knowledge of the City and its properties. He was also versed in educational matters, having served as the City's representative on the London School Board in 1885–8, and was Chairman of Christ's Hospital and a governor of Royal Holloway College. He was also a governor of St Bartholomew's and St Thomas's Hospitals.

From 1892 to 1900 he was Conservative MP for Westmoreland, and was created a baronet. He died in 1921.[3]

The Central Scheme laid down a number of requirements about how the Foundation's business was to be transacted. A Pension Committee was to be appointed and had to include the initial nominees of the Ecclesiastical Commissioners and the Bishopsgate and Cripplegate Foundations (that is, former parochial trustees). Otherwise the Central Governing Body could form any number of additional committees at their discretion provided they contained at least seven members, of whom three would constitute a quorum. Besides the obligatory Pension Committee, the trustees decided to appoint an Estate Committee and a Finance and General Purposes Committee. As its name would indicate, Finance and General Purposes was the dominant committee and determined how the Foundation's income was to be distributed. Its initial composition showed a clear bias towards education, for Hogg, Magnus, Roberts and Spicer were all chosen as members. The main business of the meetings of the Central Governing Body was to receive the reports of these committees and it was rare for their recommendations to be overturned.

This simple committee structure, decided on at its first business meeting, basically served the Foundation without change for over fifty years, during the whole period under review in this chapter. The trustees soon decided that it was reasonable for the Pension Committee to handle the business of the City Church Fund, and from time to time special committees or sub-committees, usually answerable to the Finance and General Purposes Committee, were appointed to deal with particular items of business or matters of policy.

Under the terms of the Central Scheme, the Central Governing Body was only required to meet once every two months, but at first the trustees met more frequently to clarify the administrative structure and responsibilities. At the end of 1892, however, they decided that it was only necessary to arrange six meetings for the following year, while reserving the power to call additional meetings if required, and a cycle was established in which the committees met shortly before the meeting of the Central Governing Body to which they were to report.[4] In 1894 a system was devised for handling the distribution of grants whereby special meetings were to be called in May and towards the end of the year at which the trustees would consider the recommendations of the Finance and General Purposes Committee.[5] Within two years the last meeting was found to be unnecessary, and only one special meeting was held to determine the distribution of most of the year's grants, on the same day as, and immediately before, the ordinary May meeting. Any sums left over were allocated at the last ordinary meeting of the year. This method of working, which had been established by 1897, remained virtually unchanged until the Second World War.

A list of all the trustees and the terms they served on the Central Governing Body is given in Appendix A. Some of these trustees should, however, be singled out for the particular contributions they made to the work of the Foundation. First and foremost were the Chairmen of the Central Governing Body, who, without exception, took a very active role in the Foundation's affairs. After Sir Joseph Savory's surprisingly long and successful chairmanship came to an end with his resignation in 1920, the unanimous choice fell on Sir Evan Spicer.[6] One of the original 21 trustees, as a nominee of the London County Council, Spicer had led the attempt to galvanize support for the polytechnic movement in south London even before the Foundation had been established. He was an alderman of the first London County Council and was elected chairman of its Finance Committee in 1892, Vice-Chairman of the Council in 1905–6 and Chairman in the following year. He was knighted in 1917. Spicer retained an abiding concern with the welfare of the polytechnics he had helped bring into being and was chairman of the governors of Borough Polytechnic for many years. He stepped down as Chairman of the Central Governing Body in 1934 but remained a trustee. When he died at the age of 88 in 1937, he had served the Foundation continuously for 47 years and was the last of the original trustees. In the words of his fellow trustees, as recorded in the minutes:

> Sir Evan's profound knowledge made him an invaluable colleague. He was firm and independent in his principles and commanded the love and affection of those connected with him and the esteem of all who knew him. His life was spent in the service of the Empire and of his fellow creatures, and particularly of those in a less fortunate position of life.[7]

Spicer's successor as Chairman in 1934, Peter MacIntyre Evans, was a man who 'combined exceptional business ability, a tireless energy and a quite unique charm of manner'. Appointed Clerk and solicitor to the Clothworkers' Company in succession to Sir Owen Roberts in 1907, he had also taken Roberts's place on the Central Governing Body as the nominee of King's College on the latter's death in 1915. He, too, was much involved in education and played an active part in the City and Guilds Institute, but his concerns were wider. His business interests included positions on the boards of the City of London Real Property Company and the Union Assurance Society, and he devoted much of his time to the welfare of the blind, eventually serving on a Ministry of Health advisory committee on the subject. He had been chairman of the Foundation's Estate Committee since 1920, and had also served since 1926 as Vice-Chairman of the

Central Governing Body. He held the Chairmanship of the Foundation from 1934 until his death at the age of 84 in 1944.[8] Evans's period of greatest influence on the affairs of the Foundation coincided with a time when, both by dint of an increase in the income available for distribution in grants and by inclination, the dominance of the polytechnics was coming to an end.

After the Chairman of the Central Governing Body, the chairmen of the committees were among the more active and influential trustees. The first chairman of the Finance and General Purposes Committee in 1891 was Lord Reay, a member of the Council of University College and its nominee on the Central Governing Body. Donald James Mackay, eleventh Baron Reay, had recently returned from India, where as Governor of Bombay from 1885 to 1890 he had played a major role in organizing educational services. In 1894, however, he was appointed Under Secretary of State for India and resigned his trusteeship.[9]

His successor as chairman of the Finance Committee was Richard Buckley Litchfield, a barrister, who was a nominee of the Ecclesiastical Commissioners, by whom he was employed. Litchfield's great achievements were as a teacher and administrator at the Working Men's College in Great Ormond Street, an institution which he helped to found and of which he was Bursar from 1854 to 1901 and Vice-Principal in 1873–5.[10]

Litchfield resigned because of ill-health in 1899 and was succeeded as committee chairman by Lewis Boyd Sebastian, one of the outstanding early trustees. Another barrister who was an equity draughtsman and conveyancer, Sebastian had joined the Central Governing Body as the nominee of the City and Guilds Institute in 1893. As a prominent member of the Skinners' Company, he had written a spirited defence of the City livery companies and their right to dispose of their property as they wished. In 1915, while still chairman of the Finance Committee, he was elected Vice-Chairman of the Foundation, and held both posts until his death in 1926 at the age of 74. He was also chairman of the governors of Northampton Polytechnic from 1901 to 1926 and a member of the Council of the City and Guilds Institute.[11] His concern to promote the interests of technical education meant that while he occupied such a position of influence among the trustees, there was always a presumption in favour of retaining the bias towards the polytechnics in the Foundation's affairs.

Charles James Drummond, who was Secretary of the London Society of Compositors from 1881 to 1892 and one of the original trustees, had been Sebastian's vice-chairman on the Finance Committee since 1899 and succeeded him as chairman in 1926, but died three years later at the age of 81.[12] He had previously been chairman of the

Pension Committee and was another who gave outstanding service to the Foundation. The next chairman was Sir Henry Harris, who had been appointed as a trustee by the Crown in 1921. He had been a member of the London County Council from 1892 to 1910 and had been leader of the Moderates in 1904–6 and Chairman of the Council in 1907–8; subsequently he sat as Unionist MP for South Paddington from 1910 to 1922.[13] He retired from the chairmanship of the Finance Committee in 1935 and was succeeded by Herbert Game, who had been nominated to the Central Governing Body by the LCC three years previously.[14]

The first and extremely influential chairman of the Estate Committee, Sir Owen Roberts, was one of those active citizens of the late nineteenth and early twentieth centuries whose outstanding public service has been but dimly recognized by posterity. 'An energetic, testy Welsh barrister', Roberts was Clerk to the Clothworkers' Company for over forty years. As such he actively sought to deflect the criticisms being levelled at the livery companies by using the companies' funds to promote technical education, and played a leading role in the establishment of the City and Guilds of London Institute. A zealous supporter of polytechnics, he served on the Technical Education Board which was set up by the LCC in 1893, and chaired the London Polytechnic Council on which representatives of the Board, the Foundation and the City and Guilds Institute met to discuss matters relating to the polytechnics. His main contribution to the work of the Foundation, however, was on the Estate Committee where his experience in dealing with City property proved of inestimable benefit. Frequently he had to act quickly to conclude a favourable transaction by chairman's action, and in this he always commanded the complete confidence of his colleagues. He also served as the first Vice-Chairman of the Central Governing Body, deputizing whenever Sir Joseph Savory was not available. When Roberts died in 1915, Savory, as Chairman of the Central Governing Body, spoke at length about the qualities which he had brought to the service of the Foundation, remarking *inter alia* that 'his knowledge of City property and business capacity enabled him to bring about the consolidation of various properties with great present advantage to the Foundation, and still greater to come', and pointing out that he had the remarkable record of having attended 485 meetings out of a possible 501 during a period of over twenty-three years.[15]

Roberts's successor as chairman of the Estate Committee, Edward Bond, had excellent credentials for the task. Also a barrister, he had been one of the assistant commissioners appointed by the Charity Commission to draw up the Central Scheme (see Chapter 4). Although not among the initial group of trustees, he had been appointed to the

Central Governing Body in 1895 by the LCC. At the end of his second six-year term in 1907 he was no longer a member of the Council and was not re-appointed, but two years later he returned to the Central Governing Body as a nominee of the Crown and served until his death in 1920.[16] Like Roberts before him, he was generally content for the polytechnics to receive the lion's share of the income from the estates he so carefully nurtured. He had, of course, been one of the principal architects of the scheme for utilizing the City's parochial endowments to found polytechnics, and he served briefly as Chairman of the Technical Education Board in succession to Sidney Webb in 1908.

Bond's successor as chairman of the Estate Committee, P. M. Evans, subsequently became Chairman of the Central Governing Body in 1934 (see above), when he gave up his committee chairmanship. His replacement, Charles Hogg, had served on the Central Governing Body as a nominee of the Ecclesiastical Commissioners since 1927, but his tenure of office was brief for he died in 1935.[17] His place was taken by Sir Edgar Horne, who had been a trustee, on the nomination of the Crown, since 1921. A surveyor by profession, and therefore eminently fitted for the responsibility, Horne had been Unionist MP for Guildford from 1910 to 1922, and a member of Westminster City Council, serving as Mayor in 1923–4. It was in the world of insurance that he was best known, however, for from 1928 until his death in 1941, he was Chairman of the Prudential, a company of which his father had been one of the founders and first Chairman. He was created a baronet in 1929.[18]

The first chairman of the Pension Committee, Dr Edwin Freshfield, was the solicitor who had been the most articulate spokesman for the existing trustees of the City charities and for the parochial authorities before both the Royal Commission of 1878–80 and the Select Committee which considered Bryce's bill. Characteristically, however, once the Foundation whose establishment he had formerly opposed had been brought into being and he had been appointed as a trustee by the Ecclesiastical Commissioners, he threw himself into its work with vigour. The practice in which he was a partner, Freshfields and Williams, was one of the oldest established and best known of City solicitors' firms. Freshfield himself was a scholar and antiquarian, and was awarded a Doctorate of Laws by Cambridge University for a three-volume treatise on the laws of the Roman Empire. He also played a very active part in the life of the City, and besides being a church-warden of St Margaret, Lothbury (which led to his involvement with the parochial charities), he was at one time or other Master of the Clothworkers', Needleworkers' and Vintners' Companies as well as a prominent member of the City Law Club and the City of London Conservative Association.[19]

At first, the work of the Pension Committee was almost entirely confined to the routine task of ensuring that the payments already decreed by the Charity Commissioners were made. Even though the committee was soon given the additional responsibility of administering the City Church Fund, there was still little opportunity for creative policy making. Freshfield seems to have chafed at the somewhat humdrum nature of his role, and at the beginning of 1893 he decided to present the trustees with an account of the committee's work, 'so as to relieve the excessive dryness of their Reports'. This concluded with the frank assessment that 'the Committee is therefore a strong one, and but for the additional work connected with the City Church Fund delegated to it especially by the Governing Body, and which it thankfully accepts, it might be said that an Armstrong gun has been constructed to blow away a gnat'.[20] In 1902 Freshfield quite suddenly resigned from the Central Governing Body. He was then 70 years old and taking on an increasingly senior role in his firm, but his departure may also have been prompted by a number of disagreements with his colleagues, including his opposition to a recent decision of the trustees to use £30,000 of the capital of the City Church Fund to lend to polytechnics to complete building programmes, and to a proposal to seek the demolition of All Hallows, Lombard Street, in the interests of the development of the Foundation's property holdings, even though in this case it would be the City Church Fund which would eventually benefit (see page 196). The trustees expressed their regret at his resignation.[21]

The next chairman of the Pension Committee, William Hayes Fisher, was one of the few trustees who achieved prominence in national politics. A barrister by profession, Fisher had been elected Conservative MP for Fulham in 1885 and, apart from the years 1906–10 when he lost his seat in the Liberal landslide, represented the constituency until his elevation to the peerage as Baron Downham in 1918. He was also influential in London local politics and was one of the architects of the Moderates' victory in the 1907 election for the London County Council, on which he sat as a member from 1907 to 1913. Having served as a junior minister at the Treasury under Lord Salisbury and Balfour, he was appointed Parliamentary Secretary to the Local Government Board in Asquith's coalition government of 1915 and in June 1917 was promoted to the office of President of the Local Government Board under Lloyd George. He held this important post at a crucial time during the debates over the formation of a Ministry of Health and was a deeply conservative influence, defending the poor law and its apparatus against the attempts by Christopher Addison, his erstwhile colleague on the Central Governing Body, to reform it root and branch. Lloyd George eventually engineered his resignation in November 1918, but he was too powerful to be simply dismissed, and so he was made Chancellor of the Duchy of Lancaster and Minister of Information and raised to the peerage! He died in 1920.[22]

Fisher was one of the original trustees, on the nomination of the Crown, and served continuously until his death. He was a conscientious chairman of the Pension Committee and presided over an expansion of the pensions scheme which involved a considerable amount of work (see Chapter 8); and even though he was a defender of the status quo he was quick to advocate an increase in the level of pensions to take account of the inflationary conditions of wartime.[23] As chairman of the committee which was also responsible for the City Church Fund, he took active steps to try to ensure that the Foundation's funds were not being wasted in maintaining City churches which could not support regular services. He was regular in his attendance at meetings of the Central Governing Body and retained his committee chairmanship throughout the period when he was a government minister. In a singularly busy life he was also chairman of the committee of management of the Chelsea Physic Garden, having been instrumental in persuading the Foundation to assume responsibility for the garden in 1898 when the Apothecaries' Company had withdrawn their support,[24] and chairman of the governors of the South-Western (Chelsea) Polytechnic. When he was congratulated by his colleagues on being made a peer in 1918, he remarked how the experience and information he had gained in his work for the Foundation had been of value in his other public duties, and 'laid stress on the good, though unostentatious, work done for London by the Foundation'. On his death two years later the praise of his colleagues was warm and unstinting; Bond, in a minuted comment, remarked on 'his intense devotion to Public Duty', and 'his zeal in this regard', which had probably shortened his life, adding that 'he was a valued colleague of ours, and his country has lost in him a valuable public servant'.[25] It is ironic that Fisher is now, as one historian has described him, 'one of the absolutely unknown figures in Conservative party history',[26] and does not even rank an entry in the *Dictionary of National Biography*.

Charles James Drummond succeeded Fisher as chairman of the Pension Committee, but relinquished the position on becoming chairman of the more senior Finance and General Purposes Committee in 1926. He was followed by Lady Cooper, the widow of Sir Edward Cooper, the Lord Mayor of London in 1919–20. Lady Cooper was a well-known figure in the City for her charitable work and had become known as 'the lady of the boxes' for her indefatigable efforts in collecting for the Red Cross during the First World War. In 1920 she had been appointed to the Central Governing Body by the LCC and was the first woman trustee.[27] On her death in 1932, Walter T. Prideaux was elected chairman of the Pension Committee. He was subsequently to become Chairman of the Central Governing Body and his career is described further in Chapter 10. From 1935 he presided over one of the phases of pension-giving activity on which the Foundation embarked from time to time.[28]

Of those trustees who never became committee chairmen, a few gave exceptional service in other ways. First and foremost among these was Sir Philip Magnus, who was a powerful advocate of the cause of the polytechnics and a tireless worker on their behalf. In the words of his biographer, 'to a greater or lesser degree Magnus was involved in every movement of any importance concerned with technical education before the First World War.'[29] Much of his work in this respect for the Foundation is described in Chapter 7. He resigned as a trustee in 1894 on being appointed as Joint Secretary of the London Polytechnic Council and Principal Educational Adviser and Inspector to the Central Governing Body, positions for which he received a salary from the Foundation. When he gave up these posts in 1899, however, he was immediately reappointed as a trustee by the University of London and continued to be a member of the Central Governing Body until his death in 1933 at the age of 90. As late as 1931 he was still attending meetings regularly.[30] Besides a long association with the City and Guilds Institute, he was also closely connected with the University of London. He was a member of Convocation and sat in the House of Commons from 1906 to 1922 as an MP for the University. He was created a baronet in 1917.

The name of Quintin Hogg, who was a trustee from 1891 to 1901 on the nomination of the Crown, was synonymous with the London polytechnics, and, as indicated above in Chapter 4, it would be hard to overestimate the importance of his own personal initiative in the establishment of that movement which was so to dominate the affairs of the Foundation for many years. Hogg secured a place on the Finance and General Purposes Committee where he could have most influence over the way in which the Foundation's income was spent, and, although, as a busy man, his appearance at meetings of the Central Governing Body after the first few years became increasingly infrequent, he made a particular effort to attend the special meetings at which grants were distributed. He was also an alderman of the LCC until 1895 and played a leading part in the early years of the Technical Education Board.[31]

Sidney Webb, the brilliant and multifaceted Fabian socialist, sat on the Central Governing Body as a nominee of the LCC from 1897 to 1909. Since his election to the LCC in 1892 he had taken up the cause of technical education with great enthusiasm, and was one of the principal inspirations behind the Council's development into one of the foremost education authorities in the world. Webb's involvement in the furtherance of technical education is described more fully in Chapter 7, for, despite his general radical impulse and reforming zeal, his period of trusteeship should be seen principally in the light of his preoccupation with this subject at this particular time in his life. He was a conscientious trustee, especially for a man with so many demands on his time, and attended well over half the meetings to which he was summoned. When, under the Education Act (London) of 1903, the LCC took over from the School Board for London as the education authority for the capital, and there were some tensions in its relationship with the Foundation over the polytechnics, Webb played an important role as a representative of both bodies. In 1909, when his second six-year term as a trustee came to an end, he was not reappointed by the LCC. It may be that by then he was out of favour with the Moderate-controlled Council, or he may have decided to 'slip quietly out' of the Foundation, as Beatrice Webb described his departure from the Council itself in the following year. By 1909 education was no longer his major concern and he was throwing himself into the campaign to promote the minority report of the Poor Law Commission.[32]

Another member of the polytechnic fraternity who served as a trustee for many years was Edric Bayley. As a member of the London School Board for Southwark, he had helped to organize the movement to establish polytechnics in south London, and was the first chairman of the governing body of Borough Polytechnic from 1892 to 1905. He was appointed to the Central Governing Body in 1901 by the LCC, on which he had sat since 1892 and where he had played a prominent part in the establishment of the Technical Education Board, and served continuously as a trustee until his death in 1920.[33]

Of all the trustees who did not hold the chairmanship of a major committee, none made a greater contribution to the work of the Foundation than Sir William Job Collins, who, as yet another of the brilliant nominees of the London County Council, served on the Central Governing Body from 1904 to 1945. Collins's particular field of expertise was medicine – he was a surgeon and teacher of anatomy – and his experience and knowledge of health matters were of great value to the Foundation. He was active in many spheres of public life. A member of the LCC from 1892 to 1907, he was Chairman of the Council in 1897–8 and the first chairman of its Education Committee when the Council assumed responsibility for education in London in 1904. He subsequently entered Parliament, where one of his achievements was the promotion of the Metropolitan Ambulance Act which brought the London ambulance service into being. On the Central Governing Body he was a member of virtually every sub-committee appointed to look into specialist matters and chaired several of them including those on infant welfare. He was Chairman of the Central Council for District Nursing, which at one time shared the Foundation's office premises, and also chairman of the governing body of the North-Western Polytechnic. When that institution finally opened in 1929 after many vicissitudes, Collins was praised for the considerable effort he had put into its establishment.[34]

Another trustee who had a very similar background to Collins's was Christopher Addison. He also embarked on a career in medicine, and, like Collins, taught anatomy at St Bartholomew's Hospital. His concern at the medical condition of the poor led him to enter politics to try to bring about advances in health and social welfare. In 1910 he was elected as a Liberal MP for Hoxton in east London, and was nominated as a member of the Central Governing Body by the Crown in 1911. His appointment, however, coincided with the assumption of heavy political responsibilities in connection with the passage of the National Insurance Act of 1911 and its subsequent implementation. He rapidly became one of Lloyd George's closest followers and after serving as Parliamentary Secretary at the Board of Education and, following the outbreak of war, as Under Secretary at the Ministry of Munitions, he was appointed Minister of Munitions when Lloyd George succeeded to the premiership in December 1916. In the following year he became Minister of Reconstruction to plan the social reforms of the post-war era. Not surprisingly, this busy public life restricted the amount of time which he could allot to the Foundation, but he gave what help he could on health matters. He was a member of a special committee appointed to consider grants for schools for mothers which became the important Infant Welfare Sub-Committee. In 1917, however, with such pressing affairs of state to attend to, he did not seek reappointment at the end of his six-year term as a trustee. In fact, Addison may have gained as much from the Foundation as he gave to it.

As the key to the social reforms which Addison wished to enact, he fought for the creation of a Ministry of Health, and when he finally succeeded became the first Minister of Health in 1919. Ironically, his implacable opponent in the battle to set up the new Ministry was his former colleague on the Central Governing Body, William Hayes Fisher. Addison's reforms were soon overtaken by the realities of post-war recession, but, after a largely unproductive political career for over two decades, he had a remarkable indian summer when, as Viscount Addison, he led the Labour Party in the House of Lords from 1945 to 1951 and piloted the legislation which created the Welfare State through the upper house.[35]

There were usually one or more churchmen on the Central Governing Body, looking after the very substantial ecclesiastical interests which were left after the passing of Bryce's Act and the promulgation of the Central Scheme. Among these trustees, Robert Gregory, the Dean of St Paul's, has already been noted. Another who was active in the debates over the establishment of the Foundation, the Reverend Robert Henry Hadden, vicar of St Botolph, Aldgate, and later of St Mark's, North Audley Street, Mayfair, was appointed as a trustee on the nomination of the Crown in 1895 and served until his death in 1909.[36] Another influential cleric on the Central Governing Body was Ernest Harold Pearce, rector of Christ Church, Newgate Street, who was appointed by the Ecclesiastical Commissioners in 1908. Pearce was the ecclesiastical correspondent of *The Times* and was both a respected figure in the City and a confidant of Downing Street on matters of ecclesiastical patronage. In 1911 he was appointed a canon of Westminster Abbey and was promoted to the Bishopric of Worcester in 1919, when he resigned his trusteeship.[37]

One characteristic of the trustees as a whole, and especially of the more active of them noted here, is the large number who were involved with education in general and technical education in particular. Even men with such wide and varied interests as Collins and Addison included education among their concerns. Under these circumstances it is hardly surprising that the welfare of the polytechnics was given such an overwhelming priority for so many years. No doubt the choice of trustees, and their willingness to serve, was in part dictated by the perception that certain responsibilities had been delegated to the Foundation by the Charity Commissioners, and that these should continue to be discharged by those entrusted with carrying out the Foundation's work. It was also the case, however, that support for the polytechnics coincided with a prevailing philosophy which regarded social welfare as much in terms of the contribution it could make to the health and vigour of the nation as in terms of the pursuit of social justice. The term frequently used to describe this goal was national efficiency. The polytechnics, with their emphasis on recreational as well as educational activities, seemed to be perfect vehicles for embodying the aims of such a philosophy.

One of the first tasks of the Central Governing Body in 1891 was to form an administration to conduct the Foundation's business. The Central Scheme merely required that a Clerk and such other officers 'as shall be necessary' should be appointed. At their second meeting (the first having been curtailed, as described above) the trustees chose a temporary Clerk. He was a 28-year-old barrister, Reginald J. N. Neville, who was subsequently to be a member of the Central Governing Body himself from 1929 to 1946, after having been elected to Parliament in the Conservative interest and created a baronet. Exactly what Neville's qualifications (or connections) were for the post is unclear; he had only been called to the Bar four years previously. Freshfield opposed the choice, moving instead for the appointment of Robert Pearce, the solicitor who had helped him to present the City's case to the Select Committee considering Bryce's bill, but he was unsuccessful. Neville was given a salary of £50 a month and required to devote his whole time to the affairs of the Foundation.[38]

The process of choosing a permanent Clerk and other staff proceeded rapidly. The Finance and General Purposes Committee drew up a statement of the duties of the Clerk and advertised the post, while the Estate Committee undertook similar exercises for the posts of surveyor and solicitor, the difference being that while the Clerk was to be a full-time employee of the Foundation, the surveyor and solicitor were only required to give advice as and when needed and were expected to have other professional commitments. All three appointees were to be subject to re-election annually, however.[39]

The selection of a Clerk was not an entirely straightforward matter. Six candidates were asked to attend at a meeting of the Finance and General Purposes Committee, of whom three were short-listed to be interviewed by the Central Governing Body. In the event, however, the trustees also wanted to see one of the candidates who had not been selected by the committee, Henry Howard Batten, and unanimously chose him as their Clerk. Batten was then 45 years old and had been on the staff of the Charity Commission for 25 years. He had qualified as a barrister and had been one of the officials of the Commission assigned to the task of drawing up the Central Scheme. He would appear to have been particularly well fitted to the post and the hesitation about his selection may have stemmed from an apprehension on the part of some of the trustees that, because, initially at least, they would have to deal extensively with those whose positions of power and influence had been eroded by the changes which had taken place, it might not be politic to appoint a person who had been so closely connected with the Charity Commissioners and the actual formulation of the Scheme as their principal administrative officer.[40] Neville, who seems not to have applied for the permanent post, was asked to continue to assist Batten, initially at a small salary and later on payment of an honorarium. This arrangement remained in force until 1908 when the honorarium was discontinued and Neville was appointed as standing counsel for the Foundation at a small retaining fee.[41]

Batten remained Clerk until he asked to retire at the age of 60, on his doctor's advice, in 1907. He was praised for the 'wonderfully thorough and effective' manner in which he had carried out his duties, especially in establishing an efficient office and in separating the properties which had belonged to the City Church Fund from those of the Central Fund by the exercise which was known as 'severance'. When he died in 1912 the trustees recorded their appreciation of his 'valuable services' and his obituarist in *The Times* commented how 'his tact, courtesy, and ability in dealing with those whose offices or emoluments in the old City charities were abolished or diminished by the creation of the scheme won him the esteem and affectionate regard even of those who were most bitterly opposed to the Act, while by the aged pensioners and others, to whom he acted as almoner, he was looked upon as a trusty and sympathetic friend.'[42]

When Batten retired the trustees debated whether as his replacement they should look for another Clerk who had had experience with the Charity Commission and maintain the close connection with that body which had smoothed the way during potentially difficult negotiations in the past, or whether they should seek someone qualified as a solicitor who could undertake some of the Foundation's legal work.[43] In the event they opted for the former. Ernald R. Warre was a 33-year-old barrister, the son of a provost of Eton, who had worked for the Charity Commissioners for eight years before being appointed as Clerk of the Foundation in 1907.[44] He proved to be a most effective Clerk, not only by his efficient discharge of his administrative responsibilities but also by his sympathetic character which endeared him to all who had dealings with him. When he died in 1929 at the early age of 56, the tribute the trustees put on record was unusually effusive. 'His was a fine and rare personality', the minutes record, 'and the gracious charm he radiated was felt by all with whom he came in contact. He possessed the gift of sympathy to an outstanding degree and this found a happy outlet in his work for the Foundation.'[45]

Warre's successor, Donald R. Allen, was the first (and so far only) Clerk to be chosen from among the Foundation's own staff. The son of a builder, he had been educated at William Morris School, Walthamstow, and initially pursued a career in local government and the civil service. He had served in the army during the First World War and was invalided out as a lieutenant, having been awarded the Military Cross. He joined the Foundation as an estate clerk at the age of 30 in 1925.[46] While with the Foundation he passed his Bar examinations (and was promptly awarded an honorarium of 50 guineas).[47] When Warre fell ill in 1929, Allen was appointed acting Clerk, and in the following year he was chosen from among eighteen candidates to fill the vacancy. Allen remained Clerk until 1965, and his work is discussed further in Chapter 10, but suffice it to say here that his magnificent contribution to the work of the Foundation fully measured up to that of his illustrious predecessors.

The first surveyor to the Foundation was Herbert Winstanley, a minor architect and surveyor, who had practised from an office in Basinghall Street since 1866. There were better known candidates for the post, but Winstanley had a long association with the Clothworkers' Company, and this may have commended him to Sir Owen Roberts and other members of the Estate Committee. Winstanley had been articled to Samuel Angell, the Clothworkers' surveyor, and was himself a liveryman of the Company, serving as Master in 1908–9 and chairman of its Estate Committee from 1909 to 1912. In addition to receiving a salary as surveyor to the Foundation, he was allowed to charge a fee of 5 per cent as architect of any buildings he designed for the Foundation, a role he filled only rarely, however. He died in 1913 at the age of 80, shortly after he had announced his retirement.[48]

Winstanley's successor, William Campbell Jones, was far more active as an architect and designed several buildings for the trustees and for their lessees (for which he had to obtain the trustees' dispensation). He had founded a flourishing City practice in 1887 and was the architect of a number of commercial buildings, especially head offices and branches of the major banks; additionally, as surveyor to the Skinners' Company for fifty years, he designed several of that Company's buildings. It was doubtless this connection which led to a commission from the Northampton Polytechnic to provide plans for some additions to the polytechnic's buildings as early as 1908, and this experience and the knowledge of his work by Lewis Boyd Sebastian, who was both a member of the Skinners' Company and chairman of the governors at Northampton, must have stood him in good stead with the trustees. When he was appointed as the Foundation's surveyor he was allowed an additional stipend to enable him to take on the clerk who had handled the Foundation's business for Winstanley, R. H. T. Bard. He nominally retired from the active surveyorship of the Foundation in 1937, when the work was taken on by his firm, then called Campbell Jones, Sons & Smithers (and shortly afterwards Campbell Jones & Sons), but he continued to concern himself with the Foundation's affairs and to practise as an architect until 1945, and was 89 years old when he died in 1951.[49]

The first choice as the Foundation's solicitor was, not surprisingly, Robert Pearce, thus providing him with some compensation for not having been appointed Clerk. Pearce was already an active and well-known figure in the City, but the prominent part he played in the agitation over Bryce's bill gave him a taste for political life, and in 1910 he was elected as Liberal MP for Leek in Staffordshire, a seat he held until 1918. He was knighted in 1916. He remained nominally the Foundation's solicitor until his death in 1922 at the age of 82, but his successor, Howard Bradshaw, a partner in Pearce's firm of Baylis, Pearce & Co., had in fact taken care of the Foundation's legal business for many years.[50] Messrs Martin & Farlow of King Street, Cheapside, were appointed auditors to the Foundation.[51]

The trustees naturally adopted a somewhat cautious attitude towards the appointment of staff. At first they thought that they would need an assistant clerk, an estate clerk and an office clerk with a messenger and an office boy,[52] but as Neville was asked to continue to assist Batten after the latter's appointment as Clerk they decided that they could dispense with an assistant clerk. In 1891 only an estate clerk and office clerk were appointed as permanent staff, although a salary was paid to a clerk of Neville for work for the Foundation, and it became the practice to employ two junior clerks on a weekly wage, who were normally expected to leave when they reached a certain age, though a few were taken on to the establishment.[53]

In 1892 an accountant and bookkeeper was engaged, and other clerks were added in the following year,[54] but the number of 'assistant staff', as the salaried staff other than the Clerk were known, remained modest and usually fluctuated between five and six until 1936. At that time new arrangements had to be made when the Foundation took over the direct management of part of the Packington Estate in Islington and an office was opened there, but even then no increase was permitted in the personnel of the main office, and at the outbreak of war in 1939 the total administrative staff of the Foundation, including juniors, numbered no more than twelve.[55]

The Foundation's employees were invariably loyal and long serving. James Montgomery, the first estate clerk, was 32 years old when he took up his appointment in 1891 and served until his retirement in 1925.[56] E. C. Rowland, a former employee of the Charity Commissioners, who was taken on at the same time, was still working for the Foundation at the time of his death in 1917.[57] The same was true of Albert Edward Nixon, who had been a clerk in the office of the auditors, Martin & Farlow, before becoming the Foundation's accountant in 1892; he remained on the staff until his death in 1924.[58] An even longer-serving officer was Leonard Bates, who was taken on to the permanent staff at the age of 18 in 1903 after spending some time in the office as a junior, rose to be deputy clerk and retired in 1947.[59] R. H. T. Bard did not join the salaried staff until 1932, when he was appointed as estate clerk, but he had previously assisted Winstanley and later Campbell Jones since 1900 and had brought an essential element of continuity to the management of the estates; he was still working for the Foundation at the time of his death in 1946.[60]

The first woman to become a member of staff was Miss N. Pollock, who was taken on as a temporary measure in 1914 when other staff were called away to war service and given a permanent appointment in 1917; she retired in 1944.[61] The First World War had its effect on the Foundation's personnel, as it did on the staff of many similar institutions. Howard Bodvel-Roberts, who had been appointed to the permanent staff in 1902 after two years as a junior in the office, died in 1915 of wounds received in action at Loos when serving as a lieutenant.[62]

There is no doubt that the Foundation was a conscientious and generous employer. It generally tried to follow civil service practice in setting salaries and other benefits. Annual increments were provided from the first, and salaries were frequently adjusted to reflect new responsibilities or inflationary conditions. Ex-gratia payments were often made, as, for example, when the division of property between the Central and City Church Funds had created extra work, or in 1918 'in connection with the abnormal conditions resulting from the War'.[63] At first, the trustees would not undertake to provide pensions, doubtless because they were wary of the actuarial implications of establishing a pension fund when the disposable income of the Foundation after satisfying its statutory obligations was originally so small, but instead paid half the premiums of endowment policies for each member of staff. In 1926, however, this was changed to a fully fledged superannuation scheme on civil service lines, accompanied by a compassionate fund to cover emergencies or cases of individual hardship for medical or other reasons.[64]

It is a testimony both to the attractive working conditions which the Foundation provided for its staff and their corresponding sense of loyalty that the total number of salaried employees who worked in its City office during the first 50 years of the Foundation's existence, including its three Clerks, numbered no more than 20, whose average length of service was at least 15 years.

That office, which, despite having some of the Dickensian features of a normal barristers' chambers, seems to have provided a reasonably congenial working environment, was located on the ground floor of No. 3 Temple Gardens, a block of chambers in the Middle Temple, straddling the southern end of Middle Temple Lane with a good aspect over the gardens of the Temple and the river Thames. It was built in 1878 to the designs of E. M Barry, the architect of the Charing Cross Hotel,[65] and would thus have been relatively new when the small office staff of the Foundation moved in towards the end of 1891.

Under the terms of the Central Scheme, the trustees could acquire or erect premises suitable for the conduct of the Foundation's business, and up to £6,000 from the Central Fund capital account could be spent for this purpose. An initial search having failed to reveal anything suitable, the Clerk was instructed to find a set of chambers which could be used as offices for three months at a rent of £50. No. 3 Temple Gardens was taken on this purely temporary basis from Midsummer 1891 and remained the Foundation's office until 1967.[66] Indeed, once the office had proved to be satisfactory there was little reason to change. The rent for the chambers was £200 per annum, and the trustees might well have calculated that as the £6,000 which had been earmarked by the Charity Commissioners was invested in the money market it probably produced a similar amount in interest. Even if one of the Foundation's own properties had been available, the rent foregone would almost certainly have been equivalent to that paid for Temple Gardens. The first meeting of the Central Governing Body to take place in the new offices was on 14 December 1891.[67]

A few changes were made over the years. In 1894 the Clerk reported that electric lighting had been introduced into the Temple and he was authorized to spend not more than £20 in having it laid on in the offices.[68] In 1920 the rent was raised to £250 per annum, a not unreasonable increase at a time of severe post-war inflation, and in 1933, when a neighbouring set of chambers became available, the opportunity was taken to expand over the whole ground floor at an increased rental of £400 per annum. One room in the new chambers did not become vacant until 1936, and another was let to the Central Council for District Nursing, an organization which the Foundation had assisted with grants for many years, at a nominal rent of £25.[69] The trustees' pride in their offices was shown in 1937 when they authorized the installation of some 'old marble fireplaces' from premises which were being demolished, together with new electric light fittings 'more in keeping with the chambers', at a cost of about £100.[70]

One minor item of administrative business to which the trustees had to give their attention in 1891 was the design of a common seal. The Finance and General Purposes Committee was charged with producing a design and initially decided to hold a competition among the London art schools, but the Central Governing Body widened this to include all members of the public. No record of the competition has survived, but the chosen design was by a Colonel Adams and was ready for use by 1893.[71] It has the Royal Arms in the centre representing the Crown surrounded by the heraldic shields of the nine other institutions represented on the Central Governing Body, plus the London School Board, which would have nominated members if at a future date the management of the City Church Fund had been entrusted to a separately constituted body. Around the circumference is the legend 'SEAL OF THE CITY PAROCHIAL FOUNDATION MDCCCXCI'.

The amount of their total income which is swallowed up by administrative expenses is always a matter of concern for charities, and quite properly a matter of public scrutiny. It was standard practice on the part of the Foundation to show the 'management expenses' as a separate item in the annual accounts, carefully divided between the Central and City Church Funds in proportion to the income of each. These expenses consistently accounted for less than 5 per cent of the Foundation's income. In 1909, for instance, all management expenses including staff salaries amounted to £4,112 out of a total income of £94,775 from rents and dividends, or 4.3 per cent. In 1939 the equivalent figures were £7,724 and £164,426, or 4.7 per cent. It is worth remarking that in the former year there were only some twenty applications for grants apart from the 'statutory' grants to the polytechnics and kindred institutions, while in 1939 there were over eighty. In fact such had been the increase in the Foundation's business that a new filing system had to be installed in 1938, 'the number of letters received and despatched annually having nearly quadrupled during the past eight years'.[72]

NOTES

1. Minutes, I, 1.
2. Ibid., I, 2.
3. Ibid., I, 3; XXX, 157: *Who's Who of British Members of Parliament. Volume II. 1886–1918. A Biographical Dictionary of the House of Commons*, ed. Michael Stenton and Stephen Lees (1978): *The Times*, 3 Oct. 1921, 12.
4. Minutes, II, 178.
5. Ibid., IV, 113.
6. Ibid., XXX, 158.
7. Ibid., XLVIII, 1: *The Times*, 23 Dec. 1937, 12.
8. *The Times*, 16 Nov. 1944, 7: Minutes, XXX, 149; XXXVI, 122; XLIV, 1–2: Thomas Girtin, *The Golden Ram. A Narrative History of the Clothworkers' Company 1528–1958* (1958), 317, 341.
9. *DNB*: Minutes, IV, 131.
10. Joseph Foster, *Men-at-the-Bar* (1885): Minutes, V, 85; IX, 113: J. F. C. Harrison, *A History of the Working Men's College 1854–1954* (1954), 42 and *passim*.
11. Minutes, IX, 116; XXV, 3; XXXVI, 121–2: Foster, *Men-at-the-Bar*: *The Times*, 12 Aug. 1936, 13: L. S. B. [Lewis Boyd Sebastian], *The City Livery Companies and their Corporate Property* (1885).
12. Minutes, IX, 116; XXXVI, 125; XXXIX, 41: Eric Howe and Harold E. Waite, *The London Society of Compositors: A Centenary History* (1948), 191–204: *The Times*, 27 May 1929, 21.
13. Minutes, XXXIX, 42: *Who's Who of British Members of Parliament, III, 1919–1945* (1979): *The Times*, 25 Aug. 1941, 6.
14. Minutes, XLII, 123; XLV, 58.
15. *The Times*, 8 Jan. 1915, 6: Girtin, op. cit., 268, 341: Jennifer Lang, *The City and Guilds of London Institute Centenary 1878–1978* (1978), 12, 23, 64: Frank Foden, *Philip Magnus: Victorian Educational Pioneer* (1970), 131: Minutes, XXV, 1–2.
16. *The Times*, 18 Aug. 1920: Minutes, XXX, 137.
17. Minutes, XLV, 223.

18. *Who's Who of British Members of Parliament, III: The Times*, 29 Sept. 1941, 6.

19. Judy Slinn, *A History of Freshfields* (1984), 131, 144–5 and *passim*.

20. Minutes, III, 151–3.

21. Ibid., XII, 53, 121.

22. Bentley B. Gilbert, *British Social Policy 1914–1939* (1970), 120–30, 318: *The Times*, 3 July 1920.

23. Minutes, XXVII, 110, 138.

24. Ibid., VIII, 81.

25. Ibid., XXVIII, 129; XXX, 113–14.

26. Gilbert, op. cit., 120.

27. Minutes, XXXI, 13; XXXVII, 92: *The Times*, 6 April 1932, 9.

28. Minutes, XLII, 119; XLV, 5–9.

29. Foden, op. cit., 208.

30. Minutes, IV, 100–2; IX, 41, 113; XLIII, 171.

31. Andrew Saint, 'Technical Education and the early LCC' in *Politics and the People of London. The London County Council 1889–1965*, ed. Andrew Saint (1989), 71–91: *Education for National Efficiency: the Contribution of Sidney and Beatrice Webb*, ed. E. J. T. Brennan (1975), 26–56.

32. *Our Partnership by Beatrice Webb*, ed. Barbara Drake and Margaret I. Cole (1948), 76–82, 446: *DNB*.

33. *The Borough Polytechnic News*, Aug./Sept. 1920 (in cuttings book in possession of Foundation): F. G. Evans, *Borough Polytechnic 1892–1969* (1969), 4–5: Minutes, XI, 72; XXX, 137.

34. *The Times*, 14 Dec. 1946, 7: *Who's Who of British Members of Parliament, II*: Minutes, XXXIX, 161.

35. Kenneth and Jane Morgan, *Portrait of a Progressive. The Political Career of Christopher, Viscount Addison* (1980), esp. 28–31: Gilbert, op. cit., 98–161, 317: *DNB*: Minutes, XXI, 90; XXIV, 158–60.

36. Minutes, V, 61; XI, 105.

37. Ibid., XVIII, 133; XXIX, 41: *DNB*.

38. Minutes, I, 3: *Who's Who of British Members of Parliament, III: The Times*, 3 May 1950, 8.

39. Minutes, I, 12–16, 22–3.

40. Ibid., I, 25, 26–7; XVI, 136–7.

41. Ibid., I, 37; II, 178; IV, 135; XVIII, 24.

42. Ibid., XVI, 136–7; XXII, 121: *The Times*, 29 July 1912, 9.

43. Minutes, XVI, 137.

44. Ibid., XVII, 23.

45. Ibid., XXXIX, 135: *The Times*, 23 Sept. 1929, 16.

46. Minutes, XXXIV, 143–4.

47. Ibid., XXXVII, 112.

48. Ibid., I, 28, 34; V, 28–9; XV, 116; XXIII, 51, 55: *The Builder*, 28 March 1913, 389: *The Building News*, 14 March 1913, 388: Girtin, op. cit., 336, 340.

49. Minutes, XXIII, 78, 168; XXXIX, 100; XLVII, 2: A. Stuart Gray, *Edwardian Architecture. A Biographical Dictionary* (1985), 134: S. John Teague, *The City University: A History* (1980), 171, 172, 177, 178: *Journal of the Royal Institute of British Architects*, 3rd ser., LIX (1952), 229–30.

50. Minutes, I, 28, 34; XXXII, 123, 126: *Who Was Who, 1916–1928*: *City Press*, 31 March 1906 (in cuttings book in possession of Foundation).

51. Minutes, I, 56.

52. Ibid., I, 23.

53. Ibid., I, 28, 34; II, 178; III, 135; XXIX, 93.

54. Ibid., II, 106; III, 135.
55. Ibid., XLVI, 321–3; XLIX, 252.
56. Ibid., XXXV, 95.
57. Ibid., XXVII, 1.
58. Ibid., XXXVIII, 133.
59. Ibid., XIII, 102; XLVI, 321–3.
60. Ibid., XLI, 163, 174–5; XLVI, 322.
61. Ibid., XXVII, 50–1; LIV, 16–17.
62. Ibid., XII, 15; XXV, 160–1.
63. Ibid., IX, 11–12; XXVIII, 25.
64. Ibid., XXXVII, 100; XXXVIII, 25; XXXIX, 25.
65. Nikolaus Pevsner, *The Buildings of England. London. I. The Cities of London and Westminster* (3rd ed., 1973), 339.
66. Minutes, I, 11, 24, 39.
67. Ibid., I, 69.
68. Ibid., IV, 136.
69. Ibid., XXXI, 26; XLIII, 79, 119; XLVI, 275.
70. Ibid., XLVII, 176.
71. Ibid., I, 10, 11; II, 130, 163; III, 112.
72. Ibid., XLIX, 228–9.

6   The estate and other income

We have already seen in Chapter 4 how the Charity Commissioners saddled the Foundation with a considerable financial burden even before it was formally established in 1891. The accumulated capital, that is, the stocks, funds and cash balances, but excluding the value of property, of the non-ecclesiastical charities which made up the Foundation's Central Fund, was eventually calculated to amount to over £410,000. Of this, however, some £340,000 had been appropriated, mainly for the acquisition of open spaces or the establishment of polytechnics and other institutions.[1] On top of this the annual income of the Central Fund from rents and dividends, which was, of course, correspondingly diminished by the loss of such a large proportion of its investments (by some £10,000 at the prevailing rate of return on government stock of about 3 per cent), was charged with a number of mandatory payments. These consisted principally of the compensation for vested interests which had been affected by the Scheme and the continuation of stipends and pensions to those who had received them from the old charities and who were still considered to have a valid claim to them, to an upper limit in total of £7,500, and annual compulsory grants to the polytechnics and similar bodies. These amounted initially to £24,250 per annum, reduced to £23,250 in 1900 when a grant to the Bishopsgate Institute no longer became payable, and to £22,750 in 1934 when the grant to the Chelsea Polytechnic was cut by £500 for reasons which will be given in Chapter 7.[2] In addition the trustees considered that they were under an obligation to aid the fledgling polytechnics with supplementary grants,

101

averaging some £8,000 in total during the first few years.[3] As the annual income of the Central Fund was initially estimated to amount to some £42,000,[4] those critics of the Central Scheme who thought that there would only be about £4,000 a year left over for general charitable purposes were not far wide of the mark. (It must, of course, be borne in mind that small as such a sum was as a proportion of the total charitable endowments of the city parishes, it still represents the equivalent at 1990 values of some £200,000.)

The City Church Fund, which was made up of the charities dedicated to ecclesiastical uses, was in comparatively better shape. Of its total potential capital of a little under £170,000, £111,000 remained, and of the residue, £49,355, which was the sum eventually spent on the restoration schemes for City churches already approved by the Charity Commissioners, had to be replaced by deductions from the income of the Fund over ten years. Other calls on the Fund's annual income, which was about £35,000 in the early years, were the payments to the City clergy and the sums for repairs to the fabric and the maintenance of services of their churches authorized by the Central Scheme, totalling some £21,000 initially. Any surplus at the end of the year was to be paid over to the Ecclesiastical Commissioners for use in the wider metropolis.

This financial position did not, however, become clear for a few years, and at first the trustees had great difficulty in obtaining both the information necessary to manage their own affairs and the money to meet their obligations. In May 1891 they resolved to send 'a circular of a friendly nature' to churchwardens and vestry clerks asking them to collect any rents that may be due, furnish a schedule of the properties which now belonged to the Foundation, and provide a list of the deeds relating to their properties.[5] Repeated requests were made to the Charity Commissioners for a statement of the Foundation's assets and liabilities.[6] At one point the trustees decided to borrow £10,000 from the Bank of England to meet the liabilities of the City Church Fund, but in the event it was not necessary to take up the loan.[7] Very grudgingly the Charity Commissioners agreed to advance £15,000 out of the capital of the Central Fund, ahead of the final settlement of accounts, so that grants which were considered to be essential could be paid to the polytechnics.[8]

Most of the parishes were reasonably co-operative in providing information, and by May 1892 deeds and muniments had been obtained from all but six parishes, although twenty had claimed that they had no deeds. A note of caution was, however, sounded that in the case of Holy Trinity, Minories, 'we think that nothing short of an order from the Charity Commissioners will produce the Deeds'.[9] There were some delays. The notorious parish of St Mildred, Bread Street, which, as we have seen, was frequently cited as a flagrant example of a place where charity funds had been misused, was still in the process of handing over funds in 1902, and the income from one charity of St Michael Paternoster Royal which had been overlooked in 1891 was transferred as late as 1933, the unfortunate rector having to pay back £40 which he had already spent, albeit in ignorance, at the rate of £10 per annum.[10]

The main asset of the Foundation was, of course, the property which it acquired as a result of taking over the charitable endowments of the City parishes, and one of the earliest and most urgent tasks was to compile a schedule of its estate. This was completed by the end of 1892 and a rent roll was produced containing 747 properties, mostly in the City of London but including some agricultural and outlying tenancies as far afield as Lincolnshire. As might be expected, these properties were of a very mixed character, ranging from lights overlooking churchyards which brought in a shilling a year to a group of contiguous buildings in Lombard Street and Birchin Lane which formed one item on the rent roll on lease to Glyn's Bank at a total rental of £4,300 per annum; in size they varied from a gateway in Ram Alley to a 218-acre farm at Epping.[11]

Some property to which straightforward charitable uses had originally been attached could be assigned immediately to either the Central or City Church Fund, but much of it was held under complex trusts and had to be placed temporarily in a mixed fund. The complicated task of allocating each of these properties to one or other of the Funds so that the correct proportions of income were devoted to general and to ecclesiastical uses in accordance with the original intentions of the donors took until the end of 1898. The process involved the careful valuation of property worth altogether over £1½ million, representing some two-thirds of the Foundation's entire estate. When severance, as this procedure was called, had finally been completed, the trustees acknowledged their debt to Sir Owen Roberts, the chairman of the Estate Committee, who had supervised the whole operation, and the Charity Commissioners approved the payment of gratuities totalling £500 to the staff for the extra work involved.[12]

Even before severance had been carried out, however, a number of transactions in land and buildings had taken place. From the start, the trustees, and their surveyor, did not look on the estate as a static entity, but as one in which property could be bought and sold as circumstances dictated. Likewise, the investments were regarded as flexible capital, to be augmented or diminished as the situation demanded. All transactions, of course, had to be approved by the Charity Commissioners, and the investments were held by the Official

Trustees, but after some initial circumspection the Commissioners usually, although not always, gave their approval.

In fact one of the very first actions of the trustees in 1891 was to authorize the sale of an isolated property in Cloth Fair.[13] But when, later in the same year, they were prepared to accept an offer of £15,000 for the freehold of a building in Bishopsgate, the Charity Commissioners obviously became worried and asked to have a conference on the whole question of selling property. The Commissioners eventually agreed to the sale of the building for £15,500, and the trustees were able to point out triumphantly that they had reinvested the proceeds in the purchase of ground rents in Hackney worth £643 per annum as against £450 received in rent from the Bishopsgate property.[14] The gain of an immediate increase in the annual return was, however, by no means the main consideration in the minds of the Estate Committee and their surveyor. Ground rents, especially on recently built houses like those in Hackney, were regarded at the time as a good investment, bearing in mind that this was a period of negligible inflation and relative stability in the price of government stock. The long-term well-being of their estate was always uppermost in the trustees' minds.

In general it made sense to hold on to City properties, which had risen in value so markedly over the second half of the nineteenth century and had the potential to rise still more. As the Central Governing Body's *First Report*, issued in 1900, expressed it, 'The Trustees, as a rule, are not willing vendors of City property, but a few sales have been effected where an exceptional price has been forthcoming, or where very special circumstances made a sale desirable.'[15] Such a case occurred in 1899 when £10,000 was offered for the Foundation's share in a warehouse in Crutched Friars, which the surveyor, in strongly recommending acceptance, thought 'almost a fancy price for the property', particularly as the building was in divided ownership.[16] The prevailing philosophy was, however, firmly restated in 1913 when a director of the London and South Western Bank wanted to purchase Nos. 72 and 73 Gracechurch Street, but was informed 'that it was contrary to the policy of the Trustees to sell any of their City properties, and that it would be quite useless to bring the matter forward unless he was in a position to make an offer of an exceptionally tempting nature.'[17]

One group of properties whose sale was readily countenanced, however, was the outlying rural tenancies. Not only were these a heterogeneous collection of far-flung holdings, but at a time of agricultural depression they produced a low return and created several problems of management. As early as 1892 the Central Governing Body passed a resolution moved by Hayes Fisher and seconded by Roberts, 'That it is desirable, subject to the consent of the Charity Commissioners, to take every opportunity of selling the agricultural and outlying property of the Foundation, whenever a fair price can be obtained for the same.'[18] The times were not propitious, however. Over the next two or three years there were several applications for the reduction of rents on farms as a result of the low price of produce, and many of these were granted.[19] It was clearly preferable to retain a tenant, even at a lower rental, than to risk driving him off the land. Some sales did take place in these early years – a three-quarter holding in 93 acres in Kent for £3,000 in 1893, for instance – but in the same year it was recognized that the time was unfavourable for selling.[20] By 1895, however, the pace of sales began to increase when within a short period 23 acres in Kent and 29 acres at South Mimms were sold for £1,100 and £1,650 respectively.[21] In 1896 a 110-acre farm at Stone in Staffordshire was sold at auction for £3,035,[22] and in 1897 a schedule was produced showing that 11 agricultural tenancies had been sold and had realized a little under £12,000.[23] In 1899–1900 the Foundation's largest individual holding, the 218-acre Hayley's Farm at Epping, where the rent had been progressively reduced from £180 to £100 per annum, was finally disposed of, doubtless with a sigh of relief, for £4,200.[24] The best price was £6,400 obtained for 152 acres in Lincolnshire in 1902,[25] and by 1909 only four outlying properties remained.[26] The last of these, at Ware in Hertfordshire, changed hands in 1925.[27]

If the outright sale of City property was generally eschewed, every opportunity was taken to consolidate and rationalize holdings. As the nature of its origins would suggest, the Foundation's estate did not present a tidy picture. Several buildings or parts of buildings were 'intermixed', that is, held in common with other owners. The income from Nos. 23 and 24 Old Bailey, for instance, had to be divided into twelve shares, of which eight went to the Foundation, two to the parish of Islington, and one each to the parish of Staines and the Ironmongers' Company.[28] One example of the problem was so extreme that it was described at length in the minutes. The Foundation owned a small part of No. 35 Milk Street which consisted of 'nothing more than a kind of square box on the Basement Floor (about three feet high and about ten feet superficial area), projecting from the party wall of No. 36, Milk Street, which premises belong to the Foundation. It is not known for what purpose the ground was used . . . '.[29] The 'box' brought in £1 per annum in rent and it was clearly desirable to dispose of it as quickly as possible. Likewise, in 1897 £250 was accepted for a 'little outstanding plot' consisting of two rooms in No. 89 Watling Street.[30] More frequently exchanges were made with other owners or attempts were made to buy out their interests. Also in 1897, it was resolved to offer £14,250 for Christ's Hospital's share of a group of properties, and in 1899 the Estate Committee asked to be provided annually with a schedule of properties which the Foundation owned jointly with other owners so that they could consider how best to simplify tenures.[31] Typical of their attitude was the firm request made to the Charity Commissioners in 1905 to sanction the purchase of another owner's portion of Nos. 38 and 39 Queen Street and 1 and 2 Maiden Lane for £11,000, a figure which was somewhat on the high side, 'as it is important to disembarrass the present inconvenient and complicated tangle'. In the event, approval was given.[32] One of the most valuable properties held in common, the Packington Estate in Islington, was managed by the Clothworkers' Company, which shared the income, but when the terms of the original leases began to expire, it became necessary to rationalize the position and the estate was partitioned at the beginning of 1937 (see below). Nine properties which were still held in common with others, however, remained on the rent roll in 1939.

If offers to purchase the Foundation's property were to be treated with circumspection, no such inhibition was felt about buying property if funds were available and the price was right. One of the most favoured types of purchase in the early years was of the ground rents of newly completed housing developments. We have seen how the first such transaction was the acquisition in 1892 of 67 houses and some stabling in Hackney let on 99-year leases expiring in 1983. This was followed over the next eight years by the purchase of further estates, newly built or still in building, at Battersea (consisting of a very large estate at Battersea Park), Hornsey, Thornton Heath (over one hundred houses), Muswell Hill, Hampstead and Tooting.[33] The expenditure involved was over £150,000, on which the return was only some £5,000 per annum. It is difficult at this point in time to appreciate the attraction of such investment in ground rents at or near the beginning of their terms, and contemporary justifications were given from time to time. When in 1899 the purchase of ground rents on 16 substantial houses in Frognal Lane, Hampstead, at 32 years' purchase was proposed, the Estate Committee thought the price not excessive in view of higher prices which had been paid for the ground rents of adjacent houses at auction 'and having regard to the near reduction of interest on Consols from 2¾ to 2½ per cent in 1903'.[34] The trustees' *First Report* in 1900 made a similar point, remarking that 'In the case of a Corporation the investment in Ground Rents would appear to be especially desirable; the Rentals are not subject to a reduction of interest as in the case of Consols, and the value of the reversion increases year by year, and although such increase may be of little moment to a private individual, it constitutes an important element in the case of a Corporation.'[35] This was, of course, a very long-term view of the Foundation's interests, but perhaps understandable at a time when the rate of return on conventional investments had been very low over a long period (the average rate of return on Consols having only exceeded 3½ per cent for two years in the whole period between 1828 and 1914) and when land values were static or even declining.[36] Nevertheless, after 1900 there was a marked fall off in the purchase of ground rents by the Foundation, dictated perhaps as much by lack of funds as any change of policy.

Opportunities to purchase property within the City were, of course, not ignored. A block of chambers producing £600 per annum came on the market in 1893 and was acquired for £14,500, and in the following year the Charity Commissioners agreed with the surveyor that the purchase of buildings in Fleet Street and Bolt Court contiguous to property already belonging to the Foundation was well worth the £28,750 asked.[37] When in 1900 No. 26 Walbrook, which was sandwiched between other buildings owned by the Foundation, was advertised for sale by auction, the chairman of the Estate Committee obtained the permission of the Charity Commissioners to bid for it and secured the property for £8,700 (an indication of how quickly both bodies could act when necessary).[38] A degree of discrimination was, however, always necessary. When Nos. 21 and 22 Old Bailey were auctioned in 1894, the reserve insisted on by the Charity Commissioners was exceeded and the property passed into other hands.[39]

Occasionally a particularly favourable opportunity occurred. In 1902 Sir Owen Roberts reported that the owners of No. 61 King William Street were willing to accept £40,000 for the freehold of the building, subject to a mortgage of £30,000. Despite the large amount involved the property was of exceptional value to the Foundation, for together with the adjacent Nos. 62–66 already in the Foundation's ownership, it made up an imposing block of property in a commanding position at the head of the northern approach to London Bridge. The wisdom of the investment was amply borne out when the site was redeveloped on building leases after the First World War by the Guardian Assurance Company and Lloyds Bank at a total ground rent of £14,700 per annum, to the considerable advantage of the City Church Fund, to which the property belonged.[40] The careful acquisition at an early date of properties in Fleet Street bore similar fruit in 1923 when an offer was made to take the site on a building lease at an annual ground rent of £3,400 and a premium of £5,000, the trustees' own surveyor, W. Campbell Jones, acting as architect for the new building.[41]

With all this activity in the property market it is perhaps surprising that a Licence in Mortmain was not obtained until 1912. The ancient laws of mortmain, of which the latest revisions had taken place as recently as 1888 and 1891, were designed to prevent the acquisition of land by corporations (including charitable ones). The reasons were complex, from an original concern with the evasion of feudal dues and the disinheritance of heirs to a fear of the power of corporations and the accumulation of land in their 'dead hand'. The effect was that, in general, a licence was required from the Crown for corporations to acquire and hold land, but there were so many exceptions by the late nineteenth century that it is a moot point whether the Foundation needed to obtain such a licence. The point having been raised by a nervous buyer of one of the Foundation's properties, however, it was decided to exercise due caution. The mortmain laws were finally abolished in 1960. One other legal technicality which had to be complied with occurred in 1926 when the Foundation applied to become a Trust Corporation under the terms of the Law of Property (Amendment) Act of that year, in order to be able to give a valid receipt for the purchase money when selling property.[42]

Figures produced at a later date show that in the years up to 1900, while the proceeds of sales amounted to some £135,000, over £200,000 was spent on purchases.[43] The balance came from the Foundation's capital in the hands of the Official Trustees, and, after some initial reluctance, the Charity Commissioners were usually prepared to authorize its use, no doubt mindful of the unfavourable rate of return on the limited range of securities which were open to charity trustees. The value of the Foundation's stocks, which in 1895 stood at £59,775 for the Central Fund and £75,865 for the City Church Fund, was allowed to run down to a few thousand pounds at times, especially in the case of the Central Fund.[44] This could create difficulties, however, as in 1902, when a request to provide loans for the completion of essential building plans at various polytechnics could only be satisfied by a temporary transfer of £30,000 from the City Church Fund capital account to that of the Central Fund, a measure that did not meet with the approval of every trustee.[45] In 1909 the Charity Commissioners insisted that at least £30,000 must be retained in the Central Fund capital account to meet exceptional and unforeseen demands.[46]

The practice of loaning money out of capital to the polytechnics dated back to as early as 1892, when Borough Polytechnic was offered a loan of £10,000 at 3 per cent interest, repayable over thirty years, to purchase the freehold of its site. Earlier in the same year the Finance and General Purposes Committee, following a reference to it by the Central Governing Body, had ruled that the purchase of the freehold by the Foundation itself could not be justified as an investment.[47] In 1894 the trustees resolved as a matter of policy that in view of the shortage of funds such loans would be confined to polytechnics and kindred institutions and then only in exceptional circumstances, and two years later a request for £6,000 from the South-Western (later Chelsea) Polytechnic had to be turned down.[48] Many loans were, in fact, made over the years, and at one time the trustees contemplated borrowing the money themselves to make the advances if necessary, but this recourse does not appear to have been necessary.[49] Further details of the loans which were made are given in the next chapter. Over the period up to the beginning of the Second World War some £250,000 was lent in this way, but many of these so-called 'loans' were in effect gifts, for the trustees authorized additional grants to cover the repayments and interest charges. Thus, although the capital was eventually repaid, much of it was recouped out of the Foundation's own income, being deducted at source from the grants made and meticulously remitted to the Official Trustees.

The Central Scheme had required a similar repayment out of income of the capital spent in the repair of City churches prior to the establishment of the Foundation, and such careful husbanding of the Foundation's assets was characteristic of the attitude of the Charity Commissioners. When in 1905 the freehold of the properties in Lombard Street and Birchin Lane leased to Glyn's Bank was sold to the bank for £250,000 in the largest single transaction in the period up to the Second World War, the Commissioners insisted that part of the proceeds should be used to set up a sinking fund which would realize £115,000 by 1934, when the original lease would have expired, to make the sum received up to £365,000, which was considered to be the reversionary value of the property.[50] There was no hesitation in snapping up the opportunity presented by the bank's wish to buy, however. A substantial augmentation of the Central Fund's capital account which had dwindled almost to nothing would take place at once (the income from which was approximately equivalent to the rent formerly paid by the bank), and a sinking fund was established which, when it matured early in 1930, provided another sizeable addition to the income of the Central Fund.[51]

Most of the estate was let on repairing leases of various lengths, but some direct management was necessary. There were a few properties held on short-term tenancies, described as 'agency' properties, for which the Foundation was responsible for the upkeep, rates, taxes and caretaking services. These brought in annually about £8,000 up to the First World War, but by 1926 their gross rental had increased to between £16,000 and £17,000.[52] The trustees were not loath to undertake major rebuilding schemes themselves, by utilizing their own capital, if satisfactory terms for a building lease could not be negotiated. The first major undertaking of this kind was in St John Street and St John's Lane, Clerkenwell, where, after the site had hung on the Foundation's hands for some time, £5,000 was spent in 1898–9 on building warehouses with an estimated rack-rental value of £600 per annum.[53] The 'Vestry House' in Laurence Pountney Hill was similarly rebuilt in 1899 for £2,515, and in 1905–6 the estate surveyor, Herbert Winstanley, acted as architect for the rebuilding of Clarence House in Arthur Street at a cost of £10,363.[54] The Estate Committee always preferred to let sites on building leases, however, if a satisfactory lessee could be found, but as late as 1936 when a decision was taken to rebuild Nos. 38 and 39 Queen Street and 1 and 2 Maiden Lane (now Skinners Lane), and no acceptable proposal for rebuilding was received, a new building was erected directly to the designs of the Foundation's surveyor, William Campbell Jones, at a cost of £23,866. This was quickly let on a 99-year lease at a rent of £2,500 per annum.[55]

The trustees inherited only one suburban estate which was ripe for building development. This was the Aldermary Park Estate in the vicinity of Aldermary Road and Babbacombe Road, Bromley, whose origins are indicated by the name. The land here was let in small parcels to builders and developers on 99-year building leases, but the whole development was spread over many years and was plagued by the kind of problems which frequently afflicted such undertakings. In 1901 the take-up of building plots was so slow that the surveyor recommended to the Estate Committee that a pair of houses should be built directly to encourage other offers, and in 1906 one of the builders chosen to carry out the development defaulted on his agreement. Whether the Foundation ever secured a return commensurate with the effort put in to let the land on building leases is doubtful. Even in 1926 when the Clerk submitted the *Second Report* to the trustees the development of the Bromley estate had still not been completed.[56]

A type of building which received particular attention was the public house. One of the first acts of the Congregationalist, Evan Spicer, was to request that the question of granting leases to buildings which were to be used as licensed premises should be considered by the Central Governing Body, and in 1892 it was moved by the Dean of St Paul's and seconded by Spicer that the Estate Committee should provide a special report whenever the lease of a public house came up for renewal.[57] This reforming zeal appears to have subsided quickly in the face of the rational commercial consideration that pubs commanded high rents, but it may help to explain why the Foundation's estate seems not to have been affected by the great pub boom of the late 1890s, when a large number of licensed premises elsewhere were rebuilt.[58] The trustees were pleasantly surprised when two public houses in Twickenham which they put up for sale at auction in 1903 fetched higher prices than expected, and when the lease of the Rose and Crown at Tooting expired in the following year they also sold the building at auction.[59] Any thought they may have had of divesting themselves of what some of them obviously regarded as embarrassing possessions for a charitable foundation, however, foundered on the severe recession which soon hit the licensing trade. Indeed, in 1908, in what seems on the surface to have been a complete reversal of policy, a licensee was refused permission to give up his licence, in part because of the precedent that this might create, but when two years later he repeated his application, his request was granted on payment of £300.[60] Matters did not improve for publicans, and when restrictions on opening hours were imposed in 1916 as a wartime measure, the Foundation allowed some of them rent rebates because of the losses incurred.[61]

Licensees were not the only tenants of the Foundation to suffer from adverse trading conditions during the First World War. As early as October 1914 reductions on rent were allowed for some restaurants and a manufacturers' agent, and in the following year the rent of a foreign fancy-goods merchant was reduced by a third. A few tenancies had to be terminated, but it was considered preferable to try to retain a tenant even at a lower rental than to have many properties unlet. Tailors and the proprietors of small cafés and restaurants suffered particularly badly – 'the prospect for tailors is a very bleak one' the Estate Committee was told in 1916 – and several rebates were authorized. Despite these concessions, by 1918 27 properties, an unusually large number, were empty.[62]

One aspect of the First World War which has tended to be forgotten in the light of far worse experiences in the Second World War was the threat of air raids. In 1915 it was reported that 'Some of the lessees of the Foundation have called attention to the insurance of premises held on repairing leases against possible damage by bomb-throwing from hostile aircraft.'[63] Steps were taken to effect insurance, and in a raid later that year minor damage occurred at several premises. Further raids in 1917 caused much broken glass but little structural damage.[64]

One side effect of the war which had a beneficial impact on the Foundation's finances was that it brought to an end the long period during which government securities had produced a very low return. Only two months after war was declared in 1914 the Charity Commissioners cautioned against the use of investments to purchase property, and over the next four years the policy of discouraging sales of property and encouraging purchases was completely reversed. In all, the proceeds of sales during the war years exceeded £120,000, while there were no major purchases.[65] Among the half-dozen properties sold were Nos. 72 and 73 Gracechurch Street to the London and South Western Bank, for the price which the bank had been reluctant to pay in 1913 but which, in the inflationary conditions of wartime, doubtless seemed a better proposition to the bank. Not only was the Foundation's investment capital increased during the war, but the opportunity was also taken to transfer a large proportion of it into the more profitable 4½ per cent War Loan stock.[66]

The First World War marked something of a watershed in the financial fortunes of the Foundation. The income of both the Central and City Church Funds rose slowly over the first quarter century of the Foundation's existence, but there was then a perceptible upturn in the rate of increase up to the outbreak of the Second World War. The first period was principally one of consolidation with an eye to future interests. The conservative attitude adopted by Winstanley, as surveyor, and the Charity Commissioners is illustrated by an episode in 1896 when an offer to take a large site in Fleet Street on a rebuilding lease was turned down and a repairing lease expiring in 1915 was granted instead, on the grounds that the site might be more productive at the later date 'having regard to the valuable character of the property for shops or newspaper offices.'[67]

And yet it is difficult to see how a significantly different attitude could have been taken or significantly different results obtained. This was a period, as we have seen, of low yields on the kind of investment opportunities available to trustees of charity funds, and the possession of urban property by no means produced the universal benefits that it seemed to do for preceding and succeeding generations. From about 1905 there was a severe decline in urban property values which lasted throughout the Edwardian period.[68] In 1909, for instance, the rebuilding of a site in Garlick Hill was postponed because 'the present prevailing depression' made it difficult to obtain a good ground rent.[69] The overwhelming Liberal victory in the general election of 1906, while it ushered in a period of social reform which had a profound effect on the work of the Foundation, caused deep forebodings among property owners. When Lloyd George introduced his 'people's budget' of 1909 with its taxes on incremental land values, reversions and undeveloped land, their worst fears appeared to have been realized. The Foundation itself was affected by the proposals and decided to join in protests against the bill. In the event, it only paid £1,562 in such duties and this was returned in 1920 in a dramatic reversal of policy by the post-war coalition government.[70] The government did in fact ask owners to refrain from pressing their claims where small sums were involved, but the trustees decided that they had a fiduciary duty to recover the money.

A cautious, prudent approach to estate management was doubtless wise during this long period, but one effect was to seriously reduce the possibility of the Foundation giving substantial grant aid to any cause other than that of the polytechnics. In most years up to 1914 the amount available out of the Central Fund for 'miscellaneous' grants, once pensions had been paid and the statutory and voluntary obligations to the polytechnics satisfied, rarely amounted to more than £5,000 and was frequently very much less. In 1908, indeed, the Central Government Body found itself in difficulties as a result of basing its annual grants on the estimated income for each year, and decided that in future discretionary grants should only be paid out of the previous year's realized surplus. At the same time an appeal was made to the Charity Commissioners for an advance out of capital as a working balance. The request was granted, but not without the wagging of an admonitory finger.[71]

The trough of the property cycle had passed by the outbreak of war, and the relatively buoyant conditions that followed explains why a number of advantageous sales could be made, even while the war was still in progress. The upturn continued after the armistice, although the situation was temporarily distorted by wartime and post-war inflation, and the trustees found themselves with both an increased income and a greater range of options. The careful nurturing of the estate in the early years also began to bear fruit. We have seen how a site in King William Street, which had been judiciously expanded by purchases, produced an annual ground rent for the City Church Fund of over £14,000 when rebuilt in 1919–21, and the Central Fund profited likewise from rebuildings in Fleet Street in 1923–4 to a slightly lesser extent. The chairman of the Estate Committee made a point of commenting on the benefit to the Foundation of such developments.[72]

Other rebuildings took place, such as at Nos. 45–47 Cornhill, where Campbell Jones was the architect, and the ground rent for the new buildings, at £2,050 per annum, more than doubled the rent received for the old premises.[73] So pleased were the trustees with Campbell Jones's performance as surveyor that in 1929 they resolved to raise his salary in view of the increase in the capital value of the Foundation's property, and at the beginning of the following year the chairman of the Estate Committee was able to announce that as a result of the new leases granted in the previous year alone the rental had increased by £3,000.[74]

Exactly how far the upturn in the fortunes of the Foundation could be attributed personally to Campbell Jones as surveyor is a moot point. Certainly he seems to have been more active than Winstanley and much favoured as an architect by the trustees and lessees alike, but he was operating at a propitious time. Several financial institutions, especially banks, chose to rebuild both their headquarters premises and branches in the inter-war years, usually in a grandiose style, and on sites for which they were prepared to pay high prices if freehold or high ground rents if leasehold. Among the more advantageous sales was that of a group of properties in Leadenhall Street and Creechurch Lane which the Foundation had purchased in 1912 and 1914 for under £22,000. They were sold in 1928 for £60,000 in a transaction which produced yet another favourable comment in the Estate Committee chairman's annual review.[75] Similarly, in 1935 the freehold of a group of four buildings in Gracechurch Street, of which two had been purchased in 1901 and 1913 for £24,000, sold for £76,000.[76] These examples are, however, eclipsed by the £200,000 paid by Barclay's Bank in 1931 for a large site in Lombard Street, the heartland of banking, which provided a similar boost to the City Church Fund as the sale of a plot in the same street to Glyn's Bank in 1905 had done to the Central Fund. The Ecclesiastical Commissioners, who, of course, received the surplus of the City Church Fund, wrote to Donald Allen to congratulate him on the role he had played as Clerk in the negotiations leading up to the transaction.[77]

The upward movement of the Foundation's income after the war proceeded with hardly a pause, even if there was sufficient apprehension at the time of the General Strike in 1926 to take out insurance against civil commotion and riot.[78] By 1933 not only had the income of the combined Funds increased by over 50 per cent since 1914, but there was also over half a million pounds in investments, divided between the Central Fund (£310,185) and the City Church Fund (£278,889).[79] So healthy was the general state of the Central Fund that the trustees decided for the first time to set aside 5 per cent of the income annually to form a reserve.[80]

Because the underlying performance of its estate was sound, the Foundation was only affected marginally by the depression, but there were many cases of hardship among individual tenants and some problems of estate management. The first evidence of failures 'owing to the continued depression in trade and in the textile business particularly' was brought to the attention of the Estate Committee late in 1930. In the following year there were several applications for reductions in rents, including from a picture-frame maker and a brush and basket maker, and some rents had to be written off as a result of liquidations.[81] One example was that of the manufacturing furrier paying a rent of £1,100 per annum for a 21-year lease of his premises, who had been offered a rebate of £350 for one year, but who had been forced to cease trading; there was no alternative but to obtain repossession.[82] Some particularly poignant cases were reported, such as that of the wholesale woollen and trimming merchants whose business collapsed in 1933, 'both partners, it is stated, having lost all their capital and one of them in consequence having been removed to a mental home'.[83]

As at the time of the First World War, the general policy was to accept lower rents if necessary rather than let premises go untenanted,[84] but even at the height of the depression some remarkable property deals could be concluded, as in 1932 when a property in Cannon Street and Queen Street which had previously produced an annual rent of £380 was let on a new lease at £4,200 per annum.[85] Nevertheless, the number of unlet properties increased from ten in 1931, representing a loss of rent of £1,331, to 24 in 1936 with a rental value of £5,050.[86] Thereafter, the situation eased as the worst of the depression passed. The slight decline in the Foundation's income in 1934–6 was undoubtedly due to these difficult circumstances, but the sharp increase in 1937 was the result of relettings on the Packington Estate (see below). The fact that the income of the Central Fund, despite minor fluctuations, remained very much higher throughout the course of the depression than it had been twenty years earlier meant that, without stinting the support to the polytechnics, substantial help could be given towards the alleviation of distress in ways which are described in Chapter 8.

Although the most spectacular property transactions of the inter-war years consisted of sales and rebuildings, a number of purchases were also made. The surveyor was always on the lookout for suitable City properties as and when they came on to the market, but discrimination still had to be practised. When, in 1926, there was an opportunity to buy No. 15 Watling Street, adjacent to a property of the Foundation, caution was urged as 'the Surveyor does not consider Watling Street to be flourishing' and the price which was offered at his suggestion was exceeded by another buyer.[87]

The most important purchases during these years, however, were not of buildings in the City but of playing fields and recreation grounds on the outskirts of the metropolis. Before and during the First World War loans were made to several of the polytechnics to enable them to acquire sports grounds, and as in most cases the repayments on these 'loans' were covered by increases in grants, they were in effect free gifts to the polytechnics.[88]

In 1920 there was a change of policy, largely it appears on the initiative of Edward Bond as chairman of the Estate Committee. The immediate reason appears to have been the high post-war interest rates. Battersea Polytechnic wanted to purchase 12 acres at Mitcham for an athletic ground and was offered a loan at 6 per cent interest, but the London County Council, which by this time provided most of the finance for the polytechnics, objected to the rate of interest. The trustees therefore decided to purchase the land directly and lease it to the polytechnic at a rent equivalent to a 5 per cent return on capital.[89] Similar arrangements were made for the acquisition of more land for use as playing fields by other educational institutions, as described in more detail on pages 145–6.

A logical extension of the policy of buying land for sports grounds for the polytechnics and similar institutions was the purchase of land for wider recreational purposes (see pages 165–6). In all, in the years between the First and Second World Wars the Foundation bought and equipped some 350 acres of land for various forms of sporting and other outdoor activity at a cost of well over £150,000 (a sum which is equivalent to some £5 million at 1990 values).

An important development in the history of the estate occurred in 1937 when the Packington Estate was partitioned and the trustees took over the direct management of their portion. The estate consisted of some 23 acres in Islington which had been left to charitable uses by the will of Dame Anne Packington, who died in 1563. The estate was managed by the Clothworkers' Company, which acquired some additional nearby land with the result that the two estates became intermingled. The Court of Chancery effected a degree of separation in 1827, but both estates continued to be managed by the Clothworkers and were built over in a continuous development between 1846 and 1860. In 1891 three-quarters of the income of the charity estate, amounting to £771 per annum, passed to the Foundation.[90]

The estate consisted of some 415 houses and shops held on building leases which began to expire in the 1920s and 1930s. The majority of leases fell in at Michaelmas 1936, and the Charity Commissioners decided to carry out a further partition which took effect from 1 January 1937. The increase which the Foundation could expect in its gross income from direct lettings on the estate was estimated to be not less than £18,000, from which the cost of repairs and management expenses had to be deducted. Most of the houses were multi-occupied, and although few difficulties were anticipated – 'the rooms change hands frequently at small rents, and do not remain empty for any length of time,' the trustees were told – the decision was made to open a local office with its own permanent staff of three. The income of the Central Fund enjoyed a substantial boost in 1937 from the settlement which accompanied the partition and new rents, and slightly less in the two succeeding years, when a number of repairs had to be undertaken, but the war intervened to prevent the full realization of the estate's potential.[91]

The healthy state of the Foundation's finances in the 1930s enabled the trustees to entertain thoughts of some grandiose projects of their own. The most ambitious was a proposal to build a hostel for City clerks on low wages containing bedrooms, common rooms, recreation rooms, a swimming pool and a restaurant. The cost of building was estimated to be about £200,000, and the Charity Commissioners indicated that they were prepared to approve the scheme. The site chosen, which was in Southwark, on the north side of Park Street between Rose Alley and Southwark Bridge Road, had remained unlet and unproductive for many years. When the suggestion was put to the Estate Committee in 1938, however, the vote in favour was only 5–4, and the chairman ruled that this was too close a division for such an important decision and that the proposal should lie on the table.[92] What is by no means the least interesting aspect of this episode is that the site in question is where the remains of the Rose Theatre were discovered during an excavation in 1989.

When the accounts for 1938 had been audited, the realized surplus of the Central Fund which was available for distribution in new grants during 1939, excluding the accumulated reserve and commitments from previous years and to the polytechnics and similar institutions, amounted to over £30,000[93] (equivalent at 1990 prices to approximately £1 million). The corresponding figure in 1915 had been only £7,750.[94] Only the ominous clouds gathering on the international scene, which as early as October 1938 had led to precautions against air raids being taken at the agency properties,[95] appeared to threaten the general onward and upward progression.

NOTES

1. *PP*, 1894, XXVIII, *Forty-first Report of the Charity Commissioners . . .* , 33–7.
2. CPF, *First Report of the Central Governing Body* (1900), 11: Minutes, X, 12; XLIII, 182–4.
3. *First Report, ut supra*, 12.
4. Minutes, II, 21.
5. Ibid., I, 8–9.
6. Ibid., I, 5, 67.
7. Ibid., I, 35, 36.
8. Ibid., II, 22–3, 47–8, 87, 88, 107–9.
9. Ibid., II, 76.
10. Ibid., XIII, 31; XLIII, 152–3.
11. Ibid., II, Rent Roll at rear.
12. Ibid., IV, 22; VII, 128, VIII, 12, 24: *First Report, ut supra*, 8–9.
13. Minutes, I, 16, 20.
14. Ibid., I, 16, 39; II, 5, 29, 57, 78, 96.
15. *First Report, ut supra*, 9.
16. Minutes, IX, 78.
17. Ibid., XXIII, 105.
18. Ibid., II, 59.
19. Ibid., II, 165; III 47, 65, 114–15, 119; IV, 139.
20. Ibid., III, 13, 66–7.
21. Ibid., V, 46, 50.
22. Ibid., VI, 98.
23. Ibid., VII, 42.

24. Ibid., IX, 100; X, 80.
25. Ibid., XII, 86.
26. Ibid., XIX, 26.
27. Ibid., XXXV, 137.
28. Ibid., XVII, 97.
29. Ibid., VI, 118.
30. Ibid., VII, 13.
31. Ibid., VII, 117–18; IX, 81–3.
32. Ibid., XV, 137–8; XVI, 83.
33. Ibid., V, 23–5, 81; VII, 71; VIII, 18, 133; IX, 47, 79, 106, 110; X, 74, 90, 107, 125.
34. Ibid., IX, 47.
35. *First Report, ut supra*, 9: Avner Offer, *Property and Politics 1870–1914. Landownership, Law, Ideology and Urban Development in England* (1981), 274.
36. Barry Supple, *The Royal Exchange Assurance. A History of British Insurance 1720–1970* (1970), 313, 330, 331, 335–7.
37. Minutes, III, 97, 122; IV, 64, 97–8.
38. Ibid., X, 123.
39. Ibid., IV, 47–8.
40. Ibid., XII, 121; XXVI, 96–7; XXIX, 134–5; XXXII, 67.
41. Ibid., IV 64; XXXIII, 147–8; XXXIV, 38.
42. *Second Report submitted to the Central Governing Body by the Clerk of the Foundation* (1927), 12–13: David Owen, *English Philanthropy 1660–1960* (1965), 87–8, 318–21, 584: *Report of the Committee on the Law and Practice relating to Charitable Trusts* (Nathan Report) (1952), 61–3.
43. *Second Report, ut supra*, 13.
44. Minutes, V, 39–40; IX, 36–7; XI, 43–4.
45. Ibid., XII, 53.
46. Ibid., XXIV, 154–5.
47. Ibid., II, 68, 180.
48. Ibid., IV, 103; VI, 93.
49. Ibid., XIV, 76, 95, 113, 130.
50. Ibid., XV, 94, 109, 115.
51. Ibid., XVI, 50; XL, 165.
52. Ibid., XXX, 133: *Second Report, ut supra*, 12.
53. Minutes, VI, 102; VII, 117; VIII, 73; IX, 23.
54. Ibid., IX, 103; XIV, 57; XV, 116.
55. Ibid., XLVI, 115; XLVII, 75–6.
56. Ibid., I, 17–19; III, 120; V, 134; VIII, 134; XI, 128; XII, 26; XIV, 134; XV, 71, 95; XVI, 28, 124; XIX, 100: *Second Report, ut supra*, 12.
57. Minutes, I, 72; II, 16.
58. Mark Girouard, *Victorian Pubs* (1984 ed.), 86–108 *passim*.
59. Minutes, XIII, 61; XIV, 55, 98.
60. Ibid., XVIII, 138; XX, 133, 150.
61. Ibid., XXVI, 110.
62. Ibid., XXIV, 145–8; XXV, 148; XXVI, 37–45, 69–70; XXVIII, 43.
63. Ibid., XV, 131.
64. Ibid., XV, 151–2; XVII, 133.
65. Ibid., XXV, 105–9, 111, 114, 154; XXVI, 109; XXVII, 147–8; XXVIII, 38.
66. Ibid., XXV, 124–5.
67. Ibid., VI, 60–1.
68. Offer, op. cit., 112–13, 254–82.

69. Minutes, XIX, 36.
70. Ibid., XIX, 118; XX, 136–7; XXX, 153–4, 172.
71. Ibid., XVIII, 42–3, 68.
72. Ibid., XXXVII, 69.
73. Ibid., XXXIII, 130.
74. Ibid., XXXIX, 100; XL, 70.
75. Ibid., XXII, 160; XXIV, 75–6; XXXVIII, 66; XXXIX, 67.
76. Ibid., XI, 77; XXIV, 106; XLV, 132.
77. Ibid., XLI, 135; XLII, 71.
78. Ibid., XXXVI, 99.
79. Ibid., XLIII, 71–2.
80. Ibid., XLIII, 118–19, 149.
81. Ibid., XL, 159–62; XLI, 65–6, 127, 148–9.
82. Ibid., XLII, 34.
83. Ibid., XLIII, 209.
84. Ibid., XLV, 131.
85. Ibid., XLIII, 83.
86. Ibid., XLI, 35; XLVI, 121.
87. Ibid., XXVI, 116–17, 130.
88. Ibid., XIII, 83, 107; XIV, 113; XV, 129; XXII, 28, 110; XXVII, 146, 157.
89. Ibid., XXX, 30–1, 101–2, 132–3: *Second Report, ut supra,* 23–4.
90. *The Victoria History of the Counties of England. Middlesex. Volume VIII. Islington and Stoke Newington Parishes* (1985), 23, 64: English Heritage, London Division, Historians' Files, ISL 20: *A History of the City Parochial Foundation: Trustees of the London Parochial Charities 1891–1951* (1951), 30–2.
91. Minutes, XLV, 38; XLVI, 201–2, 321–3, 326; XLVII, 75.
92. Ibid., XLVI, 265; XLVII, 181–2, 217–18; XLVIII, 149.
93. Ibid., XLIX, 85–6.
94. Ibid., XXV, 71.
95. Ibid., XLVIII, 206.

7 The polytechnics and 'kindred institutions'

The enthusiasm with which the Charity Commissioners and their officials adopted the proposal to establish a network of polytechnics on the model of Quintin Hogg's Polytechnic in Regent Street as a way of discharging their task of preparing a scheme for the utilization of the combined funds of the City parochial charities has been described in Chapter 4. The members of the Foundation's Central Governing Body, once appointed, were meant to be under no illusion about where their principal duty lay, and a substantial proportion of them were chosen from the world of education. As late as 1927, when the Clerk, Ernald Warre, prepared his *Second Report* on the work of the Foundation, he could state quite unequivocally that, 'The Polytechnics were obviously intended to be regarded as the prime concern of the Central Governing Body.'[1] The importance of the polytechnics is illustrated by the statistic that out of a total of some £2.7 million which was spent on grants of all kinds out of the income of the Central Fund in the period 1891–1939, over £2 million (approximately 75 per cent) went to the polytechnics and kindred institutions and less than £700,000 to all other causes.

The term 'kindred institutions' was used by the Foundation to describe a handful of organizations which were generally classed with the polytechnics for accounting purposes, usually because they were subject to schemes of the Charity Commissioners which required the Foundation to give mandatory annual grants for their support. These were mainly broadly educational in nature but included such diverse institutions as the Old Vic, the Chelsea Physic Garden and the Whitechapel Art Gallery.

The 'scheme' or compulsory annual grants were set out in the Central Scheme and added to or amended slightly from time to time. Those specified in 1891 consisted of £5,350 to a City Polytechnic which was to be formed by an amalgamation of the existing Birkbeck Institution and City of London College and the yet to be established Northampton Institute (in the proportions of £3,350 to Northampton and £1,000 each to Birkbeck and the City of London College); £3,500 to the Regent Street Polytechnic; £3,500 to the People's Palace; £2,500 to the Borough Polytechnic; £2,500 to the Battersea Polytechnic; £1,500 to the South-Western Polytechnic; £1,000 to the Royal Victoria Hall (or Old Vic) and Morley College; £400 to the Joint Committee for the Working Men's College and the College for Men and Women; £150 each to two smaller institutions, the Bow and Bromley and the Aldenham Institutes; and an unspecified sum to the Bishopsgate Institute which, together with the income from the Bishopsgate charities, would be sufficient to make up an annual income of £2,000 (a sum which in practice was fixed at £1,000). Several of these institutions had not yet been established, namely the Northampton, Borough, Battersea and South-Western Polytechnics and the Bishopsgate Institute, and in their cases money was to accumulate from certain specified dates. In addition, the Commissioners could direct that an annual sum not exceeding £5,000 should be paid to any future institutions of a like nature, and of this £3,000 was very quickly required for obligatory grants to the proposed Northern and North-Western Polytechnics in the proportion of £1,500 to each.

These grants were, in effect, redemptions by the Charity Commissioners of promises made to match the funds raised through local effort, by providing endowments rather than capital sums. At the prevailing rate of interest an annual endowment of £1,500 was considered to be equivalent to a capital grant of £50,000, so that in many cases the Commissioners erred on the side of generosity. It should also be remembered that they had already raided the accumulated capital of the City charities to provide over £50,000 for the establishment of the City Polytechnic, £40,000 each to the Bishopsgate and Cripplegate Foundations, £11,750 to the Regent Street Polytechnic, £6,750 to the People's Palace and £6,000 to the Victoria Hall and Morley College. Thus, by a combination of capital grants and endowments, calculated at their capitalized value, the Charity Commissioners gave the polytechnic movement the equivalent of about £1 million from the windfall available from the City charities. (Such a sum, at 1990 values, would be worth not far short of £50 million.)

From the start, however, it was clear that such largesse, munificent as it may have been, was not sufficient. The birth throes of the new polytechnics were often long and hard and they needed additional help. One of the earliest grants made by the Foundation as an independent body was £1,000 in March 1892 to the Regent Street Polytechnic (not, of course, even one of the new polytechnics) to assist in meeting an estimated deficit on the year's operations, following an appeal launched in *The Times*.[2] At their next meeting the trustees considered the applications for further assistance from the Borough (the most advanced of the new institutions and likely to be the first to open) and South-Western Polytechnics. They decided then and there to give a grant of £2,000 to the former for capital expenditure on new buildings, but deferred a decision on aid to the latter until a systematic review of the needs of the polytechnics had been undertaken.[3]

It was clear that a piecemeal approach, dealing with demands as they arose, would not be satisfactory, especially as the trustees had such a relatively small amount to give away, and they asked for a comprehensive proposal to be prepared on the subject of additional grants to the polytechnics. Predictably, Spicer, Magnus and Roberts were to the fore in urging this course.[4] Under their plan, which was formulated in June 1892, capital grants for buildings and equipment totalling £16,000, and additional annual grants adding up to £3,500 (£1,000 to Borough and £500 each to the Regent Street, South-Western, Northern and North-Western Polytechnics and the Royal Victoria Hall) were to be made. The annual grants were to be continued 'during pleasure' from year to year, and the principle of providing extra income for the polytechnics which was not likely to be withdrawn except under changed circumstances was firmly established. The opportunity was taken at the same time to remind the Charity Commissioners that it would only be possible to make these grants if the Commissioners handed over money which now rightfully belonged to the Foundation, with a hint that greater help might have been forthcoming if the Commissioners had not been so niggardly in holding on to the accrued income of the parochial charities.[5]

Another important policy which was initiated in 1892 was the provision of substantial loans to the polytechnics. Once again, Borough was the first to benefit. That polytechnic had been fortunate enough to acquire a ready-made site and buildings, although they had to be adapted and enlarged, in the premises of the British and Foreign Schools Society in Borough Road, Southwark. The site was held on lease from the City Corporation, and at a meeting of the Central Governing Body in April 1892 Sir Owen Roberts moved and Magnus seconded a resolution that the Foundation should purchase the freehold. This suggestion was eventually turned down, however, 'on the ground that the Funds of the Foundation should be invested in a more realisable class of security', a decision taken, significantly, by the Finance and General Purposes Committee rather than the Estate Committee. A way of accommodating the polytechnic was found when its governors applied for a loan of the £10,000 which was required to complete the purchase and the trustees readily agreed. They stipulated that the money was to be repaid together with interest at 3 per cent over thirty years, and that the repayment instalments were to be deducted from the annual grant payable to the institution.[6] The Northern Polytechnic quickly followed suit with a request for a similar amount, and Regent Street characteristically raised the stakes by asking for £20,000.[7]

At the very time, however, that the Foundation was groping towards a way of fulfilling its obligations to the polytechnics, events were unfolding which were eventually to lead to a complete change in the relationship of the Foundation to the polytechnics and, indeed, in the nature of the polytechnics themselves. The new factor was the intervention of the recently created London County Council.

The LCC derived its powers to aid technical education from two Acts of Parliament. The Technical Instruction Act of 1889 enabled county, county borough and urban district councils to employ the product of a penny rate for this purpose. James Bryce had indeed drawn attention to the existence of this Act when he had questioned the wisdom of devoting such a high proportion of the funds of the parochial charities to technical education in his comments on the Central Scheme (see pages 69–70). Of equal importance, however, was an unlikely bounty provided by the Local Taxation (Customs and Excise) Act of 1890. The origins of this lay in an attempt to use the proceeds of a tax on beer and spirits to compensate publicans of redundant public houses for the surrender of their licences, but such was the outcry from the temperance lobby that Parliament decreed that the money should be used instead for objects in relief of the rates or, in a clause slipped in by educational reformers, for technical education. This was the celebrated 'whisky money'.

The LCC had, in fact, been slow to seize its opportunities under these Acts, an attempt in 1891 to use some of the whisky money to grant aid the polytechnics having been overturned in the full Council.[8] It was not until the second Council was elected in 1892 with vigorous new members like Sidney Webb that attitudes changed. Quintin Hogg moved a resolution that £30,000 should be set aside for technical education, a committee was appointed, and a report commissioned from Hubert Llewellyn Smith, who had been one of Booth's assistants on his great survey and was Secretary of the National Association for the Promotion of Secondary and Technical Education. Llewellyn

Smith's comprehensive report was submitted in 1892 and, largely at Webb's prompting, the Council agreed in January 1893 to set up a Technical Education Board, on which representatives of other organizations would sit as well as members of the Council. By opening up the composition of the Board to outside bodies, the Council hoped to defuse the opposition from potential critics. The Board, which began its work in April 1893, had 35 members, 20 from the LCC and 15 others, including two to be appointed by the Foundation. The presiding genius was Sidney Webb, who was the Board's Chairman from 1893 to 1898. The Secretary was William Garnett, who had formerly been Principal of the Durham College of Technology at Newcastle upon Tyne.[9]

The Foundation's first two representatives on the Technical Education Board, selected in March 1893, were Magnus and C. J. Drummond, but the latter soon resigned, and was replaced briefly by A. Bassett Hopkins, before he, too, gave way to Lewis Boyd Sebastian early in 1894.[10] Magnus had already persuaded the Central Governing Body that the Foundation should play an active part in monitoring the educational content and examination standards of the polytechnics, but when a special meeting of the Finance and General Purposes Committee was held in February 1893 to consider how best to put this resolution into practice, it decided to await the formation of the Technical Education Board before taking the matter further. Eventually, in accordance with that procedure much beloved of the late nineteenth and early twentieth centuries, a 'conference' was called between the Foundation, the Board and the City and Guilds Institute.[11]

The conference was held at Temple Gardens in December 1893 and those present included such stalwarts of the technical education scene as Magnus, Roberts, Webb, Llewellyn Smith and Garnett. They were concerned to promote uniformity in the administration, inspection and examinations of the polytechnics, and decided to appoint a Polytechnic Joint Board (soon renamed the London Polytechnic Council) to oversee such matters. This was to consist of those members of the Technical Education Board who also sat on the Central Governing Body and on the Council of the City and Guilds Institute, plus six members to be selected, two each, by the three bodies, and the Chairman of the TEB *ex officio*. The additional representatives of the Foundation were Professor William Ramsay and Henry Hardinge Cunynghame, neither of whom were trustees (although Ramsay was to become one in 1895). Cunynghame had, of course, been the principal author of the plan to use the money available from the City parochial charities to found polytechnics (see Chapter 4).[12]

The first meetings of the London Polytechnic Council were held at Temple Gardens early in 1894. Roberts, who represented the City and Guilds Institute on the Technical Education Board, was elected Chairman and Webb, Deputy-Chairman. Magnus and Garnett were asked to act as Joint Secretaries at salaries of £100 per annum each to cover expenses and clerical assistance, and Magnus was also appointed Principal Education Adviser and Inspector at a further salary of £200. These salaries were paid by the Central Governing Body, from which Magnus thereupon resigned, presumably because he was now in receipt of a stipend from the Foundation. In addition the trustees supplied a grant of £500 to enable the Council to begin its work, and Batten was asked to act as its minuting clerk.[13]

From thenceforward, during its lifespan, the London Polytechnic Council generally determined how any additional money which could be made available for the polytechnics should be spent. The procedure was that the trustees would indicate at their first meeting in the year how much of the projected surplus should be allocated to the polytechnics (usually rubber-stamping the recommendations of the Finance and General Purposes Committee) and the London Polytechnic Council would in turn recommend how that was to be distributed, usually in the form of special grants, but occasionally by suggesting an increase in the semi-obligatory annual grants (or 'ordinary supplemental grants' as they came to be called to distinguish them from the compulsory scheme grants). The Polytechnic Council was the creation of the Central Governing Body, in effect a special committee to deal with education, and it was undoubtedly highly effective in providing a mechanism for liaison with the Technical Education Board. But its existence did mean that the Foundation's policy towards the polytechnics was driven by a small body of trustees with Roberts, Webb (a trustee after 1897), Sebastian and Magnus (no longer technically a trustee but as influential as any of the others) to the fore, all of them key figures in the burgeoning technical education movement.

Although the trustees were always concerned to ensure that sufficient provision was made for social and recreational activities at the polytechnics, the preoccupations of the Polytechnic Council were predominantly educational. In 1895 it initiated annual grants (originally £300) to help students pay examination fees. In 1897 it urged the Central Governing Body to accompany the payment of grants with a request that the polytechnics should pay particular attention to the 'literary' side of education, and three years later it questioned whether any extra grants should be given to the Old Vic, 'which is a Music Hall rather than a Polytechnic'.[14]

In 1899 Magnus intimated that he wished to give up his positions with the Polytechnic Council, and the Central Governing Body decided not to replace him as Principal Education Adviser and Inspector, on the grounds that with most of the polytechnics well established there was no longer a need for such a post. Howard Batten was asked to take over as Joint Secretary with an addition to his regular salary of £100 per annum, and Magnus was immediately reappointed to the Central Governing Body, taking the place of the existing nominee of the University of London who almost certainly deliberately stepped down to make way for him.[15] Magnus may have felt that the Polytechnic Council had already served its main purpose. Within five years it was indeed wound up as part of the changes resulting from the Education Act of 1902 and the Education (London) Act of 1903 which made the London County Council the education authority for London and also led to the demise of the Technical Education Board. Nevertheless, some important initiatives were taken in the years between 1899 and 1904.

The first, in 1901, was the introduction of City Parochial Foundation Scholarships. These were designed to assist 'the most promising students of the poorer classes' at the polytechnics or other institutes aided by the Foundation to read for degrees at the London School of Economics, and corresponded with one of the uses for the residue of the Central Fund suggested by the Charity Commissioners in the Central Scheme. It is not difficult to discern the hand of Sidney Webb behind such a move.[16] The response, however, was disappointing, and in 1914 a decision was taken to phase out the scholarships.[17]

Early in 1902 the Polytechnic Council passed a resolution calling on the Foundation and the Technical Education Board to provide capital for additional buildings for the polytechnics. This led to the decision to which reference is made in Chapter 6 to use £30,000 from the City Church Fund (in addition to £10,000 from the Central Fund) to make loans to the polytechnics, over the protest of some of the trustees.[18] It also appears to have been in connection with these loans that the trustees introduced the policy of increasing the annual grants to the polytechnics to cover the repayment and interest charges, thus, in practice, converting the loans into capital grants. In 1906 it was minuted with reference to these payments that 'it has always been understood that the Trustees would make Special Grants to enable the Polytechnics to meet the charges in question'.[19] There is no evidence that such a practice was followed before 1902, and some indications to the contrary. The catalyst may have been the knowledge that the Clothworkers' Company had paid the instalments on one of the Foundation's loans to the Northern Polytechnic before redeeming the whole amount in 1899,[20] and the suggestion that such a policy might be adopted by the Foundation may well have come from Sir Owen Roberts. Thereafter, although by no means all 'loans' were made on such favourable terms, institutions were usually informed if their grants were not going to be increased to meet the repayments.

The third initiative, which was also introduced in 1902, was the establishment of what was termed a pension and superannuation fund, for which a special grant of £1,450 was made in that year. Initially this was used to take out endowment assurance policies for the principals of the polytechnics and to set up a compassionate fund to cover cases of hardship among the staff. In 1905 a similar endowment scheme was applied to secretaries, and in the following year this was extended to all the staff of the polytechnics. Such schemes, which required matching contributions from the participants, were rare at that time, and it has been suggested that they later formed the basis of the universities' superannuation system. Eventually they were overtaken by the School Teachers (Superannuation) Act of 1918 and by the admission of non-teaching staff to the LCC's Superannuation and Provident Fund in 1929, but not before the Foundation had spent a total of £98,000 in contributions.[21]

By 1904, when the LCC assumed control of education in London, the balance of power over the polytechnics in financial terms had already imperceptibly shifted from the Foundation to the Council. In the first year of operation of the Technical Education Board, the LCC provided a mere £1,000 to the polytechnics in contrast to £29,000 from the Foundation, and in the following year the Council's grants only increased to £11,500. By 1898–9 the Central Governing Body's contribution had risen to £36,000 and the Council's to £30,000, but in 1903–4, while the Foundation's grants had remained basically static at approximately £37,000, the Council's had jumped to nearly £57,000 out of a total expenditure on technical education of all kinds of £217,000. The combined annual running costs of the dozen polytechnics or polytechnic-like institutes which were fully operational by that date were approximately £200,000. Of this sum, receipts from members' and students' fees accounted for about 30 per cent, the Council's grants about 28 per cent and the Foundation's about 18 per cent; the remainder came from Board of Education grants, contributions from City livery companies and private donations.[22]

Before examining the effect on the Foundation of the changes in the organization of London's education which took place in 1904, this is a convenient point at which to take stock of the institutions whose welfare had depended in such large measure on the support of the Foundation in the dozen or so momentous years which had elapsed since 1891.

All of the polytechnics were intended to have similar constitutions and to be bound by the 'General Regulations for the Management of an Industrial Institute' which were adopted by the Charity Commissioners and incorporated in the individual 'schemes' governing each polytechnic. These regulations described the object of the polytechnics as 'the promotion of the industrial skill, general knowledge, health, and well-being of young men and women belonging to the poorer classes' by instruction in the arts and sciences applicable to any handi-craft, trade or business, but not such as could be obtained in the workshop or place of business; instruction suitable for persons intend-ing to emigrate; instruction in such other branches of art, science, language, literature and general knowledge 'as may be approved by the Governing Body'; public lectures, musical and other entertainment, and exhibitions; gymnastics, drill, swimming and other exercise; the formation of clubs and societies; and the provision of a library, museum and reading-rooms. Each institution had its own governing body, varying in size between 12 and 17 persons, of whom three were usually appointed by the Foundation. Clearly there were not enough members of the Central Governing Body to go round, and a nominee of the Foundation did not necessarily have to be a trustee.

Membership of each institution was to be open to all persons between 16 and 25 'belonging to the poorer classes'. A distinction was drawn between members, who might wish merely to avail themselves of the recreational facilities, and students, although it was open to the governors of each institute to make attendance at classes a condition of membership. In practice the proportion of members to students varied widely from polytechnic to polytechnic.

Although much stress was laid on the fact that the polytechnics catered for the whole person, the social activities had to be of a very wholesome kind. Among a host of prohibitions were regulations forbidding drinking, smoking, gambling, and any dramatic represen-tation or dancing. In addition the buildings were not to be used for any political, denominational or sectarian purposes. Attempts were made to liberalize these rules from time to time. Moves to allow drama and dancing, for instance, were made as early as 1898, but it was not until 1911 that the schemes were finally amended to permit such activities. In 1905 a questionnaire was sent out to the polytechnics asking whether the restriction against the use of buildings for political, denominational or sectarian purposes should be removed, but a narrow majority wanted it to remain in force, and in 1908 the Old Vic was told that it could not host a temperance demonstration as this could be construed as a political event.[23]

The doyen of all the institutes was The Polytechnic founded by Quintin Hogg which, by 1891, was well settled in its Regent Street home. It remained by far the largest of the polytechnics and its demands were well nigh insatiable. Not only did it receive £11,750 out of the accumulated capital of the parochial charities, but its annual 'scheme' grant of £3,500 was one of the highest. Even so, an extra £2,000 was voted for buildings and equipment, a supplementary annual grant of £500 was quickly added, and when a request for a loan of £20,000 proved too much for the slender resources of the Foundation, the additional grant was raised to £1,000 in 1896 and £1,500 in 1900.[24] When, in 1899, the polytechnic acquired a half-finished gymnasium in Balderton Street, off Oxford Street, as an annexe to relieve pressure on its overcrowded premises, the trustees provided a loan of £7,000 to complete and fit out the building. A further loan of £1,500 was given to adapt part of the adjoining St Mark's Institute for the polytechnic, and the annual supplementary grant was raised to take account of expenditure on the annexe. One of the trustees, the Reverend R. H. Hadden, who was a governor of the polytechnic, had recently become vicar of St Mark's, North Audley Street, and was instrumental in procuring the premises in Balderton Street for the polytechnic. The loan of another £5,000 to enable the polytechnic to buy out the head lessee of its Regent Street headquarters was approved in 1904.[25]

Another institute which was much favoured by the Charity Commissioners was the People's Palace in the East End of London. It received a capital grant of £6,750 and its scheme grant of £3,500 matched that of the Regent Street Polytechnic. The origins of the Palace were romantic, it was opened with a flourish and run with flair, but financial acumen was sadly lacking from the attributes of those who directed its affairs. For many years the Foundation did no more than pay the required compulsory grant and the LCC provided no aid at all. It was left to the Drapers' Company, which had played a large part in its foundation, to come to its rescue, and it was several years before the Foundation was actively involved when steps were taken to revive its moribund recreational side (see below).[26]

The most ambitious of the new institutions which the Charity Commissioners wished to see established in 1891 was the proposed City Polytechnic. This was to be formed by the amalgamation of two existing colleges, the Birkbeck Institution and the City of London College, with the projected Northampton Institute. Birkbeck was the oldest of the evening educational institutes. It was founded in 1823 as the London Mechanics' Institution with Dr George Birkbeck as President, and changed its name to the Birkbeck Literary and Scientific Institution in 1866. In 1885 it had moved into a new building in Fetter Lane which was opened by the Prince of Wales.[27] The City of London College was a product of the year of revolutions, 1848, or to be more precise, an appeal from the Bishop of London 'to improve the intellectual and moral conditions of the industrial classes'. In the words of the college's historian, his aim was 'to set up attractions which would divert the minds of the young men of the day from "dangerous" movements and discontent to more solid and "improving" studies'. The result was 'The Metropolitan Evening Classes for Young Men' which became the City of London College in 1861. In 1882 the college, which provided a predominantly commercial education for young clerks in the City, moved into new premises in White Street, Moorfields, which were also opened by the Prince of Wales in the following year.[28] Neither Birkbeck nor the City of London College were originally intended to be recipients of aid from the Charity Commissioners, but the decision of the Goldsmiths' Company to finance entirely the proposed new polytechnic at New Cross (which became the Goldsmiths' Institute, later Goldsmiths' College) released an endowment of £2,000 per annum which was divided equally between the two institutions in the form of annual compulsory grants from the Foundation.

The Northampton Institute, on the other hand, was heavily supported. It received a capital sum of over £50,000 and its scheme grant of £3,350 was second only to those of Regent Street and the People's Palace. The Skinners' Company also took a keen interest in its fortunes and was liberal in its support. A site of one and a quarter acres between St John Street and Northampton Square, on the Northampton Estate in Finsbury, was given by the Marquess of Northampton, and a competition was held in 1892 to choose an architect for the new building. The winning design was by Edward W. Mountford, who was also the architect of Battersea Polytechnic and, more famously, the Old Bailey. His attractive essay in a Franco-Flemish eclectic style, described by Pevsner as 'exceedingly successful', was probably the best of the new polytechnic buildings; it still survives, though now somewhat overwhelmed by later buildings, and has served the institution well. It was partially ready by 1896 and completed in 1897, although its ceremonial opening by the Lord Mayor of London had to wait until 1898. Not surprisingly, in view of the liberality of the benefaction by the Charity Commissioners, the Foundation was not called on for much additional aid in the early years, but it provided an annual supplementary grant of £1,000 from 1897 and special grants from time to time.[29]

The original concept of the City Polytechnic died a natural death. A common council composed of representatives of the three institutions and the Foundation was set up, but there was little actual co-operation and the joint polytechnic was formally dissolved in 1907.[30] The City of London College was subsequently one of the constituent colleges which amalgamated to form the City of London Polytechnic in 1970, but this institution has no relationship to that proposed by the Charity Commissioners in 1891. In yet another complication of nomenclature, the Northampton Institute has become the City University.

At least two more polytechnics were planned for north London, but only one was established with any despatch. This was the Northern Polytechnic in Holloway Road, Islington, which opened in 1896. It was not overly endowed by the Charity Commissioners, with no capital grant and only a compulsory scheme grant of £1,500, but the Clothworkers' Company, which had a large estate in Islington and other interests there, provided substantial donations, and the trustees were quick to respond to requests for aid. In 1892 they gave £2,000 for buildings and equipment and a supplementary grant of £500 (increased to £1,000 in 1901). Frequent special grants were also voted, and a loan of £10,000 which was eventually repaid by the Clothworkers. An urgent appeal for assistance in 1900 was turned down for lack of funds, but when, two years later, at the prompting of the London Polytechnic Council, further borrowing was allowed out of the capital of the City Church Fund, the Northern Polytechnic benefited by over £15,000 to pay for additional buildings, and the annual grant was raised to meet the repayments.[31]

The story of the North-Western Polytechnic, to which an annual grant of £1,500 had also been awarded, was, however, a saga of delay and frustration. A site was acquired in Kentish Town Road and Prince of Wales Road but it was encumbered by leases which could not be bought out, and was subject to a mortgage. In 1894 the trustees suggested that the funds intended for this polytechnic, the plans for which 'appear hopeless and impracticable', should be diverted to the Woolwich Polytechnic, but the Charity Commissioners thought such a move premature. Four years later, however, the scheme grant was reduced to £500, which was allowed to accumulate in a building fund until such time as building appeared a real prospect, the mortgage was paid off and the Foundation entered into possession of the site, collecting rents from the existing buildings.[32]

Local support for the establishment of polytechnics on the south side of the Thames was more widespread and better organized than in north London, and the Borough Polytechnic was the first of the new institutions to be opened, in October 1892. As we have seen, it was fortunate in being able to take over suitable existing buildings in the training school of the British and Foreign Schools Society in Borough Road, Southwark, but at first its only income apart from fees and donations was its scheme grant of £2,500 from the Foundation. This was soon supplemented by a further £1,000 per annum and a one-off grant of £4,000 for adapting and fitting out the buildings. In addition, by 1904, a total of £15,500 had been lent by the trustees to purchase the freehold of the site and help pay for an ambitious building and expansion programme. The Technical Education Board also looked on Borough with particular favour once its own grants scheme was fully operational.[33]

Battersea was not far behind Borough. By 1891 a site had been chosen – a failed amusement park in Battersea Park Road – and E. W. Mountford appointed as architect. His brick and stone building, one of a number of public buildings in Battersea for which he was architect, if not quite as distinguished as the Northampton Institute, was a conspicuous and attractive adornment to the area when it opened in 1894. Also the recipient of a compulsory annual grant of £2,500, Battersea tended to be treated on a par with Borough by the Foundation. It too received a supplementary income of £1,000 per annum and grants totalling £4,000 for buildings and equipment including new workshops and a hall which was opened in 1899. Its governors, however, unlike Borough's, were less inclined to seek loans from the Foundation, although they were offered £7,700 for the purchase of the freehold of their site, and received £4,000 out of the £33,000 which was lent to the polytechnics in 1902.[34]

The Foundation's relationship with the South-Western (later Chelsea) Polytechnic was somewhat strained from the start. The Chelsea Public Library Commissioners had been instrumental in urging on the Charity Commissioners the need for a polytechnic in west London and Earl Cadogan had made a gift of a site in Manresa Road, Chelsea. An architectural competition was held and the winner was J. M. Brydon, who, like Mountford in Battersea, designed other civic and public buildings in the locality. The foundation stone was laid by the Prince of Wales in 1891 but building costs soon outran the estimates and it proved difficult to raise funds. The scheme grant awarded by the Charity Commissioners was only £1,500 per annum, and General Lynedoch Gardiner, who was a trustee and one of the Foundation's representatives on the polytechnic's governing body, complained bitterly that the South-Western was being discriminated against in comparison with other polytechnics, producing calculations of the capitalized value of the lump sums and annual endowments awarded to each to make his point. There was a strong feeling among the trustees that more local support should have been forthcoming in such a relatively prosperous neighbourhood, but in the face of a real perceived need help was proffered. The annual income was supplemented by £500 (raised to £1,000 in 1901), and £4,000 was made available as a grant and another £4,000 as a loan towards the cost of erecting and fitting out the building, which was partially opened in 1895 and completed in the following year. An application for a further loan of £6,000 was turned down in 1896, but the polytechnic benefited to the extent of over £10,000 from the 'loans' offered at the suggestion of the London Polytchnic Council in 1902, while in the following year the trustees were prepared, again on the recommendation of the Council, to buy an adjoining property for £9,000 to provide a site for an extension. In the event, as in the case of Borough Polytechnic a decade earlier, the sum was made into a loan to enable the polytechnic to purchase the site itself.[35]

There were three other institutions generally classified as polytechnics which the Foundation was not required to support under the terms of the Central Scheme. The first, the Goldsmiths' Institute at New Cross, became the sole responsibility of the Goldsmiths' Company and received no help from the Foundation whatsoever. The second, the Woolwich Polytechnic, had an unusual and troubled early history. It began life as an adjunct of the Regent Street Polytechnic on the personal initiative of Quintin Hogg with the help of local benefactors and was established in 1890 in a house in William (now Calderwood) Street, Woolwich. New buildings were erected in 1891, but its financial position was precarious and, although they were under no obligation to come to its aid, the trustees agreed to provide an annual grant of £400 as early as 1892. By 1894, however, it was forced to close with heavy debts, and a rescue plan was mounted in which the Foundation played an important part. Having failed to persuade the Charity Commissioners to transfer the scheme grant intended for the North-Western Polytechnic to Woolwich, the trustees decided to raise the annual voluntary grant to £1,000 and gave additional special grants for building projects. The War Office, the Woolwich Local Board and the Technical Education Board also provided assistance, and the polytechnic reopened in September 1894. Its position *vis-à-vis* the Foundation, however, was always as the poor relation of the polytechnic movement. A loan of £1,350 (with sufficient extra grant to cover the repayments) was made in 1903 to facilitate the purchase of the freehold of its athletic ground at Plumstead, but it was intimated that additional grants were unlikely to be forthcoming.[36]

The third institution which was accorded polytechnic status was the Sir John Cass Technical Institute in Jewry Street, Aldgate. This was established in 1898 as a result of a decision by the Charity Commissioners that the proceeds of the Sir John Cass charity, which were largely derived from a sizeable estate in Hackney, should be used for other purposes besides the maintenance of the Sir John Cass Foundation School. The Central Governing Body did not support the Cass Institute on a regular basis, but provided small grants from time to time, especially in the early years when its work was looked on with particular favour by the Technical Education Board and the London Polytechnic Council.[37]

Of the 'kindred institutions' to which the Foundation had to make obligatory grants under the Central Scheme, the Bow and Bromley and the Aldenham Institutes were soon regarded as too small and limited in scope and their grants were terminated by the Charity

Commissioners. This left the Bishopsgate Foundation, the Working Men's College and College for Men and Women, and the Royal Victoria Hall and Morley College. To these were added, under subsequent schemes of the Commissioners, the Chelsea Physic Garden, the Whitechapel Art Gallery and the Devas Institute.

Of the three institutes in the City which were built as a consequence of the reform of the City charities and opened in 1894, the Bishopsgate Institute was the most imposing and successful. Housed in a fine art-nouveau building by the architect C. Harrison Townsend, it provided an excellent library, lecture hall and meeting-room facilities. It had already been subsidized to the extent of £40,000 in the form of a capital sum, and the annual grant of £1,000 from the Foundation was only intended to make up any deficiencies in its income, which was to be principally derived from the parochial charities of St Botolph, Bishopsgate. The Charity Commissioners soon decided that the annual grant should only be continued up to 1899, by when local funds should be sufficient for the maintenance of the institute, and requests to prolong it beyond that date were turned down by the trustees.[38]

The Cripplegate Institute was also given a capital sum of £40,000 but no annual grant, and a move to introduce one in 1899 was rejected.[39] The St Bride Foundation Institute likewise did not receive an annual grant but tended to be treated more sympathetically by the trustees, partly because it had not been given a capital sum by the Charity Commissioners, partly because it served as a technical institute for the printing trades, and also doubtless because one of the trustees, C. J. Drummond, had played a major part in its establishment. In 1893 the trustees agreed to donate £2,500 towards the building fund and supplemented this on occasion with additional aid, especially to help build up a technical library to complement the collection of the London printer William Blades which had already been acquired for the institute on Drummond's initiative. The Cripplegate Foundation was supposed to support the library at the St Bride Institute, but when it failed to do so the trustees stepped in and took over the payments.[40]

The Working Men's College, which had been founded in 1854 by a group of Christian Socialists led by Frederick Denison Maurice, had undergone several vicissitudes in its fortunes and appealed to the Charity Commissioners for assistance under the 1883 Act. It was given an annual grant of £400 on condition that the college sought an amalgamation with the College for Men and Women, which had been created out of the former Working Women's College when that body had split in two in 1874. Like the City Polytechnic, the proposed amalgamation never took place and the College for Men and Women was wound up in 1901. By that time considerable additional help had been given to the Working Men's College in the form of supplementary and special grants, including an early contribution of £1,000 to a building fund which eventually enabled the college to move to a new building in Crowndale Road, St Pancras. The Foundation's readiness to provide aid was doubtless not entirely unconnected with the fact that Richard Buckley Litchfield, who was chairman of the Finance and General Purposes Committee from 1894 to 1899, was one of the founding members of the college and its Bursar for nearly 50 years. The other branch formed out of the old Working Women's College, the College for Working Women (later Frances Martin College) in Fitzroy Street, was not ignored and also received occasional grants, and when its rival closed in 1901 the scheme grant was amended so that it would receive £133 per annum and the Working Men's College, £266.[41]

The remaining institution which was awarded a compulsory annual grant or 'endowment' under the Central Scheme of 1891, the Royal Victoria Hall, or 'Old Vic' as it was even then popularly known, may seem at first sight to have been an unlikely candidate for support from the Charity Commissioners. The famous theatre in Waterloo had begun life respectably enough in 1818 as the Royal Coburg Theatre and, after 1833, as the Royal Victoria Theatre, in honour of the new heir to the throne. Its fortunes declined, however, and by the second half of the nineteenth century it had become little more than a low-life music hall, famous more for the behaviour of its audiences than for the quality of the theatrical fare on offer. By 1880 the theatre had closed and the lease was bought by the Coffee Music Halls Company, a venture of the housing reformer Emma Cons, who aimed to provide variety entertainment without the drunkenness, vice and violence that were becoming increasingly associated with traditional music halls. The Royal Victoria Coffee Hall reopened with a mixture of variety, concerts and penny science lectures. The lectures proved surprisingly popular and led to the introduction of classes which were held in rooms at the back of the stage. The Hall was constantly in financial difficulties, however, and was supported among others by the hosiery manufacturer and philanthropist, Samuel Morley, until his death in 1886. Morley had encouraged the educational side of the theatre's activities, and when this had developed by 1889 into a fully fledged college which occupied its own premises 'above, below and behind the stage', it was given the name of the Morley Memorial College.

By that time the Charity Commissioners had promised the Victoria Hall an endowment of £1,000, provided its freehold could be acquired, and a successful appeal for the purchase money was duly launched. Although Emma Cons had approached the Commissioners for aid, in one sense they had taken the initiative themselves, for it was at the

Old Vic that the conference on technical education was held in December 1887 at which a representative of the Commissioners had surprised the audience by stating that they were prepared to endow institutions providing such education and recreational facilities for the working classes out of the funds of the City parochial charities. Significantly, when the endowment came to be paid in the form of a scheme grant from the Foundation, it was not given to the college alone but to the theatre and the college in the ratio of £650 to the former and £350 to the latter. Almost immediately a supplementary grant of £500 was added, presumably in approximately the same proportions, and when the somewhat killjoy London Polytechnic Council recommended that this should be cut to £250 and restricted to the college alone, the Central Governing Body resisted on the grounds that sufficient notice could not be given. In fact the Old Vic continued to occupy a special place in the trustees' affections, and, as described below, they came to its aid on several subsequent occasions.[42]

The first additional long-term obligation taken on by the Foundation was the maintenance of the Chelsea Physic Garden. This was the second oldest physic garden in the country and had been established on land leased by the Apothecaries' Company in 1676. In 1721/2 the freehold of the site was presented to the Company by Sir Hans Sloane, who is commemorated by a statue by Rysbrack in the centre of the garden. By the 1890s the Company had decided that it could no longer afford the upkeep of the garden and recommended that the site should be sold and the proceeds used to endow scientific research and teaching. Widespread concern was voiced and a departmental committee was appointed by the Treasury to look into the situation. In 1898, W. H. Fisher (later Lord Downham), a trustee who also happened to be a Junior Lord of the Treasury in Lord Salisbury's government, introduced a motion before the Central Governing Body urging the trustees to take over the garden from the Apothecaries' Company. He stressed its importance as an open space and as a source of botanical study for students at the Battersea and South-Western Polytechnics. The trustees were convinced and asked the Charity Commissioners to draw up a scheme. This was published in 1899 and required the Foundation to give an annual grant of £800 to the garden. The government provided a small supplementary grant, but from this time the Chelsea Physic Garden was essentially the Foundation's responsibility, a state of affairs which was reflected in the composition of the garden's managing committee, over half of whose members were to be appointed by the Foundation. In 1900 a loan of £4,000 was advanced to pay for new buildings including a curator's house, laboratory, lecture room and greenhouse.[43]

The next undertaking to attract the support of the Foundation, the

Whitechapel Art Gallery, would also seem to be a somewhat unusual choice. Art and design were, however, regarded as very important components of technical education, and the appreciation of art was looked upon as a means of enlightenment for the working classes. The Whitechapel, indeed, was not the first art gallery with which the Foundation was concerned. The South London Art Gallery, a private venture, was one of the first recipients of a grant in 1891 and continued to be aided until 1896 when it was taken over by the Library Commissioners for Camberwell and provided with a new building in association with the Camberwell School of Arts and Crafts by the munificence of John Passmore Edwards. Even then the Foundation gave considerable help in buying out existing interests.[44]

The Whitechapel Gallery grew out of the annual exhibitions which were held from the early 1880s by Samuel Barnett, the vicar of St Jude's, Whitechapel, in the parish schools. The Foundation sometimes supported the exhibitions with a small grant, until, in 1896, Barnett took the decision to build a gallery. The promise of a site and a sum to cover the cost of building was obtained on condition that an endowment of £500 per annum could be secured. Accordingly, in 1897 an appeal was made to the trustees, who readily agreed to make an annual grant of this amount. C. Harrison Townsend designed his second outstanding art-nouveau building in east London and a scheme for the gallery was approved by the Charity Commissioners in 1899. A brief period of uncertainty followed when Passmore Edwards, who was one of the gallery's principal benefactors, uncharacteristically refused to provide an additional sum which he had previously offered, on the grounds that his name was not included in the gallery's title. An early payment of the Foundation's grant helped to resolve the problem and Lord Rosebery opened the gallery in 1901.[45]

The Devas Institute in Battersea started out as a boys' club and was handed over to the Foundation by its trustees in 1901 to be run as a junior educational and social institute. The Foundation gave it an annual grant of £250 and this was frequently supplemented by special grants.[46] Other institutes were also aided from time to time but not on a continuous basis.

In 1904, in accordance with the criteria usually adopted by contemporaries, there were 12 polytechnics in London, including such institutions as Birkbeck, the City of London College, the Goldsmiths' Institute and the East London Technical College of the People's Palace. Most of them were by then housed in new buildings of considerable architectural distinction which contributed to their prestige and standing in the educational world, and if those buildings were rapidly proving inadequate to meet the growing needs of the various institutions, this was an inevitable consequence of their success. Sidney

Webb, writing in 1904, praised the remarkable strides made by the polytechnics since Quintin Hogg had moved his pioneering institution to Regent Street in 1882 and estimated that they were attended by some 40,000 members and students in all. A little later Sir Michael Sadler, the noted educationalist, described the polytechnics as 'the most characteristic educational achievement of the last twenty years'.[47]

Thus, when the London County Council took over as the education authority for London in May 1904, it inherited a flourishing polytechnic movement. Even before it began work alarm bells started ringing in Temple Gardens when the trustees discovered that there would be no representatives of the Foundation on the new Education Committee in contrast to the old Technical Education Board. At least they hoped that the London Polytechnic Council would be allowed to continue, but the LCC decreed otherwise and replaced it with the less formal mechanism of the occasional 'conference' to discuss matters of mutual concern, to which the Council and the Foundation would each send up to four representatives.[48]

At the first of these in December 1904 Magnus voiced concern over the degree of control which the Council seemed to want to exercise over staff appointments at the polytechnics, and further disquiet was aroused when it was realized that the Council's numerical representation on the governing bodies of each institution would be much enhanced because it had taken over the places formerly allocated to the London School Board and the Technical Education Board. On being approached over the issue, the Council responded that it chose its nominees on the governing bodies for their fitness to serve and did not instruct them how to act and vote, and that in view of the size of its grants, which were likely to increase, it felt disinclined to reduce its representation.[49]

An uneasy truce then seems to have prevailed until 1909 when the LCC wanted to alter the basis on which it gave its grants. Instead of providing fixed grants, the Council decided that it would base them on an approved programme of work for each institution and annual budgets which were to be vetted by the Council, with any surplus which had accrued from previous years being deducted from the current year's grant. The proposals were almost certainly a consequence of the change in political control of the Council which had take place in 1907 when the Progressives were finally ousted by the Moderates, who were less committed to the polytechnics and more inclined to seek ways to economize. As soon as they were announced, the trustees appointed a sub-committee consisting of Edric Bayley, Edward Bond and, inevitably, Magnus, Roberts and Sebastian, to consider the implications. Their forthright report suggested that these were so far-reaching in giving virtually total power over the polytechnics to the Council, including, through the control of budgets, the amounts to be spent on the social and recreational activities which the Foundation regarded as its particular responsibility, that the trustees should even consider 'whether it is desirable to perpetuate a dual, and in the case of the Central Governing Body, shadowy suzerainty over Polytechnics'. They reminded the trustees that there were several other ways in which the Foundation's income could be used for public benefit and contemplated the withdrawal of most of the supplementary and special grants.

To some extent there was an element of bluff in this threat. The report made the point that even though the Council's total grants to the polytechnics in the previous year amounted to £77,000 (twice the sum provided by the Foundation) this still represented only 38 per cent of the overall receipts of the polytechnics, and concluded that as the Central Governing Body was representative of so many public authorities, it should maintain its involvement with the polytechnics. As a way forward, the sub-committee recommended that the Council should consider voting the sums for its annual block grants triennially so that institutions would retain a degree of certainty and independence, and this formed the basis of a compromise.[50]

Two years later, the university studies controversy, which had been simmering for some time, came to a head when Battersea Polytechnic, without consulting the Foundation, submitted a petition to the senate of the University of London asking to be recognized as a school of the university. By the University of London Act of 1898 and the Statutes of 1900 which followed from it, the university had been reconstituted as a teaching institution rather than solely an examining body as it had been previously. Provision was made for certain institutions within 30 miles of central London to become schools of the university and for teachers in polytechnics with the requisite qualifications to be recognized as teachers of the university so that their courses, if approved, would count towards internal degrees. Tension subsequently arose between the traditional work of the polytechnics and higher grade or university teaching, and the latter was more wholeheartedly embraced by some institutions than others. Individuals, too, differed in their reactions. Webb and Garnett were very much in favour of this development, Magnus was equivocal, and Hogg and C. T. Millis, the influential Principal of Borough Polytechnic, were strongly opposed, as indeed was Robert Blair, the Education Officer of the LCC.[51]

In a separate but related development, under the Board of Education Act of 1899, endowments which were primarily of an educational nature were transferred from the Charity Commissioners to the jurisdiction of the Board of Education, but the Commissioners were successful in retaining most of the polytechnics under their authority on the basis that their social and recreational activities formed a major part of the trusts under which they were governed. Only the City of London College and Birkbeck Institution were transferred, when the City Polytechnic was formally dissolved in 1907. The Northampton Institute successfully resisted such a move, but in the same year the Commissioners, apparently on the prompting of the Board of Education, questioned whether the Battersea and South-Western Polytechnics had not become so overwhelmingly educational in nature that their jurisdiction ought to be changed. Nothing came of this, but it alerted the trustees to the need to be wary of certain tendencies at work within the polytechnics.[52]

Thus when they received the information in 1911 that Battersea had made moves to become a school of the University of London, they immediately instructed the Clerk to prepare a report on whether the polytechnics were fulfilling their purpose in assisting the 'poorer classes'. The trustees indeed had a duty under the Central Scheme, as Warre reminded them in his report, to notify the Charity Commissioners of any institution in which due regard was not being paid to the interests of the poorer classes, a concept which, although not easy to define, Warre interpreted as meaning 'the artizan and wage-earning classes'. In a detailed and thoughtful report, Warre sided with the view of William Garnett that it would be wrong to discourage work of university calibre in the polytechnics, as this was a means of making such education accessible to the poorer classes, but that the tendency to concentrate on such teaching to the exclusion of other courses should be resisted and that it would be quite wrong for polytechnics 'of the ordinary type' to become schools of the university.

If, then, a case could be made out that the polytechnics were still fulfilling their obligations to the poorer classes, Warre went on to question whether the extent to which their educational work could now be aided out of public funds should not lead to a change in policy on the part of the trustees. He cited as an example a new scheme which was just being promulgated for the People's Palace in which the educational side as represented by the East London College was intended to be separated from the recreational activities carried on by the Palace, the Foundation's responsibility in future being confined to the latter. As the grants of the LCC were at this time restricted to educational objects by law, this was a logical step, and from this report stemmed the distinct policy on the part of the Foundation of aiding the social and recreational activities of the polytechnics rather than their educational work, although an exception was certainly made in the support of building projects, and it was, in any case, not always possible to make a clear distinction. Meanwhile, Battersea Polytechnic was informed in no uncertain terms by the Charity Commissioners that its approach to the University of London was entirely inopportune.[53]

Although the LCC had adopted the trustees' recommendation that it should give triennial block grants to the polytechnics, when it came to spelling out the conditions under which these should be awarded they included such minute control over the smallest items of expenditure that the governors of the polytechnics rebelled and sought the aid of the trustees. Typical of the Council's attitude was a letter to the Northampton Polytechnic rejecting virtually every item in the estimates submitted and asking for economies to be introduced. In addition, the Council tried to use the block grants as a means of furthering its policy of rationalizing educational provision in the capital by enforcing the closure of some departments at institutions, to avoid duplication where it considered that the subject was better taught elsewhere. In 1912, the thoroughly exasperated trustees, when confronted with what they regarded as little short of perfidy on the part of the Council, passed a resolution questioning whether they should not immediately stop any non-compulsory grants to the polytechnics and ask the Charity Commissioners to alter the schemes to release them from their obligatory grants. Instead, in time-honoured fashion, they appointed a sub-committee with Bond as chairman and including Sir William Collins, Roberts, Sebastian and Evan Spicer, to examine the problem. As Bond remarked, the issue which had to be faced was whether 'the proper course would be for the Trustees to cut themselves adrift from the Polytechnics'.

In the event, of course, neither the sub-committee nor the whole Central Governing Body, which still numbered among its members several staunch supporters of the polytechnics, were prepared to take such a drastic step. A solution was hammered out with the Council whereby the conditions were relaxed, and by 1914 when block grants for the period 1914–17 were announced, the polytechnics were satisfied that their criticisms had for the most part been accepted. In addition, it was proposed to hold six-monthly conferences between representatives of the LCC, the Foundation and the governors of the polytechnics to seek to resolve future differences.[54]

Thus, for the first ten years of the period when the LCC was the education authority for London, the Foundation frequently – at times it must have seemed almost constantly – found itself at odds with the Council over the polytechnics. To some extent this was a case of a young authority flexing its muscles and the Foundation indulging in a fair amount of bluster to try to preserve as much independence as possible for its young progeny. There were, however, some serious differences of policy, and beneath the surface there was a political dimension, especially after 1907 when the Moderates defeated the

Progressives in the LCC election. Although originally there were undoubtedly mixed motives in the eager embrace with which the Charity Commissioners had greeted the infant polytechnic movement, the espousal of their cause by the Young Turks of the LCC through the Technical Education Board was a product of the reforming impulse which was characteristic of the Progressives with their Liberal–Fabian Socialist core. The Moderates, on the other hand, were naturally less inclined to be warm in their support of institutions which had been favoured by their predecessors, and were more concerned with financial rectitude than social engineering. There may also have been an element of the local–national conflict which was so often a feature of the political scene in London, for this was a period when social reform was very much on the agenda of the Liberal government. By 1914, however, an equilibrium had been reached between the Foundation and the Council, which, despite some strains, generally persisted into the late 1920s.

In the meantime, individual institutions continued to be aided by the Foundation, often on a generous scale, by grants and especially by loans, usually with an accompanying increase in grant to meet the repayments. The biggest single loan which was made up to the First World War was £20,000 to the Regent Street Polytechnic for the rebuilding of the front of the institute, which the Howard de Walden Estate had made a condition of extending its lease. The loan was made subject to a matching sum being provided by the LCC, to which the Council agreed, and the premises were rebuilt in 1910–11 to their present-day appearance.[55] At approximately the same time, £13,000 was lent to the Northampton Institute for the purchase of a freehold site which had come on to the market and which was suitable for an extension, even though building was delayed for several years.[56]

Whether an institution was assisted with the repayment of a loan depended on its status in the eyes of the trustees. In 1907, £15,000 was offered to Birkbeck to acquire the lease of adjoining premises, but it was made quite clear that no help would be given in the repayment of the loan, an attitude that was hardly surprising in view of the college's recent transfer from the jurisdiction of the Charity Commissioners to that of the Board of Education.[57] Five years later, however, when the chairman of the governors of the college asked for an increase in its annual grant, which was still required to be paid despite the change in circumstances, he was informed that while this would not be possible, if the college wished to acquire a sports ground, which it lacked, the Foundation would be prepared to consider making a loan and might even subsidize the repayments.[58] The apparent change of heart was a product of the trustees' new policy of concentrating their aid on recreational activities. Similar help had been given to the Woolwich and Northampton Polytechnics to acquire athletic grounds.[59]

Battersea was treated in a similar manner to Birkbeck. When it applied for a further loan of £2,500 in 1908 to build an extension, it was told that the advance would only be made on the strict understanding that no grant would be made for the repayment of the principal and interest.[60] The trustees were concerned that there was an over-concentration on higher-level university teaching at Battersea, and this may have affected their attitude. When Woolwich Polytechnic, to which the Foundation was under no obligation to provide assistance, asked for funds towards the purchase of the freehold of its site in 1913, the trustees' first reaction was to turn down the request, but after the Charity Commissioners had intimated that the acquisition of the freehold would make possible a rebuilding programme in which social activities could be better accommodated, the Central Governing Body relented and agreed to lend £10,000, with the proviso that the repayment instalments should be the first charge on its existing annual grant.[61] No such qualification, however, applied to the small Devas Institute, which was lent £7,500 for rebuilding and informed that the repayments would be covered by a grant.[62]

The circumstances surrounding the aid which was given to one of the 'kindred institutions' deserve special mention. In 1913 the Old Vic, then under the management of Emma Cons's niece, Lilian Baylis, was in financial difficulties, and there was a possibility that it might have to be let to another proprietor. Instead, an appeal was launched and an ambitious programme undertaken including the experiment of staging Shakespearian plays. By 1914 this appeared to hold out such promise of success that the Foundation gave a special grant of £1,000 to top up the appeal and agreed to raise its annual grant from £1,000 to £1,500. Three years later another £500 was given in the exceptional circumstances produced by the war, when the threat of air raids seriously reduced the theatre's takings. The trustees were informed that the theatre now not only put on works by Shakespeare, Goldsmith, Sheridan and other famous dramatists, but that school matinees of Shakespeare were given twice a week and had been attended by more than 90,000 children in a season. In the following year the Carnegie United Kingdom Trust promised further aid if the Foundation would increase its own grant, which was duly raised to £2,000 per annum in 1918. An additional £500 was made conditional on the receipt of a favourable report, and was promptly paid when the governors cited the 'marked success which has been attained throughout the war by our Shakespearian productions and operatic works'.[63] Thus was the Old Vic launched on that period of brilliance as the home of classic

English drama – a national theatre in all but name – with the blessing, and the sponsorship, of the Foundation.

The war had an adverse effect on the polytechnics. The inevitable reduction in the size of classes as men were called away to battle led to a loss of income from fees, and to help make up the deficiency, by the end of the war the level of annual grants from the Foundation had been raised to £42,500.[64] Inflation, which persisted into the post-war years, brought its own problems, and help was given particularly to the smaller institutions which existed closer to the margins of solvency. Additional grants were made to the Chelsea Physic Garden (making the annual total £2,000 by 1921), the Working Men's College, the College for Working Women, the St Bride Institute (for its library), the Whitechapel Art Gallery, the Devas Institute, and a new candidate, the Hampstead Garden Suburb Institute, whose persistent importuning brought a limited reward, although by no means on the scale hoped for by its promoters.[65]

At the Old Vic and Morley College the problem was of a different order. For some time the LCC had been unhappy about the coexistence in the same building of the theatre and the college, and in 1921 it insisted on a number of alterations which meant that the college would have to move. An appeal was launched and the trustees immediately offered a loan of up to £15,000, but the governors of the two institutions were reluctant to take on this commitment. Eventually a single donor, Sir George Dance, stepped in with £30,000, and the trustees gave another £4,000. New premises were found for the college in the former schools of the Yorkshire Society in Westminster Bridge Road, but even after receiving a share of the appeal fund, the college still required £5,000 to complete building operations. The trustees initially considered providing a loan of the full amount, but then promised a grant of £2,500 if the LCC would give an equal amount. The Council complied, and the problem was resolved.[66]

Many of the polytechnics embarked on ambitious expansion schemes in the inter-war years and the Foundation usually came to their aid with grants and loans. The loans were so numerous and the sums involved were frequently so large that there was no longer a presumption that the repayments would be taken care of by increased grants, but several of the grants which were given in fact served that purpose. The Regent Street Polytechnic was lent £50,000 in 1925 to help pay for an extensive building programme which was expected to cost some £250,000, and its annual grant was also increased by £2,000, to £7,000 in all.[67] Borough Polytechnic, too, received support on a large scale; it was situated in one of the poorest parts of London and had a Principal in C. T. Millis who believed in adhering to the ideals of the founders of the movement. Additionally, it had not benefited from a new building in 1892 but had had to adapt an existing one. When rebuilding became a possibility in 1925 the Foundation made a grant of £2,000 towards the building fund and followed this up with loans of over £20,000, and an increase of £1,000 in the annual grant to help ease the pain of repayment.[68]

When the Northern Polytechnic had the opportunity to purchase a site for an extension in 1920, the Foundation offered a loan on condition that the LCC would accept the repayment instalments as a legitimate charge on the income of the polytechnic. The Council, in an economizing mood, was reluctant to agree, but the trustees decided to make a loan of £8,000 in any case and cover the repayments by grants. Ten years later the same policy, and for the same reasons, was followed in a further loan of £5,250 towards the cost of the extension. Events at Northampton Polytechnic followed a similar course. In 1929 it finally became possible to contemplate building on the site which had been acquired with the help of the Foundation in 1908, and a loan, initially of £5,000 and later of £10,000, was offered. When it became clear that accepting even the smaller sum would prove difficult for the institution, the trustees responded by making a grant of £5,000 over two years and a loan of £3,000 to acquire more property, and, in addition, donated smaller sums to the building fund. The Connaught Building, as the extension was called, was built to the designs of the Foundation's surveyor, W. Campbell Jones.[69]

Woolwich was given a loan of £6,500 in 1933 to purchase the site of a public house which stood in the way of expansion, and early in the next year was awarded a grant of £1,500, followed shortly by a further £4,800 to augment the sum of £20,000 which the LCC had provided for a building fund.[70] Other loans for building schemes included £5,000 to Battersea and £4,000 to Chelsea.[71]

Most of the special grants which were made at this time were specifically directed towards the social side of the work of the polytechnics. The Northern Polytechnic was given £1,450 in 1930 for the equipment of its social rooms, and £2,500 in 1934 for the erection and equipment of a building 'for social purposes'. The Northampton Polytechnic was given £1,000 to pay for filtration plant for its swimming pool in 1928, and three years later the same amount was given to the City of London College to help cater for the considerable expansion of its social and recreational activities.[72] Many smaller amounts were given for similar purposes, but the majority of such grants (over £15,000 in total between 1920 and 1939) were designed to meet expenses involved in maintaining the playing fields of the various institutions.

This sum, however, represented only a fraction of the Foundation's expenditure on sports grounds for the polytechnics, and the vigorous manner in which the trustees sought to ensure that each institution was properly provided with such amenities must be regarded as one of their major policy initiatives of the inter-war years. Up to 1920 their policy was generally to give loans for the acquisition of recreation grounds, with, in most cases, additional grants to cover the repayments. In that year, however, the LCC refused to give its consent for Battersea Polytechnic to accept such a loan to purchase 12 acres at Mitcham because the prevailing rate of interest was too high, and so the trustees decided to purchase the land directly and let it to the polytechnic. In the same year 8 acres at Greenford were acquired for use as playing fields by Birkbeck College, and additional land at Mitcham was bought for letting to Chelsea Polytechnic. In all some 34 acres at Mitcham and 8 acres at Greenford were purchased by the Foundation for £14,923 and £4,000 respectively.[73]

An athletic ground at Grove Park, Lewisham, was purchased in 1924 for £3,147 for the use of the City of London College, and in 1925 an additional 10 acres were added to Birkbeck College's grounds at Greenford for £3,200. In the same year an 8-acre site at Palmer's Green was acquired for Northampton Polytechnic, and in 1930 £12,000 was paid for 21 acres of playing fields at Stanmore for North-Western Polytechnic.[74] The expense of laying out the grounds and providing facilities was either met by a combination of grants and loans to the institutions or paid directly by the Foundation and recouped in rents. Campbell Jones designed the pavilions at Mitcham, Grove Park, Palmer's Green and Stanmore.[75]

In 1935 the Foundation mounted a successful defence at a public inquiry against an attempt by the local council to acquire 15 acres of the playing fields at Mitcham by compulsory purchase for the erection of housing in connection with a slum clearance scheme.[76] Fifty years later that victory was to have a significance which could not remotely have been foreseen, when, under very different circumstances, the playing fields were sold (see page 255). At the time it was a matter of principle to defend amenities which, in the opinion of the Foundation, served such a useful social purpose. The trustees may from time to time have doubted the wisdom of devoting so much of their limited resources to the polytechnics, but on one aspect of that support they never seemed to waver, namely their commitment to ensure that each institution had adequate provision for sport and other forms of physical recreation.

During the inter-war years the Foundation found itself supporting two new institutions while one old one was substantially recast. One of the new ones, indeed, should hardly be called that, for the North-Western Polytechnic had been planned from the start, but it was not until 1929 that its doors finally opened. There had been several earlier attempts to establish this long-delayed institution, but all to no avail. The site had been cleared in 1911 after the existing leases had expired, an architectural competition had been held and a design chosen. The Charity Commissioners were unhappy, however, that the plans did not make sufficient provision for social activities and recreation, a sentiment that was endorsed by the trustees, and by the time adjustments had been made to the design, war had broken out, prices had risen and materials had become difficult to obtain. When tenders were eventually submitted in 1915, even the lowest proved beyond the governors' means, despite the offer of additional grants and loans from the trustees and a generous level of aid from the LCC. Attempts to revive the project in 1920, and again in 1924, came to nothing, and it was 1927 before the Clerk could report that the building was finally under way. By the time the institution opened in 1929 the Foundation had provided it with over £50,000 in accumulated annual grants and special sums. Its support did not stop there, for not only were further grants made in succeeding years, but also a recreation ground was purchased and fitted out at Stanmore at a cost to the Foundation of over £21,000, and let to the polytechnic.[77]

The other new institution, Sadler's Wells Theatre, was an offshoot of the Old Vic. Sadler's Wells was an old theatre which had fallen on hard times. Lilian Baylis had long had the ambition of creating an Old Vic for north London, and in 1925 an appeal was launched to convert Sadler's Wells for this purpose. There was an enthusiastic response, including the promise of a substantial grant from the Carnegie United Kingdom Trust, and in May 1936 the Central Governing Body committed £3,000 to the project. The old theatre had to be virtually completely rebuilt and by the time the new Sadler's Wells opened on 6 January 1931, appropriately with a performance of *Twelfth Night*, the Foundation had contributed £8,000 and promised £3,000 more (approximately 10 per cent of the cost of the whole venture). The Charity Commissioners drew up a scheme under which the Foundation nominated three members to a 15-strong governing body.

The theatre alternated drama with opera and ballet in an extension of the repertoire of the Old Vic. In 1933 Lilian Baylis wrote to the Foundation to inform the trustees that although the previous season at the Vic and the Wells had been very successful, there was still need for further subsidy for the production of opera, and that she was preparing a new season of plays 'in which Charles Laughton, an actor of the highest distinction and reputation, has offered to play leading roles at great financial sacrifice to himself'. The trustees immediately ordered that any outstanding grant should be paid and offered a loan which was not in the event needed. The practice of mixing plays with opera and ballet posed difficulties, and in 1934 the Charity

Commissioners announced that they were proposing to amend the scheme so that Sadler's Wells would concentrate on the production of opera and ballet and the Old Vic on drama. In 1935, the trustees resolved to give 'final grants' of £500 per annum for three years to Sadler's Wells, but when Lilian Baylis died in 1937 they not only expressed their deep regret but also gave £3,000 in grants and a loan of £20,000 at the preferential rate of interest of 3½ per cent to the Lilian Baylis Memorial Fund, which was set up to improve backstage facilities at the theatre by building an extension.[78]

The old institution which was given a different form was the People's Palace. From the beginning there had been tension between the social activities of the Palace, with their emphasis on popular entertainment, and the increasingly academic work being done at the East London Technical College. In 1907 the college, which by then catered almost entirely for full-time students, was given temporary status as a school of the University of London. The Charity Commissioners decided to separate the two bodies, and while the Drapers' Company continued to support the college, the Foundation's grant was allocated to the Palace. East London College (now Queen Mary College) was confirmed as a school of the university in 1915.

The trustees seemed little inclined to give any additional support to the Palace beyond the obligatory scheme grant, refusing in 1922, for instance, to cover a deficit of £600 on a series of experimental concerts, but the destruction by fire of the Queen's Hall at the centre of the Palace in 1931 created a crisis which demanded a response. The Drapers' Company was inclined to favour the adaptation of the whole complex for educational use, but the trustees were adamant that their grant should not be transferred to East London College, which catered for university students. After holding a public inquiry, as recommended by the trustees, the Charity Commissioners decided that there was sufficient support to warrant reviving the old institution. The Queen's Hall, of which the shell remained, and other buildings of the Palace were transferred to the college, and a new People's Palace was erected on the site of a nearby terrace of houses which belonged to the Drapers' Company. The Company also took care of the monetary compensation involved in the transfer of property to the college. The new building, which was designed by Campbell Jones & Smithers, the firm of the Foundation's surveyor, was erected in 1936. Almost immediately the governors appealed for an increase in grant, but they were turned down, although the trustees provided loans totalling £14,000 by the outbreak of war.[79]

For nearly a decade after the end of the First World War the trustees do not seem to have questioned that their primary role was to be providers for the polytechnics, in contrast to the years immediately before the war when they were assailed by all kinds of doubts. Relations with the LCC appear to have been relatively cordial, despite the effect of the Council's own economizing measures and the implementation of the 'Geddes axe' (the recommendations of the committee on national expenditure of 1921–2, chaired by Sir Eric Geddes) which fell just as heavily on higher education as on other aspects of public expenditure. One result was the introduction of the policy of purchasing playing fields, when the Council indicated that it was not prepared to accept the repayment of loans as a legitimate expense in the budgets of the polytechnics.[80] The Council also rigorously pursued its policy of rationalizing educational provision at the polytechnics with the aim of producing a comprehensive London-wide system of technical education in which each institution would specialize in certain subjects. This frequently led to disputes with governing bodies when the Council wanted to close down departments to avoid duplication,[81] but the trustees, in keeping with their aim of concentrating their efforts on the social and recreational side of the polytechnics, generally kept out of such arguments. The Council's policy, however, had more general implications which were certainly to trouble the trustees before the end of the 1920s. In the meantime, as expenditure on the polytechnics rose, an increasing proportion of their income came from rates and taxes, and the Foundation's financial contribution declined as a percentage, with a corresponding diminution in its real influence.

In 1927, His Majesty's Inspectors produced a report on the provision of engineering education in London which brought all the old issues to the fore. One of the institutions examined was the Northampton Polytechnic, where engineering courses had been concentrated in accordance with the LCC's policy, and the inspectors questioned whether, in view of the large number of students on the courses who were reading for university degrees, the aims of the founders of the polytechnics were still being realized. They were particularly concerned that many of the students were ones who would normally have attended university but were attracted to the polytechnic by its very much lower fees, and were not from the 'poorer classes'. The trustees immediately responded by placing a moratorium on further special grants to the polytechnics, and Sir Philip Magnus undertook to prepare a memorandum on the subject.

Magnus's memorandum, when it appeared in the following year, was highly equivocal and basically fudged the issue. He certainly agreed that 'From any point of view, however, it would seem undesirable that the Polytechnics, largely maintained from public funds, should compete with the University Colleges by charging fees lower than those of the Colleges for courses of instruction that equally prepare students for University degrees.' On the other hand, the use of buildings, staff and equipment during the day helped to meet the costs of overheads and enabled fees for evening classes, which were largely attended by the 'poorer classes', to be kept lower than they would otherwise have been. He thought that one answer might be to expand the part-time day courses for apprentices and young workers – the so-called 'sandwich' courses which had been introduced at Northampton – and made the point that the policy of the LCC in concentrating certain subjects at particular institutions was bound to lead to a change in the nature of the polytechnics. The trustees thanked Magnus, circulated his report to various bodies, and renewed their grants. There, for the moment, the matter was allowed to stand, but it had been put firmly on the agenda once again.[82]

In 1930, perhaps as a sign of the times, when loans were approved to the Chelsea and Northampton Polytechnics, it was expressly stated that no assistance would be given with the repayment and interest charges. Thereafter, this became the trustees' standard policy, although exceptions were sometimes made.[83] In the following year, with financial storm clouds gathering, the LCC refused to authorize the acceptance of loans, in case repayments fell to the Council.[84]

At about the same time the trustees decided to make their own unobtrusive 'visits' to the polytechnics. Their new Clerk, Donald Allen, may have been behind this initiative, for he was later to state that on taking office he had been 'so indignant' that mandatory grants had to be paid to the polytechnics. When it appeared that in some polytechnics 'due regard is not being paid to the interests of the poorer classes', a sub-committee was appointed to enquire further.[85] A working definition of the 'poorer classes' as persons who had been educated at public elementary schools and/or whose parents were in receipt of incomes not exceeding £250 per annum was adopted for this purpose, and a questionnaire was sent to each polytechnic asking *inter alia* how many students fitted this category. The replies indicated that, overall, some 75 per cent of students satisfied these criteria, and the sub-committee was 'satisfied that generally speaking, due regard is being had to the interests of the Poorer Classes'. However, at Chelsea Polytechnic fewer than half of the students had attended an elementary school, and at Regent Street only just over half. In the latter case there were considered to be special circumstances arising out of the size and origins of the institution and the high proportion of members who did not take courses, but the trend at Chelsea was so worrying that the trustees decided that they had to draw the attention of the Charity Commissioners to the situation.

The LCC, worried about the direction which the Foundation's enquiries were taking, defended the polytechnics and pointed out that its own attempts to organize higher education had led in the case of Chelsea to a concentration on natural sciences, which attracted students 'of a more highly educated type'. The Charity Commissioners did not doubt that this interpretation was correct and that educational benefits might have resulted, but they had to adopt a strictly legalistic view, so that 'if when grants are authorised by an Act of Parliament (or by Schemes made under an Act) for a special purpose that purpose is changed, the authorities responsible for the change must be taken to make it with the full knowledge that they run the risk of losing the grants.' They decreed that the scheme grant to Chelsea should be reduced from £1,500 to £1,000 per annum, and presumed that the Central Governing Body would withdraw its supplementary grant. Indeed, they could not resist a criticism of the Foundation, 'having felt somewhat hampered by the apparent inconsistency between the representations made to them that Chelsea is not catering for the poor and the existence of an additional grant made voluntarily by the Central Governing Body in substantially the existing circumstances which they could only properly make if satisfied that the Polytechnic was catering for the poorer classes.'

The Commissioners asked the Foundation to look at the possibility of awarding grants on a per capita basis according to the number of students of the poorer classes at each institution, but on examination the trustees decided that such a method was impracticable. They adhered to the current arrangements with the exception of Chelsea, whose protestations and suggested changes to accommodate the Foundation's wishes were to no avail. But this was merely the first step. The polytechnics were to be kept under periodic review, and, as Donald Allen remarked to representatives of Borough Polytechnic, which had shown up well in the questionnaire, 'in general it was plain that the Trustees would sooner leave financing the polytechnics to the LCC so as to turn their own resources to the Social Services Fund and the assistance of the unemployed'.[86]

In 1935 a special sub-committee of trustees produced a comprehensive report on the policy relating to grants which included the polytechnics in its terms of reference.[87] One of their recommendations was:

> That the Trustees' general policy should be to continue to refrain from subsidising Schemes which can be financed out of the rates and/or the Exchequer, and that if and when grants are made in aid of Schemes for which statutory provision exists the object should be not merely to relieve local authorities of expenditure which primarily falls upon them but to encourage the undertaking of Schemes which the Trustees desire to promote.

Moreover, 'the principles enunciated above should be applied to the grants, other than Scheme grants, made to Polytechnics and Kindred

Institutions.' The implications were not spelt out but could be deduced from the review of the effect of legislation on the trustees' past policy which was included in the report. This referred specifically to sections of the Education Acts of 1918 and 1921 which gave powers to local education authorities for the first time to promote social and physical training at educational institutions which came under their jurisdiction. To reinforce the point, the relevant sections of the Acts were given in full in the report. Previously the Foundation had refrained from using the existence of these powers as a reason for reducing its own grants for social and recreational purposes, because only students appeared to be covered by the Acts, but the proportion of non-students who used the facilities of the polytechnics (with the exception of Regent Street) was now quite small and by no means all of them belonged to the poorer classes.

A conference was held with representatives of the LCC who fully understood what was afoot. The Council was apprehensive that if the Foundation's grants for social and recreational activities were withdrawn precipitately, it might have to make up the deficiency out of its expenditure on education. The trustees saw the wisdom of this argument and in effect gave three years' notice that they were likely to introduce changes in 1938, but promised to hold further discussions in 1937.[88]

A meeting was duly held in the spring of 1937 and in the following autumn two deputations were received, one representing the polytechnics generally and the other, Regent Street alone. The trustees were, however, not to be deflected from their chosen course and resolved to withdraw all the non-obligatory grants. 'Having regard, however, to the continuance during many years of these payments to the Polytechnics . . . and to the embarrassment which may be caused to the London County Council and the Polytechnics by the sudden withdrawal of such grants', they agreed to reduce the payments gradually over a number of years. In the cases of Battersea, the City of London College and Regent Street, 'where the proportion of poorer-class students is somewhat low', the supplementary grants were to be withdrawn over five years, and at Borough, Northampton, Northern, North-Western and Woolwich Polytechnics and Birkbeck and Morley Colleges, over ten years. These decisions were not taken without much debate and, unusually for the Central Governing Body, the issue was put to the vote, ten voting for the recommendations and two against. The polytechnics were also told that applications for special grants for 'such activities as the Trustees may desire to promote' would be entertained, and, in a final magnanimous gesture, £20,000 of the debt of the Regent Street Polytechnic to the Foundation, which amounted to nearly £40,000, was written off.[89] Nevertheless, it was quite clear that the dominance of the polytechnics was at an end.

NOTES

1. CPF, *Second Report submitted to the Central Governing Body by the Clerk of the Foundation* (1927), 34.
2. Minutes, II, 36.
3. Ibid., II, 48–51, 66–8.
4. Ibid., II, 35, 48.
5. Ibid., II, 47–8, 88.
6. Ibid., II, 59, 68, 180: F. G. Evans, *Borough Polytechnic 1892–1969* (1969), 6–7.
7. Minutes, III, 28, 40; IV, 60–1.
8. Andrew Saint, 'Technical Education and the early L.C.C.' in *Politics and the People of London. The London County Council 1889–1965*, ed. Andrew Saint (1989), 74–5.
9. Ibid., 71–91: Bernard M. Allen, *William Garnett A Memoir* (1933), 46–54: Beatrice Webb, *Our Partnership*, ed. Barbara Drake and Margaret I. Cole (1948), 76–82: *Education for National Efficiency: the Contribution of Sidney and Beatrice Webb*, ed. E. J. T. Brennan (1975), 23–56.
10. Minutes, III, 50, 62; IV, 27.
11. Ibid., II, 96; III, 128–9.
12. Ibid., IV, 26–7, 29, 40.
13. Ibid., IV, 58–9, 70–1, 100–2.
14. Ibid., V, 58; VII, 52; X, 51–8.
15. Ibid., IX, 41, 98, 113.
16. Ibid., XI, 126; XII, 131–2.
17. Ibid., XXIV, 135–6.
18. Ibid., XII, 53, 94.
19. Ibid., XVI, 99–100.
20. Ibid., IX, 98.
21. Ibid., XII, 61, 112–13; XVI, 120–1; XXXI, 21; XXXVIII, 92–3; XXXIX, 112–13; XLIX, 181: *Second Report, ut supra*, 26–7.
22. Minutes, VIII, 35; XIII, 67: London County Council, *Annual Report of the Technical Education Board of the London County Council 1903–1904* (1904), 44, 62: Sidney Webb, *London Education* (1904), 143–4.
23. Minutes, VIII, 66–7; XV, 90–1; XVIII, 85; XIX, 26; XXI, 125–6.
24. Ibid., II, 88; VI, 47–50; X, 51.
25. Ibid., IX, 136; X, 70; XI, 57, 72, 93; XIII, 67; XIV, 63, 76, 95, 130: *Survey of London. Vol. XL. The Grosvenor Estate in Mayfair, Part II, The Buildings*, ed. F. H. W. Sheppard (1980), 110–11.
26. George Godwin, *Queen Mary College: An Adventure in Education* (1939): G. P. Moss and M. V. Saville, *From Palace to College. An Illustrated Account of Queen Mary College* (1985).
27. C. Delisle Burns, *A Short History of Birkbeck College* (1924).
28. *The City of London College. An Historical Account of the College from its Foundation in 1848 to the Present Day* (2nd ed., 1964).
29. S. John Teague, *The City University: A History* (1980): Nikolaus Pevsner, *The Buildings of England. London except the Cities of London and Westminster* (1952), 116: Minutes, VIII, 35; XIV, 63–5.

30. Teague, op. cit., 24–5, 41: Minutes, XVII, 92.
31. *Northern Polytechnic 1892–1967* (1967): *The Victoria History of the Counties of England. Middlesex. VIII. Islington and Stoke Newington Parishes*, ed. T. F. T. Baker (1985), 130–1: Minutes, II, 88; V, 42; IX, 98; X, 84; XI, 57–9; XIV, 129.
32. Minutes, IV, 115, 148; VII, 73; IX, 16: *Second Report, ut supra*, 29–30.
33. Evans, op. cit.: Minutes, II, 88; VIII, 35; IX, 97; XIV, 129.
34. H. Arrowsmith, *Pioneering in Education for the Technologies. The Story of Battersea College of Technology 1891–1962* (1966): Minutes, III, 91; IV, 59; VI, 81; VIII, 45–50; XIV, 129.
35. *Chelsea College – a history*, ed. H. Silver and S. J. Teague (1977): Minutes, II, 66–8, 88; IV, 82; VI, 93; XI, 57; XIII, 137; XIV, 129; XVIII, 142–3.
36. Collin Brooks, *An Educational Adventure. A History of the Woolwich Polytechnic* (1955): Minutes, II, 161–3; IV, 148; VIII, 35; XIII, 83, 117; XV, 129.
37. *Annual Report of the Technical Education Board . . . 1903–1904*, 11–12, 15–16: Minutes, VIII, 90; XI, 57; XII, 61.
38. *The Builder*, 24 Nov. 1894; Minutes, X, 12, 69.
39. Minutes, IX, 54.
40. Ibid., III, 13; IV, 10–12, 81; V, 10–11; VII, 54–7; VIII, 38.
41. J. F. C. Harrison, *A History of the Working Men's College 1854–1954* (1954), esp. 109–10, 138–41: Minutes, III, 65, 90; V, 58, 124; VI, 9–10; VIII, 35; XI, 57, 126; XII, 85.
42. Cicely Hamilton and Lilian Baylis, *The Old Vic* (1926): Denis Richards, *Offspring of the Vic. A History of Morley College* (1958), esp. 80–2, 103–4: Minutes, II, 88; X, 51–8.
43. Minutes, VIII, 81; IX, 41, 74–5; X, 100, 115–16: *Second Report, ut supra*, 31–2.
44. Minutes, I, 75; IV, 12; V, 131–2; VI, 58, 109–10.
45. Ibid., IV, 60; VII, 82; IX, 73; X, 69: Asa Briggs and Anne Macartney, *Toynbee Hall. The First Hundred Years* (1984), 3, 24, 57–9.
46. Minutes, XI, 48, 92; XII, 16: *Second Report, ut supra*, 32–4.
47. Webb, *London Education*, 134–74: C. T. Millis, *Technical Education: Its Development and Aims* (1925), 73.
48. Minutes, XIV, 34, 61, 77, 93–5, 114, 126–7.
49. Ibid., XV, 26–7, 92, 132–5, 171.
50. Ibid., XIX, 114, 143–6, 151.
51. Webb, op. cit., 168–71: Allen, op. cit., 99–102: Millis, op. cit., 129–33: Stephen F. Cotgrove, *Technical Education and Social Change* (1958), 63–5: Teague, *City University*, 61–4.
52. Minutes, XVII, 22, 92.
53. Ibid., XXI, 110, 125–33.
54. Ibid., XXII, 119, 131, 153–7; XXIII, 27–30; XXIV, 28–30, 69: Teague, op. cit., 64–6.
55. Minutes, XVII, 61; XVIII, 104: Ethel M. Hogg, *The Polytechnic and its Founder Quintin Hogg* (1932), 300.
56. Minutes, XVII, 60, 160: Teague, op. cit., 172–4.
57. Minutes, XVII, 117.
58. Ibid., XXII, 28.
59. Ibid., XIII, 83, 117; XIV, 113, 130; XV, 129: Teague, op. cit., 71–2.
60. Minutes, XVIII, 137.
61. Ibid., XXIII, 119; XXIV, 30–1; XXV, 31: Brooks, op. cit., 90–1.
62. Minutes, XVI, 80, 120.
63. Ibid., XXIII, 103–4; XXIV, 80–2; XXVII, 157–60; XXVIII, 74–6, 110; XXIX, 27: Hamilton and Baylis, op. cit., 191–215.

64. Minutes, XXIV, 137–8; XXVIII, 74–6.
65. Ibid., XXIX, 28, 71–5, 115, 144–5; XXX, 81, 85–6, 165–6; XXXI, 75–9; XXXII, 136; XXXIII, 74–8.
66. Ibid., XXXI, 115–16; XXXIII, 74–8; XXXIV, 67, 117, 137: Hamilton and Baylis, op. cit., 215–22: Richards, op. cit., 198–207.
67. Minutes, XXXIV, 137; XXXV, 114–15; XXXVI, 70–3; XXXVII, 76–9; XXXVIII, 72–4: Hogg, op. cit., 350.
68. Minutes, XXXV, 72–5; XXXIX, 123–4; XL, 67–8, 78–82; XLIV, 76–81: CPF, *Report on Policy Relating to Grants* (1937), 19: Evans, op. cit., 39–41.
69. Minutes, XXX, 123–4; XXXII, 27–8; XXXIX, 99, 114–15; XL, 151–2; XLI, 74–81; XLII, 24, 76–82: Teague, op. cit., 173–5.
70. Minutes, XLIII, 153–4; XLIV, 76–81, 143.
71. Ibid., XXXVIII, 25; XL, 151–2: *Report on Policy Relating to Grants* (1937), 19.
72. Minutes, XXXVIII, 111; XL, 78–82; XLI, 74–81; XLIV, 76–81.
73. Ibid., XXX, 30–1, 69, 101–2, 132–3, 146, 152, 156: *Second Report, ut supra*, 24–6.
74. Minutes, XXXIV, 27; XXXV, 121; XL, 106.
75. Ibid., XXXI, 75, 152; XXXII, 109–10; XXXIV, 76, 149; XXXVI, 70, 146; XL, 68–9, 143; XLII, 24–5; XLIII, 88–9, 119–20: *Second Report, ut supra*, 24–6.
76. Minutes, XLV, 193, 274.
77. *Second Report, ut supra*, 29–31: Minutes, XX, 110–12, 152; XXII, 80; XXIII, 82, 119, 122–5; XXIV, 154–5; XXV, 74; XXX, 80–1; XXXIV, 66–7; XXXVI, 25–7; XXXIX, 74–8; XL, 106; XLII, 24–5.
78. Minutes, XXXVI, 74–84; XXXIX, 146; XL, 85–92; XLII, 108–9; XLIII, 151–2; XLIV, 142; XLVIII, 84–5, 197–8, 235; XLIX, 33: Edward J. Dent, *A Theatre for Everybody. The Story of the Old Vic and Sadler's Wells* (1945), 82, 95–6: Dennis Arundell, *The Story of Sadler's Wells 1683–1977* (2nd ed. 1978), 184–215.
79. Minutes, XXXII, 74–6; XLI, 119–21, 145, 163–4; XLII, 125–6, 171–3; XLIV, 26; XLVII, 155–6, 193; XLVIII, 231–6: Godwin, *Queen Mary College*, 78–88, 90–2, 183–4.
80. Minutes, XXXII, 27–8.
81. Teague, op. cit., 64–6, 72–3.
82. Minutes, XXXVII, 148–9; XXXVIII, 108–11: Teague, op. cit., 75–6.
83. Minutes, XL, 151–2: *Report on Policy relating to Grants* (1935), 6.
84. Minutes, XLI, 74–81.
85. Ibid., XLII, 64–5; PRO, CAB 124/142, q. 5986.
86. Minutes, XLIII, 120–7, 182–4, 212–14; XLIV, 160–6: *Report on Policy Relating to Grants* (1935), 27–43: Silver and Teague, op. cit., 45–6: Evans, op. cit., 44–5.
87. *Report on Policy Relating to Grants* (1935).
88. Ibid., 51–2: Minutes, XLV, 189, 207–8.
89. Minutes, XLVII, 195–214; XLVIII, 30–1: *Report on Policy Relating to Grants* (1937).

8 Pensions, open spaces and miscellaneous grants

To provide assistance to the aged poor has always been one of the principal and worthiest objects of charity. Defenders of the City parochial charities in the last quarter of the nineteenth century concentrated on the extent to which they helped to satisfy this need at least among those who had lived or worked in the City of London. The Charity Commissioners, however, enquired very closely into the eligibility of the pensions being provided by the old charities and eliminated a large number of them. Some thought the Commissioners had been too stringent – their hand 'fell heavily on a large class of recipients' was how the Foundation's own Pension Committee described it – but they eventually produced lists of 97 individuals whose pensions or emoluments had to be continued and a further 274 whose pensions they considered to be justified but where continuance was left to the discretion of the trustees.[1] The difference between the two categories was that the first group of pensioners had been appointed under charities dedicated to the provision of pensions and the second group under trusts which were not so specific. The trustees naturally felt disinclined to make such a fine distinction and were prepared to pay all of the pensions listed, nominally totalling £6,400 per annum (although £6,000 was the maximum payable according to the Central Scheme). All the named pensioners, however, had been appointed prior to the passing of the City Parochial Charities Act in 1883, and the Central Scheme allowed the trustees to spend a further £1,500 in payment of any additions made to those pensions over the succeeding five years or of any new pensions allocated in that period. Finally, an additional £500 could be applied to provide pensions 'or occasional or temporary grants in case of emergency' to poor persons who had been residents of, or employed in, the City parishes which were subject to the scheme.

If all this seemed to be a recipe for confusion, such certainly proved to be the case. In the early years there were quite wide variations in the number of pensioners on the Foundation's books from time to time, not least because many of the named pensioners may have died before the Foundation began its work. The maximum number at any one time was 406 early in 1892, on whom £1,839 had been spent in the previous quarter. At the same time as reporting this, the Pension Committee commented that several pensioners whose names had been submitted by the Charity Commissioners were not properly qualified, and that it had had great difficulty in obtaining all the necessary information.[2] What was clear, however, was that through natural attrition the number of pensioners would be bound to decrease until only the £500 allotted for new pensions could be spent on this service – a matter of no little frustration to the Pension Committee.[3]

By early 1895 the number of pensioners had diminished to 325, costing £1,405 in the previous quarter,[4] but the Royal Commission on the Aged Poor, which reported in that year, changed the whole situation. The Commission had been convened as the result of a growing concern over the plight of the elderly in society. For most of the nineteenth century the prevailing wisdom had been that the aged would be taken care of by their own providence in earlier life, by the support of their dependents or relatives, by charity, or, if these failed, by the poor law. An increasing awareness that a large proportion of old people were having to seek poor law relief, however, led to an agitation for the introduction of old-age pensions, which was given added momentum in 1890 when the first figures with any degree of reliability (a day count of paupers) suggested that nearly a fifth of the population aged over 65 was in receipt of some form of poor law relief.

The resulting ideas about how best to introduce a scheme of old-age pensions ranged across a broad spectrum of opinion from Charles Booth's advocacy of a universal, non-contributory pension averaging 6s per week at age 65, paid for out of national and local taxes, to the views of Charles Loch, the Secretary of the Charity Organisation Society, who believed that voluntary effort, utilizing if necessary more of the proceeds of endowed charities, was all that was required. The government predictably appointed a Royal Commission under Lord Aberdare to investigate the whole question of the aged poor.[5]

The Aberdare Commission met in 1893–4 and one of its witnesses was Sir Henry Longley, the Chief Charity Commissioner. He referred to a scheme which was operative in the parishes of Hammersmith and

Fulham whereby the funds of two endowed charities were used to provide pensions of between 5s and 10s per week to 'poor persons of good character', who from 'age, ill-health, accident, or infirmity, shall be unable to maintain themselves by their own exertions', if they had shown 'reasonable providence' and had not received poor law relief for five years. Charles Loch, who was a member of the Commission, asked Longley whether he thought such a scheme could have a wider application, and enquired whether any part of the funds of the City parochial charities could be made available for this purpose 'in the event of the money not being required for technical education on existing lines'. Longley responded that such a use was permitted by the Central Scheme and indeed that 'there could not be a better application of the money'. The surprising nature of this statement, in view of the recent preoccupations of the Charity Commissioners, was not lost on the Radical, Henry Broadhurst. In some perplexity he asked, 'But your recent epidemic of educational enthusiasm, I understand, is likely to break out again in another way; is that so? in technical institutions?', quickly adding, 'However, I fear this is not quite the place where we ought to fight that battle.'[6]

The Commission's report appeared in 1895 and was a conservative, not to say reactionary, document. It saw no reason to change the present system of poor law relief as it affected the aged, except to urge that there should be greater discrimination between 'the respectable poor who become destitute and those whose destitution is directly the consequence of their own misconduct'. But it also recommended that some of the funds of the City parochial charities should be used to provide pensions in other parts of London outside the City, on the lines of the scheme for Hammersmith and Fulham.[7] At the same time, not entirely coincidentally, the annual report of the Charity Commissioners drew attention to the new legislation which reduced the need to use charitable funds for educational purposes and added that, 'in the case of Doles, other applications are now more favoured, as, for instance, to Old Age Pension Funds, which have the recommendation of being nearer in object to the present application, and do not tend, if rightly safeguarded, to pauperise the recipient'.[8] The Commissioners were probably entirely unaware of the irony that an appendix to the same report contained the final statement of accounts of the City parochial charities, showing how much had already been spent on educational and allied institutions.

The Foundation's Pension Committee, which had previously had only the gradual reduction of its own pension-giving responsibilities to look forward to, seized on the recommendations of the two reports with alacrity. It initially suggested that the annual sum available for pensions within the City parishes should be raised to £2,000, and that a further £3,000 should be provided for the same purpose in the wider metropolis. The Charity Commissioners baulked at increasing the former sum beyond the £500 already allotted, but were prepared to agree that, in addition, up to £4,500, or a larger sum with their specific approval, could be spent on pensions in the Metropolitan Police District, which was the area of jurisdiction of the 1883 Act.[9]

An amending scheme of 1897 laid down the principles which were to govern the award of the new pensions. The recipients were to be 'deserving poor persons' who had lived or worked in the metropolis for at least five years, had not received poor law relief for five years, and who were not less than 60 years old unless disabled by sickness, accident or infirmity. The pensions were not to be less than 5s or more than 10s per week, and the total income of any pensioner from all sources including the Foundation's pension was not to exceed 10s a week. (This was not an ungenerous provision in the light of the sums suggested for pensions by other authorities, but should be measured against the average wage at this time of about 25s per week.) Pensions were to be granted initially for three years but were to be renewable.

The scheme left it to the discretion of the Central Governing Body to determine how it was to choose its pensioners, but there were such complex stipulations about how to give notice, how to vet applicants for their 'character and circumstances' and evidence of 'reasonable providence', and how to make appointments once vetted, that the trustees were paralysed into inactivity, and nothing happened until 1900. By then the number of pensioners supported by the Foundation had decreased to 215 and the annual expenditure on pensions had declined to £4,000, leaving £1,000 which could be allocated to new pensions within the limit imposed by the Commissioners. The trustees themselves were reduced to bickering about how best to implement the new scheme; some thought it had to be amended before it could become operative, while others wanted to turn over all responsibility, including the funds, to local pension societies.[10]

Eventually they decided to rely heavily on the services of the Charity Organisation Society and especially of its district committees. Notices advertising the availability of the pensions were placed in a number of daily and weekly newspapers, and 876 applications were received. About a quarter of these, chosen primarily on the basis of age, were investigated by the COS, and some 170 were selected for pensions while over 40 were rejected.

The minimum age of the first group of pensioners, except for a few cases in which there was exceptional hardship, was 77, but even those above that age had to be of good character and show ample evidence of previous thrift. They included an 81-year-old widower who had been a member of the Loyal United Friends for 42 years and had also put money in a savings bank when young, but had had to use up all his savings because his wife had been an invalid for 30 years. Another was an engine driver of 'thoroughly good character' who had belonged for 43 years to a friendly society which had gone out of business, while a 'very feeble' widow, whose husband had been in the Foresters for 42 years and who received 2s a week from a son, was given a pension of 8s to make her income up to 10s. A considerable number of the successful applicants had belonged to provident or friendly societies which had failed. The youngest pensioner was a 42-year-old pattern maker who suffered from locomotor ataxy and had to have morphia injections two or three times a day. Probably of equal importance was the consideration that he belonged to the Hearts of Oak Benefit Society which paid him 4s a week.[11]

At first, the trustees were required to readvertise for new applications approximately every three years – receiving 327 in 1903 and 366 in 1905 – but could not award new pensions out of any funds which accumulated in between. This soon came to be seen as a rather cumbersome way of proceeding, and they were subsequently allowed to fill vacancies as they occurred through the death of pensioners or their removal to an infirmary, or in the occasional cases when pensions were taken away for deception or serious lapses in behaviour. In this way the annual sum spent on pensions approximated closely to the £5,000 which had been specified by the Charity Commissioners (equivalent at 1990 values to some £250,000).

The operation of the Foundation's pension scheme was scrutinized by the Royal Commission on the Poor Laws, when W. Hayes Fisher, the Chairman of the Pension Committee, appeared as a witness in 1906. He was at pains to point out that although the Foundation relied heavily on the recommendations of the Charity Organisation Society, it did not feel bound by them and had at times decided to grant a pension against the Society's advice. Nevertheless, he admitted that the character traits of the applicants were a major factor in selection, including 'the cleanliness of their homes'.

Fisher produced some statistics from a wide sampling of the Foundation's pensioners which showed that 39 per cent belonged broadly to the class of tradesmen, 22 per cent had been domestic servants, and 15 per cent were mechanics. Married couples accounted for 36 per cent of the sample, while 54 per cent were widows or spinsters, thus producing an overwhelming preponderance of women. One reason for this was undoubtedly the advanced age of the recipients, for under normal circumstances the relative paucity of funds available meant that no one under the age of 77 could hope to receive a pension; as Fisher pointed out in response to a question why the proportion of the pensioners who were labourers was so small, very few labourers could in fact expect to reach that age. Nevertheless, there was a suggestion that perhaps the Foundation's pensions did not reach the poorest class.

The Commission enquired about the system used by the Foundation, which Fisher thought worked 'admirably'. Prompted by some sympathetic questioning from Charles Loch, he dwelt particularly on the way in which the promise of small weekly amounts from the Foundation had produced offers of assistance from relatives and others. The figures he gave, doubtless calculated by the COS, were that in 398 cases £3,865 provided by the Foundation had resulted in pensions totalling £8,334. Some of the members of the Commission, in particular Beatrice Webb, were unhappy about the implication that undue pressure was being placed on relatives to contribute.

Fisher was also prepared to criticize the amount which the Foundation was spending on polytechnics, although making it clear that he could only give a personal opinion. 'There are some people who think that the Polytechnics now had better look more to the rates and less to our funds, and that we might utilise our funds more for pension purposes,' he responded to one questioner, adding, 'but that is a matter of policy on which I certainly should not feel myself entitled to speak on behalf of the body which I represent.' Octavia Hill was anxious to pursue this line of questioning.

Fisher had to admit, however, that the Foundation's pensions reached only a fraction of the aged poor in London. He had a particularly sharp exchange with Beatrice Webb when he tried to extend his defence of his committee's work into a general criticism of state pensions, and she might have cynically wondered whether the Foundation's scheme was designed less to make inroads into the vast problem of the aged poor than to bolster the Charity Organisation Society's view about the efficacy of voluntary effort and the lack of any necessity for governmental intervention.[12]

Despite the opposition of C. S. Loch and his ilk, however, the Liberal government finally secured the passage of an Old Age Pensions Act in 1908. This was a modest measure which provided a non-contributory pension of up to 5s per week to all persons aged 70 and over whose income was below a certain level and who satisfied other criteria, including a 'thrift test' that they could show some evidence of having tried to provide for themselves and their dependents.[13]

Virtually all of the Foundation's pensioners were eligible for the new state pensions, and a reappraisal of its scheme was necessary. Sir Owen Roberts, with the support of Sidney Webb, took the opportunity to try to have the sum set aside for pensions reduced to £500 once more, but instead the Finance and General Purposes Committee was asked to take a more studied view of the matter.[14] Loch, having lost the main battle, was still dedicated to the promotion of thrift and wanted any funds released by the discontinuance of pensions to be used to estabish centres for the collection of small savings from labourers. He was told, however, that the Foundation's financial position would not allow it to support 'experimental charitable work'.[15] The trustees eventually came to the conclusion that the level of income necessary to support a pensioner in London was 10s per week, whereas the government pension only provided a maximum of 5s (and, in its defence, it must be said that this was also the view of the COS). Accordingly most of the Foundation's pensioners had their weekly amounts reduced by the 5s they received from the state, but they were not removed from the lists altogether.[16] Nevertheless, no new pensioners were subsequently appointed under the amending scheme of 1897, and the annual amount spent on pensions sharply declined, to £2,850 in 1910, for instance, and £1,640 in 1915.[17]

In that year, however, the Pension Committee decided to raise the earnings limit for its pensioners from 10s to 13s per week, which, 'besides being valuable in cases of great age or infirmity . . . is now necessary owing to the increased cost of living'.[18] The maximum pension was subsequently raised twice, to 15s in 1917 and 20s in 1920, to take account of wartime and post-war inflation. When the rate of state pension was increased in 1919, however, it was only to 10s per week, still below the Foundation's figure.[19]

In 1934, when the number of pensioners had diminished to 24 and the money spent on them added up to little more than £500, David Romain, who was the nominee of the Bishopsgate Foundation on the Central Governing Body, successfully moved that the amending scheme of 1897 should be revived.[20] The background to this surprising reassertion of the role of the voluntary sector in the field of pensions lay partly in the growth of distress as a result of the depression, and partly in the realization that the complex arrangements for the public provision of pensions had created some alarming gaps. A contributory pension which was payable at age 65 had been introduced in 1925 for those insured under the National Insurance Act of 1911, but only insured persons were eligible and this scheme operated alongside the older non-contributory one, in which the qualifying age was 70. In both the maximum pension was 10s per week (£1 for married couples), which was soon acknowledged to be woefully inadequate.[21]

The Charity Commissioners approved of the trustees' initiative and drew up a new scheme in 1935 which differed little from that of 1897 except that the maximum pension payable was to be 25s per week. The total sum to be set aside annually for pensions was still limited to £5,000 despite the growth in the Foundation's income, and applicants were once more expected to be of good character and to have shown evidence of thrift.[22]

There was an overwhelming response to the first advertisements later in 1935. Over 1,500 applications were received, most of which revealed 'great need'. Two investigators were appointed at salaries of £5 per week each, one a retired inspector with the Ministry of Health and the other an experienced social worker, and the first 74 pensioners, all aged at least 80, were appointed before the end of the year. All were in receipt of a state pension of 10s and were given additional sums of between 5s and 15s a week. Although they had to state on their application forms whether they had belonged to a provident or friendly society, need appears to have been the only criterion on which the pensions were based.[23]

Early in the following year a second group of pensioners was appointed, making 255 in all, while an even greater number, 330, were placed on a waiting list.[24] The pensions were paid by local almoners who were generally attached to settlement houses, Toc H or local churches, and the total sum expended quite quickly reached the £5,000 allotted, and even a little beyond that figure when expenses were included.[25]

In 1939 the Pension Committee produced a short report on its recent work. It acknowledged that by the Poor Law Act of 1930 local authorities had the power to provide relief to the elderly and disabled poor, and, perhaps responding to criticism, admitted that a case could be made that in giving pensions the Foundation was relieving those authorities of a statutory duty. However, it was convinced that its own pensioners were the kind of persons who would never have recourse to public assistance and concluded that 'there is little doubt that the addition of a few shillings weekly to the income of the poor and aged does result in very much greater happiness and health to those whose lives are often uninteresting in the extreme.' In the same year Arthur Greenwood moved a resolution in the House of Commons pointing out the inadequacy of state pensions and regretting the refusal of the government to increase them.[26]

The manner in which the open-space protagonists had persuaded the Charity Commissioners to part with £161,000 of the accumulated capital of the City parochial charities for their favoured causes is described in Chapter 4. This was far from being the limit of the Foundation's obligations in this direction, however. The only specific purpose named in the rather nebulous clause of the Central Scheme permitting the residue of the Central Fund to be used 'for the benefit of the poorer classes of the Metropolis' was 'for preserving, providing, and maintaining open spaces and recreation grounds or drill grounds within the

Metropolis', and when in 1935 a sub-committee produced a report on the policy to be adopted in the allocation of grants it reaffirmed that 'the Trustees have always regarded the preservation, provision and maintenance of Open Spaces in the Metropolis as of importance, second only to that of assisting Polytechnics'.[27]

Even during the difficult early years, money was found to provide grants for the acquisition of open spaces – £2,000 each for Hackney Marshes and Paddington Recreation Ground, and £1,500 for Hilly Fields, Deptford, for instance.[28] In 1894, when the trustees devised a system for the annual distribution of grants, they decided to divide the applications into three categories – polytechnics and educational institutions; open spaces; and miscellaneous – and to allocate a proportion of the funds available to each.[29] In this way a definite sum was set aside for open spaces each year, and up to 1901 grants totalling £19,450 were given towards the acquisition or laying out of some twenty parks, recreation grounds, churchyards and square gardens.[30] A favoured method of proceeding was for the Foundation to promise the final sum needed to purchase an open space, thus encouraging other donors to make contributions up to that amount, and it was quite prepared to co-operate with local councils and district boards which would eventually own the land in question.

The trustees preferred to utilize the services of well-established societies or other organizations whenever possible, and the one they turned to for this purpose was the Metropolitan Public Gardens Association, which had been founded in 1882 and had rapidly become both an effective pressure group and a body which actively bought up and laid out churchyards, disused burial grounds and garden squares before handing them over to local authorities.[31] As early as 1893 a grant of £500 was given to the Association towards the laying out of St Thomas's Square, Hackney, and The Triangle, Caledonian Road, and in 1895 the Central Governing Body resolved to give £1,000 per annum to the Association for five years for the purchase or laying out of minor open spaces.[32]

In 1901, the two categories of open spaces and miscellaneous grants were merged, and for several years, when few funds were available for grants of any kind once the obligations to the polytechnics had been met, relatively little went to open spaces. Projects which tended to attract support were generally those seeking to extend the major metropolitan open spaces such as Hampstead Heath (for which a grant of £1,500 was given in 1906) and Wimbledon and Putney Commons. In 1905, in a somewhat surprising move, the trustees appointed a special sub-committee to look into the possibility that the Foundation might itself purchase freehold ground in the vicinity of the metropolis suitable for open spaces and recreation grounds. Nothing came of this at the time, but it did anticipate a future policy initiative.[33] In all, between 1901 and 1920 only £7,000 was spent on open spaces in the sense of parks and gardens.[34]

What this calculation excludes, however, is the very important support which was given to the London Playing Fields Society in the form of annual grants from 1895 onwards, although these were not at first included in the category of grants for open spaces. The work of the Society, which had been founded in 1890 as the London Playing Fields Committee, grew in importance as the desire to provide opportunities for young people to indulge in physical recreation took on an added urgency with the revelations about the poor conditions of recruits for the Boer War, and later the First World War. Its initial grant in 1895 was £100, but this was increased to £200 in the following year, and £600 in 1906. Three years later the trustees authorized a loan of £12,500 to the Society to enable it to purchase a recreation ground of 34 acres in Walthamstow, and, in a similar gesture to the help given to the polytechnics, its grant was increased to £1,000 to assist with the repayment and interest charges, as there appeared to be 'no better outlet for fulfilling the Trustees' obligations as regards "Open Spaces and Recreation Grounds" '.[35]

This remained the standard level of annual grant until 1930, but in 1919 and the three succeeding years it was temporarily raised to £3,000 to help meet the additional expenses of bringing back into recreational use ground that had been used for growing produce during the war. In addition, the Society claimed that 'for young men at work in the office, factory or shop, back from the open-air life of the war, health-giving out-of-door recreation is more than ever seen to be a necessity.'[36] After 1930 the grant was reduced and fluctuated annually until 1938 when it was decided not to give grants as a matter of course but only for special purposes. The reasons for this change in policy were partly that the Society itself had become largely self-supporting as its playing fields were becoming more intensively used, and partly because the Foundation was by then assisting directly with the costs of many recreation grounds including those in its own ownership.

In fact, the Foundation itself had taken on a similar role to that of the Society shortly after the First World War when the trustees decided to acquire playing fields and recreation grounds, initially for the polytechnics and then for wider use. The details of the purchase of land for playing fields and sports grounds for the polytechnics and other educational institutions are given in Chapter 7. This led naturally to the acquisition of land for general recreational purposes. The first such instance occurred in 1932 when the National Association of Boys' Clubs asked the Central Governing Body to either make a grant for the purchase of the former Merchant Taylors' sports ground at

Bellingham, or buy the site themselves. The Estate Committee, to which the matter was referred, promptly chose the latter course, and the playing fields were bought for £15,000. One of the London County Council's large out-of-centre estates had been built at Bellingham and such a facility was considered to be much needed there.

Other, similar, ventures quickly followed. In 1935, 50 acres at Chigwell Row in Essex, suitable for use as a camping site, were purchased for £10,000 and let at a rent of £25 per annum to the National Council of Girls' Clubs and the Girl Guides' Association with a covenant that the land was to be used for the London members of those organizations. A grant of £1,000 was made for fitting out the camp. In the following year an even larger site of nearly 80 acres at Cudham in Kent was purchased for £6,000 and let on similar terms, £3,000 being also made available for the erection of a warden's dwelling and huts. The philosophy behind such initiatives was expressed particularly well in a report from the Chigwell Row camp in 1937. 'There is at present', stated the report, 'a great "drive" all over the country towards better health and improved physique. The nation at large has woken up to the fact that it has neglected the physical education of its youngest members. Great Britain in this respect dropped behind several of the other European countries and is now determined to make up the leeway.'[37] What was perhaps also implied but not stated in the report was the concern that some of those European countries were ones with which Britain might soon find itself at war.

With such views as those expressed in the report reflecting the national mood, the trustees had no hesitation in 1938 in accepting an opportunity to purchase a 106-acre farm, Grange Farm, at Chigwell as a venue for camping and sporting activities. The cost, including the redemption of tithes and the land tax, was £21,430. Ambitious plans for adapting the site had to be deferred on the outbreak of war. Additionally, in 1938 a sports ground at Leyton formerly used by the Essex County Cricket Club, which had been the subject of negotiations for many years, was finally acquired for £15,000 and let jointly to the National Association of Boys' Clubs and the National Council of Girls' Clubs at a rent of £10 per annum.[38]

In the meantime, support for public parks, commons and woodlands was not neglected. During the 1920s, grants totalling £5,000 were made for bringing more land on the edge of Hampstead Heath into public ownership, including parts of the Kenwood estate, and, among other causes aided, £1,000 was given towards the £12,000 required to preserve 97 acres of Pett's Wood as a memorial to William Willett, the originator of 'summer time'.[39]

In 1930, when a sub-committee drew up a policy to guide the trustees in making grants, it asserted that the preservation, provision and maintenance of open spaces were of such 'paramount importance' that a separate category was once more created for grants towards those ends. The sub-committee commented that the shortage of recreation grounds for young children in the more congested parts of the metropolis was a particularly pressing problem, and over the course of the next few years the Foundation contributed £14,600 to the large sum of money which was required to preserve Coram's Fields, the site of the Foundling Hospital in Bloomsbury, as a children's playground and recreation ground. Another scheme which served more than one purpose was the creation of Parsloes Park out of 100 acres of land near the LCC's Becontree Estate, toward which the Foundation gave £5,000. This was just one of several measures which were designed to assist in tackling the many social problems of these vast out-of-centre housing estates (as described below), and an added bonus in this case was that the laying out of the park provided work for the unemployed.[40]

The sub-committee which reported on a policy for grants in 1935 reaffirmed the importance of open spaces but warned against assisting schemes which, under various new statutes, should now be financed out of rates or by the Exchequer. Two years later another sub-committee appointed for the same purpose spelt out more clearly what was meant by urging that 'no further grants towards the acquisition and laying-out of open spaces by Local Authorities be made except to encourage the undertaking of Schemes which the Trustees desire to promote and which, without such encouragement, would not be attempted.'[41] The report also pointed out that under the Physical Training and Recreation Act of 1937, local authorities had increased powers to provide facilities for these and allied activities.

Thereafter, applications for grants from public bodies for open spaces were invariably turned down, and the Foundation's assistance was confined to those playing fields and camps established by voluntary effort, and, of course, its own camping grounds.[42] This did not entail any lessening of the overall commitment to support outdoor activities, as the promotion of these had become an increasingly important part of the work of youth organizations, to which the Foundation had pledged its aid, but it does indicate that, even before the outbreak of war, the trustees' policy on open spaces was taking a new direction.

Surprisingly, the trustees did not draw up a policy to assist them in making general grants until 1930. One reason was that at least until the First World War there was so little money to give away. Up to 1914, once the polytechnics had been taken care of and pensions paid, the average amount available for distribution in grants was less than £5,000 per annum. Of that, between one-third and one-half was spent on open spaces, leaving some £3,000 for a wide variety of needs in the whole metropolitan area. Of course, it must be remembered that this sum was equivalent to £150,000 at 1990 values, so it was not entirely nugatory, but it was certainly not a sufficient amount to justify creating an elaborate policy to guide the trustees in its allocation. In addition, and understandably, there was no rush to advertise the availability of grants, so that it took some time for a consistent pattern of applications to be established. Nevertheless, even though the trustees' approach to grant-making was initially somewhat *ad hoc*, it is possible to single out certain fields of activity in which they tended to concentrate their efforts and certain principles that came to be adopted in making decisions well before these were formally codified.

One of the areas to which the trustees soon turned their attention was education, where, despite the prodigality of their support for the polytechnics and other institutions for technical education, they still felt that there was additional work to be done. For several years small grants were given to some of the City ward schools which had previously received support from the parochial charities, but these were brought to an end in 1901.[43] One-off grants were also made for educational purposes, such as £100 in 1892 to the National Home Reading Union to provide books and establish reading circles for working men and women in poorer districts, and £250 in 1897 for the library of the London School of Economics (which was voted at the very first meeting Sidney Webb attended as a trustee).[44]

By far the most important series of educational grants, apart from those to institutions, however, were made annually to the London Society for the Extension of University Teaching. The Society had been established in 1876 to provide a metropolitan organization for promoting the university extension lectures which had been instituted, largely on the initiative of Cambridge University, in the early 1870s. The lectures, which were designed to bring the benefits of university teaching to people who had no possibility of attending the universities themselves, proved very popular and were well attended.[45]

The Society was given a grant (of £300) as early as April 1892 and it was one of the first organizations to attract consistent support from the trustees. For the first few years the grant fluctuated between £200 and £300, and in 1895, when only £200 was given, the criticism was made that the fees for the lectures were rather too high and should at least be reduced at those institutions supported by the Foundation. In fact, it was a general criticism of the extension lectures that the charges imposed put them beyond the reach of all but the upper echelons of artizans, and that their appeal was largely to middle-class audiences. The trustees appear to have been satisfied that the money was being well spent, however, for in 1897 they raised the grant to £400 and it remained at that level until 1902. At that time the work of the Society was taken over by the Board to promote the Extension of University Teaching under the auspices of the University of London and the grant was increased to £500. It was, however, suggested that in organizing the lectures the desirability of concentrating them in polytechnics and similar institutions should be considered and that a reasonable number of courses should be given in poorer districts.[46]

Thereafter, £500 was given annually on a virtually automatic basis until 1912, when the trustees asked for a report on the advisability of continuing their support. They were told that the Board employed lecturers of high standing who had to be well remunerated, and as the Foundation's grant accounted for a fifth of total receipts, the continuance of its subsidy was of considerable importance. Although only a minority of those attending could be classed as artizans and labourers, women made up a high proportion of the audiences (a factor which may have helped to make the trustees well disposed to the lectures), and part of the grant was used for tutorial classes which were organized in conjunction with the Workers' Educational Association and at which the majority of students were working class. The trustees decided to continue their grant, which was maintained at the rate of £500 per annum, until 1930 when the sub-committee appointed to formulate a policy on grants recommended that no further grants should be made for educational purposes apart from those to the polytechnics, and that year's grant for the lectures was given on the understanding that it would be the last.[47] The university extension lecture movement was aided continuously by the Foundation for almost forty years – an unusually long period of support for a single cause – and the level of grant, which in most years was the equivalent of some £15,000 at 1990 values, represented a sizeable share of the cost of the lectures.

The aid to the settlement movement in the early years should also be seen as primarily educational in nature. There is an obvious affinity between the university extension lectures and the university settlements, of which Toynbee Hall, founded in 1884, was the first. The settlement houses embraced a wide social purpose, but adult education was an important part of their work and one on which the trustees focused.[48] As befitted the doyen of the settlements, Toynbee Hall received the most assistance (over £900 in a series of grants between 1893 and 1904), but other settlements were also aided from time to time. These included the Bermondsey Settlement, the Passmore Edwards (later Mary Ward) Settlement, Bloomsbury, Oxford House (once the Charity Commissioners had decided that it passed the non-denominational test), the Women's University Settlement and the Robert Browning Settlement, Walworth. Grants to settlements ceased after 1904 (until they were resumed in the 1930s for different reasons which are explained below), not because their work fell out of favour, but because at a time of very great pressure on the modest income of the Foundation, it was considered that they could command other sources of support.

In 1899 a grant of £100 was made to the Passmore Edwards Settlement specifically for the first non-residential school for invalid children which Mrs Ward had established in the settlement in the previous year.[49] The welfare of children was another major concern of the trustees and one which, of course, frequently overlapped with education. The Ragged School Union (later Shaftesbury Society), which was given £100 in 1894 and £50 annually between 1895 and 1899, had started out in 1844, for instance, with aims that were primarily educational but soon expanded into other aspects of children's welfare. Another organization which was also aided for the first time in 1894 was the Children's Country Holiday Fund, which had been founded in 1884 by Samuel and Henrietta Barnett in St Jude's, Whitechapel.[50]

Within the general category of the welfare of children, however, the most constant and lasting support was given to the London Schools Dinner Association, which also first received a grant in 1894. The feeding of hungry schoolchildren touched many of the springs of social action. A survey undertaken by the London School Board in 1889 had revealed that some 12 per cent of children attending its schools went short of food, and the London Schools Dinner Association was formed in that year to co-ordinate the activities of the various voluntary feeding societies that operated in the capital. Not only was the plight of hungry children guaranteed to arouse the charitable conscience but the realization that a large proportion of the young were chronically undernourished raised apprehensions about the future of the national stock, which were reinforced by the revelations about the poor physical condition of recruits for the Boer War. Thus, the provision of meals for necessitous schoolchildren became bound up with the drive for national efficiency. As a co-ordinating body, the Association was the kind of organization which the Foundation favoured, and it was given an annual grant of £100 between 1894 and 1910. This sum, which was sufficient to feed some 150 needy children on school days throughout the year, accounted for slightly under a tenth of the Association's income.

Such was the scale of the problem, however, that voluntary effort could only make slight inroads, and in 1904 an Interdepartmental Committee on Physical Deterioration urged that municipal authorities should combine with voluntary agencies to provide meals. The end result was the Education (Provision of Meals) Act of 1906, which was the first of the major measures of social reform passed by the Liberal government elected in that year. The trustees allowed time for the Act to become effective, but discontinued its grants to the Association after 1910, except in 1913 when £50 was given specifically for the provision of meals in vacations, a service which was not covered by the 1906 Act but authorized in a further Act passed in 1914.[51]

Other organizations which catered for children were aided as funds became more readily available. Foremost among these in terms of the length and generosity of support was the movement to provide evening play centres at schools in London, which, perhaps not entirely coincidentally, was first given a grant of £100 in 1911 when the former grant of the same amount to the London Schools Dinner Association came to an end. The first play centre was opened in 1897 at the Passmore Edwards Settlement by Mrs Humphrey Ward, and the Children's Play Centre Fund was inaugurated in 1904. An application to assist with the cost of running the centres in London was not made until 1911, but at once elicited a sympathetic response from the trustees. As the LCC allowed the premises to be used rent-free and did not charge for heat or lighting, this seemed to be an ideal instance of co-operation between the statutory authorities and a voluntary body, and a grant was given every year from 1911 to 1940. The amount was quickly raised to £400, at which it remained until 1924 when it was increased to £500, and still further to £600 in 1927. By then the Foundation was providing about one-sixth of the income of the centres raised from voluntary sources, although the bulk of their costs were met from public funds. In 1941 the centres were taken over by the LCC, by which time the Foundation's total contribution to their running costs over 30 years had amounted to £13,750.[52]

A service of a not dissimilar kind was undertaken by the London Children's Gardens Fund, which was started in 1911–12 with the aim of creating small gardens out of waste ground in the poorest districts of London, both to occupy children after school hours and provide them with a healthy outdoor activity. The children were allocated small individual plots on which they were encouraged to grow flowers and vegetables under supervision. The Foundation gave the Fund a grant of £50 in 1914 and followed this up with a similar sum in most years up to 1938. The overall costs of the scheme were not large and even this relatively small annual grant was regarded by the organizers as a great boon in that it encouraged other contributions.[53]

To give help to disabled and invalid children was always high on the charity agenda. There were a number of organizations devoted to this purpose which received occasional assistance from the Foundation, such as the Moore Street Home for Crippled Boys, and one, the After-Care Association for Blind, Deaf and Crippled Children, was grant-aided on a more consistent basis between 1907 and 1920, latterly at the rate of £200 per annum. The Invalid Children's Aid Association, perhaps the best known of the societies dealing with sick and crippled children, which was founded as an offshoot of the Charity Organisation Society in 1888, received only intermittent aid from the Foundation in the early years, the trustees doubtless considering that the Association was able to take care of its own fundraising. Once the pressure on the Foundation's own income had eased, however, applications from the society were treated more sympathetically and it was given an annual grant between 1921 and 1935, at the rate of £100 from 1921 to 1924, £200 from 1925 to 1931, and thereafter £300. In 1936 a grant was refused on the basis that the Association's finances were in a satisfactory state and there were other calls on the Foundation's resources, but it was renewed in 1938–9 to enable the organization to extend its work to the new LCC housing estates, in which the trustees were taking particular interest at that time (see below).[54]

The needs of sick and disabled children impinged on the whole vast area of health and medical services, to which in the widest sense the trustees devoted most of the resources available for miscellaneous grants in the long period up to the Second World War. The level of overall demand within this field was wellnigh insatiable, even though, as a recent historian of English philanthropy has expressed it, 'medical agencies were more generously supported by the British public than any other secular charities'.[55] More particularly, it was the needs of the voluntary hospitals that dominated the philanthropic scene, but, after an early rash resolution to allocate £5,000 out of the surplus for 1892 or 1893 to provident, convalescent and other hospitals and infirmaries that benefited the poorer classes of the metropolis had been referred back to the Finance and General Purposes Committee, the trustees decided that the funds available to them were much too limited to be able to offer any tangible aid in this direction. Instead, they looked for ways in which they could assist the small convalescent homes which catered for poor patients discharged from metropolitan hospitals, as their more modest demands for funds presented more realizable goals. At first, grants were made to a wide scattering of convalescent homes on no firmer basis than that they were the ones from which applications were received. This culminated in 1897 in applications from homes in Dover, Eastbourne, Littlehampton, Seaford and Limpsfield, Surrey – the word presumably having spread around – and although grants were given to them all, the Central Governing Body was asked to provide some guidance in dealing with such applications.[56]

Fortunately for the trustees, an organization to which they could turn for assistance was founded in 1897. This was the Prince of Wales's (later King Edward's) Hospital Fund for London, which was established to commemorate Queen Victoria's Diamond Jubilee and was at least in part designed to provide a more orderly way of distributing the outpouring of voluntary aid to hospitals in the metropolis. Early in 1898 Edwin Freshfield moved that in lieu of making grants to individual convalescent hospitals, £1,000 per annum should be granted 'during pleasure' to the Fund on condition that the money should be used for the maintenance of convalescent hospitals. The Central Governing Body agreed and asked if the trustees could be represented on the committee of the Fund. £1,000 was a very much larger sum than the total grants made previously to convalescent homes and over twice as much as the highest individual 'miscellaneous' grant made before that date. Freshfield was duly appointed to the Fund's committee and the grant of £1,000 was repeated annually until 1908, when it was still by far the largest of the Foundation's general grants. The Fund reported each year how the grant had been spent. In 1899, for instance, 13 convalescent hospitals were aided with sums ranging from £200 to £25.

By 1902, following gifts on the King's accession and a special coronation appeal, a considerable amount of capital had accumulated in the Fund, and the trustees resolved to withdraw their grant, but the problem of adjudicating on the myriad claims from convalescent homes proved so intractable that the motion was rescinded later in the year. In 1908, however, when the Foundation was in financial difficulties as a result of basing its grants on the anticipated surplus for the year, the grant to the King's Fund was made with the stipulation that it would have to be the last. By that time the Fund's income from its own investment generally exceeded the contributions from other sources, and the wisdom of continuing for so long to provide it with a sum of money which in most years accounted for about a third of the Foundation's residual income for general causes must be questioned. It may be that the prestige of the Fund, with its royal connections, somewhat overwhelmed the trustees. Certainly, there was never any attempt thereafter to grant-aid any individual convalescent homes.[57]

Substantial assistance was also given at an early stage to the Metropolitan Provident Medical Association, which was founded in 1879 as a result of a campaign by the Charity Organisation Society to promote and support provident dispensaries in the poorer parts of London. Dispensaries were an important source of medical services for the working classes, and provident dispensaries, which involved an element of self-help, were naturally favoured by the COS. After some initial grants to individual dispensaries, the trustees soon settled on a regular subvention to the Association as the best means of assisting the dispensary movement, and gave it £300 per annum between 1893 and 1908. Provident dispensaries were not an unalloyed success, however, and the Foundation's grant soon accounted for a sizeable proportion of the Association's income. Accordingly, the trustees decided in 1908 that any future grant should be limited to 50 per cent of the subscriptions received by the Association. Thereafter, the annual grant varied between about £120 and £160 until the introduction of health insurance under the National Insurance Act of 1911 reduced the need for provident dispensaries. In 1914, the trustees questioned whether the dispensaries still served a useful purpose, but it was pointed out to them that only employed persons were covered under the Act and not women and children. They thereupon decided to make a grant of £50 in that year, but it was the last.[58]

The largest measure of support – and the longest-lasting – for any medical service, however, was that given for district nursing. Once more, occasional help was given at first to local organizations such as the East London Nursing Society, which was founded in 1868 as a pioneering body to provide home nursing for the sick poor in the East End, but its applications were by no means always approved.[59] Similarly, the Metropolitan Nursing Association, a more ambitious undertaking, which was one of the first to send nurses into schools, was awarded grants in 1895–6, but subsequent applications were also unsuccessful.[60] In fact it was not until 1910 that a consistent level of aid began to be given to district nursing. By then grants to the King Edward's Hospital Fund had ceased, and those to the Metropolitan Provident Medical Association were diminishing, and normally the time would have been ripe for other medical agencies to stake a claim. Unfortunately, however, when the Queen Victoria Jubilee Institute for Nurses first applied for a grant in 1909, the Foundation was switching from a policy of allocating grants on the estimated surplus for the current year to one based on the previous year's surplus, and there were simply no funds available to accede to the request.[61]

The Queen's Institute was, however, just the kind of co-ordinating body which generally found favour with the trustees. It had been founded out of the surplus of the Women's Jubilee Offering of 1887 and incorporated in 1889 as a body which set standards of service and training, and to which most local organizations would affiliate. Doubtless encouraged to renew its application for a grant, it was given £500 in 1910 specifically for distribution among the nursing associations which catered for the sick poor in London. Thereafter, the grant was repeated annually and raised to £1,000 in 1913, by when it was the highest of the 'miscellaneous' grants.[62]

The Queen's Institute was a national body, however, and the organization of district nursing in London still left much to be desired. Consequently, in 1914 a Central Council for District Nursing in London was formed, and the Foundation's grant (plus an extra £300 for administrative expenses) was transferred to the new body in 1915.

It no doubt greatly assisted the Council's standing with the Foundation that Sir William Collins was elected as its first Chairman and Addison as its Vice-Chairman. Indeed, in 1919 the Council was given a *pied-à-terre* at Temple Gardens, which by the mid-1930s had become a room specifically set aside for its own use at a nominal rent. In the meantime, the grants to the Council were increased with unfailing regularity, to over £2,000 in 1918, £3,000 by 1925 and £4,700 by 1935, and invariably made up the bulk of its income.[63]

Under the Local Government Act of 1929 the London County Council was given increased powers over district nursing in London, and in 1932 the Central Council was warned that if the service came under municipal control or was largely maintained out of the rates, the Foundation's financial aid might be withdrawn. In fact the LCC chose to work through the Central Council by providing it with a grant, and the trustees were satisfied that the principle of voluntary action was not compromised. As Elizabeth Macadam commented in *The New Philanthropy*, published in 1934, 'District nursing . . . is a remarkable instance of a very efficient service, recognized and largely utilized by the public authority, which is and appears likely to remain under voluntary control.' The Central Council continued to be grant-aided by the Foundation until the financing of the service was taken over by the LCC in 1948, by which time it had received in total over 33 years some £115,000. This works out at an annual average of £3,500, which would be equivalent at 1990 values to at least £100,000 per annum.[64]

In 1918 a small part of the annual grant to the Central Council for District Nursing was specifically earmarked for maternity nursing, and in the 1930s some of the grant was used to enable district nurses to undergo training in midwifery.[65] This was not the first time that the trustees had turned their attention to these services. Between 1907 and 1914 they had given occasional small grants to the Home for Mothers and Babies and Training School for District Midwives in Woolwich, and followed these up in 1914 with £500 for an expansion programme. The home, which provided virtually the only residential maternity services in south-east London, also aspired to become a school for midwifery for the metropolis.[66] Another maternity home, the East End Mothers' Lying-in Home, persistently importuned for funds but was rarely given a grant because it received aid from other sources, including the King's Fund. The Maternity Nursing Association in Myddelton Square was given grants in 1911 and 1913 and then aided on an annual basis from 1915 to 1929, at £50 until 1919 and then £100 per annum, on the recommendation of the Foundation's own Infant Welfare Sub-Committee which first met in 1914.[67]

Maternity and infant welfare were accorded considerable importance in the early twentieth century. The realization at the end of the nineteenth century that infant mortality was not only very high, at over 150 deaths per 1,000 births, but had not declined since the middle of the century, produced widespread concern. Very soon this was reinforced by the more general anxiety about the physical state of the populace and the future well-being of the nation. Efforts to improve infant welfare concentrated on the need to educate the mother, and after the first School for Mothers had been established in St Pancras in 1907 a number of similar institutions with various names were founded by voluntary action. These came to be generically known as infant welfare centres.[68]

The first applications for grants from such organizations came from the Bermondsey and Stepney Schools for Mothers in 1914 and were referred to a special sub-committee on which Collins and Addison, the two trustees with a medical background, both sat. Addison provided the information that the government was contemplating state aid to infant welfare centres, and the sub-committee called in Sir George Newman, the Medical Officer of the Board of Education, who said that any assistance from the Board would be limited to 50 per cent of approved expenditure. He was also 'very emphatic' that 'maternal management' was the key to the problem. The sub-committee decided that this was a cause to which aid must be given and recommended that £500 should be devoted to schools for mothers. A particularly well-attended meeting of the Central Governing Body (at which both Collins and Addison were present) adopted the recommendation despite an attempt to reduce the amount. The sub-committee had looked for an organization to distribute the grant, but although one existed in the form of the Association for Infant Consultations and Schools for Mothers (a branch of the significantly named National League for Physical Education and Improvement), the committee was concerned that it was not sufficiently well informed about the fifty or so institutions which might lay claim to assistance from the Foundation. So, although the Association was given £10 per annum to assist it with its expenses, the committee decided that it would determine how the money was to be allocated itself and was reconstituted on a semi-permanent basis as the influential Infant Welfare Sub-Committee under the highy capable chairmanship of Sir William Collins.[69]

For the next ten years amounts ranging from £500 to £1,000 were given annually to infant welfare centres and carefully distributed by the sub-committee. In 1915, for instance, 29 centres received amounts between £45 and £10, and 25 were grant-aided in 1916.[70] In the following year the sub-committee produced a special report on day nurseries – a subject with which Collins had been concerned during

his time as an LCC councillor and one which was of particular importance in wartime – but concluded that because these could now attract
grants from public funds, the Foundation would not be justified in
subsidizing their running costs. Nevertheless, it was agreed to set aside
£1,000 in 1918 to aid the establishment of new nurseries or to meet
particularly deserving requests for assistance. In fact, it proved very
difficult to spend this amount and half of it was given to the Central
Council for District Nursing for maternity nursing.[71] Likewise conscious of its wider purpose, the sub-committee allocated £100 a year
to the Association for Promoting the Training and Supply of Midwives
in 1918–21.[72]

The reports of the Infant Welfare Sub-Committee were long and
detailed, and reflected the trustees' pride in their involvement in this
area of social welfare. In 1918, for instance, they reported that they
had arranged a series of lectures on the subject at various venues and
articulated the principles behind their activities in words which could
be taken as a policy statement about much of the Foundation's work:

> We desire to call attention to the fact that since the Trustees interested themselves
> in the question of Infant Welfare, assistance from the Government, London County
> Council and Borough Councils has become increasingly available. The help given
> by the Foundation has undoubtedly been of great service to numerous Institutions
> – more especially in assisting them to qualify at an earlier period than would
> otherwise have been possible for the receipt of substantial grants from the State –
> the effort of the Foundation has in fact had the merit of being of a pioneer
> description.

Thereafter, the trustees' main aim was to assist institutions to the
point where they would become eligible for public aid and then transfer
their support to other new centres which were struggling to achieve
the standard necessary for recognition. Finally, in 1925, when, after
an initial period of post-war austerity, grants from public funds became
readily available under the Maternity and Child Welfare Act of 1918,
the trustees decided that their support was no longer needed and
withdrew from the field of infant welfare. This in itself, considering
how enthusiastically they had embraced this particular activity, was
a bold decision and showed that they now had the maturity to base
their grants on real perceived need rather than simply continuing to
assist favoured causes.[73]

The establishment of infant welfare centres has been cited as an
excellent example of co-operation between the voluntary and public
sectors, and in particular of the pioneering role of voluntary agencies
in founding a service which could then be taken over by the state.
Certainly, there was a dramatic improvement in the statistics of infant
mortality – from over 154 per 1,000 live births in 1900 to 51 on the

outbreak of the Second World War – and even those latter-day critics of the infant welfare movement who have questioned whether the focus on the failings of the mother was not a way of avoiding tackling environmental conditions which may have been responsible for more deep-seated but less easily eradicable causes of infant mortality, recognize that the centres were popular and successful. As a recent historian of the movement has expressed it, 'Regardless of the purpose of centres and whether education was the best way of preventing infant mortality, there is no doubt that the centres provided information, much needed nourishment, companionship and a measure of reassurance for many women.'[74]

The welfare of the blind was another area in which there was successful co-operation between voluntary agencies and public authorities. Under the Blind Persons Act of 1920 county and county borough councils had a duty to ensure that there was at least a minimum level of provision for the blind within their areas, but they were encouraged to work through the various voluntary agencies which had been active in the field for many years.[75] Up to the end of the First World War the Foundation's support for blind charities had, like their work in several other spheres, been confined to the occasional grant rather than any continuous level of assistance. The Association for Promoting the General Welfare of the Blind received £100 in 1893, the Royal School for the Indigent Blind 50 guineas in 1896 and £100 in 1917, and the Royal Normal College £200 in 1917 (specifically in this instance to help the college to raise enough money to qualify for a grant from the Carnegie United Kingdom Trust).[76] Apart from the more regular grants given to the After-Care Association for Blind, Deaf and Crippled Children described above, this represented up to that time the sum total of the trustees' support for charities catering for the blind.

One consideration in their minds may have been that with so many calls on the funds at their disposal, there were other causes which made a less obvious appeal to the donors to charity than the needs of the blind. In 1918, however, for the first time the Foundation gave a grant of £50 to the highly successful National Library for the Blind, which had been founded by voluntary effort in 1882 and recently provided with new premises by the Carnegie United Kingdom Trust. The grant was renewed on an annual basis and rose to £350 by 1928, at which it remained until the Second World War.[77] In 1928 the trustees also gave a grant for the first time to the Greater London Fund for the Blind, which had been established in 1920 to co-ordinate the activities of the numerous, and often competing, organizations collecting money for the blind in the metropolis. It was, of course, the kind of body which was tailor-made for the trustees' support and continued to receive annual grants varying between £300 and £500.[78]

Two other areas to which the trustees gave particular attention from an early date were the welfare of women and young girls, and the welfare of boys above school age. In the first category one of the societies which received the most constant support was the Metropolitan Association for the Befriending of Young Servants, which helped girls to find and keep work and aimed to protect them from corrupting influences by providing lodging houses where they could stay if necessary. In 1917, when employment opportunities for girls had become more varied and as many as 6,000 were in the Association's care, it changed its name to the MABYS Association for the Care of Young Girls. The Foundation first gave the society a grant in 1894 and assisted it intermittently until 1910 and then on an annual basis, with £100 until 1917 and thera;fter £200 up to 1939.[79]

An institution of a more unusual kind which received regular aid from the Foundation was a hostel for disabled and invalid women workers in Camberwell, which provided residential accommodation for some women and work opportunities for others who were mobile. The hostel, or group of hostels as it became, was given a grant on its first application in 1913 and this was repeated, with one exception, every year until 1939. As funds became more plentiful, other organizations could also be helped. The Women's Holiday Fund received grants from 1922, and Normand House, West Kensington, a reception centre for female first offenders, between 1921 and 1935. Aid for rescue work was, however, chiefly concentrated on the Central Council for Rescue and Preventive Work in London (later the Central Council for the Social Welfare of Girls and Women in London), which was founded in 1922 and received an annual grant of £300 from that year onwards.[80]

Aid was also given to numerous organizations connected with the welfare of youths, of which only a few can be singled out. The Homes for Working Boys in London, which had been established in 1870, catered predominantly for boys between 14 and 18 on low wages. They received £100 in 1893 and occasional grants subsequently until 1917, when annual grants began to be given on a regular basis. Sometimes these were as high as £500 when appeals were launched to open new homes.[81] A similar organization dating from the 1920s was the Hostels for Youthful Employees of Limited Means (or HYELM movement) which catered mainly for middle-class boys who, through loss of parents or other circumstances, had to depend on their slender earnings at the beginning of a career. Although not aided on an annual basis, HYELM was given very substantial grants from time to time – £500 in 1929, £2,000 in 1936 and again in 1937, and £500 in 1939.[82] The Association for Befriending Boys, which visited and helped boys discharged from poor law schools, received a lower level of grant but on a more constant basis between 1915 and 1932.[83]

In the general field of the welfare of the adolescent, boys', and later girls', clubs came to occupy an increasingly important place. The Foundation began to aid individual clubs in 1914 when it gave £200 to the Hampshire House Trust in Hammersmith, which had become 'a centre for social service in a poor riverside district', to purchase a site for a boys' club and recreation ground. From 1920 the Highway Clubs in East London, a new project to establish mens', boys' and girls' clubs in Shadwell, were given grants averaging £100 a year for ten years. Through the 1920s the Foundation also gave small grants to the Federation of London Working Boys' Clubs, and from 1925 the metropolitan area of the YMCA (having been deemed to be non-denominational by the Charity Commissioners), including £500 in 1928 to purchase ten acres at Sandwich Bay to provide a summer camp for boys.[84] These, and occasional grants to other clubs, marked the first tentative intervention in a field which, during the 1930s, was accorded considerable priority, as described below.

Among the bodies which received grants but do not fall easily into categories, mention might be made of two. The Charity Organisation Society appealed for assistance for the first time in 1914, when it found that the expense of training volunteers was exceeding its income from voluntary contributions. In view of the service given by the COS in distributing the Foundation's pensions, the trustees had no hesitation in making what was at the time a very substantial grant of £500. The society was subsequenty given grants on a number of occasions, rarely in amounts less than £250 and in 1924 as high as £1,000 to help pay for the expenses of taking over the Trinity Almshouses in Brixton, to which in return the Foundation was to have a right of nomination.[85] A more unusual but no less important grant was the £1,000 given in 1928 to the London School of Economics on an appeal from Sir William Beveridge to help meet the costs of the new survey of London life and labour which was carried out on the lines of Booth's great work. The Carnegie United Kingdom Trust gave a matching grant.[86]

Before considering the trustees' first attempt to formulate a specific policy for the distribution of grants in 1930, it may be useful to look back at the principles which had evolved in the course of grant-making over the previous forty years. In the first place the grants were for the most part demand-led. Applications had to be made for them, and these were not always repeated from year to year. The few exceptions were when the trustees decided to allocate a specific sum for a number of years to an organization, such as the King Edward's Hospital Fund, and in some other cases, even though applications still had to be made, the grants were regarded as commitments which were not to be withdrawn without due notice, as for example those for university extension lectures, district nursing and infant welfare.

Invariably, many more applications were received than could be satisfied, even after those which did not come within the terms of the Central Scheme had been eliminated. The Clerk and his staff carefully vetted the applicants and made a rigorous assessment of their financial position. Even those who were given grants on a regular basis were sometimes turned down if their finances were considered to be in a satisfactory state, although sometimes such refusals may also have been intended to remind the recipients of grants that they should not expect them to be given as a matter of course.

Under the terms of the 1883 Act and the Central Scheme, the Foundation's funds were to be used to assist the poorer classes of the metropolitan area, and there was a reluctance to aid national organizations unless they had London branches or it could be clearly demonstrated that the money was spent on residents of the metropolis. So, for instance, when the Central Council for District Nursing in London was formed, the annual grant for district nursing was transferred to that body from the Queen's Institute. Conversely, however, purely local societies were rarely aided, and the Foundation, in the spirit of charity organization, preferred to work through metropolitan-wide co-ordinating bodies such as the Greater London Fund for the Blind or the Central Council for the Social Welfare of Girls and Women in London. In such cases, the trustees required the submission of detailed reports showing how the money had been allocated and why.

As with most grant-giving bodies, the Foundation liked to use its grants to encourage the liberality of others. In cases of extensive capital expenditure it would frequently promise to provide the final sum needed if the remainder could first be raised from other sources. After the Carnegie United Kingdom Trust had been formed in 1913, the two bodies often collaborated, either by making matching grants, or, because the Trust operated in a similar manner, the Foundation would assist in providing the initial sum which had to be raised to attract a grant from the Trust.

On the whole, with limited funds at their disposal, the trustees generally confined their support to ventures which had been tried and tested, but from time to time they were prepared to assist new schemes in that pioneering spirit which social historians frequently cite as one of the most important attributes of the voluntary sector. The evening play centres movement is an example of just such an activity which received generous assistance, but perhaps the principal one was infant welfare. When, however, as in this instance, services, which in their early stages had been largely sustained by voluntary effort, came to attract an increasing degree of public support, the trustees would have to decide at which point their grant should be discontinued. As more and more services became eligible for government or municipal grants, the extent to which they should continue to be aided by the Foundation became increasingly difficult to determine. It was this consideration, and in particular the acquisition of extensive new powers in several areas of welfare by the London County Council under the Local Government Act of 1929, as much as the increase in the funds at its disposal, which, in December 1929, led the Central Governing Body to appoint a sub-committee to report on 'the policy to be adopted in the future allocation of grants'.[87]

After affirming the importance of open spaces, especially playing fields and recreation grounds, and recommending the discontinuance of grants for educational purposes (other than to the polytechnics), the report focused on four main areas of activity on which support should be concentrated, at least until the LCC had had time to develop its recently acquired powers. These were medical and health services; the welfare of women, girls and children; charities for the blind; and boys' and girls' clubs. The only fundamental change of practice it recommended was in the last category, where it advocated that, instead of individual clubs receiving assistance, grants should be made to the London committees of the National Association of Boys' Clubs and the National Council of Girls' Clubs for allocation among local clubs, with, of course, the trustees' approval.

In terms of procedure, the sub-committee considered that any member of the Central Governing Body should have the right to ask for a copy of the annual report of any organization applying for a grant, and that successful applicants should be visited by a trustee or other representative of the Foundation, although, doubtless on past experience, it was strongly of the opinion that the names of the trustees should not be divulged to applicants. Finally, it recommended that a similar committee should be appointed every five years to consider the allocation of grants, thus instituting the practice of holding a quinquennial review of the policy on grants, which was also adopted by the Carnegie United Kingdom Trust.[88]

The report was endorsed by the Central Governing Body and, thereafter, grants were divided into categories corresponding to the areas recommended for support, although a number remained 'unclassified'. Apart from the cessation of the grant for extension lectures, however, the only significant immediate effect was that grants of £500 each were made to the National Association of Boys' Clubs and the National Council of Girls' Clubs. In the following year the grant to the former was increased by £1,000 specifically for the establishment of a boy's club on the new LCC housing estate at Becontree, and in 1932 a similar amount was given to the National Council for a girls' club on the same estate. These were the first actions by the trustees in an area that was increasingly to occupy their attention in the years ahead.[89]

The LCC's policy of dispersing people from the overcrowded city centre to the outskirts of London, beyond the LCC's own boundaries but within the Metropolitan Police District (and therefore within the area to which the 1883 Act applied) had resulted in the development of huge suburban estates. Of these, Becontree and Dagenham, which housed some 100,000 people by the time it was completed in 1934, has been described as 'the largest planned residential suburb in the world'.[90] No matter how substantially the physical amenities of their homes might have been improved, the enforced migration of so many people who existed largely on low incomes was bound to create a great deal of dislocation. It was this that led to the trustees' concern in the 1930s.

Boys' and girls' clubs clearly served a useful purpose in such circumstances and those at Dagenham received additional grants, including £3,500 in 1934 and £1,550 in 1936, but there were other social needs on these vast estates which the Foundation sought to alleviate. The formation of Parsloes Park at Dagenham, for which a grant of £5,000 was made in 1933–4, was designed to serve such a purpose, and in 1933 the trustees also gave £500 for a training school and nursing centre at Dagenham as part of their support for district nursing. In the same year a grant of £2,000 was made to the New Estates Community Committee to establish a community centre and boys' club on the Downham Estate near Lewisham, with the hope that such a gift might 'stimulate further action' by the LCC. Two years later a further grant of £2,800 was made for the same centre, but an additional £8,000 which was requested to help meet the cost of establishing similar centres on all the large LCC suburban estates proved to be more than the trustees were prepared to contemplate.[91]

If the needs of these housing estates were a new area of social policy for the Foundation in the 1930s, so was the relief of the unemployed. It is perhaps surprising that the Foundation had not been involved in this field before, but the problem of unemployment was so vast and intractable that it was probably only because the funds at its disposal increased markedly at the very time that the onset of the depression seriously exacerbated the problem that the Foundation could begin to make a worthwhile contribution. The first step was taken late in 1932 when a relatively modest grant of £500 was given to the Central Allotments Committee which operated through local allotment societies to provide the unemployed with plots of ground to cultivate and supplies of seed and fertilizers.[92]

In January 1933 the Prince of Wales made an appeal at the Royal Albert Hall for funds to help the unemployed to find a use for their enforced leisure time. A month later, at their first meeting of the year and ahead of the annual round of grant distributions, the trustees took the exceptional step of ordering £5,000 to be placed at the disposal of the National Council of Social Service for allocation to schemes for providing occupational centres for the unemployed in the metropolis. The Council, which had been formed in 1919 to foster co-operation between the various voluntary agencies and between them and the statutory authorities, took a particularly active role in establishing such centres, or unemployed clubs as they came to be known. The Council explained at length how it had spent the grant and was promptly awarded a further £4,000 in 1934 and £3,500 in 1936–7.

The National Council of Social Service was one of the main vehicles used by the government to distribute its aid to the unemployed, on the basis that the voluntary principle behind the establishment of centres or clubs for the unemployed, involving as it did the payment of a small membership subscription, fostered their self-esteem. This policy on the part of the government attracted criticism on the grounds that it concentrated on tackling the effects rather than the causes of unemployment, but there was nothing that voluntary agencies could do about the latter, whereas they could at least assist in mitigating some of the worst consequences of unemployment.[93]

Once the principle had been established, other grants were soon made by the Foundation to help the unemployed, including £5,000 in 1935 to the Land Settlement Association, which had been formed in the previous summer at the direct request of the Ministry of Agriculture to carry out experiments of resettling some of the unemployed on smallholdings. The Association produced a scheme for resettling some forty families from the metropolis, for which it estimated it would need £20,000. The government was prepared to provide £15,000, leaving the rest to be raised by voluntary effort.[94]

It must have come as a disagreeable surprise to an organization which preferred to stay out of the public gaze to find that questions were being asked in the House of Commons in 1933 about its attitude to the unemployed. The reason was that an application for a grant from Toc H for relief work based at All Hallows Church had been turned down. This had annoyed an MP, Major Carver, who demanded an explanation. A ministerial reply, that the trustees had the right to decide how the Foundation's income was to be spent and that they had chosen to make a grant to the National Council of Social Service for the benefit of the unemployed in the metropolis, did not appease the major, who trumpeted that 'London, the greatest city in the World, has handed over its ancient charities, which are intended for the poor, to a committee who are not disposing of them as they should.'[95] It was an outdated expression of an old complaint and could be safely ignored.

In the following year, however, the trustees had to turn down a specific request from the government for aid in setting up hostels in London to house young people from the depressed areas who were being encouraged to migrate to the capital where more work was available. After holding a special meeting, they decided that they could not comply with the request because the government's scheme was designed to assist the poor of other areas rather than the poor inhabitants of the metropolis. It was a fine point, but the trustees were determined to adhere to the letter of their statutory powers and duties as they interpreted them.[96]

In 1935, a second sub-committee reviewed the policy relating to grants. It produced a long and thorough report which was printed as a 'private and confidential' document.[97] The committee, obviously concerned at the new relationship which was emerging between voluntary bodies and statutory agencies in the 1930s, examined at length the various Acts of Parliament which affected the welfare activities supported by the Foundation. Its conclusion was that the Foundation should not support services which could be financed out of the rates or by the Exchequer, except to encourage the development of certain aspects of the work which the trustees particularly wished to promote. Nevertheless, it did not recommend that any of the present grants should be discontinued, but focused on certain activities it thought were particularly deserving of support, many of them ones to which the Foundation had only recently begun to give aid. Among these were work among the unemployed and the establishment of community centres on new housing estates. The report also recommended that, whenever possible, funds for district nursing and boys' and girls' clubs should be increased, especially for the training of club leaders. In fact, the report emphasized the 'supreme importance' of the welfare of children and young persons, adding that many social workers 'believe this to be the greatest present need'.

Many of the areas of work which the report singled out as especially worthy of assistance fell into this broad category. Despite the rejection of the plea from the Ministry of Labour to grant-aid hostels for juveniles transferred from other areas, there was now thought to be a more general need for hostels in London for which funds could usefully be employed. Likewise, although the policy for some years had been not to give grants to settlement houses, it was now recognized that they served a similar function in their districts to community centres, and that applications from them should not necessarily be rejected but 'considered on their individual merits'. Similarly, the work of holiday homes and country holiday funds had been given a low priority for many years, but was now thought to be of great value. One new area was what was described as the moral welfare of children, and arose mainly from the recognition in the mid-1930s of a problem which has been receiving a great deal of attention at the present day, namely the sexual abuse of children. Apart from these relatively new concerns – or revived older ones – the report advised that grants should continue to be given to charities for the blind, invalid aid societies, children's play centres, MABYS and the Central Council for the Social Welfare of Girls and Women.

Some effects of this policy were immediately apparent in the grants made in 1935. That for district nursing was increased by £1,000, and besides the £2,800 given for a community centre on the Downham Estate already mentioned, a further £2,000 was made available for the establishment of community centres in Kensington, Paddington and Poplar, while Toynbee Hall was given £4,000 towards the cost of building an extension. In connection with the Foundation's new-found concern for the moral welfare of children, a first-time grant of £250 was made to the Children's Central Rescue Fund, which had been started in 1912 among members and officers of the LCC to help child victims of sexual assault.[98]

In 1936 the grants for boys' and girls' clubs were increased to £1,500 each, besides £1,550 for the clubs at Dagenham, and a further £1,000 was given to the YMCA for boys' clubs in London. In addition the HYELM movement received £2,000 for a hostel at Tufnell Park (attracting a matching sum from the Carnegie Trust). One of the largest grants made in the year was £3,000 for a proposed London Council of Social Service to co-ordinate voluntary services in the capital, especially those concerned with the unemployed.

But what was as striking as any new grants which were given in 1936 was the number of applications which were turned down, even from organizations which had long come to expect assistance, such as the Invalid Children's Aid Association or the Homes for Working Boys. The reason usually given was 'the satisfactory condition of the finances of this Society, and the number of urgent calls which have been made upon the Trustees for the present year'.[99] What this does indicate is that even though more money was becoming available for grants as the Foundation's income increased, this difficult period was also one of very great need.

Yet another sub-committee was appointed in 1937 to draw up a policy for grants 'in view of the possible increase in the available surplus for distribution in the near future', a reference to the changes about to take place on the Packington Estate.[100] The committee's main recommendation was that the non-statutory grants to the polytechnics should be withdrawn, on which the trustees took a firm decision at the end of the year, as has been described in Chapter 7. The report also dealt at length with the new Physical Training and Recreation Act passed in that year which gave powers to both the government and local authorities to assist various services for the young besides those associated directly with physical fitness, including community centres, holiday camps and camping sites, youth organizations and the training of youth leaders.

Although, as the report recognized, in the long term the Act might reduce the need for voluntary support in some of these areas, its immediate effect was to highlight the importance attached by the government to the provision of various services for youth. The most obvious ones were those encouraging the pursuit of physical fitness, a matter in which Britain's potential enemies, Germany and Italy, were making great strides, and to which the government had devoted its own national fitness campaign in the previous year. This was a major consideration behind the Foundation's own policy of providing gymnasia, swimming pools, playing fields, camping grounds and other facilities for recreation, which became a very important adjunct of its support for youth organizations throughout the 1930s. Probably of no less importance at this time, however, was the role played by youth organizations in what one observer has called 'social ambulance work', that is, the efforts to combat the incidence of juvenile delinquency and the rootlessness of unemployed youth.[101]

Thus, far from advocating the cessation of grants for those activities on which the Act focused, the committee, if anything, thought that aid should be stepped up, particularly for youth organizations, community centres, and the training of 'leaders in social service work'. Other recommendations were that the new London Council of Social Services should continue to be supported, and, on a procedural point, that a Grants Sub-Committee of the Finance and General Purposes Committee should be appointed.

The distribution of grants in the three years up to the outbreak of the Second World War firmly reflected the priorities of the moment. Apart from district nursing, which continued to receive substantial amounts totalling over £14,000 in the course of the three years, and Toynbee Hall, which was given £6,000 towards its building fund, the largest sums were reserved for youth organizations and community centres. Grants to boys' and girls' clubs, including those to individual clubs and national and local organizations, totalled over £30,000 (equivalent to nearly £1 million at 1990 values) and ones for community and social centres over £15,000. Some grants were made either because an additional sum had been promised by the National Fitness Council, which had been set up under the Physical Training and Recreation Act, or on condition that a grant was also made by that body. In line with the recommendations of the sub-committee, the London Council of Social Service was also particularly well supported, with grants in excess of £6,000 over the three years. There was, of course, also a multitude of smaller grants to various organizations.[102]

It is instructive to compare the number of grants which were made at various dates. In 1899 'miscellaneous' grants totalling £2,250 were made to 11 organizations out of 28 which applied. In 1929, 22 grants were made totalling £6,685, and only six applicants were rejected. By 1939, £25,000 was available for miscellaneous grants, and out of 64 applicants 44 were approved and given sums varying between £4,800 (for district nursing) and £25.[103]

NOTES

1. Minutes, III, 151–3: Guildhall Library, MS. 7230, 144–58: *PP*, 1909, XL, *Royal Commission on the Poor Laws and the Relief of Distress, Appendix, vol. III, Minutes of Evidence*, q. 30936 (3–4).
2. Minutes, II, 2–3.
3. Ibid., III, 151–3.
4. Ibid., V, 3.
5. Ronald V. Sires, 'The Beginnings of British Legislation for Old-Age Pensions' in *The Journal of Economic History* (U.S.), XIV (1954), 229–53: Doreen Collins, 'The Introduction of Old Age Pensions in Great Britain' in *The Historical Journal*, VIII (1965), 246–59: David Owen, *English Philanthropy 1660–1960* (1965), 244–5, 505–10: Bentley B. Gilbert, *The Evolution of National Insurance in Great Britain: The Origins of the Welfare State* (1966), 159–232: James H. Treble, *Urban Poverty in Great Britain 1830–1914* (1979), 102–10.
6. *PP*, 1895, XIV, *Report of the Royal Commission on the Aged Poor, Minutes of Evidence*, qq. 7642–7818.
7. Ibid., pp. li, lxxxiii.
8. *PP*, 1895, XXVI, *Forty-Second Report of the Charity Commissioners for England and Wales*, 42.
9. Minutes, V, 62–3; VI, 22–4.
10. Ibid., IX, 27–8; X, 3, 28, 60–3, 109.
11. Ibid., X, 127–70.
12. *RC on the Poor Laws, Appendix, vol. III, Minutes of Evidence*, qq. 30936–31063.
13. Sires, op. cit., 252 and n.: Collins, op. cit., 258: Sir Arnold Wilson and G. S. Mackay, *Old Age Pensions: An Historical and Critical Study* (1941), 46: Derek Fraser, *The Evolution of the British Welfare State: A History of Social Policy since the Industrial Revolution* (2nd ed., 1984), 150–4, 154n.
14. Minutes, XVIII, 120, 143.
15. Ibid., XIX, 97.
16. Ibid., XIX, 77–80, 86–91.
17. Ibid., XXI, 26; XXVI, 52–3.
18. Ibid., XXV, 136.
19. Ibid., XXVII, 110, 138; XXX, 141: Wilson and Mackay, op. cit., 50, 57–9.
20. Minutes, XLIV, 2, 10, 190.
21. Wilson and Mackay, op. cit., 93–115, 207, 215: Fraser, op. cit., 204: Bentley B. Gilbert, *British Social Policy 1914–1939* (1976), 235–54.

22. Minutes, XLV, 5–9, 50, 181–3, 201.
23. Ibid., XLV, 225–6, 245–59.
24. Ibid., XLVI, 7–84, 126–73.
25. Ibid., XLVI, 298; XLVIII, 59–60; XLIX, 75–6.
26. Ibid., XLIX, 204: Wilson and Mackay, op. cit., 207.
27. CPF, *Report on Policy Relating to Grants* (1935), 8.
28. Minutes, II, 16, 69, 89, 159; III, 13.
29. Ibid., IV, 113.
30. CPF, *Second Report submitted to the Central Governing Body* (1927), 49.
31. H. L. Malchow, 'Public Gardens and Social Action in Late Victorian London' in *Victorian Studies*, XXIX (1985–6), 97–124.
32. Minutes, III, 13, 50; IV, 149; V, 11.
33. Ibid., XV, 131.
34. *Second Report, ut supra*, 50.
35. Ibid., 39: Minutes, XIX, 121, 151.
36. Minutes, XXIX, 76.
37. Ibid., XLII, 124, 162; XLV, 190, 195–6, 210; XLVI, 331–2; XLVII, 29, 137.
38. Ibid., XLIII, 50–1; XLVI, 331–2; XLVIII, 152, 163–6, 175–6: *A History of the City Parochial Foundation* (1951), 66–7.
39. Minutes, XXXI, 152–5; XXXII, 77–81, 124; XXXIV, 79–88; XXXV, 116; XXXVI, 76–84.
40. Ibid., XL, 63, 153; XLI, 147; XLIII, 32, 80–1; XLIV, 23, 140–1: *History of the City Parochial Foundation*, 66.
41. *Report on Policy relating to Grants* (1935), 14: *Report on Policy Relating to Grants* (1937), 10.
42. Minutes, XLVIII, 87–9; XLIX, 103–7.
43. Ibid., I, 54–5; V, 59; XI, 60.
44. Ibid., II, 68; VII, 56.
45. J. F. C. Harrison, *A History of the Working Men's College 1854–1954* (1954), 103–6: Asa Briggs and Anne Macartney, *Toynbee Hall: The First Hundred Years* (1984), 29–31, 50–1.
46. Minutes, V, 124; VI, 50; XII, 61–70: Briggs and Macartney, op. cit., 51: Harrison, op. cit., 106.
47. Minutes, XXII, 149; XL, 65, 85.
48. Briggs and Macartney, op. cit., 28–33: Minutes, XIII, 72.
49. Minutes, IX, 96.
50. Ibid., IV, 10, 40, 79; V, 59; VI, 10, 49; VIII, 38–44; IX, 96.
51. Ibid., XX, 76–80; XXIII, 88: John Hurt, 'Feeding the hungry schoolchild in the first half of the twentieth century' in *Diet and Health in Modern Britain*, ed. Derek J. Oddy and Derek S. Miller (1985), 178–206: Gilbert, *The Evolution of National Insurance*, 102–17: *The Times*, 11 Dec. 1901, 7.
52. Minutes, XXI, 76–80; XLVI, 222; L, 114: Violent Creech-Jones, 'The Work of Voluntary Social Services among Children before School-leaving Age' in *Voluntary Social Services Since 1918*, ed. Henry A. Mess and Gertrude Williams (1948), 115–16.
53. Minutes, XXIV, 83–8; XLVII, 90.
54. Ibid., XVII, 73; XLVI, 220; XLVIII, 94: R. M. Wrong, 'Some Voluntary Organizations for the Welfare of Children' in *Voluntary Social Services: Their Place in the Modern State*, ed. A. F. C. Bourdillon (1945), 39–40, 49–50.
55. Owen, *English Philanthropy*, 479.
56. Minutes, II, 97, 117; VII, 54–7; XX, 78–80.
57. Ibid., VIII, 31, 91; IX, 98–9; XII, 52, 85; XVIII, 70–4: Frank D. Long, *King*

Edward's Hospital Fund for London: The Story of its Foundation and Achievements 1897–1942 (1942): Owen, op. cit., 487–9: Brian Abel-Smith, *The Hospitals 1800–1948: A Study in Social Administration in England and Wales* (1964), 182–5.

58. Minutes, III, 63; IV, 39; XVIII, 70; XXIV, 83: Charles Loch Mowat, *The Charity Organisation Society 1869–1913: Its Ideas and Work* (1961), 60–1: Gilbert, *Evolution of National Insurance*, 304, 306–8: Owen, op. cit., 232.

59. Mary Stocks, *A Hundred Years of District Nursing* (1960), 25, 45–6: Minutes, III, 40; IV, 79–80; VI, 109–10; VIII, 44; X, 55.

60. Ibid., V, 59; VI, 109–10; XI, 64; XII, 70; XIII, 74: Stocks, op. cit., 42–60, 139.

61. Minutes, XIX, 40.

62. Stocks, op. cit., 64–77: Minutes, XX, 76–80; XXIII, 84–5.

63. Minutes, XXVIII, 77, 137; XXIX, 131; XXXV, 76; XLV, 148–9; XLVI, 275: Stocks, op. cit., 154–7: *History of the Central Council for District Nursing in London 1914–1966* [1966]: London County Council, *A Survey of District Nursing in the Administrative County of London* (1931).

64. Minutes, XLII, 85: Elizabeth Macadam, *The New Philanthropy: A Study of the Relations Between the Statutory and Voluntary Social Services* (1934), 288–9: Constance Braithwaite, *The Voluntary Citizen: An Enquiry into the Place of Philanthropy in the Community* (1938), 199–323: *A History of the City Parochial Foundation* (1951), 74: Stocks, op. cit., 155.

65. Minutes, XXVIII, 137; XLV, 148.

66. Ibid., XVII, 73–6; XX, 78; XXIII, 89–90; XXIV, 83–8.

67. Ibid. XXV, 88–94.

68. G. E. McCleary, *The Early History of Infant Welfare* (1933) and *The Maternity and Child Welfare Movement* (1935): Madeline Rooff, *Voluntary Societies and Social Policy* (1957), 29–75: Jane Lewis, *The Politics of Motherhood: Child and Maternal Welfare in England, 1900–1939* (1980).

69. Minutes, XXIV, 158–60.

70. Ibid., XXV, 162–4; XXVI, 135–7.

71. Ibid., XXVII, 163–4; XXVIII, 137.

72. Ibid., XXVIII, 136; XXIX, 145–6; XXX, 163–4.

73. Ibid., XXVIII, 137, XXXV, 86: Rooff, op. cit., 50–2.

74. Rooff, op. cit., 30, 69: Lewis, op. cit., 100.

75. J. F. Wilson, 'Voluntary Organizations for the Welfare of the Blind' in *Voluntary Social Services*, ed. Bourdillon, 57–72: Rooff, op. cit., 173–250.

76. Minutes, III, 64; VI, 109–10; XXVII, 80–8, 120.

77. Ibid., XXVIII, 77–82; XXXVIII, 75–84: Rooff, op. cit., 178, 188–9.

78. Minutes, XXXVIII, 75–84; XLVI, 227–8.

79. Ibid., IV, 10; XXVII, 80–8; XLVI, 224.

80. Ibid., XXIII, 87–90; XXXI, 80–6; XXXII, 77–81; XLVI, 155.

81. Ibid., III, 90; IX, 96; XXVII, 80–8; XXVIII, 136; XLV, 173; XLIX, 136–7.

82. Ibid., XXXIX, 79–90; XLVI, 236–7, 276–7, 305; XLVII, 191; XLIX, 137.

83. Ibid., XXV, 88–94.

84. Ibid., XXIII, 86–7; XXX, 86–92, 166–9; XXXV, 76–86; XXXIX, 66.

85. Ibid., XXIV, 83–8; XXXIV, 79–88.

86. Ibid., XXXVIII, 75–84.

87. Ibid., XXXIX, 169: Gilbert, *British Social Policy*, 229–35.

88. Minutes, XL, 63–6: Simon Goodenough, *The Greatest Good Fortune: Andrew Carnegie's Gift for Today* (1985), 175.

89. Minutes, XL, 85–92; XLI, 85–96.

90. John Burnett, *A Social History of Housing 1815–1985* (2nd ed., 1986), 234: Andrew

Saint, ' "Spread the People": The LCC's Dispersal Policy, 1889–1965' in *Politics and the People of London: The London County Council 1889–1965*, ed. Andrew Saint (1989), 223–4.

91. Minutes, XLIII, 32, 80–1, 93–108; XLIV, 85–111; XLV, 164–70; XLVI, 229.
92. Ibid., XLII, 174.
93. Ibid., XLIII, 32–3; XLIV, 25–6, 141–2; XLV, 234–5; XLVI, 239–40; XLVII, 113–14: Henry A. Mess, 'Social Service with the Unemployed' and John Morgan, 'The National Council of Social Service' in *Voluntary Social Services Since 1918*, ed. Mess and Williams, 40–54, 88–9: A. F. C. Bourdillon, 'Voluntary Organizations to Facilitate Co-operation and Co-ordination' in *Voluntary Social Services*, ed. Bourdillon, 179–91.
94. Minutes, XLV, 173–4; XLVI, 305–6.
95. Ibid., XLIII, 150.
96. Ibid., XLIV, 180, 194–5.
97. *Report on Policy Relating to Grants* (1935).
98. Minutes, XLV, 147–77.
99. Ibid., XLVI, 198–9, 215–44, 276–7, 281–2.
100. *Report on Policy Relating to Grants* (1937).
101. Pearl Jephcott, 'Work among Boys and Girls' in *Voluntary Social Services since 1918*, ed. Mess and Williams, 131–2, 136–7: P. F. Beard, 'Voluntary Youth Organizations' in *Voluntary Social Services*, ed. Bourdillon, 139–40, 148.
102. Minutes, XLVII, 28, 95–125, 193; XLVIII, 29, 31, 72–4, 89–127, 166–8; XLIX, 107–45.
103. Ibid., IX, 38–40, 96; XXXIX, 79–90, 161–9; XLIX, 107–45.

9 The City Church Fund

The management of the City Church Fund was always intended to be a largely independent part of the work of the Foundation. The Charity Commissioners had indeed envisaged that once the difficult task of dividing property between the Central and City Church Funds had been completed, a separate body with its own trustees might be constituted to administer the City Church Fund. In such an event, the two members of the Central Governing Body nominated by the Ecclesiastical Commissioners were to be replaced by ones appointed by the School Board for London. Ironically, however, while the Foundation has continued to exercise responsibility for the City Church Fund down to the present day, and two nominees of the Church Commissioners as successors to the Ecclesiastical Commissioners continue to sit on the Central Governing Body, the London School Board itself met with an early demise in 1904.

Nevertheless, the trustees' role in relationship to the Fund has remained very largely a passive one; they look after its assets, and husband its resources, but have very little say in how the income is spent. The Central Scheme stipulated that after certain annual payments had been made any surplus should be handed over to the Ecclesiastical Commissioners for application by them to the purposes specified in the 1883 Act. Most of the payments were mandatory. These consisted of £4,935 for ten years in repayment of the sums spent out of capital in carrying out essential repairs to the City churches; £4,475 to some forty named individuals, mostly incumbent rectors and vicars, during their tenure of office, in compensation for vested interests; and about £16,000 (equivalent at 1990 values to some £800,000) for the maintenance, repairs and general upkeep of the fabric of the churches and for the costs of services, according to a schedule attached to the Central Scheme.[1] There were 48 parish churches named in the schedule. Excluded were the churches of the five parishes which had kept their own endowments and had not contributed to the City Church Fund, and additionally St Bartholomew-the-Less, which served as a chapel to St Bartholomew's Hospital, St Benet, Paul's Wharf, which had been used by Welsh Episcopalians since 1879 and had ceased to be parochial, and All Hallows, London Wall, for reasons which are not now apparent.

Besides having to make these mandatory grants, the trustees were given the discretionary power to continue to make any payments to a minister or lecturer appointed since the passing of the 1883 Act which they had received from parochial charities (of which there were in fact just two), and to pay certain specified sums to the future ministers of 13 churches and the holder of the Campden lectureship at St Lawrence Jewry. These were the only payments over which the trustees had any choice, and they exercised it to the full.

The annual grants which were to be made for the maintenance of the fabric and services of the City churches had been very carefully assessed by the Ecclesiastical Commissioners' architect, Ewan Christian (for the fabric) and by a committee headed by the Archdeacon of London (for the services). By the terms of the Central Scheme, however, if, within two years, these sums were found to be insufficient, the Charity Commissioners could authorize an increase, provided the new total did not exceed the amount the church would have received from its old ecclesiastical charities, except in the cases of churches 'of historical or architectural interest not possessed of sufficient funds for the maintenance of their fabric and ornaments'. This important concession had been allowed by a clause which Bryce, acting largely out of his own personal interests, had managed to insert in the 1883 Act (see page 45). Two supplementary orders were indeed issued by the Charity Commissioners in 1893 raising the amounts payable for the upkeep of the fabric of St Stephen, Coleman Street, and St Bartholomew-the-Great, and in the latter case the sum was higher than it would normally have been because the church was considered to be of historical and architectural interest.[2]

The Pension Committee, to which the business of the City Church Fund was delegated, soon found the restrictions on its freedom of action to be irksome. Its chairman, Edwin Freshfield, was a forceful personality, who was not content to accept a role which he described as 'merely perfunctory', and he was soon asking for more discretion to be allowed to the trustees in the matter of allocating money for repairs.[3] When the first opportunity to exercise any degree of choice occurred he accepted it with alacrity and submitted a long report to the Central Governing Body. The occasion was the appointment of a new minister at St Mary Abchurch in 1893. This was one of the thirteen churches where the trustees were empowered to continue to make allowances (in this case up to £180 per annum) when the living changed hands. Freshfield recommended that the new incumbent should continue to receive the full amount provided he lived in the rectory house and did not let it, on the grounds that:

> The church is one of the most interesting specimens of the church architecture of Sir Christopher Wren, and is one of those which is not likely will be pulled down. The Committee consider that as there must be a Rector of the parish, it is proper that he should be put into such a position that he can reasonably be expected to live in the parish and to discharge his duty.[4]

Freshfield was seeking to establish a principle that when the trustees had the option of continuing to make payments they should do so if they could thereby encourage the new ministers to live in the parishes concerned. As a City man through and through, he was not particularly anxious to make savings which would merely be handed over to the Ecclesiastical Commissioners. In most cases, however, there was no such choice. When an incumbent died or resigned, the payments he received ceased and the sum was added to the annual surplus.

If the sum total of the allowances made to individual ministers was bound to diminish, however, the grants made for the fabric and services were fixed by the Central Scheme and would only change if benefices were united and churches demolished. In 1897 the Pension Committee made another attempt to exert some influence over the situation, claiming that it was by no means satisfied that all the payments were justified. It pointed out to the Charity Commissioners that some churches were closed for long periods and could hardly be said to be maintaining the requisite degree of public worship. The Commissioners acknowledged that there was a problem and issued an amending scheme in 1899 which gave them the power to modify or discontinue payments to any church which had been closed for six months, and to suspend or reduce any other payments upon representation from the Central Governing Body, provided both the Bishop and Archdeacon of London gave their consent.[5] It was at least a partial victory in Freshfield's campaign to give the trustees more say in how money was allocated to the City churches.

Meanwhile, Freshfield's policy on the continuance of payments to new ministers was being scrupulously implemented. By 1899, when he made a progress report to the Central Governing Body, two applications had been turned down because of non-residence in the parish, and an allowance to the new rector of St Mary-at-Hill had been initially approved but subsequently withdrawn for the same reason. There had also been a saving of about £650 in the grants made to churches through the union of benefices, and some £1,400 as ministers had died or resigned.[6] Freshfield had also been able to persuade the Charity Commissioners to adopt some flexibility in the administration of the fixed payments by agreeing to authorize a loan of £3,000 to St Augustine, Watling Street, provided the money was repaid over 30 years out of the annual grants.[7]

The main duty of the trustees as far as the City Church Fund was concerned was to manage the property which belonged to the Fund and maximize the surplus payable to the Ecclesiastical Commissioners at the end of each year. This task was principally undertaken by the Estate Committee and has been described in Chapter 6. As we have seen, at first much of the property of the Central and City Church Funds was intermingled, and it was not until the process known as 'severance' had been completed in 1898 that the assets of the two Funds could be properly separated. At this point a decision had to be taken whether the Foundation should be relieved of its responsibility for the City Church Fund and a new body set up for the latter.

As the use of the term 'severance' indicates, this was a distinct possibility, but as early as March 1897 Freshfield had moved a resolution at a meeting of the Central Governing Body, seconded by the Dean of St Paul's, pointing out that the Charity Commissioners were not obliged to follow this course of action and urging them not to do so. He argued that, as the trustees and their staff had acquired considerable experience in managing the Fund's property, citing in particular the exceptional aptitude of Sir Owen Roberts and C. T. Harris, as chairman and vice-chairman of the Estate Committee, and as the costs of management were low, it would not be in the public interest to create a separate body. The resolution was passed unanimously, and the Charity Commissioners were duly convinced.[8]

The surplus income which was paid over to the Ecclesiastical Commissioners rose, with minor fluctuations, over the years, not so much at first because of any substantial increase from rents and dividends, but more as a consequence of a diminution in the payments out. In 1893 it was a little over £4,000, in 1895 £8,000, and in 1900, after severance, £12,500.[9]

Under the terms of the 1883 Act the surplus was to be applied by the Ecclesiastical Commissioners:

to the maintenance of the fabric of churches or the better endowment of existing benefices or for giving theological instruction to persons preparing for holy orders or generally to extending the benefit of clerical or spiritual ministrations in accordance with the doctrines or by the Ministers of the Church of England as by law established in the more populous districts of the Metropolis.

From 1897 the annual reports of the Ecclesiastical Commissioners contained details of how the money had been used. An appendix to that year's report listed all the grants given up to and including 1896, showing that 126 churches had been aided, mostly with money for repairs, but also with amounts for the acquisition of sites and the erection of new churches, which was probably contrary to the spirit, if not the letter, of the 1883 Act. The report for 1900 likewise showed that 53 churches had been assisted in the previous year, mostly again with grants for repairs, but sometimes with sums towards the cost of sites for mission halls, parish rooms and new churches.[10]

In 1902 questions were asked in Parliament about the use of some of the funds to rebuild denominational schools in Southwark, and the Reverend Robert Henry Hadden, the vicar of St Mark's, North Audley Street, who, as a trustee, considered that he had a particular responsibility to see that the Commissioners adhered to the terms of the Act, wrote a letter of complaint in the same vein to *The Times*. The official response, however, was that the Commissioners had been given a wide discretion in how they applied the funds made over to them, and thereafter it was assumed that they had a virtual *carte blanche* to use the money as they wished.[11]

Toward the end of 1902 Freshfield suddenly resigned from the Central Governing Body. He had increasingly found himself at odds with some of his colleagues over a number of matters. Wanting more pensions to be made available to those who lived or worked in the City, he had seemed to some of the trustees to be less than enthusiastic about introducing the new pension scheme; he was unhappy about the use of the capital of the City Church Fund to provide loans to the polytechnics; and, as a final straw, a decision had been taken in October of that year, in a meeting at which he was not present, to seek a union of benefices which would enable All Hallows, Lombard Street, to be demolished, thereby making its site available for a highly advantageous property transaction which would be of considerable long-term benefit to the City Church Fund. Sir Owen Roberts had drawn the attention of the trustees to the opportunity, which had occurred as a result of the death of the late rector, but it was Hadden, in his self-appointed role as guardian of the ecclesiastical interests of the wider metropolis, who pressed the matter strongly. Hadden had recently resigned as a member of Freshfield's committee and there was clearly some animus between them. Before the end of the year, having resigned his trusteeship, Freshfield was presiding at a meeting of the

City Churches Preservation Society, convened specially to oppose the Foundation's desire to demolish All Hallows.[12]

All Hallows, Lombard Street, was a Wren church, and a spirited public defence of it was mounted. In this instance, at least, the architectural interest of the church counted for less with the trustees than the value of its site, but short of a special Act of Parliament, the consent of its parishioners was needed to achieve the necessary union of benefices, and this was not forthcoming. The respite for the church lasted until 1938 when it was demolished for the rebuilding of Barclay's Bank, with far less opposition than had been aroused in 1902–3.[13]

The new chairman of the Pension Committee, William Hayes Fisher, had no ties to the City and was determined that as much money as possible should go to poorer parishes in greater London. Hadden, who, on Freshfield's departure, rejoined the committee as its vice-chairman, was of like mind, despite having previously held livings in the City. One of Fisher's first acts was to seek a meeting with the Bishop of London and the Archdeacon of London to see whether there was any scope for changes in the allowances made to the City churches. In 1905 he reported on the results of his discussions and of some studies which had been carried out in the meantime. These showed that while payments had been suspended to only one church, which had been closed for over a year, under the amending scheme of 1899, a number of churches had such small attendances at services that the continuance of their payments should be 'seriously reconsidered'. A league table of the worst examples was produced for the benefit of the Central Governing Body. Top of the list, once again, was St Mildred, Bread Street, where the average size of congregation was 16, all of them church or parish officials, but there were another six with average attendances of under 30. Between them they received grants totalling £2,500.

The Bishop and Archdeacon had informed Fisher that a number of amalgamations of benefices had been recommended, only to be thwarted by parishioners using their right of veto. They all agreed that where this happened, the trustees should take the initiative by asking the Charity Commissioners to reduce or stop the annual payments concerned, and the Central Governing Body endorsed this stance. Fisher was at pains to point out that he was not seeking to penalize those churches with active incumbents who held well-attended lunchtime services on weekdays and whose allowances were fully justified.[14]

The best of intentions, however, came to naught against the effective obstructionism of the City vestries, and the only effective way of making savings proved to be the adoption of a more rigorous attitude to the continuation of discretionary allowances to new ministers once the mandatory payments had come to an end. In 1911, when the incumbent of St Clement Eastcheap died, the trustees decided not to exercise the power to pay his successor £235 per annum, in view of the relatively prosperous state of the benefice as measured against the requirements of the parish and the desirability of increasing the surplus payable to the Ecclesiastical Commissioners. Attempts to persuade them to change their mind failed.[15] Over the next two years, discretionary payments were withdrawn from three more churches, producing a saving of £287 per annum. In the case of St Mary Abchurch, the new rector pleaded that his church was of historical and architectural interest (as Freshfield had earlier acknowledged) and that the grant for the maintenance of its fabric was insufficient; he even offered to devote the money he had received as a testimonial on leaving his former office to the interior decoration of the church, but to no avail. Only if he agreed to live in the parish, he was told, would the situation be reconsidered.[16] In the meantime the surplus paid over to the Ecclesiastical Commissioners rose steadily, if not spectacularly, from £18,846 in 1903 (once the last instalment of the capital sum spent on repairs had been repaid) to £22,956 in 1910, and £26,467 in 1920, the year of Fisher's death.[17]

In 1920 the report of the latest commission on the City churches under the chairmanship of Lord Phillimore was published. Its recommendations, which included the demolition of 19 churches, were more drastic than those of any preceding commission. One of its members was the ubiquitous Sir William Collins, although he was not appointed to represent the Foundation. He dissented from some of the findings on the grounds that he considered two or three at least of the threatened churches to be of sufficient architectural or historic interest to be worthy of preservation, and he was concerned that the commission's recommendation, that any savings created by the demolition of churches should go to the Central Board of Finance of the Church of England, would give increased authority to yet another fund-raising and distributing body in addition to the City Churches Fund and the Ecclesiastical Commissioners. The report also recommended that more flexibility should be given to the Foundation to determine what grants should be made to the City churches, and with this, of course, he was in entire agreement. But in this, as in its main recommendations, the Phillimore Commission, like its predecessors, actually accomplished very little.[18]

Nevertheless, the payments to the churches remained a live issue. In 1921 a question was asked in the House of Commons about the sums provided and whether they were properly accounted for, and in the following year the trustees enquired whether any changes should be made. The Pension Committee, by now under the chairmanship of C. J. Drummond, who had a number of connections with the City, reminded them that the payments were fixed, and advised against seeking an amending scheme on the grounds that the Charity Commissioners still had the option of removing the City Church Fund from the trustees' jurisdiction and might just do so if they were asked to consider an amending scheme.[19]

In fact, the whole situation had changed since pre-war days. In the first place, a substantial rise in rent on the rebuilding of property belonging to the City Church Fund in King William Street had boosted the surplus of the fund by nearly £10,000. At the same time the effects of inflation and the age of the fabric of most of the churches were pushing up the cost of repairs. So, while severe doubts remained about whether any payments at all should be made to a handful of churches, the question no longer seemed to be whether too much was being made over to the generality of City churches, but rather whether it was sufficient to meet their needs. From 1919 onwards a number of appeals were made for an increase in the grants made, but the trustees were powerless to vary the amounts, although they sanctioned loans to St Stephen Walbrook, and All Hallows, Barking, for urgent repairs, on the security of the annual payments.[20]

In 1929, when a number of churches pressed the matter, advice was sought from the Charity Commissioners. The Phillimore Commission had recommended that any savings made in the church allowances through the implementation of its proposals for the demolition of several churches should be applied firstly to the maintenance and repair of the remaining City churches, and although the actual savings had been negligible, the recommendation still lay on the table. The Charity Commissioners were not unsympathetic but pointed out once again that to vary the amounts would need parliamentary approval of an amending scheme. They suggested instead that the Ecclesiastical Commissioners might be persuaded to set aside an annual sum out of the surplus they received for this purpose.[21]

Protracted negotiations followed, the successful outcome of which was undoubtedly aided by yet another windfall for the City Church Fund when Barclay's Bank agreed in 1931 to pay £200,000 for properties in Lombard Street to facilitate the rebuilding of its premises. In the following year, the Ecclesiastical Commissioners congratulated Donald Allen on the part he had played in concluding such an advantageous transaction, and shortly afterwards agreed to make £5,000 per annum available for a period of five years out of the surplus revenue of the City Church Fund for repairs to City churches, the individual grants to be made on the recommendation of the Bishop of London. In 1937 they agreed to extend the scheme for a further five years.[22]

Because the whole issue of payments to the City churches had been raised in such a fundamental manner, the trustees considered that they were under an obligation to enquire whether satisfactory arrangements were being made for worship at these churches which were proving so expensive to maintain. Accordingly, in 1932 a questionnaire was sent to the incumbents asking for details of the services and other activities taking place in their churches and how long they were open. Most of the replies were satisfactory, but in the case of seven churches, including, not surprisingly, St Mildred, Bread Street, the trustees questioned whether, on the information supplied, the continuation of payments was justified. The Charity Commissioners were asked to take appropriate action, but their response was perhaps predictable. Having consulted the Archdeacon of London, who said that he would take steps to ensure that the ministers were more active and the churches kept open longer, the Commissioners decided that, 'although the Trustees were fully justified in bringing the facts before the Commissioners . . . it might not be in the best interests of the Church in the City to pursue the matter further at present and that it would be better to let it rest for a time in the hope that more will be done in the future.'[23] Nothing in fact was done until the advent of war, when the catastrophic bombing of the City of London changed the whole situation.

The last of the mandatory payments to named ministers ceased in 1922, and by 1939 the discretionary allowances to incumbents sanctioned by the Central Scheme had been reduced to £635. Of the 48 churches which had been named in the Central Scheme, nine had been demolished since 1891, and the payments for the maintenance of the fabric and services of the remaining 39 now added up to £14,657 (some £1,500 less than in 1891). Meanwhile, as the careful management of the property and investments of the City Church Fund bore increasing fruit, the surplus paid over to the Ecclesiastical Commissioners rose from £35,604 in 1921 (when the much-enhanced rents from the rebuilt properties in King William Street were first added) to £48,894 by 1939.[24]

NOTES

1. CPF, *First Report of the Central Governing Body* (1900), 10.
2. Supplemental Orders to the Central Scheme dated 26 May and 29 September 1893.
3. Minutes, V, 4–5.
4. Ibid., III, 80–3.
5. Ibid., VII, 77; VIII, 31: Amending Scheme of 3 March 1899.
6. Minutes, IX, 88–92: *First Report, ut supra*, 10.
7. Minutes, VII, 24–5; VIII, 92.
8. Ibid., VII, 44–5.

9. *First Report, ut supra*, 10: *Second Report submitted to the Central Governing Body* (1927), 45.
10. *PP*, 1897, XXIV, *Forty-ninth Report from the Ecclesiastical Commissioners for England*, 83–7: *PP*, 1900, XVIII, *Fifty-second Report . . .* , 93–5.
11. *The Times*, 14, 18 Nov. 1902.
12. Minutes, XII, 120, 122, 133–4: *City Press*, 13 Dec. 1902.
13. Press cuttings book in possession of Foundation.
14. Minutes, XIII, 76, 139; XV, 98–101.
15. Ibid., XXI, 9, 84.
16. Ibid., XXII, 8, 89, 123–4; XXIII, 8, 110.
17. *Second Report, ut supra*, 45.
18. Minutes, XXX, 115–17: *Report of the City of London Churches Commission 1919* (1920): *The Times*, 7, 13, 14, 17 May 1920.
19. Minutes, XXXI, 10; XXXII, 117.
20. Ibid., XXXI, 45–6, 127–8; XXXII, 67, 71; XXXIX, 161.
21. Ibid., XXXIX, 178–9: *A History of the City Parochial Foundation* (1951), 39–40.
22. Minutes, XLI, 135; XLII, 71, 116; XLVII, 131.
23. Ibid., XLIII, 113–14, 215: *History of the Foundation*, 41–4.
24. Minutes, XXXII, 8; XLIX, 16; L, 73.

Part III
The Foundation 1939–1991:
The emergence of the Welfare State

10 Trustees and administration

The outbreak of the Second World War led to the introduction of new ways of conducting the Foundation's business. That was only to be expected. What is more surprising is that the system which was created in response to the conditions of wartime has survived basically intact to the present day, although overladen in recent years with additional structures designed to cater for the vast expansion in the work of the Foundation and the wish of trustees to be more actively involved.

Since 1891 meetings of the Central Governing Body had been regularly held on a Monday, and under the Foundation's own standing orders the committees were required to meet beforehand, the Pension and Finance and General Purposes Committees at least ten days and the Estate Committee six days before the ordinary meetings of the Central Governing Body. This was so that the reports of the committees could be circulated and digested by all the trustees in advance of their meetings. After the declaration of war, the next meeting of the Central Governing Body, in October 1939, was switched to a Friday, and this remained the favoured day right up to the present time. Moreover, such was the difficulty of travelling that the meetings of the main committees were scheduled for the same day, prior to that of the Central Governing Body, and this, too, has continued to be the common practice.

There was nothing in these arrangements that was contrary to the Central Scheme, but the position was not regularized until 1943 when the standing orders were amended to take account of the changes. At the same time a new standing order was adopted allowing any member of the Central Governing Body to attend a committee meeting and to have the right to speak, by leave of the chairman, but not to vote. This was to take care of the awkward situation that had arisen whereby trustees were present to attend meetings of the Central Governing Body and any committee to which they had been appointed, but were technically not entitled to take part in the deliberations of other committees.[1]

What was contrary to the Central Scheme, however, was that from 1940 onwards only five ordinary meetings of the Central Governing Body were held each year instead of the required six. The Charity Commissioners had agreed that, in the exceptional circumstances then prevailing, the last meeting scheduled in 1940 should not be held, but the practice continued after the war, and it was not until 1957 that an order was obtained from the Charity Commissioners authorizing this departure from the Central Scheme 'for the time being'. By 1965 even five full meetings a year had come to seem too many, and the Commissioners were asked to sanction just four. Accordingly, they issued a new scheme in the following year requiring only four meetings to be held each year, one in each period of three months.[2]

In practice, although this arrangement helped to ensure that there was a high turn out at meetings, it meant that when the trustees gathered together as a body they had a great deal of business to go through in a short amount of time. There was little opportunity for extended debate on any issue. One result was to give greater prominence to the role of sub-committees, which met separately, and to the handful of trustees who sat on them or held the positions of chairman or vice-chairman of the main committees, frequently one and the same persons.

In terms of seniority and the far-reaching effects of their deliberations, the foremost of these sub-committees were those appointed approximately every five years to determine the policy on grants for the next quinquennium. After the war, these were usually presided over by the Chairman of the Central Governing Body, the only exceptions being in 1971 and 1976, when Lord Cottesloe, the Vice-Chairman, took the chair. The policies decided upon by these committees are discussed in Chapters 13 and 14.

The most important of the standing sub-committees was the Grants Sub-Committee whose formation was recommended by the policy review committee of 1937 and which first met in 1938. The intention was that the main meeting of the sub-committee would be held before the special meeting of the Central Governing Body which was summoned in the spring to allocate grants, but that it would also meet at other times to consider additional applications. Understandably, during the war its activities were generally confined to the spring meeting, and, indeed, in 1943 the practice of holding a special meeting of the Central Governing Body to consider grants was abandoned and never revived. Thereafter, for many years, it was understood that the main business of the trustees' second meeting of the year would be to allocate grants.

With the revival in grant-making activity after the war, the Grants Sub-Committee began to meet more frequently, usually about ten days before each meeting of the Central Governing Body (or technically the Finance and General Purposes Committee to which it reported), although primacy was still given to the second meeting. In 1966, when the number of full meetings each year was reduced to four, an attempt was made to systematize matters by decreeing that the sub-committee would normally meet twice a year, and in between times only if it was necessary to consider emergency applications. Within a very short time, however, it was found necessary to hold another meeting before the regular July meeting of trustees. This pattern persisted until 1987, when, with the considerable increase in requests for aid, new procedures were devised by which another meeting of the Grants Sub-Committee was convened before the first main meeting of the year and the work on grants was spread evenly throughout the year.[3]

The composition of the Grants Sub-Committee was generally kept to between seven and ten persons, including the Chairman and Vice-Chairman of the Central Governing Body (who were ex-officio members of all committees) and the Chairman of the Finance and General Purposes Committee, who was always a member. The chairman of this very important and influential sub-committee, whose recommendations were very rarely questioned, was always a senior trustee but not at first the holder of any particular position. Indeed, during the war years the chairmanship frequently changed hands, but from 1946 to 1959 it was held by Charles Robertson, who, in 1949, was also elected chairman of the Finance and General Purposes Committee. When he stepped down on account of advancing years in 1959, his place was taken by Sir Arthur Howard, the Chairman of the Central Governing Body, and from that time henceforward the chairmanship of the sub-committee was always held by the Chairman of the Foundation.

Other sub-committees were appointed from time to time. An Emergency Sub-Committee, chaired by Sir William Collins, met during the war, largely it appears to consider abnormal requests for assistance which were specifically related to wartime conditions. Towards the end of the war a sub-committee of the Estate Committee was appointed to look into the problems of post-war reconstruction, and another to plan for the reintegration of staff who had been on active service. The only one that took on the stature of a standing committee, reappointed each year, was the Investment Sub-Committee which first met in 1947 with Robertson again as chairman. Originally it reported to the Finance and General Purposes Committee, but in 1973 its terms of reference were changed so that henceforth it would report to the Estate Committee and all its members would be drawn from that committee.[4] Its work is described in Chapter 11.

Among the trustees who made particularly significant contributions to the work of the Foundation in the years since 1939, pride of place must be given to the Chairmen of the Foundation. Peter MacIntyre Evans remained Chairman throughout most of the war, until his death on 21 October 1944. Walter Prideaux, who had been his Vice-Chairman since 1935, referred, in a glowing tribute, to the unforgettable impression made by 'the great ability, wide experience, sound judgment and understanding spirit which he brought to the deliberations of the Trustees or the devotion which he showed to the work here and the welfare of those for whose benefit this Body exists'.[5]

Prideaux himself was immediately elected to fill the vacancy. Walter Treverbian Prideaux was a solicitor and had been Clerk of the Goldsmiths' Company from 1919 to 1939. He came from a distinguished family which had long associations with the Goldsmiths', his father, Sir Walter Sherburne Prideaux, having also been Clerk and a noted historian of the Company. Walter T. Prideaux had sat on the Central Governing Body since 1926 as the nominee of the City and Guilds of London Institute, and had been chairman of the Pension Committee since 1932 and, as indicated above, Vice-Chairman of the Foundation since 1935. He and the Clerk, Donald Allen, struck up a close and successful working relationship. Prideaux served as Chairman until 1957 when he felt compelled to step down on account of advancing age (he was then 82) and the difficulties of journeying to London. His colleagues were quick to praise his achievements, remarking, *inter alia*, that 'His gracious charm and courtesy had endeared him to them all and the Trustees would be ever grateful for the incalculable benefits derived from his wise guidance.'[6]

Prideaux's successor, Sir Arthur Howard, was appointed to the Central Governing Body by the Crown in 1942 and had been Vice-Chairman since 1945. The son of Baroness Strathcona and married to a daughter of Earl Baldwin (Stanley Baldwin), he brought an air of patrician formality to the proceedings of the Foundation. A tall, upright man, who had served as a captain in the Scots Guards in the First World War (in which he had been awarded the Croix de Guerre), he exuded authority and has been described as a very good chairman of meetings. He also brought with him a wealth of experience in many fields. He was Mayor of Westminster in 1937, a Conservative Member of Parliament from 1945 to 1950, a Justice of the Peace for Sussex and Deputy-Lieutenant for London. Among many other interests, he was Joint Treasurer of St Thomas's Hospital for many years and Chairman of the Teaching Hospitals Association. He, too, collaborated well with successive Clerks, all of whom had also served in the armed forces. He died on 25 April 1971 while still holding the office of Chairman.[7]

On Howard's death, Sir Edward Chadwyck-Healey, who had been his Vice-Chairman since 1957, stepped up to the chairmanship. He had been appointed as a trustee by the Crown at the same time as Howard, but fell victim to the unwritten rule that Crown-appointed trustees should not serve beyond their seventy-fifth birthday, and had to retire from the Central Governing Body at the end of his current six-year term in 1972. He had been an active trustee, firmly supportive of Donald Allen, for instance, in his battle to rid the Foundation of its obligation to the polytechnics. As the Chairman of Charringtons from 1949 to 1959 and President of the London Chamber of Commerce in 1955–7, he also brought considerable business experience to bear, especially on the deliberations of the Estate Committee, on which he sat for many years.[8]

The new Chairman elected at the first meeting of 1972 was Walter Arbuthnot Prideaux, the son of Walter T. Prideaux, whom he had succeeded as the nominee of the City and Guilds of London Institute in 1957. He had previously been chairman of the Finance and General Purposes Committee since 1964. Like his father, Walter A. Prideaux was a solicitor and the Clerk of the Goldsmiths' Company, a post he held from 1953 to 1975. A man of great charm and engaging personality, Walter Prideaux was an excellent Chairman who provided firm direction without ever appearing obtrusive. Increasing deafness led him to step down as Chairman in 1981, when he was described as having brought to the post 'knowledge, experience, expertise and wisdom tempered with courtesy and dignity'; he continued as Vice-Chairman until 1984, when he decided not to seek renomination as a trustee.[9]

John Smallwood, who succeeded Prideaux in 1981, had been Vice-Chairman since 1977, and before that vice-chairman successively of the Pension and Finance and General Purposes Committees. His career had been spent in the Bank of England, where he rose to be Deputy Chief Accountant, but he was also active in Anglican church affairs, becoming a member of the General Synod and a Church Commissioner. Appointed a trustee by the Commissioners in 1969, he was the first of their nominees to be Chairman of the Foundation. During the period of his chairmanship, which has continued to the present day, several quite momentous developments in the history of the Foundation have taken place, some of which are discussed at the end of this chapter, and he has performed a skilful role in guiding the Foundation through these; he has, indeed, been described as a chairman for change.

Most of the trustees who were elected Vice-Chairman of the Central Governing Body eventually became Chairman, but of those who did not, special mention should be made of Lord Cottesloe. First appointed as a trustee by the Crown in 1953, when he was the Honourable John Fremantle, he was a member of the Grants Sub-Committee from 1956 and, as Vice-Chairman of the Foundation from 1971 to 1977, presided over the Quinquennial Policy Sub-Committees of 1971 and 1976. When he retired in 1977 he was praised for 'his very concise and apposite summaries of many of the more difficult matters under discussion, as well as for a quick but often humorous intervention at many a timely moment'.[10] Among many other public positions, he was the first Chairman of the South Bank Board, and the Cottesloe Theatre is named after him.

When Walter Prideaux retired in 1984, Dr Ronald Tress became Vice-Chairman and held the position until his own retirement in 1989. As a former Master of Birkbeck College and Director of the Leverhulme Trust, he brought both sagacity and a wide experience of philanthropy to the trustees' deliberations. His successor was Lady Marre, whose long service to the voluntary sector, including ten years as Chairman of the London Voluntary Service Council (formerly the London Council of Social Service) made her a deeply knowledgeable and highly influential member of the Central Governing Body from the time of her appointment in 1975.

Well over one hundred trustees sat on the Central Governing Body at one time or other in the second half-century of the Foundation's existence, and it is obviously only possible to single out a handful here, although all are listed in Appendix A. Some of the active trustees of the 1930s carried their work over into the war period, such as Sir William Collins, who, after Sir Evan Spicer, was the longest-serving trustee. In 1944 his fellow trustees paid him a special tribute on his completion of 40 years' service, and when he finally resigned in the following year, the minutes record that 'Mr. Prideaux, in a devoted tribute to Sir William's services to the Foundation, stated that he was a very great Londoner and that it was difficult to express adequate appreciation of the benefit which had accrued to the Body by reason of his association with it.'[11]

Herbert Game, who became a trustee in 1932 and was chairman of the Finance and General Purposes Committee from 1935 until his death in 1949, was another of the trustees of high calibre who were appointed by the London County Council. Yet another was Charles Robertson, who was already 60 years old when he was first nominated in 1934 and who finally retired at the age of 90 in 1965, having been persuaded to wait until the London County Council had been superseded by the Greater London Council. In between, he was chairman of the influential Grants Sub-Committee from 1946 to 1959, and of the Finance and General Purposes Committee (in succession to Game) from 1949 to 1959. A 'convinced Socialist', he was chairman of the Education Committee of the LCC from 1937 to 1945 and was one of the main architects of the plan for reorganizing education in London after the war.[12]

The first group of post-war trustees included Sir Cosmo Parkinson, the former Permanent Under-Secretary of State for the Colonies, who was appointed by the Crown. He remained a trustee for 20 years and was vice-chairman of the Finance and General Purposes Committee from 1959 to 1963 and chairman in 1963–4.[13] T. C. Harrowing, a Common Councilman of the City of London, sat on the Central Governing Body as the nominee of the Bishopsgate Foundation from 1947 to 1981. His position as chairman of the Corporation's Public Health Committee greatly facilitated the smooth handover of Isleden House to the Corporation in 1953, and from 1967 until his retirement he was vice-chairman of the Foundation's Estate Committee, to whose proceedings he could bring the benefit of his wide experience of the City.[14]

The tradition of having at least one outstanding churchman on the Central Governing Body was continued in 1944 when the Ecclesiastical Commissioners, as they were then still called, appointed the Reverend Allan John Macdonald Macdonald, the rector of St Dunstan-in-the-West. A noted ecclesiastical historian with many publications to his credit, he was also Rural Dean of the City of London and, from 1950, a prebendary of St Paul's. He chaired the Foundation's Pension Committee, which at that time was still largely responsible for policy matters in connection with the City Church Fund, from 1948 until his death in 1959.[15]

Macdonald's replacement as a trustee was the Venerable O. H. Gibbs-Smith, the Archdeacon of London, and from that time henceforward it became common practice for the Church Commissioners to appoint the current Archdeacon to the Central Governing Body. This was an eminently sensible arrangement as the Archdeacon had a considerable say in the distribution of that proportion of the City Church Fund which went to the City churches (see Chapter 15). An exception occurred when the Very Reverend Martin Sullivan, who, as Archdeacon, had been a trustee since 1963, was appointed Dean of St Paul's in 1967, but remained a member of the Central Governing Body. The Dean always found time for the work of the Foundation, which he greatly admired, and was vice-chairman of the Pension Committee from 1967 to 1972 and then chairman until his retirement as Dean in 1977, when he resigned as a trustee. His place on the Central Governing Body was taken by the Venerable Sam Woodhouse, the Archdeacon of London, thus reverting to what had by now become the normal state of affairs.[16] When Woodhouse retired as Archdeacon in 1978, his place as a trustee was taken by his successor, Frank Harvey, who was an active member of the Central Governing Body with perceptive views on a wide range of issues, until his sadly premature death in 1986. His place as a trustee was taken by the new Archdeacon, George Cassidy, who rapidly made his mark on the Foundation's deliberations, particularly through his pronounced views on the rights and wrongs of the distribution of the income of the City Church Fund.

Other long-serving trustees in the post-war period included Lewis F. Sturge, who was appointed by the LCC in 1950 to replace Herbert Game and continued to be the nominee of the LCC and then the GLC until 1973. He was chairman of the Pension Committee from 1959 to 1972 and chairman of the Finance and General Purposes Committee in 1972–3. Sir Lionel Denny, 'a very distinguished and well-known Londoner', who was Lord Mayor of London in 1965–6, was a nominee of the City Corporation from 1952 to 1977, and sat on the Estate Committee for the whole period and on the Finance and General Purposes Committee from 1968 onwards.[17]

Peter Shaw, who served as the nominee of King's College for 29 years between 1958 and 1987, was one of a number of distinguished academic trustees, whose contributions extended well beyond the world of education. Shaw was successively vice-chairman of the Finance and General Purposes Committee from 1964 to 1975 and chairman from 1975 to 1985. The next chairman of the committee, Lord Henniker, had been appointed as a trustee by the Crown in 1973. He had a strong and enthusiastic commitment to the voluntary sector, with a deep understanding of its workings. His associations with Toynbee Hall and the Wates Foundation, of which he was Director for many years, were invaluable to the Foundation, which benefited considerably from his wise counsel until his retirement in 1990.

The chairmen of the Estate Committee, who carried a special responsibility because of the frequent need to act quickly (in consultation with their professional advisers) in transactions affecting the Foundation's property, generally held the position for long periods. On the death of Sir Edgar Horne in 1941, the chairmanship passed to Francis Allen, a trustee since 1935, who had a wide knowledge of property. When he died in 1945, one of the trustees appointed by the City Corporation, Cyril Turner, took over, and retained the chairmanship until his retirement on account of ill-health in 1967.

The next chairman, Sir John Russell, a barrister, was a well-known figure on the LCC and had been a member of the Central Governing Body on the Council's nomination since 1950. He was vice-chairman to Turner from 1959, and chairman from 1967 to 1977, when he retired at the age of 83. A special tribute, recorded in the minutes, remarked how, 'His great interest, profound knowledge and quick support of the staff and advisers in the day to day administration of the Foundation's considerable estate had resulted in a steadily increasing income to the Foundation for distribution to the many deserving and needy appellants throughout Greater London.'[18] His successor, John Udal, who had been appointed as a trustee by the Greater London Council in 1973, also served as chairman for ten years. During that time he sought consistently to protect the long-term value of the Foundation's endowment at a time of great volatility in the City property market. When he stepped down in 1987, Gerald Manners, Professor of Geography at University College London, who had been one of the principal architects of the diversification policy and vice-chairman of the committee since 1985, was elected chairman.

Of the many other trustees, several held very important positions in other walks of life, sometimes, indeed, to the extent that the time they could devote to the Foundation was limited, but whenever possible they brought their experience to bear on individual issues. A number of them also represented the Foundation on the governing bodies of many of the institutions which received grants, where they performed a very important function in looking after the Foundation's interests and frequently rose to positions of considerable authority in their own right. Some were politicians, but they rarely allowed their political differences to obtrude on the Foundation's business, and as trustees they sought to put the Foundation's interests (or, rather, those of the people it existed to serve) first. As Donald Allen expressed it before the Nathan Committee in 1951, 'It is an extraordinary thing that when the trustees are first appointed they come up representing their appointing body, the London County Council if you like, but within a year they are really representing the City Parochial Foundation on the London County Council.'[19]

We have seen how the concentration of the business of the main committees and the Central Governing Body into five, and subsequently four, days of the year, tended to give particular authority to a small number of trustees. Perhaps more importantly, it gave added power and influence to the Foundation's staff and advisers, and especially the Clerk. It is by no means a coincidence that measures which were introduced as a temporary response to wartime conditions were continued well after the principal reasons for their adoption had ceased to apply, during the tenure of a particularly forceful and dominating, but widely respected, Clerk in the person of Donald Allen. Although he was always punctilious and correct, in seeking the authority of his senior trustees for all that he did, it may not be too much of an exaggeration to characterize the later period of the long clerkship of Allen as an enlightened despotism.

Early in the war he was called up for the reserve, but the War Office was quickly persuaded that his services to the Foundation were far too valuable for him to be spared. Characteristically, however, he agreed to do voluntary work among the troops stationed in Essex at the request of Eastern Command, and, equally characteristically, he sought the trustees' approval first. The circumstances of the time meant that he exercised considerable discretion in such matters as the adjustment of rents, and many of the steps which were undertaken by the Foundation to alleviate wartime suffering were the result of his own first-hand observations of the distress of those whose homes had been bombed. His efforts (and, of course, those of his staff) to keep the office open and the Foundation functioning at the height of the Blitz received the unstinting admiration of the trustees, which was given tangible manifestation by the award of frequent bonuses.[20]

Towards the end of the war, when the prospect opened up of new legislation which would expand the statutory provision of social services, Allen gathered together with the secretaries of the major charitable trusts and others, whom he described as his 'friends in London', to discuss what were likely to emerge as major problems after the war and how best the voluntary sector could help to tackle these. Several of the initiatives which were pursued by the trustees after the war, which are described in Chapter 13, including the building of Isleden House, stemmed from those discussions. The attempt to remove the residual obligations to the polytechnics, which was also a cardinal feature of the trustees' post-war policy, as detailed in Chapter 12, also reflected the determination of Allen to make better use of the money which had to be spent on these compulsory grants.[21]

A recognition of the standing which Allen had achieved in the world of philanthropy occurred in 1950 when he was invited to be a member of the Nathan Committee. This committee, which was appointed by the Prime Minister to inquire into the law and practice relating to charitable trusts, owed its origins to a debate in the House of Lords on the role of the voluntary sector in the Welfare State, which had in turn been stimulated by the publication of Beveridge's book on *Voluntary Action*. Besides its chairman, the lawyer and Labour peer, Lord Nathan, the dozen members of the Committee included B. E. Astbury of the Family Welfare Association, Eileen Younghusband, probably the foremost authority of the day on social work, leading barristers and central and local government officials. Allen more than held his own in this company, and his incisive questioning of witnesses contributed to what was generally acknowledged to be a successful inquiry. He was asked to be a member of the small drafting sub-committee, and large parts of the Nathan Report, which was widely respected, were written or suggested by him. The Report was published late in 1952 and led, belatedly, to the Charities Act of 1960.[22]

Allen did not hesitate to make the Committee aware of some of the matters which concerned him as Clerk of the Foundation, both in his questioning of witnesses, and when he stepped down to give evidence himself. The main issue which rankled with him – the need to continue to give grant-aid to the polytechnics – is covered in Chapter 12, but it is worth remarking here that the chapter in the Nathan Report which deals with the alteration of trusts bears all the hallmarks of his influence.

His own evidence before the Committee, although brief, gives a fascinating insight into the way he ran the Foundation and what he saw as his own role. He considered that there was an optimum size for trusts like the Foundation, because it was important to retain a personal touch. 'To-day,' he explained, 'I know intimately every application which comes before the trust and I know them well, I see their accounts and I go to see their work or as much of it as I can and I do know the applicants.' He was also proud of the low administrative costs and small staff, which numbered only one more than in 1891. This was one reason why he was opposed to publicity, which tended to encourage enquiries from applicants who couldn't be helped and create unnecessary work. As he put it, 'The Trustees, rightly or wrongly, hide their light under a bushel. They like to do good by stealth.' Lord Nathan, who favoured publicity to let others know what work was being done and to prevent any possible duplication, declared himself not to be 'over-impressed by that'.

Allen explained that when the policy committees met, he informed them what budget was likely to be available and suggested ways in which the money should be spent. 'They will have their own ideas and we shall get round the table and decide it' was how he described it. 'What I do is find out the gaps in the social services. I meet my colleagues, we foregather and discuss these matters and find out the gaps in the social services and decide how we are going to meet them.' His 'colleagues' were men like Astbury, Jimmy Mallon of Toynbee Hall, Sir Wyndham Deedes, or government officials and officers of the LCC and Essex County Council, with whom he had close ties as a resident of Snaresbrook. He liked to think that he took an active role, 'working out schemes', rather than simply responding to requests for help, and thought that there was a particular part to play in encouraging local authorities to use the powers they possessed. 'There are plenty of local authorities who have the power to do certain things but are not doing them and they will not do them. Well, we can probably make them do these things.' There was no problem in using the funds available, and he thought that the Foundation could spend double or treble its income with comparative ease, always with the caveat that it must not lose the personal touch or end up with an inflated bureaucracy.[23]

One by-product of Allen's evidence to the Nathan Committee was the private publication in 1951 of a short history of the Foundation, written, of course, by himself. He had provided a memorandum for the Committee and Lord Nathan had expressed a request for such a history. As might be expected, the booklet which Allen produced was an excellent brief summary, but its distribution was for the most part confined to those individuals and bodies which already had dealings with the Foundation, and its preparation was not the result of any change of heart on the subject of publicity.

Allen's was a commanding presence in the Foundation's office. Two years after the publication of the Nathan Report, he was awarded a knighthood in the Birthday Honours List. It was a signal recognition of his qualities and his standing in the wider community of those engaged in philanthropic work. He was then nearly 60, and he agreed to continue as Clerk until he was 65, but it was difficult for him to relinquish the office, and, indeed, difficult for the trustees to let him go. In 1959 they asked him to remain for another two years until he was 67, but when the time came it seemed to be accepted without question that he should continue for a few more years. One factor behind his desire to carry on may have been the wish to see the successful conclusion of his campaign to abolish the scheme grants to the polytechnics, an accomplishment which occurred in 1962.[24]

Finally, in 1963, steps were taken to choose a new Clerk who would take over on Allen's seventieth birthday in August 1964, and, from 40 applicants, George Anthony Carpenter was appointed Clerk Designate. But, as so often happens after a long reign, the succession proved to be fraught with difficulties. In July 1964 Allen stayed away from a meeting of the Central Governing Body for the first time since he had entered the Foundation's service so that Carpenter could act in his place, but within two weeks the Clerk Designate had asked to be released from the appointment and was given permission to apply for another post. A major factor behind his decision appears to have been the awareness that two very long-serving members of the existing staff were finding it difficult to work with him, and with such a small staff this created an impossible situation.[25]

Allen agreed to soldier on, and the post was readvertised. Out of over one hundred enquiries, the field was narrowed to two candidates,

Hugh Anthony Stephen Johnston, the Director of the Overseas Services Resettlement Bureau, and Bryan Hamersley Woods, the Assistant Clerk (to Walter Prideaux) of the Goldsmiths' Company. They were interviewed by the Central Governing Body and Johnston was chosen. 'Tim' Johnston had spent his working life, apart from war service with the Royal Air Force, in the overseas civil service, especially in Nigeria, where he was a much respected figure. On returning to England in 1961 he had headed the Overseas Services Resettlement Bureau, which was set up to seek out re-employment opportunities for those who, like himself, had retired from service overseas. He was appointed Clerk Elect from 1 April 1965, and Allen was finally able to retire on 30 June, after 40 years' service with the Foundation, 35 of them as Clerk.[26]

At the close of business at the last meeting of the Central Governing Body attended by Sir Donald Allen, the Chairman, Sir Arthur Howard, paid him a long and warm tribute. In the following month a dinner was given in his honour at Goldsmiths' Hall, to which most of the leading figures in the world of charity were invited. Howard once more gave the main speech, which his fellow trustees asked to have recorded in the Foundation's minutes. It was a moving occasion, leavened by much humour, but suffused with deep affection and admiration. There was no doubting the genuineness of the sentiments expressed by Howard:

> We of the City Parochial have indeed cause for profound gratitude to Donald Allen. We are grateful for the superb administrative competence of his work. We are no less grateful for the invariable courtesy of the man. Above all we are grateful for his perceptive awareness of the needs of his less fortunate fellow men and his fiercely burning zeal to remove the causes of their inadequacy and, should that prove impossible, at least to mitigate the consequences.

Even in retirement Allen continued to devote his time to the cause of philanthropy and carried out a review of some of the smaller City charities for the Corporation of London. When he died on 24 September 1983 at the age of 89, the obituary that appeared in *The Times* was reprinted in the minutes.[27]

It would be difficult to overemphasize Donald Allen's contribution to the work of the Foundation. For 35 years his was the dominating influence on those activities which are principally described elsewhere in this book. If, from the perspective of the 1990s, questions might be asked whether some of the causes which he championed, boldly innovative as they may have been, should have been given quite such a high priority, no one could doubt the sincerity of his motives. In addition, Allen was the first to acknowledge that there were times when favoured schemes had to be discarded and new ones introduced, for, in terms used by Howard and repeated in Allen's obituary, one of his principal attributes was an awareness of how changing conditions affect the changing needs of the poorer classes.

If Allen's was the longest tenure of the Clerkship, Johnston's was the shortest. Tragically, after barely two and a half years in the post, he died suddenly at the age of 54 on 9 December 1967. At a sombre meeting early in 1968 the trustees deplored their premature loss, remarking how Johnston had 'combined to a rare degree administrative ability of the highest order with a deep and genuine concern for the lot of his less fortunate fellow beings.' They decided not to readvertise the post but to approach Bryan Woods, who had been interviewed with Johnston when the latter was appointed in 1964. He accepted and took up his duties on 1 May 1968.[28]

Bryan Woods, who was 47, had been a Sandhurst-trained career soldier up to 1958, when an attack of polio led him to resign his commission. He was appointed Assistant Clerk of the Goldsmiths' Company in 1962. Although different in personality to Donald Allen, Bryan Woods brought some similar characteristics to his management of the Foundation, in particular a strong personal direction and a determination to familiarize himself with the circumstances of all the applicants, either by seeing them in the Foundation's office, or, when he considered it to be necessary, by paying them visits.

Woods managed the Foundation's affairs from 1968 until his retirement at the age of 65 in 1986. As such he presided over its fortunes at a time of great change and of great pressure on its slender resources. These were the years which in national terms witnessed the transition from a relatively buoyant economy and the growth of welfare services to a situation in which the Welfare State has come under increasing stress and, some would claim, has actually gone into retreat. Both periods posed their problems for the Foundation, but the latter in particular was characterized by the emergence of a host of new needs as society appeared to be becoming increasingly complex. It was, too, a period in which there was a good deal of confusion between the role of the state and that of the voluntary sector. Woods also steered the Foundation through the difficult period leading up to the abolition of the Greater London Council and the concerns produced by that action, leading to the creation of the Trust for London.

Apart from displaying the obvious virtues of flexibility and responsiveness to new situations as they arose, Bryan Woods also brought rigour and consistency to bear on the business of grant-making. Grants were to be made for a purpose – to fund a post or a specific aspect of the work of an applicant – and were not to be swallowed up in general expenditure; financial discipline was to be introduced if it didn't already exist; and if managerial expertise was lacking, a legitimate use of funds was to try to fill the gap. Over-dependence on the Foundation was to be avoided; 'pensioner' applicants were to be discouraged. Conversely, there was always room for risk-taking, for the support of a new and untried venture. In fact, in the opinion of those who worked with him, Bryan Woods was exceptionally adept in assessing what was likely to succeed and what not, and in ensuring that the Foundation's funds had been properly spent. There were remarkably few outright failures.

Woods's successor, Timothy Cook, was appointed Clerk Elect in 1985 and took over as Clerk in May 1986.[29] Having spent his working life in the voluntary sector, in prisoners' welfare and aftercare work, as director of an alcoholics recovery project and as Director of Family Service Units, Tim Cook's background was fundamentally different from that of his predecessors. Partly by accident and partly by design, his assumption of the Clerkship coincided with greater publicity for the work of the Foundation, a quickening of the pace of change and a vast broadening of the constituency for its support. His open, informal approach soon began to communicate itself to the entire workings of the Foundation. Together with the Chairman, John Smallwood, he sought to involve the trustees far more widely in decision making and to ensure that the Foundation was accessible to a wide range of organizations that had previously been either unaware of its existence or inhibited from applying to it. Some of the mechanisms by which these changes were accomplished are described at the end of this chapter.

The surveyorship of the Foundation continued in the hands of Campbell Jones & Sons until 1951. William Campbell Jones himself finally relinquished his residuary role in 1945 when he was 83, and the Foundation's work was then basically handled by Mervyn Campbell Jones, who had already been associated with it for over thirty years, and a new member of the firm, Frank K. Hewitt, who joined them in 1945. A third member, R. N. Wakelin, virtually acted as in-house architect, both for projects handled directly by the Foundation and for some of those undertaken by outside developers.

When Mervyn Campbell Jones retired in 1951, Frank Hewitt was appointed surveyor personally instead of the firm. It was a recognition even at this early date of his outstanding qualities as a surveyor which were to serve the Foundation so well for over thirty years. In 1967 the firm of Campbell Jones & Sons was dissolved and Hewitt joined Collins & Collins & Rawlence, which amalgamated with Hampton & Sons in 1970. Throughout, his position with the Foundation remained unassailable. He worked closely with successive Clerks who all respected him greatly. A reticent, almost shy, man, he was professionally extremely astute and could drive a hard bargain on behalf of his clients. He always took a long-term view of the Foundation's affairs

and sought to build up the value of its endowment by using development opportunities to expand its freeholds, especially in the City. This
process, which was generally referred to as consolidation, is described
in detail in Chapter 11, as are other aspects of his work for the
Foundation. When he died suddenly in 1982 at the age of 63 he was
described as 'a major architect of the well-being of the Foundation'.[30]

For several years Hewitt had been able to call on the assistance of
Bill Killick, who had joined Collins & Collins & Rawlence in 1968
and became a partner in Hampton & Sons in 1972. Killick was
appointed acting surveyor on Hewitt's death and was confirmed as
his successor in 1983. He provided that continuity and experience
which had been essential ingredients in the successful conduct of the
Foundation's estate business. Killick guided the Foundation through
the development boom of the 1980s and the diversification policy
introduced in the same decade, and concluded several complex transactions on terms which were highly favourable to the Foundation.
During his surveyorship there has been a great leap forward in the
Foundation's income, but he would be the first to acknowledge that
this owed much to the patient build-up of his predecessor.

Howard Bradshaw, who had been appointed solicitor in 1922 but
had in practice been the Foundation's legal adviser for several years
before that, continued to hold the position until his death in 1947. In
his will he left the residue of his estate to the Foundation for charitable
purposes, with the suggestion that an appropriate use might be to
assist elderly ladies in reduced circumstances – a need of which he
had become particularly conscious in the changing post-war world.
Donald Allen wrote of the bequest that, 'No finer tribute could be
paid to the Trustees than an action of this kind by a London solicitor
who had been associated with their legal work for more than fifty
years.'[31]

Bradshaw's replacement as solicitor, J. W. French, was another
partner in the firm of Baylis, Pearce & Co., which he had joined in
1931. He remained legal adviser until his impending retirement. The
trustees then turned to Mark Farrer, of the long established and much
respected firm of Farrer & Co., who was appointed solicitor in 1972,
although French was asked to assist in concluding outstanding business
until he formally retired in May 1973. Mark Farrer was an experienced
charity lawyer, who had undertaken work for the Fishmongers' Company, of which the Chairman of the Central Governing Body, Sir
Edward Chadwyck-Healey, was a past Master. Chadwyck-Healey
introduced him to Walter Prideaux, who was about to take over
as Chairman, and the appointment was sealed. While Mark Farrer
concentrated on general aspects of the Foundation's business, including
amendments to the Central Scheme eventually leading to the new

and much simplified scheme of 1989, and relations with the Charity Commissioners, with whom he established a good rapport, the legal aspects of the management of the estate were handled by Raymond Cooper, another partner in his firm and an outstanding property lawyer. Cooper worked closely with Frank Hewitt and Bill Killick, and must share the credit for the advance in the Foundation's fortunes. He was particularly praised by the trustees for his part in the sale of the playing fields at Mitcham in 1988.[32]

Of other professional advisers, the Foundation retained basically the same firm of auditors, although through mergers it underwent several metamorphoses and is now Peat Marwick McLintock. In 1970 Messrs Mullens & Co. were officially appointed stockbrokers to the Foundation, although they had previously advised on investments, and in a further step in 1987, Baring Investment Managers were appointed investment managers.[33]

One of the most remarkable features about the staff of the Foundation is that their numbers actually diminished over most of the post-war period. Five members of staff were called up during the war and one, Douglas Garnham, was killed in action. Temporary staff were appointed, and two of the older employees, H. J. Sleigh, the accountant, and R. H. T. Bard, continued past retirement age. The strenuous efforts of the staff to keep the office functioning, especially at the height of the Blitz, were much praised by the trustees, and they were given annual bonuses.[34]

After the war, as the younger members of staff returned from the services they were given positions of responsibility, at first in tandem with those who were due to retire. Sleigh retired in 1946; he had been taken on to the staff in 1925, but had spent the previous 23 years in the service of the Foundation's auditors, Martin & Farlow. Bard died in 1946 shortly before he was about to retire; he had been connected with the Foundation for 34 years, 19 of them as assistant to successive surveyors and 15 as a direct employee. When Leonard Bates retired late in 1947 he had put in 45 years' service.[35]

In the meantime, J. S. Burt, who had joined the staff as a junior clerk in 1927, was appointed assistant clerk, W. Greatorex, who had begun his service also as a junior in 1929, was reinstated as office clerk on demobilization, and H. E. G. Goddard, yet another who had started out as a junior clerk in 1930, became officer-in-charge at the Packington office. R. Wilcock, the former head of the Packington office, who had been an employee since 1937, was promoted to be accountant in place of Sleigh. They all maintained that tradition of longevity of service which had been such a feature of the pre-war years. Burt resigned from the Foundation in 1960 to take up the important post of General Secretary of the Family Welfare Association, but Wilcock,

Greatorex and Goddard (who replaced Burt as assistant clerk) continued until they reached retirement age. Wilcock retired in 1964, Greatorex in 1973 after 43 years' service, and Goddard in 1974 after 44 years with the Foundation, interrupted, in both the last two cases, by war service. Other long-serving members of staff were the secretaries, Mrs Meek, Mrs Norman and Mrs O'Brien, who were employed for 29, 27, and 26 years respectively.[36]

The presence of such a band of able, dedicated employees with a very low turnover was one of the factors that enabled staff numbers to be reduced. When the war ended, the trustees decided that a complement of ten (seven at Temple Gardens and three at Packington) in addition to the Clerk was needed. From 1953, however, as staff left or retired they tended not to be replaced. In that year the number was reduced to nine, in 1958 to eight, in 1959, when the business of the Packington office was virtually wound up, to seven, and in 1960, when Burt left and Packington was about to be sold, to six. In 1962, when their salaries were increased, Allen stated, 'The staff is small, selective and well qualified. Each member has his or her individual duties but each is capable in emergency of assuming additional responsibilities; for example, in cases of sickness and holidays the work is not allowed to get into arrear.' In fact, even the positions the staff held were regarded as flexible and their titles were frequently changed as they took on new areas of responsibility.[37]

Donald Allen and Bryan Woods were proud of the fact that they could run the Foundation with such a small staff. As late as 1984 the only addition was a part-time post, which was made full time in that year. Despite the growth in income (and the demand for grants) in the 1980s the number of assistant staff remained seven until 1988. By then, however, the assumption of the responsibility of the Trust for London and the growth in the volume and complexity of the Foundation's normal business, which had led to its office services being 'seriously stretched', necessitated a significant increase. At the time of writing the total staff, including the Clerk, number 14.[38]

We have seen that before the war the cost of administration accounted for less than 5 per cent of the Foundation's income. As staff salaries made up the major part of the administrative expenses and staff numbers were kept down, these expenses remained very low for much of the post-war period and in the early 1960s were less than 4 per cent of the gross income. In fact, so little was being spent on administration at this period that the question might be asked whether it was sufficient for the proper conduct of the Foundation's business. The figure had risen to about 7 per cent by the mid-1980s, but with the considerable increase in income at the end of the decade dropped to about 5 per cent again.

In 1967 the Foundation finally had to give up the 'temporary' office which it had acquired in 1891, when the Middle Temple, faced with a severe shortage of accommodation for barristers, decided to repossess all its chambers let to other bodies. Alternative rooms were quickly found nearby, on the second floor of No. 10 Fleet Street, a late-Victorian block of offices, which, although not ideal and providing more space than was actually required, were considered to be adequate 'until a permanent office could be found'. The move took place in January 1967. The surplus space was let to the Elderly Invalids Fund, later Counsel and Care for the Elderly, a client of the Foundation, until 1980, and subsequently to the Esmée Fairbairn Charitable Trust.[39]

The rent of the office, although subject to periodic review, was low by central London standards, but the accommodation fell below the standards which were increasingly coming to be expected in up-to-date offices, and as it looked unlikely that the lease would be renewed after 1991, when the premises were intended to be redeveloped, a search was made for new offices. In 1975, indeed, the trustees had considered renovating the listed historic buildings at Nos. 27 and 28 Queen Street in part for the Foundation's own use, but the Charity Commissioners had cavilled at the likely cost of some £250,000, and the buildings were let to Haslemere Estates for refurbishment as a commercial venture.

Finally, in 1989 a satisfactory new location was found at No. 6 Middle Street, Smithfield, where a modest-sized building was then under construction, which would provide a basement and two floors of excellent office accommodation for the Foundation and additional floors which could be let, in an area which was conveniently situated and well served by public transport. Part of the proceeds of the sale of playing fields at Mitcham were used to purchase the freehold (see page 255), and the staff moved in on 18 December 1989. Thus, after nearly one hundred years, the original aim of the Charity Commissioners that the Foundation should have its own freehold offices was fulfilled.[40]

In terms of office administration, perhaps the most significant event in recent years has been the introduction of computers. This took place in February 1986 and has, as in most offices, revolutionized procedures. One by-product has been to make it much easier to disseminate information, as desk-top publishing has replaced conventional printing, and this has coincided with the emergence of an ethos which favours greater publicity for the Foundation's activities.

The change in the complexion of the Foundation's business as its income increased, voluntary groups proliferated, and demands multiplied can be traced back to at least the beginning of the 1980s, but the abolition of the Greater London Council gave an added dimension to the process of change. In 1984, when the decision to abolish the GLC had been taken, a letter was sent to the Secretary of State for the Environment, Patrick Jenkin, on the recommendation of the Grants Sub-Committee, to express the trustees' concern about the lack of any clear statement from the government on how it proposed to replace the Council's funding of the voluntary sector. The response from the government, intimating that individual boroughs were to be responsible for funding voluntary organizations which operated within their own boundaries, and that the London Boroughs Association would take care of those which catered for people in more than one borough, was considered to be less than satisfactory. The Foundation was not alone, of course, in expressing unease about the government's proposals and the matter was debated at length in Parliament. Another letter was sent from the Chairman, this time to the Minister for Local Government, Kenneth Baker, pointing out the need for 'an independent, central grant-making body capable of taking an overall and impartial view of the funding needs of the voluntary sector in London', and asking for a meeting.[41]

The upshot was that a meeting was held at which the government asked the Foundation to take on the trusteeship of a new trust, which was eventually called the Trust for London. This was expected to have an income of about £1 million and an initial endowment of 'at least' £10 million. Some trustees were opposed to the acceptance of the government's proposition, but the majority were in favour. Their decision was influenced by the freedom from any restrictions on how the income was to be applied, and the agreement of the Charity Commissioners that it could be used with flexibility to aid a wide variety of organizations and not necessarily be confined to those that were registered charities. In addition, those who attended the meeting at which the formation of the trust was announced came away with the distinct impression that more money was likely to be forthcoming once the sale of the GLC's assets had taken place. Indeed, it was pointed out that an endowment of £10 million invested in equities would be likely to yield only some £600,000 in income and that has proved to be the case. Further approaches to the government, however, produced an adamant refusal to add to the original endowment. The trustees were left with a feeling of acute disappointment.[42]

The trust deed setting up the Trust for London was sealed on 12 May 1986, and the Trust began to function in 1987, although its first full year of grant-making did not occur until 1988. The Trust for London is separate from the City Parochial Foundation although it is managed by the latter and shares the services of its administrative staff. Indeed, the two field officers who were appointed in January

1988 were expected initially to devote all their time to the work of the Trust. It is too soon to assess the impact of the Trust, and not appropriate in this history of the Foundation to enter into detail about its policies and priorities, but there is some indication that the existence of the Trust has led to an increase in the number of organizations applying for grants from the Foundation.

The abolition of the GLC also set in train a series of changes in the procedures and constitution of the Foundation which were eventually to lead to a wholesale revision of the Central Scheme. The first issue was how to replace the four trustees who had been nominated by the GLC when their terms came to an end. A number of alternatives were canvassed, from leaving the total number at 17, or increasing the nomination of some of the existing bodies, to finding a new nominating body or bodies, but the trustees decided that the most satisfactory method was to appoint replacements themselves. Previously, as a general rule, the only appointments over which their views were sought were those of the Crown, when they were sometimes asked to indicate particular areas of concern. By having a right to name some additions to their number, however, they considered that they could better fill gaps in knowledge or experience.[43] The Charity Commissioners agreed with this solution, and the first three trustees to be appointed under the new procedure were all women – Ros Howells, Rabbi Julia Neuberger and Maggie Baxter – thus helping to redress the traditional male dominance of the Central Governing Body.

One procedural change that was approved late in 1986, on the recommendation of the Quinquennial Policy Sub-Committee for 1987–1991, and introduced in 1987 was the introduction of a three-tiered grant system. This was a response to the increase in the number of applications, both present and projected, and allowed for a greater degree of delegation. Henceforth, approval for grants up to £5,000 could be given by the Chairman of the Grants Sub-Committee and one other trustee, and the grant could be released immediately and reported to the Sub-Committee. For grants between £5,000 and £15,000 (soon afterwards raised to £25,000) approval could be given by the Grants Sub-Committe and the grant released immediately and reported to the Finance and General Purposes Committee. Grants of a higher denomination, however, had to be approved by the Finance and General Purposes Committee and the Central Governing Body.[44]

The adjustments that were made necessary by the abolition of the GLC and the impact of other changing circumstances prompted a wholesale revision of the Central Scheme. Some amendments were agreed with the Charity Commissioners quite quickly, before the main body of changes. These included the amalgamation of the Pension Committee – whose separate existence when there were few if any pensions to dispense had come to seem increasingly pointless – with the Finance and General Purposes Committee, and the abolition in 1987 of the denominational restriction contained in Clause 47 of the Central Scheme.[45]

This clause prevented the Foundation from giving grants out of the Central Fund to any organization whose membership was limited to the followers of any one denomination, and had long been thought to rule out many worthy causes from receiving grant aid. Donald Allen had been critical of this limitation in his evidence before the Nathan Committee in 1951, and the trustees had questioned its usefulness on other occasions.[46] The Charity Commissioners continued to place a strict construction on the clause, and the publication of *Faith in the City* by the Church of England and the increasing amount of welfare work being undertaken by the churches and religious bodies of other faiths had made its continuance seem even less desirable. In the case of ethnic minorities especially, some of the most vital work in this respect was being undertaken by groups which were construed as being denominational. One immediate result of its removal was to produce a substantial increase in the applications for grants, even though there was still a strict bar on giving any aid for the advancement of religion. Other procedural changes affecting the consideration of grants which were advocated by the Quinquennial Policy Sub-Committee for 1987–91 are described on page 316.

The new Central Scheme which came into force on 18 April 1989, and which owed much to the drafting skills of Mark Farrer and Christopher Jessel of Farrers, was very much shorter and simpler than that of 1891. The Charity Commissioners had already given the trustees and their professional advisers much greater freedom in the management of the estate (see page 256) and this was now extended to all the business of the Foundation. The Official Custodian for Charities (who had replaced the Official Trustees under the Charities Act of 1960) was to transfer all the Foundation's investments to its investment managers, and was discharged from his trusteeship of the land and buildings which were henceforth to be vested in the Central Governing Body.

Instead of the complex provisions of the original scheme, the new one merely required the income of the Central Fund to be applied 'in furthering any charitable purposes other than the advancement of religion which are directed to the benefit of poor inhabitants of the area of benefit' (namely the Metropolitan Police District) and, at the trustees' discretion, for purposes which benefit poor persons 'who are for the time being' located in the area. The substitution of 'poor inhabitants' for 'poorer classes' removed a somewhat outdated connotation which could raise problems of definition. Another long-overdue simplification was the dropping of the alternative name of the 'Trustees of the London Parochial Charities' for the Central Governing Body, which had originally stemmed from differences in nomenclature between the City of London Parochial Charities Act of 1883 and the Central Scheme of 1891. Additionally, henceforth the Central Governing Body was to be free to adopt whatever standing orders and form such committees as it considered necessary for the discharge of its business, and, in an important innovation, persons other than trustees could be appointed to committees provided that a majority on each committee were members of the Central Governing Body.

The new Central Scheme is remarkable for its clarity and conciseness, and reflects the entire satisfaction of the Charity Commissioners with the way in which the Foundation was being managed. Equally importantly, however, is its demonstration of how far the prevailing philosophy about the legitimate objectives of charity had changed since the 1890s. Complete discretion could now be allowed the Foundation in the utilization of its income for charitable purposes, and there was no longer any need to channel it in 'safe' directions.

Shortly after the revised Central Scheme came into force a new committee structure was instituted by which two of the former sub-committees were elevated to full committee status. To the Finance and General Purposes Committee (the addition of Pension to its title having been sensibly dropped) and the Estate Committee, which continued to meet on the same day as the Central Governing Body, were added the Grants Committee and the Investment Committee, although, as before, these met on different days from the other committees. In addition, there was a greater readiness to appoint sub-committees as and when necessary, and, as part of the process of encouraging greater participation on the part of the trustees, attempts were made to ensure that each member of the Central Governing Body served on at least one main committee and one sub-committee.

NOTES

1. Minutes, LIII, 74–6.
2. Ibid., LI, 37; LXVII, 165–6, 195–6; LXXV, 142; LXXVI, 110–11.
3. Ibid., LXXVI, 16–18; LXXVIII, 152; XCVII, 41.
4. Ibid., LVII, 146–7; LXXXIII, 179.
5. Ibid., LIV, 103.
6. Ibid., LXVII, 1–2.
7. Ibid., LXXXI, 37–8: *The Times*, 27 April 1971, 18: *Who's Who of British Members of Parliament. Volume IV. 1945–1979*, ed. Michael Stenton and Stephen Lees (1981).
8. Minutes, LXXXII, 1–2: *Daily Telegraph*, 24 Aug. 1979, 12.
9. Minutes, XCI, 1.
10. Ibid., LXXXVII, 2.

11. Ibid., LIV, 69; LV, 109.
12. Ibid., LXXV, 33–4: *The Times*, 9 Jan. 1968, 8.
13. Minutes, LXXVI, 130: *The Times*, 17 Aug. 1967, 10; 19 Aug. 1967, 12.
14. Minutes, LXIII, 97; XCI, 2, 49.
15. Ibid., LXIX, 35: *The Times*, 24 Feb. 1959, 13; 25 Feb. 1959, 12.
16. Minutes, LXXXVII, 141: *The Times*, 6 Sept. 1980, 14.
17. Minutes, LXXXVII, 2.
18. Ibid., LXXXVII, 2: *The Times*, 20 April 1978, 20.
19. PRO, CAB 124/142, q. 6011.
20. Minutes, L, 54, 172, 183, 190, 192; LI, 24, 94; LII, 12; LIII, 26: LIV, 41; LV, 13.
21. PRO, CAB 124/142, q. 6018.
22. The work of the Nathan Committee, and events leading up to the passing of the Charities Act, are described in David Owen, *English Philanthropy 1660–1960* (1965), 573–97. The records of the Committee, including the Minutes of Evidence, are in PRO, CAB 124/137–201.
23. PRO, CAB 124/142, qq. 5964–6117.
24. Minutes, LXIV, 119; LXIX, 123–4.
25. Ibid., LXXIII, 137–8; LXXIV, 111, 143–4.
26. Ibid., LXXIV, 175; LXXV, 2, 38: *The Times*, 12 Dec. 1967, 12; 15 Dec. 1967, 10; 28 Dec. 1967, 8.
27. Minutes, LXXV, 112, 136–7; XCIII, 305–6.
28. Ibid., LXXVIII, 2–3, 50–1.
29. Ibid., XCV, 79–80; XCVI, 62.
30. Ibid., LV, 88; LX, 168; LXI, 2, 23; LXXVIII, 20–1; XCII, 275: *Chartered Surveyor Weekly*, 20 Jan. 1983, 157.
31. Minutes, LVII, 18: *A History of the City Parochial Foundation 1891–1951* (1951), 21–2.
32. Minutes, LXXXII, 2; LXXXIII, 48; XCIX, 335.
33. Ibid., LXXX, 16; XCVII, 112–13, 257.
34. Ibid., LI, 24, 86; LIII, 74; LIV, 109–10.
35. Ibid., LVI, 18–25, 119–20; LVII, 157.
36. Ibid., LVI, 18–25; LXX, 38–9; LXXIX, 44; LXXXII, 118, 161; LXXXIII, 135, 177; LXXXIV, 22; XCVIII, 159.
37. Ibid., LVI, 21; LXIII, 200–1; LXVIII, 47; LXIX, 110, 132; LXX, 38–9; LXXII, 177–8.
38. Ibid., XCIV, 17, 220; XCVII, 143; XCVIII, 13.
39. Ibid., LXXVI, 113, 138–9; LXXVII, 209; LXXIX, 45; XC, 149, 220–1.
40. Ibid., LXXXV, 109; XCIV, 74; XCIX, 18–19, 203–9, 500–1, 515–20, 667.
41. Ibid., XCIV, 213–14, 296; XCV, 2–4.
42. Ibid., XCV, 80–1, 233–4, 347; XCIX, 357–9.
43. Ibid., XCVI, 87, 364–5.
44. Ibid., XCVI, 452–3.
45. Ibid., XCVI, 362; XCVII, 2, 139.
46. PRO, CAB 124/142, q. 6116: Minutes, LXVII, 155, 165.

11 The estate and other income

For a Foundation whose assets were largely tied up in property in the City of London the Second World War had literally devastating consequences. Already, by October 1939 public houses were closing through lack of trade, and some tenants were giving up their leases while others were asking for rent rebates.[1] The process continued throughout the period of the phoney war with a wide variety of lessees – accountants, auctioneers, solicitors, restaurateurs, booksellers, iron-mongers, several furriers, tobacconists and others – asking for, and invariably receiving, concessions. Nevertheless, rent arrears were rising and a large number of properties remained unlet.[2]

If this situation was worrying enough, however, it became vastly worse when the Blitz began on 7 September 1940. The Foundation's properties were in the front line. By early October, when the trustees met for what was to be the last meeting of the year, some thirty buildings had been affected by bombing, some of them totally destroyed. The heavy air raid on the commercial heart of the City on 29 December 1940 took an enormous toll, and by the time the succession of raids slackened off in 1941, 103 City properties belonging to the Foundation had been totally destroyed and a further 25 seriously damaged. On the outlying estates 60 buildings had been destroyed and 113 badly damaged. The loss of rent amounted to £27,000, most of it from the Central Fund.[3]

Under the terms of the Landlord and Tenant (War Damage) Act of 1939 most tenants were released from any obligation to repair in cases of war damage and could surrender their leases if the buildings were rendered unusable. The Foundation tried as far as possible to avoid this by accommodating tenants through reductions in rents, making temporary repairs, granting new lettings of usable rooms or finding them alternative premises. When all else failed they sought to negotiate surrenders of leases rather than go through the courts. Some lessees, of course, wanted to hold on to their ground leases, and one lessee of a building which had been very badly damaged seems to have shown an unusually charitable disposition. 'We considered one-fifth of the ground rent to be the amount we would be prepared to pay', he wrote, 'but in view of the grievous losses which we understand the London Parochial Charities have sustained and their many commitments, we are prepared to pay one-half of the rent instead of one-fifth, as the amount of money involved is not large.' Sometimes the changes in rent were very considerable. At Nos. 1 and 2 Gracechurch Street, which had been let at a ground rent of £1,500 per annum and now represented a loss to its lessees, the rent was reduced temporarily to £300.[4]

The open spaces which the Foundation had acquired were generally requisitioned for other uses. The sports ground at Leyton was initially claimed by the Royal Air Force and shortly afterwards turned into a training ground for the Home Guard. Grange Farm and Cudham were taken over by the Army, and at Chigwell Row part of the land was used for cultivation by the Ministry of Agriculture and the remainder by the local Home Guard. In each case the negotiation of an equitable rent was not an easy matter.[5]

In 1942 it was possible to begin the process of clearing up, both physically and financially. Tenants began to drift back to the residential estates, including the Packington Estate in Islington which had been heavily bombed, although they were 'still nervous of occupying the upper floors of larger houses, and it is practically impossible to let rooms on top floors.'[6] Rent arrears remained a serious problem and by midsummer 1942 amounted to over £13,000, but the Clerk still strove to avoid litigation and was prepared to continue to reduce rents when necessary. Despite its financial losses, however, the Foundation was prepared to make a contribution to the war effort by waiving its, albeit modest, claim to compensation for the removal of iron railings.[7]

The decline in income was indeed a serious matter. At its lowest point in 1943 the gross income of the Foundation was £35,000 less than in 1939, a decrease of over one-fifth, almost entirely accounted for by the loss of rents.

There was a slight recovery in 1944, sufficient to appoint a small sub-committee of trustees headed by Francis Allen, the chairman of the Estate Committee, to consider the problems of post-war reconstruction. No sooner had they begun to confer, however, when a second wave of destruction occurred, this time by V1 flying bombs and V2 rockets. There was some damage in the City but the outlying estates took the brunt of the attacks. On the Packington Estate, for instance, a flying bomb which landed on 2 August 1944 destroyed a further 19 houses and severely damaged 23 others.[8]

Nevertheless, there was sufficient confidence by the end of the year that matters were slowly returning to normal for ten houses in Battersea which were held on long leases to be bought for £600 to add to the Foundation's other domestic property in the area. Of far greater importance, however, was the report of the redevelopment sub-committee which was presented to the trustees in December 1944, for it established some important principles which were to guide the management of the estate in the post-war period. Great as the destruction by bombing had been, the committee, doubtless well advised by the Foundation's surveyor, recognized that it did provide an opportunity to rationalize the Foundation's holdings in the City. The report advocated the consolidation of City freeholds by purchases or exchanges of property, even though this might involve a sacrifice of income in the short term until the consolidated sites were ripe for redevelopment. It also favoured using investments to finance direct rebuilding on some sites in a strong affirmation of the view that the key to future prosperity lay in maximizing the potential of the Foundation's property holdings. The trustees welcomed the report and authorized the Estate Committee to act directly if any opportunities for purchases or exchanges occurred.[9]

Another important event in 1944 was the passing of the first of two important Town and Country Planning Acts. Under the 1944 Act local authorities could apply for certain badly damaged areas to be declared comprehensive redevelopment areas in which widespread powers of compulsory purchase could be exercised. Although it would be some time before the powers afforded by the Act could be utilized, and by then its scope had been expanded by the more comprehensive Act of 1947, the City Corporation was quick to announce its intention to take advantage of the opportunities presented as soon as the war ended in the spring of 1945. The Foundation, anticipating that this might assist its policy of consolidation, supplied the Corporation with a map of its properties with a view to entering into discussions on possible exchanges. It doubtless also helped that Donald Allen was invited to sit on the City's Reconstruction Advisory Council.[10]

In the meantime, the surveyor kept a sharp look out for any properties which could be added to likely development sites, while seeking to dispose of isolated or unpromising vacant plots where buildings had been demolished, of which there were some eighty in the City at the war's end. In the former category, efforts were initially concentrated on two closely adjacent areas on the north side of Cannon Street, around Walbrook and Abchurch Lane. By a slow and patient process some dozen largely vacant sites were acquired by purchase or exchange in Cannon Street, Walbrook, Budge Row, Bond Court, Oxford Court and Abchurch Lane, while an equivalent number elsewhere were sold or offered in exchange. The sums involved, because the sites were unproductive, were not large. There was no incentive to hurry because restrictions on building meant that redevelopment would have to be delayed.[11]

Lessees gradually returned to those buildings that were still intact or could be repaired, and rents which had been temporarily reduced were raised again. In 1945 21 new leases and tenancy agreements were negotiated, and in 1946 a further 62, producing in the latter year an increase in rents of over £11,000. Not all the new lettings were quite as favourable as that of Cannon Street Buildings, which had been badly damaged and where the head lessee had chosen to disclaim the lease even though it was not due to expire until 1963. The Foundation had taken over the building and the few tenants who chose to remain, and in 1945 the Ottoman Bank offered to take a 21-year lease of the unlet parts on condition that they were repaired and modernized. As the cost of this was only estimated to be some £4,000, and the increase in rents over that received under the old lease would be some £6,000 per annum, the offer was accepted with alacrity.[12]

Another important source of income in the immediate post-war period was war damage compensation from the government. Although it took about five years to settle all the claims, the sum eventually received was some £478,000, four-fifths of it payable to the Central Fund.[13] This purely coincidental disparity in the fate of buildings belonging to the two Funds meant that initially more of the Central Fund's sites were developed, but the imbalance was corrected in later years.

The bombing of the Foundation's outlying estates left 180 sites vacant at the end of the war. Some of them were taken over by the London County Council to erect prefabricated houses (the 'prefabs' which remained a familiar part of the urban landscape for many years),[14] and the wisdom of retaining these scattered 'ground rent' estates, as they were termed, began to be questioned. A decision was taken early in 1946 to sell the very first properties purchased by the Foundation, a block of 67 houses in Stamford Hill, Hackney, which at the time of acquisition was 'considered a good class residential estate, but the neighbourhood has gradually deteriorated and at the present time practically every house is sub-let in floors to more than one family'. The money received, it was stated in justification, could be used to help purchase redevelopment sites in the City, and later in the year the estate was sold at auction for £28,160, about £12,000 more than the price paid for it in 1892.[15]

The Packington Estate in Islington, which had suffered particularly severe damage, was a different proposition because the properties there were managed directly rather than let on long leases. Nevertheless, the net income was depleted by the need to undertake repairs, and a substantial part of the estate was appropriated for Isleden House, an experiment in housing the elderly which is described in Chapter 13. In 1947 the surveyor was instructed to consider the desirability of redevelopment, if necessary in conjunction with neighbouring owners.[16]

The playing fields and other open spaces were gradually brought back into the uses for which they had been intended. The Leyton sports ground, however, was singled out for special treatment. A short lease of the ground had already been granted in 1943 to Essex County Council for use in connection with what was described as the new youth movement, and in 1946 this was converted into a deed of gift on condition that the land would be made available in perpetuity to the youth of east London as an open space and recreation ground, or, if it ever ceased to be so used, that the capital value of the land and buildings would be devoted to a like purpose as determined by the trustees.[17]

In 1947 the City Corporation announced that it was applying to the Ministry of Town and Country Planning for substantial parts of the City to be declared comprehensive development areas. A large number of the Foundation's properties were affected, and its surveyor considered that objections to compulsory purchase should be lodged in the case of those which he thought capable of individual redevelopment. In the event, well over two hundred acres in seven separate areas were covered by the Declaratory Order, and the Foundation began to serve notices on the Corporation, requiring it to purchase sites within the areas concerned. The value was restricted to that of the existing uses, but under the 1947 Town and Country Planning Act it was also possible to claim limited compensation for the loss of development rights. In all, over several years, 45 of the Foundation's sites in the City were disposed of under the terms of the Act and another 40 by private treaty, netting altogether over £600,000. Together with the sums received in compensation for war damage and loss of development rights, the many unproductive sites which were left at the end of the war realized over £1.1 million which was reinvested in the enlargement of sites capable of redevelopment. If the net result was a contraction in the number of properties owned by the Foundation, several of those that remained were rendered substantially more valuable by the judicious acquisition of neighbouring plots.[18]

The first sites where this process had proceeded to the extent that redeveloment was a practical proposition were on the east and west sides of Walbrook at its junction with Cannon Street. Late in 1948 the trustees decided to test the water by embarking on the direct rebuilding of the eastern corner, an unusual step but one dictated by the unfavourable climate for development under building leases as a result of the difficulty in obtaining building permits and the uncertaint-ies created by the proposal in the Town and Country Planning Act of 1947 to levy a development charge. The shortage of steel caused delays, but Campbell Jones & Sons were instructed to prepare working drawings, and a building licence was granted late in 1949. Before a start was made, however, an offer was received to take the site on a 99-year building lease at a ground rent which would ultimately amount to £10,000 per annum, and this was readily accepted. It was 1956, however, before Walbrook House, as the new building was named, was completed. On the western side of Walbrook an unexpected bonus occurred when the small sites pieced together at relatively low cost were required for the largest of the early post-war redevelopment schemes, that of Bucklersbury House, and the Foundation was paid £185,000 for the freeholds.[19]

The first building to be completed on the Foundation's estate after the war was Lumley House in St Mary Axe in 1952. It was also the first instance of a policy which was later to be adopted to considerable effect – the expansion of a site as part of a development package. In this case the Foundation already owned Nos. 43–45 St Mary Axe, and the adjacent vacant site of Nos. 47–51 was purchased for £30,000 so that the whole could be let on a 99-year building lease at a ground rent of £2,500 per annum. When completed, the building was described as an addition to the estate of which the Foundation could be proud, but 40 years later, having outlived its usefulness, it was demolished in 1990 in preparation for a new development on a much larger scale.[20]

As the Foundation entered the 1950s the opportunities for invest-ment in City freeholds became increasingly limited as post-war recon-struction gathered pace once the period of restrictions ended. At one point the trustees even decided to reverse their long-established policy of not investing in agricultural land, but fortuitously, or perhaps because their professional advisers were loath to implement what they may have regarded as a somewhat maverick decision, no landholdings which were considered to be suitable came on to the market. Unde-terred, the trustees resolved to depart once more from established policy and authorized the surveyor to treat for the leasehold interests of office buildings which were sub-let to substantial tenants, or for the freeholds of modern blocks of business premises in the suburbs of London or the provinces let on 14- or 21-year leases. The reasons given for this early manifestation of what was later to be called 'diversification' reflect both global concerns at a stage of the Cold War which is now all too easily forgotten and an apprehension of the effects of mounting inflation. 'It is suggested', reads the report recommending the new policy, 'that under present conditions, and with the risk of war, it might be desirable to hold properties distributed over a somewhat wider area than at present and that such properties might, as leases expire, serve to off-set to some extent the effects of inflation.' The same report also raised the spectre of leasehold reform and cautioned against acquiring any more suburban residential estates.[21]

Later, in 1951, the first such commercial leasehold was purchased, that of King's House, King Street, which was held on a lease from the Mercers' Company expiring in 1985. The price was £225,000, and after allowing for the establishment of a sinking fund to replace the capital plus a sum for dilapidations by the end of the lease, and another fund to safeguard against a rise in maintenance costs, which were required by the Charity Commissioners, the net income from rents of about £14,000 provided a return on the investment of some 6 per cent, which was regarded at the time as eminently satisfactory.[22]

Another transaction in 1951 was an example of the 'sale and lease-back' arrangement which was common at a time of credit shortages and which could be of considerable ultimate benefit to an institution with long-term rather than short-term interests. This was the purchase of the freehold of Peek House, Eastcheap, for £315,400 on behalf of the City Church Fund from its current owners, Peek Brothers, a firm of wholesale grocers and tea blenders, who agreed in return to take a 99-year lease at a ground rent of £16,000 per annum. Peek House was a substantial stone-fronted edifice which had been erected in 1884–5 and was thought to have a virtually indefinite life. Nevertheless, as a matter of prudence a sinking fund was set up to replace the capital over some sixty-five years, and, after deducting the contributions to this, the net return was only about 4½ per cent. Taking the long-term view, however, the Foundation had acquired a valuable freehold in a part of the City where, by assiduously following a policy of consolidation over many years, it was to put together a block of properties with enormous future potential.[23]

In 1952 the block in Holloway Road containing Jones Brothers department store was bought for £290,000 from John Lewis, who, like Peek Brothers, wished to realize the capital value of their asset and took a 99-year lease instead at an annual rent of £16,500. Three years later, £320,000 was paid for the long leasehold interest in York House, Queen Square, Bloomsbury, the net income from which provided a return of about 5 per cent after allowing for the establishment of a sinking fund. Towards the end of the decade two buildings in High

Street, Kingston, were purchased for £93,500, in accordance with the policy of acquiring out-of-centre business premises, and one in Mansion House Place was acquired for £127,500.[24]

Most of the money for these and other purchases came from the gradually accumulating proceeds of the sale of vacant plots, but the process of selling the freeholds of houses on the outlying estates was pursued with increasing vigour throughout the decade. Initially these properties were only sold in blocks, but in 1956 the decision was taken to sell to individual lessees on all the estates except for those in Holloway Road and Tooting High Street, where the properties consisted of shops with living accommodation above, and parts of the Bromley Estate with development potential. The residential estates were for the most part let on controlled tenancies and the general trend of legislation in favour of lessees meant that this type of investment was becoming progressively less attractive. By 1960 170 such freeholds had been sold for £63,770. The loss in ground rents amounted to £1,224, but it was estimated that by the reinvestment of the proceeds the actual income had been doubled.[25]

The Packington Estate in Islington had always been regarded as a separate entity. The war damage was gradually repaired and the estate restored to good heart and condition, but rent controls held down the income, direct management imposed an administrative burden, and the return on the estate of some £22,000 by the end of the 1950s was not expected to show much of an increase for some time. Moreover, the age of the houses meant that substantial structural repairs might soon be necessary, and there was a threat of compulsory purchase as a large part of the estate was earmarked for public housing in the County of London Plan. Isleden House had already been sold to the City Corporation in 1953 (see page 278), and when a reasonable offer was made for the remainder of the estate in 1959, the surveyor recommended acceptance on the grounds that the money could be reinvested in other property which was not subject to the same uncertainties. The sale was completed in 1960 for £377,250. No one at that time could have foreseen the steep rise in the value of residential property in such an area, and the Foundation was at least spared involvement in the bitter dispute that marked the demolition of many of the Victorian houses for the construction of the large public housing scheme which was named the Packington Estate.[26]

A number of sites in the City were redeveloped in the 1950s. Besides Lumley House and Walbrook House, already mentioned, Roman House was erected in Fore Street to the north of London Wall, where, in the now familiar manner, the site was enlarged at a cost of £40,000 before development began, and a small building was also erected in Salter's Hall Court. Just outside the City, on the Southwark side of

Southwark Bridge, the ground in Park Street and Rose Alley which had lain undeveloped for many years, was finally let on a building lease for 125 years at a ground rent of £2,250 per annum. Southbridge House, as the new building was called, was completed in 1958.[27]

At the corner of Cannon Street and Abchurch Lane, where a good-sized plot had been created as one of the first fruits of the policy of consolidation, the trustees decided to build directly in two stages, initially at Nos. 135–137 Cannon Street and later at Nos. 139–141. Richard Wakelin of Campbell Jones & Sons, who also designed Roman House, was appointed as the architect, and the first building was completed in 1957 at a cost of approximately £65,000 and let to the Ottoman Bank at a rent of £6,500 per annum.[28]

Some important policy decisions were taken towards the end of the decade. For some time Donald Allen had felt that the type of investments to which the trustees of charities were limited was unduly restrictive, a view shared by the Nathan Report which he had helped to compile. Accordingly, in 1958 he persuaded the Charity Commissioners to issue a new scheme permitting two-thirds of the Foundation's endowments to be regarded as a 'free part', able to be invested in land, government securities of the United States and Canada and their states or provinces, or in shares of companies in the United Kingdom, United States and Canada, and public corporations in this country, provided the companies concerned had a paid-up capital of £750,000 and had paid dividends of at least 4 per cent for five years. Significantly, this special dispensation anticipated the greater freedom given to trustees in general by the Trustee Investments Act of 1961.

In 1959 a Special Investments Committee was convened consisting of the chairmen and vice-chairmen of the Central Governing Body and the main committees to decide what changes they should make in the light of the new powers given them by the Charity Commissioners. They compared the performance of investments in property over the years since the war with that of gilt-edged securities and concluded that while the former had proved eminently satisfactory, both the income and capital value of the latter had declined in real terms. They reaffirmed earlier decisions to invest primarily in property, and gave instructions that £150,000-worth of gilt-edged securities were to be sold and £100,000 reinvested in short-dated securities or Treasury Bills, or held as cash, so as to be readily available for the purchase of property, while £50,000 was to be invested in equities.[29]

The Foundation entered the 1960s on a buoyant note. Its gross income had risen from £133,000 in 1945 to £362,000 in 1960, a rate of increase well above the rise in the retail price index over the same years, and a number of large-scale developments were in the offing as the first post-war property boom neared its peak. Nevertheless, such had been the enormous set-back caused by the war and the distorting effects of high inflation that the income still did not compare with that of 1938 in real terms, and was, indeed, not to do so until 1985. To some extent, however, such a comparison is misleading in that the 1930s were a period of falling prices, and if the 1920s are used as a yardstick a different picture emerges. It should also be remembered that in the management of the estate an attempt had to be made to balance the desire to maximize current income with the need to ensure that the value of the Foundation's endowment for the future was maintained. In general, if it came to a conflict between the two, present benefits were invariably sacrificed for long-term potential. A further distorting effect was created by the decision, taken for social purposes, very much on the initiative of Donald Allen, to invest heavily after the war in the building of Isleden House (to the extent of £157,000 from capital, in addition to £100,000 from income) in the knowledge that such an investment could never be fully recouped.

The 1960s opened with negotiations in train for three major redevelopment schemes involving the acquisition of large blocks of property at considerable expense. The first, for which the preparations took several years, was in King William Street and Arthur Street and involved the closure of the ancient Crooked Lane. The Foundation's original holdings in the area, which was described by the surveyor as 'one of the best pieces of undeveloped land in the City', were minimal, but it suited the developers' purposes for the Foundation to acquire the freehold of the rest of the site for £350,000 and let the whole on a 99-year building lease at a ground rent of £26,000, representing a return of about 6½ per cent. The new building erected on the site was known as Sovereign House.[30]

The other two schemes were in Cheapside and resulted in the building of Mitre House on the north side and Bolsa House on the south side. In both cases, once again, the Foundation only owned a small part of the development site, and in the former had acquired a frontage to Cheapside as recently as 1950 for £12,500. The additional landholdings required cost £480,000 and £475,000, and the ultimate ground rents under the building leases amounted to £38,150 and £34,750 respectively. Mitre House and Mitre Court behind were designed by Richard Wakelin and together constitute one of the few developments of this era which has generally been praised for its architectural quality.[31]

The development of Mitre House and Court involved two important innovations. The building lease negotiated in 1961 was for 125 years, with provision for the ground rent to be reviewed after 33, 66 and 99 years so that it bore the same percentage relationship to the rack rent as the original ground rent. The Foundation's greatly respected surveyor, Frank Hewitt, is generally credited with being the first to introduce such reviews in building leases as a way of dealing with inflation. The other innovation was that the purchase money was taken from both the Central and City Church Funds and the ground rent allocated proportionately between them, thus ending the policy of the strict separation of the properties belonging to each fund which had commenced with 'severance' in the 1890s.[32]

The Foundation's outlay on these major redevelopments was over £1.3 million, and to recoup some of the money the trustees decided to sell isolated holdings whenever favourable offers were received. Between 1960 and 1965 some twenty such properties in the City were sold for over £800,000. Some were held on leases which had several years to run and represented rapidly depreciating assets at a time of continuing inflation, while others were of greater value to their purchasers than to the Foundation and could therefore command prices in excess of their nominal value. Many were acquired by the City Corporation as part of its accumulation of property for the widening of Upper Thames Street.[33] With these extensive purchases and sales in mind, the conclusion was drawn in 1962, prematurely in the event, that 'the policy of consolidation has now been fulfilled'.[34]

In 1965 the policies of the new Labour Government, especially the restrictions on office building, the Rent Act and the proposal to introduce legislation favouring leasehold enfranchisement, resulted in a sharp diminution in activity on the estate, and the following year was a particularly difficult one because of a sterling crisis and stringent financial restrictions.[35] The property boom was over and there was little in the way of new development for the rest of the decade. The buying and selling of property continued, however, though on a reduced scale.

An offer of £250,000 for the freehold of Walbrook House by its lessees in 1967 caused much heart-searching. The building stood on one of the first sites to be developed after the war in accordance with the policy of consolidation and was described as 'one of the Trustees' best freehold properties', but the price was exceptionally high because the lessees owned the adjacent site, and the lease still had 85 years unexpired at a fixed ground rent. So the offer was accepted and the surveyor sought guidance on whether he should seek other opportunities to dispose of freeholds which were subject to long leases at fixed rents.[36]

A number of smaller properties, principally in Aldersgate, were sold to the City Corporation for a total of some £170,000, and other sales realized £140,000. On the other hand, No. 27 Martin Lane, in the area towards the eastern end of Cannon Street where much of the Foundation's property was now concentrated, was bought for £168,250, the leasehold interest in No. 17 Abchurch Lane was acquired at auction for £85,000 in order to facilitate future development, and an exchange which the trustees had been trying to make since 1964 was concluded in 1970 when No. 34 Coleman Street was conveyed to Christ's Hospital in return for the larger site of No. 48 Cannon Street, the Foundation having to pay an additional £110,000 to compensate for the difference. Nevertheless, there was a dearth of suitable property to purchase in London, and the surveyor was asked to consider investing in growth areas elsewhere; Ashford and Ipswich were specifically mentioned.[37]

The only one of the Foundation's holdings where significant changes took place in the later 1960s was the large residential estate at Bromley. Although a substantial part of the estate consisted of houses held on long leases which were gradually being enfranchised, a process speeded up by the Leasehold Reform Act of 1967, there were also streets where the houses were let on short tenancies and these were considered suitable for redevelopment. This process had begun in 1963, and other plots were let on building leases in 1966 and 1968. Several of the remaining houses did not come up to the standard specified in the Housing Act of 1964, however, and to the trustees' chagrin, and doubtless some embarrassment, Bromley Borough Council declared a clearance area covering some of them on the grounds that they were unfit for human habitation and acquired them by compulsory purchase. When, therefore, an offer was made in 1969 for the remaining undeveloped sites, it was accepted, although not without remarking that the transaction marked the end of an epoch in the history of the Foundation in that these were the last residential properties let at rack rents. The price paid was £127,000.[38]

Confidence returned to the property market at the beginning of the 1970s and there was a pronounced increase in the volume of transactions in land and buildings. The most immediately noticeable effect on the estate was the receipt of attractive offers for some of the Foundation's City freeholds, but, as the surveyor expressed it, 'the Trustees have decided recently, as a matter of general policy, to preserve and improve their capital position, albeit that this might result in a temporary reduction of income', and he presumed that they would not be interested in selling. This principle was upheld, fortunately in the event, even when £250,000 was offered for Bouverie House, Fleet Street, which was held on a long lease at a fixed rent. In 1972, indeed, the trustees even contemplated the possibility of borrowing money to finance purchases, but this never proved to be necessary.[39]

The principle of not selling did not extend to the residential estates where the disposal of individual freeholds proceeded apace. Whenever possible, this was done outside the Leasehold Reform Act when better terms could invariably be obtained, but some enforced enfranchisements under the Act also took place. Accordingly, when the opportunity occurred to sell all of the remaining houses in Battersea for £153,000 in 1972–3 it was seized eagerly.[40] This left a laundry and an employment exchange which the trustees have retained ever since for the future development value of the site.

The early 1970s also witnessed the first consideration of a possible change in attitude towards the open spaces and playing fields owned by the Foundation. From about 1956 as the leases of these facilities had come up for renewal, it had been the policy to charge economic rents, as far as these could be determined, largely because the level of rents could affect the price paid if they were ever subjected to compulsory purchase. In the case of those that were held predominantly for a social purpose, such as the camping grounds at Chigwell Row and Cudham let to the Girl Guides or the sports ground at Bellingham let to the London Federation of Boys' Clubs, it was made clear to those organizations that any rises in rents would be covered by increases in grants. With the ending of the Foundation's obligations to the polytechnics and the transformation of those institutions which was taking place as part of the continuing changes in the nature of higher education, however, the playing fields which were let to them fell into a somewhat different category. In 1970 Chelsea College of Science and Technology, as it had become, was considering amalgamating with St George's Hospital Medical School, and enquired whether the Foundation would consider relinquishing the playing fields at Mitcham for use as the site of a new campus. The trustees replied in the negative, and reaffirmed that it was their policy to continue 'to preserve, provide and maintain open spaces and recreation grounds within the metropolis, unless such a policy is shown to conflict with the public interest.' Nevertheless, the future of the playing fields could be said to be on the agenda.[41]

The status of the large Grange Farm Centre, occupying over a hundred acres, was again a different matter. Its development, out of the income available for grants, is described in Chapter 13, but it did constitute one of the Foundation's more sizeable holdings. Originally administered by a committee of management with direct responsibility to the trustees, it had been let to Chigwell Urban District Council in 1965 on a 60-year lease at a nominal rent of £25 as the result of a decision to adopt a more arm's length approach. Subsequently, the Council made several overtures to purchase the freehold, and an offer of £125,000 was accepted in 1973, although this was well below the costs of the Centre to the Foundation. But the Centre was about to be cut in half by the M11 motorway, several years of the lease at a nominal rent remained, restrictions were placed on the conveyance to preserve its original purpose, and some parts were retained for institutions to which the Foundation regularly gave grants, as described further in Chapter 13.[42]

Some of these actions on the periphery of the Foundation's estate may have had important long-term consequences, but the most significant events at the time were happening in the City. The first proposals for redevelopment in the decade, although they were provisions for future redevelopment, occurred in 1971 in Fetter Lane and Lovat Lane, and both established important principles for future transactions. In each case the Foundation only owned part of the site earmarked for development, which complicated matters further. At Fetter Lane the surveyor advised that a 99-year building lease should be granted as usual, but not at a ground rent based on the rental value, reviewable at intervals, but instead at a rent which would be a proportion of the income derived from the occupational tenancies of the building and therefore variable. He advocated this because, at a time of rapidly escalating inflation, any increases in ground rents which could be imposed at the time of rent reviews invariably lagged behind the continuously rising rack rents. There was, of course, an element of risk involved. If the occupational rents fell, so would the Foundation's income. As Hewitt expressed it, 'I would like the Trustees to enter into this transaction upon the basis of a direct share in the equity, but I am, I realise, advocating speculation against security.' They agreed to the proposal on the basis that it should not form a precedent for future transactions. It was, indeed, a very early instance of the 'side-by-side' arrangement whereby both freeholder and leaseholder share the success – or failure – of a development, which has now become a common method of proceeding.[43]

At least at Fetter Lane there was a prospect of early rebuilding, although, in the event, the transaction proved less advantageous than had been hoped because the completion of the building coincided with the mid-decade slump when rental values declined even though building costs had escalated during its construction.[44] At Lovat Lane, however, there were several factors which were likely to impede development, not least that listed buildings were involved elsewhere on the site; and so, simultaneous leases were granted, the one providing for modernization and the other a 99-year building lease to become operative on rebuilding, at an initial ground rent of £15,000 with a provision for upward reviews every five years based on that sum plus a proportion of the rack rents calculated by a complex formula.[45]

Another development which was negotiated in the boom years of the early 1970s was at Nos. 9–11 Lime Street, which had been let on an 80-year lease expiring in 1976 at a ground rent of £1,600 per annum. Terms were agreed for the granting of a building lease from

1975, or earlier if the building was completed before that date, at an initial ground rent of £131,650 with an upward revision to 40 per cent of the rack-rental value in 1985 and every seventh year thereafter. Such a high gearing could only have been achieved at the peak of the property cycle, and the quite phenomenal increase in the rent helps to explain why the income of the City Church Fund, to which the property belonged, surged ahead in the mid-1970s and briefly overtook that of the Central Fund.

The developers, the City of London Real Property Company, also owned No. 8 Lime Street, which was included in the rebuilding. The surveyor had unsuccessfully tried to obtain its freehold for the Foundation during negotiations, but when the new building was completed in 1975 the company found that in the less favourable economic climate that then prevailed the differences in tenure between parts of the building inhibited the disposal of it. Accordingly, the company agreed to convey the freehold to the Foundation for £1 in return for a new 120-year lease of the whole of the building at the ground rent previously agreed.[46]

One other development for which terms were agreed before the worst effects of recession began to be felt was at Nos. 48–50 Cannon Street and 11–12 Great St Thomas Apostle. Three of these were 'agency' properties of the Foundation which brought in about £15,000 per annum, while the fourth belonged to the Skinners' Company and was to be acquired for the Foundation by the Hammerson Group, who proposed to develop the site. The rebuilding of these properties was highly desirable and was, indeed, actively promoted by the surveyor to the extent of having architect's drawings prepared. The agreement concluded with Hammersons also involved the surrender of leases in Eastcheap and St Mary-at-Hill to facilitate possible development there, and provided for the payment of a ground rent of £167,000 per annum from the time of the new building's completion, subject to revision upwards every seven years to 49 per cent of the rack-rental value. In the middle of 1974 Hammersons pulled out, almost certainly because of the worsening economic climate, but fortunately for the Foundation, which stood to reap a considerable benefit from the deal, a new developer, GRE Compass Ltd, came forward and agreed to take a building lease on identical terms.[47]

The surrender of leases in Eastcheap and St Mary-at-Hill was part of a process whereby the Foundation gradually accumulated a block of properties on the south side of Eastcheap between St Mary-at-Hill and Idol Lane for redevelopment. The consolidation of holdings in the area required some freehold purchases which, the surveyor warned, 'would involve the Trustees in a material temporary loss of income'. The acquisition of Nos. 30–36 Eastcheap was, indeed, a highly complex matter in which the trustees had to purchase a company, Cavendish Laboratories Ltd, whose assets consisted of the Eastcheap building and another small building, No. 11 St Christopher's Place, Westminster. The price was £397,850, but No. 11 St Christopher's Place was a modern building let at a rent of £10,000 per annum, and the occupational rents in Eastcheap could nominally be negotiated upwards pending redevelopment.[48]

Any such increases in rent had to be nominal, however, because of the rent freeze introduced by the government in November 1972. The freeze lasted until March 1975, and although several rents which were subject to review were raised in this period, sometimes by very large amounts, the Foundation could not immediately enjoy the benefits. New lettings and building leases were exempted from controls, and so there was not exactly a standstill in these years. Nevertheless, it was estimated in 1975 that the ending of the freeze would result in an increase of over £130,000 in the gross income of the Foundation.[49]

Throughout the early 1970s the performance of the Foundation's capital assets was carefully monitored both at meetings of the Investment Sub-Committee and at special meetings of the Estate Committee. A decision was taken in 1973 which, while it might seem to be primarily an administrative matter, indicated the investment priorities of the Foundation. This was that the Investment Sub-Committee was to report in future to the Estate Committee rather than to the Finance and General Purposes Committee and that its membership was to be drawn from members of the Estate Committee. The primacy of investing in property was invariably upheld. At one point the trustees even questioned whether the sale of residential ground rents should be stopped in view of the very great increase in the value of house property, but the surveyor advised against any change in policy, pointing out that leasehold enfranchisement still applied and that the Rent Acts generally favoured tenants.[50]

Such was the concern at the sluggishness of the Foundation's non-property investments, that the trustees sought unrestricted freedom of investment, with the particular intention of transferring money into unit trusts. The Charity Commissioners were reluctant to grant such powers, and while they gave permission for the Foundation to apply to the Courts, enquiries indicated that such an approach was unlikely to be successful and the issue was not pursued. Nevertheless, at a special meeting of the Estate Committee in 1974, while it was agreed that the emphasis should continue to be on investing in property and that the opportunities of purchasing sound commercial property in the Home Counties and the provinces should be more actively pursued, it was also emphasized that other investments should not merely be regarded as a temporary repository for funds earmarked for the purchase of real estate but ought to be given more attention as a separate portfolio in their own right.[51]

The committee's chairman, Sir John Russell, had opened this meeting with an unrelieved picture of economic gloom, remarking how, over the past few months:

> the country has experienced a strike by power workers and by miners, an oil fuel crisis, a proposal to change the tax laws affecting property development, a general election, a change of government, two budgets, a standfast in the field of property development, further proposals to change the tax laws affecting property development, a loss of confidence of crisis proportions, an inflation rate variously estimated at between 16 and 20 per cent, a second general election and, in consequence, a downward slide on the stock market not experienced for 25 years.

He returned to the same theme in the annual review he gave to the Estate Committee in each of the next three years, and there was, indeed, a pronounced slowdown in activity.[52]

The development at Nos. 48–50 Cannon Street was not completed until 1979, and another rebuilding on the north side of Cannon Street, at the west corner of Salter's Hall Court, for which negotiations commenced in 1974 was not finished until 1978. It was, however, yet another instance of a very favourable transaction by which the Foundation acquired a new building occupying double the site area it had previously owned, but at 150 years the building lease was the longest yet granted.[53] One definite casualty of the slump was at Nos. 30–40 Eastcheap, where the proposed developer withdrew, citing as reasons the liability to development gains tax and capital gains tax.[54]

Even during these 'quiet' years, however, one or two highly profitable transactions took place. For instance, in St Swithin's Lane an isolated property which had been acquired by an exchange in 1959 was let on a lease with almost thirty years to run at a fixed ground rent of £1,750 per annum. The lessee, however, wanted to rebuild and agreed to take a new long lease at a ground rent of £37,500, which would become payable on completion of the building, and which was thereafter to be revised every five years to 23 per cent of the rack rental value until 2004 (the date of expiry of the original lease), when the proportion was to rise to 50 per cent. Other buildings were modernized and let at much higher rents, while the listed eighteenth-century buildings at Nos. 27 and 28 Queen Street, which had threatened to hang on the Foundation's hands, were let on favourable terms to Haslemere Estates, who specialized in the restoration of such buildings. In addition, the opportunity was taken to purchase No. 3 Skinners Lane for £250,000 and thus complete the consolidation of another block of properties which had the potential for redevelopment.[55]

Despite what was described by its chairman as 'the virtual collapse of the market in property suitable for redevelopment', the Estate Committee still affirmed its belief in the desirability of investing in real estate, and even in the unpropitious circumstances of 1975 went on record as saying that 'there could be considerable advantage in the Trustees switching out of Stock Exchange securities and Local Loans . . . into real property.'[56]

The recovery towards the end of the 1970s was marked by a number of overtures to the Foundation. Some lessees who held buildings on long leases granted several years ago at fixed rents wanted to extend their leases in return for a small increase in ground rent immediately and regular reviews. Despite the short-term increase in income which would result, the surveyor advised against acceding to their requests:

> I think that the commercial owner of property will normally negotiate with lessees to improve his present income and free himself from rents which are fixed over a long period, but that the Trustees are guided by longer-term considerations. Historically, it has proved right to wait for one's reversions when they fall due, and although the past few years have been exceptional and may not be repeated, they have provided good examples of this in the case of a number of the Trustees' sites.[57]

Such a policy, however, was soon to be overtaken by events as older buildings proved unsuitable for the new technology and space requirements of the 1980s, and offers for rebuilding or refurbishment were received on such favourable terms that it would have been foolish to reject them.

Two new development proposals were received in 1978. In Lovat Lane Nos. 25–26 were to be rebuilt and Nos. 27–28 substantially reconstructed, the Foundation thereby gaining the freehold of No. 27 and a 30 per cent share in the rack rents of the buildings once completed and let. The other scheme concerned the group of buildings at the eastern corner of Cannon Street and Abchurch Lane, which included some of the Foundation's original holdings together with others added in the first phase of consolidation after the war. The corner building, Nos. 135–137 Cannon Street, had been rebuilt directly in 1957, and Nos. 139–141 (Cannon Street Buildings) was an 'agency' building which had been renovated after extensive war damage. The development, by Haslemere Estates, involved the rebuilding of Nos. 135–141, but incorporating the structure of 135–137, and the modernization and reconstruction of Nos. 19–22 Abchurch Lane behind. Once the work had been completed in 1981, the Foundation received an immediate increase in income of over £180,000, with provision for quinquennial rent reviews.[58]

This last development illustrates the complex arrangements which were now becoming the norm in the City and which frequently caused both the negotiations and their subsequent implementation to be protracted affairs. The two projects instituted in 1979 were both of this nature. The first was for the rebuilding of Clarence House, Arthur Street, which had been built directly in 1905–6 to the designs of Herbert Winstanley, the Foundation's first surveyor, together with adjoining premises in Martin Lane. Here the developers, Miller Buckley Developments Ltd, agreed to convey to the Foundation at no cost another recently modernized adjacent property. During building, a licence fee was to be paid which would more than cover the rents previously received from the buildings, and on completion the Foundation stood to gain an increase in income of some £75,000 with the prospect of five-yearly reviews, besides the capital asset of one brand new building and one substantially refurbished one.[59]

The other was on the north side of Cannon Street to the west of Abchurch Lane, resulting in the erection of Sherborne House. As the former buildings on the site had been let on long leases at low rents, some of which were due to expire shortly but others not for some years, the advantage to the Foundation was very considerable. The developers, who were once again Haslemere Estates, paid for the long leasehold interests, and the increase in income was initially some £200,000, but due to rise every five years to a proportion of the occupational rents.[60]

Both these developments were eventually completed in 1983 and 1984 respectively, but not without a lengthy delay, caused in part by planning difficulties but equally by the second financial crisis of the decade in 1979–80 which led to a steep rise in interest rates and another sharp recession. It is against this background that the crucial decision, taken late in 1980, to pursue a positive policy of diversification and to set aside £5 million for the purpose, should be seen.

The occasion was a special meeting of the Estate Committee, which was summoned from time to time to consider what policy to adopt towards the Foundation's investments, both in real estate and stocks and shares. The predominant trend since the war had been to consolidate holdings, with a handful of exceptions, in a number of lucrative commercial premises within the City of London, and to safeguard capital appreciation even at the expense of current income. On the latter principle there was to be no wavering, but as perhaps 90 per cent of the Foundation's wealth was at that time tied up in office buildings in the City, some doubt was expressed at the wisdom of such a concentration. After a debate, the surveyor was instructed to seek opportunities to purchase freehold commercial properties outside the City, and the £5 million which was deemed to be a suitable sum to allocate for this purpose was to be raised by the sale of other investments, by selling properties on the outskirts of the City, and if necessary by borrowing on mortgages, even if this led to a temporary reduction in income.[61] The meeting was very well attended, and there was a general consensus in favour of the decision, which was supported by John Udal in the chair, but one of the prime movers was undoubtedly Gerald Manners, the Professor of Geography at University College, and later chairman of the Committee. Frank Hewitt, the surveyor, on the other hand, was a City man through and through and had mixed feelings about the new policy.

Looking back with hindsight from 1990, after a decade which has witnessed the greatest amount of construction activity in the City's history, the desire to achieve a wider geographical spread of property holdings might seem to have been somewhat premature. But it must be seen in the context of the 1970s, a decade of political instability in which there had been two oil crises and when enormous building booms had been punctuated by severe economic slumps. There had been no shortage of siren voices warning that the paramountcy of the City of London as a financial centre should not be taken for granted, especially when new technology was making the concentration of offices in one or two locations far less necessary, and when it was government policy to encourage the dispersal of offices. Another factor was that the cost of property in the City had risen so steeply that the Foundation could hardly compete in that market, whereas it could afford to buy reasonably-sized freeholds outside central London.

Once the policy decision had been taken it was scrupulously adhered to and set the agenda for the first half of the 1980s. The principal characteristics of the period were the sale of several properties to provide the funds for diversification, the purchase of large office complexes in the London suburbs and elsewhere in the south of England, and the promotion of half a dozen major developments in the City as part of the unprecedented boom that preceded the 'Big Bang', or deregulation of the Stock Exchange, in 1986, and was eventually to continue well beyond it. Each of these will now be considered in turn.

In 1981 a schedule was drawn up of some twenty properties which were either isolated, on the City fringes, or let on long leases at fixed rents, and their sale was actively canvassed. Such was the volume of activity in the property market that there was little difficulty in disposing of the majority of these, together with one or two others where the opportunity presented itself, by the end of 1985, which was the date specified for the completion of the first phase of diversification agreed in 1980. Many of the properties were in the area of Clerkenwell and Smithfield, one or two were elsewhere in the City and others in Holloway, Camden, Chiswick, Kingston and Hampton Hill. No. 11 St Christopher's Place, which had been purchased as part of the complicated deal entered into to acquire Nos. 30–36 Eastcheap, was included, as were the remaining long-leasehold residential properties in Bromley. Just under £1 million was raised from the sale of stocks and shares, and the target of £5 million was easily achieved.[62]

A milestone in the history of the estate was reached in 1985 when an agreement was concluded for the sale of the last residential properties in Bromley which were still on the Foundation's books. In all, since the decision to dispose of most of the so-called ground rent estates in 1956, over 700 such properties were sold at an aggregate price of about £700,000. All that was left of this once far-flung series of residential estates was a block of flats in Shepherd's Bush let to the Metropolitan Police, who showed no inclination to wish to purchase.[63]

The first possibility of an out-of-town purchase which took the surveyor's eye was in Worthing, but concern at some of the terms of the head lease caused the trustees to withdraw. Worthing was not a happy hunting ground for the Foundation, for an isolated and somewhat bizarre decision to invest in a supermarket there 20 years earlier had also fallen through.[64] A suitable alternative was not found until 1983 when Miller Buckley, with whom the Foundation had had satisfactory dealings in the City, proposed to build an office block in Horsham. Satisfactory terms were quickly concluded by which the Foundation paid some £2 million for the freehold, and a 20-year lease was granted to a major insurance company at a rent which represented an immediate return of about 6 per cent and which was reviewable every five years.[65]

The first stage of diversification was completed with the acquisition of an office block in Swindon. Here the arrangements were more complex, involving not merely the purchase of the freehold, but the payment of development costs, up to a total capital commitment of £3 million. In return the developer was to take a head lease and the rental was to be shared on a 'side-by-side' basis. Previously the Charity Commissioners had indicated that they would not look favourably on the direct funding of development projects even on the Foundation's own freeholds, but this view was in response to a theoretical approach, and when faced with a concrete example they gave their consent. The building was completed early in 1987.[66]

The developments which were instituted in the 1980s tended to take on some different characteristics from those of the 1970s. Most were also, for various reasons, subject to long drawn-out negotiations. Even the straightforward rebuilding of No. 21 Godliman Street, for which terms were agreed in 1980, ran into difficulties over the provision of a fire escape and rights of light, and was not begun until 1983. On completion in 1985, the Foundation received a proportion (initially about a third) of the net rental income.[67]

The redevelopment of Monument House in Monument Street and Fish Street Hill by Speyhawk Land and Estates Ltd was more protracted and involved several changes of plan. At first it looked as though rebuilding would have to be confined to the Foundation's own freehold, and the developer agreed to pay a premium of £400,000. As this was unusual an explanation was provided:

> It has been the Trustees' aim, in developments of this nature in the City, to enlarge the site in their ownership by the inclusion of adjoining land acquired at the expense of the developer. This has served, not only to increase the Trustees' holding, but also, as it is the equivalent of a premium, to reduce the ground rent to a level which the market will bear. In this case, the adjoining land . . . cannot be acquired at the present time, and therefore the Surveyor considers that a monetary premium in this instance has to be regarded as appropriate.

Eventually it proved possible to obtain the adjacent properties to the south and these were conveyed to the Foundation, but the premium was still paid on the grant of the lease and the ground rent gearing was adjusted to reflect the addition of the freehold properties. The payment of a premium was in part dictated by the general reluctance of institutional lenders to finance schemes with the high gearings of the 1970s. The long leasehold term of 150 years which was granted was also a reflection of the increasingly stringent demands of financing bodies. The new building was completed in 1987 when it was renamed Gartmore House.[68]

The rebuilding of No. 16 Coleman Street, a building previously let on a lease expiring in 2009 at a low fixed ground rent, is typical of the new needs of the 1980s, both in terms of the kind of offices required and their financing. Because the building was 'old fashioned and lacking in modern amenities' the lessees wanted to rebuild despite the extremely favourable terms of their present tenure. Accordingly, terms were agreed by which a premium of £700,000 was paid for a 150-year lease at a ground rent which was ultimately to amount to 10 per cent of the rack-rental value, subject, as usual, to quinquennial review. Once more, the start was delayed and rebuilding was not completed until 1987.[69]

Subject to delay and complications as these developments may have been, they could not better illustrate the benefit to the Foundation of the boom of the 1980s. Not only had it gained two new buildings, one on an enlarged site, and premiums of over £1 million but the immediate increase in annual income over the old rents on completion was more than £100,000.

Another protracted development at Nos. 36–39 Queen Street and 3 Skinners Lane involved the rebuilding of Nos. 38–39 Queen Street, which had been built as a direct venture in 1936 to the designs of the then surveyor, William Campbell Jones, and incorporated No. 3 Skinners Lane, which had been acquired in 1976 because of its development potential. The arrangements were more than usually complex and included neighbouring sites, but as a result the Foundation acquired a long leasehold interest in Nos. 36–37 Queen Street (having failed to obtain the freehold).[70] One other project undertaken in these years, the extensive refurbishment of Nos. 1 and 2 Gracechurch Street, is worth commenting on because it was financed directly to the extent of some £885,000, the money coming from the excess obtained from the sales of property for diversification. As the building was fully let shortly after completion in 1986 for rents totalling £159,000, the recoupment of the capital investment was not likely to be long delayed.[71]

A review of the history of the estate in these years would not be complete without reference to the death of the Foundation's surveyor, Frank Hewitt, in October 1982. The basic history of the post-war surveyorship is given on pages 219–20, but it is also appropriate to refer here to the outstanding part he had played in the management of the estate for over thirty-five years. He had been the main architect of the post-war recovery and had nurtured the estate to the very sound position it had reached by the time of his death. Among his many achievements, perhaps the most important was the consolidation of the Foundation's holdings in the City, initially by purchases, sales and exchanges, and later in negotiations with developers through which he was frequently able to obtain an enlargement of the Foundation's freehold as part of the redevelopment scheme. On his death the trustees were extremely fortunate in being able to call on the services of Bill Killick, who had been Hewitt's associate and partner for 14 years. Hewitt and Killick between them not only assiduously put together an outstanding portfolio of properties as a solid base for the growth of the Foundation's endowment, but also ensured that those properties were always let to 'first-class', financially sound, lessees.

Some concern was aroused in the middle of the decade by the publication of the City of London's draft local plan, which, to the mind of the Clerk and surveyor at least, was too conservation-oriented. Many of the Foundation's buildings were in conservation areas, and the draft plan included a schedule of buildings which, although not listed, were to be preserved in order to protect the appearance of those areas. Fifteen of these belonged to the Foundation, and a formal objection was lodged on the grounds that the plan would be too inhibiting to development. The Foundation was not alone in making such representations and, following revision, the amended plan which was deposited in 1986 was deemed to be much more acceptable. The emphasis on the preservation of unlisted buildings in conservation areas was removed and the offending schedule was dropped entirely.[72]

Early in 1986, with the diversification policy approved in 1980 having been brought to a successful conclusion, the trustees took stock. There is some evidence of a certain ambivalence of attitude, which is not surprising in the light of the highly volatile circumstances of the time. In the middle of January the Investment Sub-Committee met and recommended 'that the Estate Committee should consider whether to continue the Diversification Policy for a further period in order to continue to reduce the risks consequent upon the bulk of the Foundation's properties still being located within the City of London.' At the end of the month, however, the Estate Committee received a report which concluded:

> It may be that the Trustees were being unduly cautious when, in 1980, they considered that the City of London and Inner London might become less attractive as commercial areas but, as a consequence of their diversification policy, they have disposed of their least attractive properties and have acquired two properties in expanding provincial centres offering good prospects for capital appreciation and income growth over the years to come.[73]

One problem, although it was hardly an unwelcome one, was that there was likely to be a large accumulation of funds available for investment in the near future. Substantial premiums on some development schemes were shortly due to be collected and negotiations were in train which could result in the payment of even bigger ones. It had always been a firm policy to preserve the reversionary value of buildings held on long leases and not to extend those leases, but such was the demand for up-to-date office space that lessees were offering extremely attractive terms to secure the extensions that would make it possible for them to redevelop or refurbish if desired. This coincidence of interests between the freeholder and the lessee which made it profitable for both of them to renegotiate leases is described as the 'marriage value' and was coming to apply in an increasing number of cases. As a result the trustees decided to take each case on its merits and vary their policy where necessary.

This review of the policy was prompted by a proposal to take a new lease of Nos. 113–116 Leadenhall Street which in the end came to nothing, but it soon bore fruit. At Bouverie House in Fleet Street, held on a lease which still had nearly forty years to run at a fixed ground rent of £3,400 per annum, the lessees sought a new 150-year lease, and in return for a ground rent of some 10 per cent of the occupational rents were prepared to pay a premium in excess of £2 million.[74] In the light of the receipt of this 'unexpected bonus', as it was called, it is worth recalling that in 1971 an offer to purchase Bouverie House had been rejected.

Other sizeable additions to the 'suspense account' which was kept free for reinvestment in property came from the sale of York House, Queen Square, for £1.83 million and some quite remarkable sums for compensation for loss of right of light arising out of developments on property adjoining that of the Foundation, amounting to £175,000 in one case, £170,000 in another and £120,000 in a third.[75]

In deciding how to utilize these capital accretions, the trustees reaffirmed their commitment to the City of London, resolving 'That the Surveyor be instructed to continue to look principally at the acquisition of freehold properties in the City of London but also to investigate, as appropriate, the possibility of acquiring properties in provincial centres such as County Towns.'[76] The next opportunity that occurred, however, was in neither of these but in Sunbury, where a newly completed office block containing 25,000 square feet of offices let to a major bank was acquired for £5.85 million. Speed was of the essence in the property market at this time, and as authority had been given to the chairmen and vice-chairmen of the Central Governing Body and the major committees to act for the body of trustees in such circumstances, they rapidly concluded the deal.[77]

It was, in fact, acknowledged that opportunities for further developments or purchases in the City were limited. Two new developments were completed before the end of the decade, however. One was the construction of a new building on the site of Sovereign House, King William Street, itself only erected in 1962, but now 'dated in terms of the quality of accommodation demanded in the market'. Rebuilding took place in 1987–8 and, as a result of a favourable pre-letting to a Japanese bank, the Foundation stood to gain an increase in rental income of about £300,000 as well as a premium of £750,000. The other was at Nos. 14–18 Eastcheap where rebuilding (with a replica of the former facade) was completed in 1990 under the terms of a 150-year lease granted in 1978 which provided for such a development; on the letting of the new building a considerable increase in the Foundation's rent was to be expected.[78]

At the time of writing, redevelopment is also taking place at Nos. 30–40 Eastcheap, on the freeholds so assiduously gathered together for just such an opportunity, and at St Mary Axe, where a large development by Speyhawk encompasses the site of Lumley House and an adjacent one belonging to the Leathersellers' Company.

One development outside the City achieved quite unanticipated notoriety. This was the rebuilding of Southbridge House (or Rose Court as it has now become) in Southwark Bridge Road. The circumstances themselves were unusual enough. Southbridge House had been built in 1955 on a 125-year lease at a fixed ground rent. This was an exceptionally long term for the time, but the site had stood empty for several years previously. When its rebuilding was proposed in 1988, therefore, and the Foundation was offered a premium of at least £1.3 million (depending on the lettable floor area) for an overriding lease at a peppercorn rent which added 60 years to the original term, the offer was readily accepted. Perhaps fortunately, this arrangement meant that the Foundation had such a remote interest in the building that it was in no position to intervene, even if the trustees had wished to do so, when the remains of the Rose Theatre were discovered on the site early in 1989.[79]

In terms of the estate, however, the most stirring events of the end of the decade took place in connection with the playing fields. In 1984 the Estate Committee considered what its attitude should be if a lessee of one of the grounds wanted to determine its lease, in the light of changing attitudes to sport and the provision of leisure facilities. All of the playing fields were now let at economic rents, mostly to educational institutions, but that at Palmer's Green had been let to Metal Box since 1973, originally for conversion into a car park although it had remained in recreational use. The committee decided that while it would not positively promote any changes in the use of the fields, if circumstances altered it would be prepared to consider granting building leases of them, or letting them to other charities or commercial organizations, or, in the last resort, their sale.[80]

If there seems to be an element of indecision in this response, it probably reflects the uncertainty of the trustees as a body about what attitude they should take towards these facilities which had been acquired by their predecessors for a definite social purpose. In 1986 a consultant was appointed to report particularly on the potential for development of the sites at Mitcham and Palmer's Green. The circumstances were that King's College, which, following its amalgamation with Chelsea College, was now the lessee at Mitcham, also owned adjoining playing fields, and had intimated that the whole site was surplus to its requirements. The trustees were concerned that they might be left with playing fields on their hands which were difficult to let and expensive to maintain, a fear which was reinforced by a lengthy, vexatious and 'ridiculous' lawsuit which had just taken place over repairs to the pavilion at Mitcham. They resolved that, short of finding any other charitable body to take it over, any site that was no longer required by its current lessee should be sold or, if that wasn't possible, let for commercial use.[81]

In the meantime discussions were held with the London Borough of Merton about the possibility of residential development taking place at Mitcham, with totally unforeseen consequences. The Council's attitude was favourable, conditional planning consent for a scheme covering both the 34 acres belonging to the Foundation and the 14 owned by King's College was granted in July 1988, and by November 1988 the whole site had been sold for £47 million of which the Foundation's share was over £32 million.[82] For a site which had cost under £15,000 in 1920 this was a quite phenomenal increase in value, which undoubtedly took the trustees and their advisers by surprise.

Shortly after the sale had been completed, a special meeting of the Estate Committee and Investment Sub-Committee was held to decide how best to invest the proceeds, together with other capital sums which would shortly be received. For virtually the first time there was a strong body of opinion among the trustees that every effort should be made to maximize the present income in view of the difficulties which were likely to be faced by the voluntary sector at a time of declining support from local authorities. Other trustees, however, advocated adhering to the time-honoured strategy of maintaining the value of the endowment so that there would be a steady increase in income over the years ahead. The latter policy meant essentially reinvesting the money in property which would yield an immediate return of 5 to 6 per cent with the prospect of substantial long-term growth. After considerable debate the committees decided to divide the available capital in the proportion of 6:4 between property and a mixture of other investments including cash which at that time yielded the highest rate of interest of all.[83]

In the course of 1989 the money that had been allocated to the purchase of property was spent on three major acquisitions: No. 10 Arthur Street, an office block in Windsor and the freehold of the Foundation's new offices in Middle Street, Smithfield. The first of these was a new building immediately adjacent to the Foundation's property in Arthur Street, King William Street and Martin Lane, and it not only constituted a sound present investment but also improved the development potential of the Foundation's existing holdings in the distant future; as such, of course, it illustrates how the policy of consolidation has been followed right up to the present day. The office block in Windsor had also recently been completed and was similar to the other outlying properties acquired in the course of diversification. The purchase of No. 6 Middle Street in advance of completion meant that at long last – after nearly a hundred years – the Foundation would actually own its own offices as had originally been envisaged in the Central Scheme, and in addition had extra lettable space in the building which would be income producing.[84]

Following the Mitcham sale, the question of what policy should be adopted towards the remaining playing fields was re-examined. With the exception of Palmer's Green, all were let to bodies which could be said to be pursuing charitable objects, and the trustees considered that it was desirable to retain open spaces which were of benefit to poorer Londoners. Nevertheless, a flexible attitude had to be adopted in case any of the lessees decided not to renew their leases and the Foundation was left with vacant possession of large areas of playing fields and associated facilities which were costly to maintain. The sports ground at Palmer's Green had fallen into that category several years ago, and in the course of 1990 negotiations were undertaken with a view to its sale. The acreage was far less than at Mitcham and the price suggested was less spectacular but was still a sizeable amount.[85] Nevertheless, the trustees were concerned about the loss of playing fields and open spaces in Greater London and took the view that the income from any capital prospectively realized from the sale of playing fields should be used if possible for open space or amenity purposes, preferably in inner London.

One other occurrence in the late 1980s which is worth noting was the decision of the Charity Commissioners in 1988 to allow the trustees much more discretion in the management of the estate. It was in the Charity Commissioners' nature, for very sound reasons, to exercise caution in their oversight of charitable bodies, but in the case of the Foundation such caution had perhaps come to seem excessive. The need to obtain the consent of the Commissioners to most property transactions had proved time-consuming, and the insistence on advertising properties for sale had merely tended to depress the initial offers. Other requirements, too, sometimes proved unhelpful. In 1982, for instance, the Commissioners had at first insisted on replacement accounts being established to recoup out of income the potential reversionary value of all the properties which were sold to provide money for diversification. This would have made a nonsense of the whole rationale for diversification or, indeed, of any flexible approach to buying and selling, and, after discussion, they agreed to judge each case on its merits and not necessarily insist on the setting up of a sinking fund. We have also seen how they frowned on the possibility of the Foundation helping to finance a development itself until presented with a virtual *fait accompli*.

A more permissive atmosphere prevailed in the latter part of the decade, however. First, in 1987 the Commissioners decided that no more recoupment accounts needed to be set up, and that the consolidated sinking fund which had been formed from earlier ones could be wound up and the money released. Then, in the following year, they elected to exercise the power given them in the Charities Act of 1960 to confer a general authority on the Foundation's trustees which removed the need to refer the vast majority of transactions in land and buildings to the Commission. One of the criteria under the Act for allowing such freedom of action was that past transactions should, in their judgement, have been conducted entirely satisfactorily, and the decision was a huge vote of confidence in the trustees and their professional advisers.[86]

The Commissioners were doubtless also persuaded by the sound position to which the estate had been brought by careful management in the post-war period, and the very healthy state of the Foundation's finances in consequence. From a portfolio of some 750 scattered holdings in 1891 the estate had been transformed into a solid core of about sixty properties in the City, most of them grouped together in clusters where the contiguity enhanced the value of each one, together with a handful of buildings in inner London, four office blocks in the wider south-east which showed every sign of rapidly increasing in value, and seven playing fields or camping grounds within the Metropolitan Police District. Moreover, most of the properties consisted of prime buildings with first-class tenants, let at rents which were subject to frequent review, on sites which were likely to rise considerably in value on redevelopment.

It has already been remarked that such was the adverse effect of the war on the Foundation's revenues, that it was not until 1985 that the income recovered in real terms, after allowing for inflation, but since that date it has more than doubled. If the post-war period alone is taken, however, the real income of the Foundation quadrupled between 1945 and 1989, and, even before the windfall from Mitcham, was two and a half times higher in 1987 than it had been in 1945. Just as importantly, this growth in income has been achieved as a result of a policy which has always placed the protection of the value of the Foundation's endowments first; the long-term interest of securing a steady advance in funds which can be used to improve the condition of the poorer elements of the population of London for an indefinite period in the future has never been sacrificed for short-term expediency.

NOTES

1. Minutes, XLIX, 217, 221–7.
2. Ibid., L, 43–51, 144–9, 166–9.
3. Ibid., L, 182–3; LI, 28–9, 42, 87–8; LII, 60.·
4. Ibid., LI, 30–4, 89, 146–7, 149.
5. Ibid., XLIX, 219; L, 186; LI, 92, 113.
6. Ibid., LII, 17; LIII, 63.
7. Ibid., LII, 21–2, 65, 87; LIII, 65–6.
8. Ibid., LIV, 67, 97; LV, 62.
9. Ibid., LIV, 113–15.

10. Ibid., LV, 82; LVI, 124–5.
11. Ibid., LV, 64–5, 82–4, 124–5; LVI, 33, 91; LVII, 30, 111–2, 160–4; LVIII, 34, 87–8.
12. Ibid., LV, 86, 127–9; LVI, 90; LVII, 84.
13. Ibid., LXXI, 188.
14. Ibid., LV, 22–4, 64, 105.
15. Ibid., LVI, 32, 128.
16. Ibid., LV, 18; LVII, 85.
17. Ibid., LIII, 76–7; LVI, 129, 141.
18. Ibid., LVII, 161; LVIII, 119–20; LXI, 32–4; LXX, 98–9: London County Council, *Administrative County of London Development Plan 1951. Analysis* (1951), 245–52.
19. Minutes, LVIII, 173–8; LIX, 97–8, 125–6, 167; LX, 101–2; LXI, 26–7; LXVI, 215.
20. Ibid., LX, 101–2; LXI, 97–8; LXIII, 117–18.
21. Ibid., LIX, 163–4; LXI, 32–6.
22. Ibid., LXI, 120–1, 153.
23. Ibid., LXI, 121–2: Oliver Marriott, *The Property Boom* (1967), 39–40.
24. Minutes, LXII, 138–40; LXV, 139–41, 206; LXIX, 25–6, 149; LXX, 135–9.
25. Ibid., LXVI, 208–10; LXX, 98–9.
26. Ibid., LXIII, 17; LXIX, 174, 199–200; LXX, 130, 160: *Victoria History of the County of Middlesex. Volume VIII. Islington and Stoke Newington Parishes*, ed. T. F. T. Baker (1985), 24.
27. Minutes, LXIV, 111–12; LXV, 99–100, 139–41; LXVIII, 161.
28. Ibid., LXIII, 156; LXIV, 113–14; LXVI, 99–100; LXVIII, 111–12.
29. Ibid., LXVIII, 171, 204; LXIX, 164–7: *Report of the Committee on the Law and Practice relating to Charitable Trusts* [Nathan Report] (1952), paras 277–98. Some of the phrases used by Allen in his report to the trustees were taken virtually word for word from the Nathan Report.
30. Minutes, LXVIII, 32–3; LXX, 183–5; LXXI, 103.
31. Ibid., LX, 120, 164; LXXI, 105–9, 185–6; LXXII, 97–8, 179–80; LXXIII, 97–8: Nikolaus Pevsner, *The Buildings of England. London. I. The Cities of London and Westminster* (3rd ed., 1973), 226: *Save the City. A Conservation Study of the City of London*, ed. David Lloyd (1976), 52.
32. Minutes, LXXI, 185–6; LXXII, 179–80.
33. Ibid., LXX, 182–3; LXXI, 141–4, 183–4; LXXIII, 20–2; LXXIV, 23; LXXV, 105–6, 157.
34. Ibid., LXXII, 182.
35. Ibid., LXXVI, 93–4; LXXVII, 159.
36. Ibid., LXXVII, 252–3; LXXVIII, 117.
37. Ibid., LXXIV, 165–6; LXXV, 27; LXXVII, 185–6; LXXVIII, 29–32, 138, 153–4; LXXIX, 30, 145–6, 189–90; LXXX, 87–8.
38. Ibid., LXXIII, 132–3, 156; LXXVI, 118–20; LXXVIII, 35–6, 141, 204–6; LXXIX, 192–3; LXXX, 86, 87–8, 136.
39. Ibid., LXXX, 131; LXXXI, 141; LXXXII, 119.
40. Ibid., LXXXI, 240–2; LXXXII, 151; LXXXIII, 41.
41. Ibid., LXVI, 141–2, 163–4; LXVIII, 34–5; LXXX, 151–2.
42. Ibid., LXXV, 160; LXXX, 135; LXXXIII, 37–40; LXXXIV, 19, 32–3.
43. Ibid., LXXXI, 26–8, 134–8; LXXXII, 100.
44. Ibid., LXXXVIII, 159.
45. Ibid., LXXXI, 245–7.
46. Ibid., LXXXII, 192–3; LXXXIII, 27; LXXXV, 160.

47. Ibid., LXXXII, 19–20; LXXXIII, 165–6, 210–12; LXXXIV, 97–8, 143–5.
48. Ibid., LXXXII, 20–2, 201–3; LXXXIII, 34–5.
49. Ibid., LXXXIII, 41–2, 214–15; LXXXV, 31, 104.
50. Ibid., LXXXIII, 179, 205–6.
51. Ibid., LXXXIII, 15–16, 136; LXXXIV, 192–3.
52. Ibid., LXXXIV, 192; LXXXV, 103–4; LXXXVI, 112–13; LXXXVII, 125–6.
53. Ibid., LXXXIV, 148–50; LXXXVI, 121–2; LXXXVIII, 163.
54. Ibid., LXXXIV, 195–6.
55. Ibid., LXXXV, 33–4; LXXXVI, 112, 160–1; LXXXVII, 125.
56. Ibid., LXXXV, 219–20; LXXXVI, 112–13.
57. Ibid., LXXXVIII, 24–5.
58. Ibid., LXXXVIII, 105–6, 107–8; XC, 36; XCI, 153–4.
59. Ibid., LXXXIX, 115.
60. Ibid., LXXXIX, 170–2; XC, 133–4; XCII, 177–8.
61. Ibid., XC, 266–7.
62. Ibid., XCI, 224–5, 320–1; XCVI, 51.
63. Ibid., XCI, 146; XCV, 313; XCVII, 232.
64. Ibid., LXXIII, 177–8; LXXIV, 24; XCI, 319–21; XCII, 183–4.
65. Ibid., XCIII, 49–51; XCIV, 189–90, 409–10.
66. Ibid., XCII, 335–6; XCIV, 38; XCV, 44–6, 55; XCVI, 49; XCVII, 230.
67. Ibid., XC, 136, 204–5; XCIII, 187; XCIV, 183–4; XCVI, 213–14.
68. Ibid., XCI, 308–10; XCII, 188–9; XCIII, 387–9; XCVII, 231.
69. Ibid., XCIII, 397–8; XCVIII, 288.
70. Ibid., XCI, 34–6; XCV, 205; XCVII, 230–1.
71. Ibid., XCVII, 231.
72. Ibid., XCV, 69–70; XCVI, 341–2.
73. Ibid., XCVI 48–50, 72–4.
74. Ibid., XCV, 46–8; XCVI, 55–6; XCVII, 343–4; XCVIII, 290.
75. Ibid., XCIII, 389; XCIV, 423–4; XCVI, 476; XCVII, 253.
76. Ibid., XCVII, 107–8.
77. Ibid., XCIV, 409; XCVII, 340–2.
78. Ibid., XCV, 318–20; XCVIII, 306; XCIX, 333.
79. Ibid., XCVIII, 296–7; XCIX, 503–4.
80. Ibid., LXXXIII, 213–14; XCIV, 40.
81. Ibid., XCVI, 481; XCVII, 109–10.
82. Ibid., XCVIII, 127–31, 589–97.
83. Ibid., XCIX, 153–6.
84. Ibid., XCIX, 203–9, 487–90, 667–8.
85. Ibid., XCIX, 156–7, 160–1.
86. Ibid., XCII, 184–5, 252; XCVII, 130; XCVIII, 141–2.

12 The phasing out of the polytechnics

It was in about 1930 that the trustees began, not for the first time in the Foundation's history, to question whether the support they were giving to the polytechnics was really helping the poorer classes of London. This time, however, they refused to let the matter subside, but pursued it with vigour and determination, largely, it appears, at the instigation of their new Clerk, Donald Allen, to whom the issue took on the nature of a personal crusade. In 1937 the decision was taken to phase out the supplementary and special grants, but the Foundation had no power to remove the compulsory annual grants laid down in the Central Scheme, and had to seek authority from outside to do so. The main story of the post-war years as far as the relationship between the Foundation and the polytechnics is concerned is the attempt to obtain that authority, and the official obduracy and bureaucratic lethargy which delayed its realization until a quarter of a century after the first steps to remove the non-compulsory grants had been taken. Thereafter, the polytechnics could be treated like any other supplicant, and their appeals for assistance dealt with strictly on their merits, sometimes, indeed, with a sympathy that was often conspicuously lacking when the element of compulsion was present.

The offending scheme grants were restricted to those which were paid to the polytechnics and other educational institutions and did not include the handful which went to the 'kindred institutions' such as the People's Palace, the Old Vic, the Chelsea Physic Garden, the Devas Institute and the Whitechapel Art Gallery, whose relevance to the needs of the poorer classes was not, at that stage at least, called into question. What was at stake was a sum of £18,600 per annum, which, in the immediate post-war years, made up over a quarter of the total amount available for grants of all kinds. By the time the grants were withdrawn in 1962, however, such had been the decline in the value of the pound and the increase in the Foundation's income that they only represented about a tenth of the sum available overall, and their removal had become in large measure a matter of principle.

Even during the war years the attitude to the kindred institutions had been subtly different. Sadler's Wells Theatre, which tended to be classed as such because of its associations with the Old Vic, was excused the repayment of instalments on its loan of £20,000 until further notice and given a grant of £1,000 in 1940, in recognition of its attempts to stay open in difficult conditions. The Old Vic and the People's Palace were forced to close as a result of enemy action, but, with the consent of the Charity Commissioners, their scheme grants continued to be paid in order to reduce outstanding loans. When Chelsea Polytechnic asked for a reduction in the rate of interest payable on its loan, however, the request was refused.[1]

In 1944 the Regent Street Polytechnic, which had been particularly vigorous in its opposition to the withdrawal of the supplementary grants, asked for help with the payment of debt charges arising out of its pre-war rebuilding scheme. Its appeal coincided with the passage of the 1944 Education Act, and a sub-committee was appointed to consider the polytechnic's request and the ramifications of the new legislation. Its conclusion was that the 1944 Act imposed a clear duty on local education authorities to secure the provision of adequate facilities for further education. As it was the trustees' policy to refrain from subsidizing activities which could be financed out of the rates or national taxes, there was no reason to depart from the view that support for the polytechnics should be reduced. Accordingly, the application from Regent Street was turned down, as was one from Chelsea Polytechnic in the following year for funds to provide accommodation for a new College of Physical Education.[2]

The Act also required education authorities to provide adequate recreational and social facilities at their institutions of further education, but the Foundation recognized that this would take some time, and continued to assist with additional items of expenditure on the playing fields. Grants were made to Birkbeck for repairs to the pavilion at its ground, to Chelsea for the reinstatement of tennis courts, to Northampton for necessary works at Palmer's Green, and to Morley College to spend on its sports ground, while the Northern Polytechnic was offered both a grant and a loan for improvements to its playing fields at Tufnell Park.[3]

In 1948, when the last supplementary grants were paid in accordance with the programme of phased withdrawal, Donald Allen made a point of informing the trustees that since 1891 the grants made to the polytechnics added up to £2,130,002, of which £1,291,288 had been in the form of scheme grants.[4]

Two years later Allen was asked to be a member of the Nathan Committee on the law and practice relating to charitable trusts, and he took the opportunity to refer in both general and specific terms to the Foundation's obligations to the polytechnics. He submitted a memorandum to the Committee urging that where grants were required to be made to organizations or institutions for which responsibility was subsequently assumed by statutory bodies under an Act of Parliament, trustees should be free to withdraw such grants and apply the money to other purposes specified in the original trust deed or scheme. He returned to the charge in his questioning of several of the witnesses, and when he changed places and gave evidence to the Committee himself early in 1951 he deftly turned his fellow members' questions to his advantage and made his position quite clear by his answers. He thought that the Foundation's continued involvement with the polytechnics was 'unfortunate' and that the money saved by discontinuing the grants to them could be used 'for experiments in social services generally for the benefit of the poor'. When the Committee's report came to be written it advocated that a power to alter the objects of charitable trusts should be conferred with appropriate safeguards, although it should be stressed that this recommendation did not arise solely, or even principally, from the Foundation's experience with the polytechnics, as there were many more flagrant examples of outdated trusts.[5]

The second post-war quinquennial policy review took place in 1951, and the subject of the scheme grants to the polytechnics was placed high on the agenda. Allen wrote to the various institutions informing them that their grants were under review and asking for comments. All regretted the move, and stressed how important the Foundation's grants were, as much in a symbolic as a practical way, to the preservation of their independence from the London County Council. He also sought the views of the Ministry of Education, which urged the Foundation to continue the grants but had to concede that, 'if the Foundation withdrew its aid to the Polytechnics it would be the duty of the London County Council to see that this reduction in income did not prevent students from obtaining satisfactory technical education.'[6]

An attempt to reach a compromise with the polytechnics, whereby the scheme grants would be withdrawn but an equivalent amount would be set aside to assist them in any 'special works' for which statutory support would not be forthcoming, met with a frosty response. Accordingly, when the sub-committee reported towards the end of that year it ignored the negative aspects of the letter from the Ministry of Education and merely cited the phrase quoted above as a vindication of its view that positive steps should be taken to withdraw the grants. The reasons for the sub-committee's stance were spelt out clearly: 'The funds of the City Parochial Foundation are intended to benefit the poorer inhabitants of the Metropolitan Police Area and with the present organisation of the statutory system of public education it would seem without doubt that the continuance of these Scheme Grants tends to relieve the Exchequer and rates of expenditure for which they are responsible.'[7]

Under the Ministry of Education (Transfer of Functions) Order of 1949 jurisdiction over the polytechnics and similar institutions had passed from the Charity Commissioners to the Minister of Education – a move which had filled Allen with foreboding that the money freed would be required to be used for educational purposes[8] – and so an application was made to the Ministry for an order terminating the grants. The Ministry referred the matter to the Charity Commissioners, but neither body could decide, or wanted to decide, which had the authority. Instead they suggested that the Foundation should make an application to the High Court. So began the long and tedious business of preparing a legal case, which was not assisted by the determination of each of the polytechnics to mount a separate defence, a tactic which led Allen to remark to the Foundation's solicitor, J. W. French, 'what a nuisance it all is'.[9]

Eventually the case was heard by Mr Justice Roxburgh on 1 December 1954, but he ruled that the Courts had no jurisdiction in the matter because the Central Scheme, which had the force of a statute, gave no such power to the Courts and stated that it was up to the Charity Commissioners to issue any amendments to the Scheme. As Allen testily remarked when he reported the matter to the trustees, 'This was of course the view of the trustees in 1951 to which point we now return.' They resolved to pursue the matter, and concurrent applications were made once more to the Charity Commissioners and the Ministry of Education to withdraw the grants. Informal contacts suggested that the former were amenable, or at least they gave that impression, but that the latter was opposed. Eventually, in April 1955 a long letter was received from the Commissioners which was a masterpiece of obscurantist language. It concluded, apparently on the grounds that there had been no general allegation that the institutions in question were not being conducted in conformity with their governing schemes, that 'the Commissioners and the Minister are of one mind that at this point the application made to them is not justiciable in form.' Even the indefatigable Allen must have felt deflated.[10]

Another policy sub-committee was shortly due to be appointed and it was decided to defer to that committee. In the meantime, a White Paper was issued by the Government which indicated that at long last some of the recommendations of the Nathan Committee were likely to be embodied in legislation, including a widening of the grounds on which trusts could be altered. Rather than start another long, and possibly profitless, round with the Charity Commissioners, the trustees decided to await the enactment of legislation, although they asked for a letter to be sent to the Commissioners recapitulating the reasons for wishing to withdraw the grants, which, they thought, had been 'wholly disregarded'.[11]

If some time had elapsed between the publication of the Nathan Report and the subsequent White Paper, however, there was an even longer gap between the appearance of the White Paper and the passage of legislation based on it. In the interval, significant changes occurred at some of the polytechnics. As part of the drive for the expansion of technical education from the mid-1950s, Battersea, Chelsea and Northampton Polytechnics were designated Colleges of Advanced Technology with a considerable enhancement in status that made them national rather than local or even London-wide institutions. Other institutions no longer had even a token connection with the polytechnic movement. Birkbeck College, for instance, had become a school of the University of London in 1920, but still received its annual scheme grant.

Thus, by the time the Charities Act of 1960 came into force at the beginning of 1961 the polytechnic movement had already begun that process which was to transform it beyond measure over the next 20 years. Section 13 of the Act stated that the original purposes of a charitable trust could be changed where they have since 'been adequately provided for by other means'. Allen decided that this clause gave him sufficient reason to approach the Commissioners again, but as another quinquennial policy review was about to take place it seemed politic to refer the matter to the sub-committee which was appointed to undertake the review. Accordingly, he prepared a long report which reviewed the whole history of the Foundation's relationship with the polytechnics, and recommended that application should be made to the Charity Commissioners to withdraw the scheme grants under Section 13 of the Charities Act and apply the money instead for other educational purposes which were outside the scope of local education authorities. The last stipulation was probably necessary because the Act only allowed trusts to be varied *cy près*, and Allen, anticipating opposition, was anxious not to be caught out on these grounds.

The report was duly approved by the sub-committee and subsequently by the full Central Governing Body, and was forwarded to the Charity Commissioners in June 1961 with an application to withdraw the grants. The institutions concerned were informed, and all initially decided to oppose the application. This time, however, the Commissioners were at one with the Foundation and drew up an amending scheme. When it was published, most of the institutions, including the three Colleges of Advanced Technology, withdrew their objections, and only the Regent Street, Northern, North-Western and Borough Polytechnics and Morley College persisted in formally petitioning against the proposed scheme. No other objections were received, however, and the Commissioners announced that they intended to establish the new scheme, whereupon the remaining polytechnics chose not to press their opposition. An order was sealed on 30 July 1962, and Allen could barely contain his satisfaction and relief. His reply to the Commissioners struck an uncharacteristically personal note. 'I could hardly believe my eyes,' he began, 'when I read in your letter this morning that the Scheme relating to the withdrawal of the grants to the Polytechnics had been sealed.'[12]

Under the new scheme, Clause 44 of the Central Scheme was amended to read:

> The Central Governing Body shall, out of the residue of the Central Fund, apply an annual sum of not less than £18,600 for educational purposes for the benefit of the poorer classes of the Metropolis for which provision is not made by local education authorities.

This 'Education Fund', as it came to be known, tended to be used to provide grants which the trustees would have wanted to make in any case and which could be said to have a vaguely educational purpose.

Relations with the polytechnics remained cordial, and were perhaps more friendly once the compulsory grants had ceased than they had been during the protracted period when the Foundation was seeking to bring them to an end. One of the first acts of the trustees once the new scheme had become official was to write off a debt of just under £2,000 which was owed by the Northern Polytechnic, and in the following year a loan of £10,000 repayable over ten years was approved for the modernization of the kitchens at the North-Western. It had been intimated to some of the smaller institutions, indeed, that more favourable consideration might be given to their needs once the whole business of the scheme grants had been cleared up, and the first grant to be made out of the Education Fund was £1,500 in 1962 to the Working Men's College, which was in some financial difficulties.[13]

The educational institution which received the most generous support from the Foundation was Morley College. As an evening institute with a low level of fees, there was no doubt that Morley had adhered to its original purpose and still catered for people who worked by day, many of whom could be said to be among the poorer elements of the population of London, although by no means the poorest. Moreover, the college buildings had been largely destroyed by bombing and their reconstruction had been beset with difficulties and had not been completed until 1958 (when the trustees gave a grant of £250 for the reopening ceremony). Thus, when the college appealed for assistance in acquiring land for a future extension its request was received sympathetically, and in 1962–4 grants of £5,500 and loans of £10,500 were approved for this purpose. The loans were quickly repaid, and when it came to the allocation of grants for the next quinquennium (covering the years 1967–71), £25,000 was set aside (from the Education Fund) to help pay for the construction of a new building on the site which would include a gymnasium, a theatre-cum-concert hall, and a canteen. The whole of the grant had been claimed by 1969.

This was not the end of the story, however. In the 1972–6 quinquennium another £20,000 was given towards the costs of the next phase of building on the site, and, in 1978–80, £1,000 a year was provided to meet the costs of the Morley College Youth Theatre productions at the Old Vic. Finally, in 1982, £50,000 was given towards the cost (estimated at £450,000) of a new Community Education building, in which facilities and courses designed for people living in one of London's more deprived areas could be accommodated. These included 'Fresh Start' courses, literacy classes and family workshops. As the report recommending the award of a grant commented, 'In its new and extended role, Morley College nowadays makes much more provision for the people in whose interests the City Parochial Foundation works.'[14]

The non-educational institutions were treated differently, and separately. The People's Palace never really recovered from its closure during the war. It struggled on for a few years, but was losing money so rapidly by 1953 that the governors informed the Charity Commissioners 'that in their view the Charity has failed'. The Commissioners asked the Foundation to assume the trusteeship of the Palace to see it through liquidation, and to take over the endowment for the benefit of the poorer inhabitants of the East End. The charge was accepted, debts amounting to over £13,000 were paid off, and an agreement was made to sell the freehold to Queen Mary College for £95,000.

The scheme grant was cancelled, and a new scheme was drawn up whereby the money that was left after the sale had been completed, amounting to £91,000, was to be invested and the income applied for objects which would be 'beneficial to the poorer inhabitants of the Metropolitan Boroughs of Stepney, Bethnal Green, Poplar and Shoreditch'. The Charity Commissioners expressed their gratitude to the

Foundation for its 'public spirited action' in stepping into the breach even though by doing so they faced the possibility of adverse criticism. 'Fortunately,' their letter of thanks continued, 'this possibility did not materialise. That was perhaps to be expected from the high repute in which the City Parochial Foundation and its management are held in the metropolis.' The People's Palace and Four Boroughs' Fund, as it was called, has continued to be accounted for separately, and now produces about £10,000 per annum which is available for modest grants.[15]

After 1962 the only institution to which a mandatory grant was still payable under the terms of the original Central Scheme was the Old Vic, but this state of affairs did not last very long. The theatre had a chequered post-war history, and this is reflected in its relationship with the Foundation. In 1946 the proposal was mooted that the Old Vic and the Shakespeare Memorial Theatre should amalgamate to form the National Theatre; the trustees were concerned, but nothing came of this suggestion in the short term. The building in Waterloo had been badly damaged during the war and remained dark for nearly a decade. Provincial and overseas tours were mounted by the company, however, and the scheme and supplementary grants amounting to £2,000 per annum continued to be paid.

In 1950 strenuous efforts were made to raise money for the necessary repairs so that the theatre could be open during the Festival of Britain in the following year. The Foundation gave a grant of £5,000 and a loan of £10,000, and matching grants were also made by the Pilgrim Trust and the Carnegie United Kingdom Trust. The theatre duly reopened and had a highly successful decade in which a complete cycle of Shakespeare's plays was performed. When the National Theatre Board was appointed in 1962 and reached an agreement with the governors of the Old Vic to take over the theatre as the temporary home of the National Theatre, however, the trustees decided that both their scheme and supplementary grants should be withdrawn, and the Charity Commissioners agreed. At the same time, the trustees indicated that if the theatre reverted to its former status they would be prepared to consider sympathetically any applications for assistance, and that if the National Theatre undertook activities which could be shown to benefit the poorer inhabitants of the metropolis it, too, might be eligible for grants.

In fact, no grants were made until the new National Theatre opened in 1976 and the company moved from the Old Vic. The theatre was used by the Prospect Company as its London base, and a grant of £30,000 over three years was approved for refurbishment. Only £10,000 was paid before the company ran into difficulties, and the remaining £20,000 was converted into the offer of a loan, which was, however, withdrawn in 1981 when the company went into liquidation. In 1982 the Old Vic was bought by the Canadian businessman, Ed Mirvish, and the Royal Victoria Hall Foundation was reconstituted as a purely grant-making body with which the Foundation was no longer associated.[16]

The first of the additional institutions to which the Foundation was required to pay a mandatory grant under supplementary schemes was the Chelsea Physic Garden. The original grant fixed by a scheme of 1899 was £800, but this was soon supplemented by additional sums, which from the early 1920s made the total up to £2,000 per annum. Damage from bombing was sustained during the Second World War, several plants were removed to Kew, and the extra grant was actually reduced as the Garden was placed on a care and maintenance basis. After the war the grant was gradually restored to its pre-war level, and eventually beyond it, as the effects of inflation began to be felt; in addition, in 1948, the Foundation agreed to accept responsibility for repairs and redecorations to the buildings of the Garden.

By the mid-1970s the trustees were becoming concerned about both the rising cost of repairs and the amount of grant now needed (although in real terms it was no more than in the 1930s). There was also a nagging doubt, once the connections with the polytechnics had been severed, whether the Physic Garden could be said to serve the purposes of the Foundation any longer, if indeed it ever had done. The sub-committee which was appointed to prepare a policy for the quinquennium 1977–81 was asked to include the future of the Garden in its deliberations. It recommended that funds should be made available for the modernization of the Garden, but that the Charity Commissioners should be informed that the Foundation wished to withdraw further financial support. In the meantime the trustees would actively seek another sponsor.

This task, of course, fell to the Clerk, Bryan Woods, whose attempts to find a solution to what soon came to appear a somewhat intractable problem mirrored on a smaller scale Donald Allen's earlier efforts to rid the Foundation of its obligations to the polytechnics. His first proposal to establish a Garden School and Centre for Plant Studies came to naught, other schemes proved equally abortive, and overtures to the National Trust foundered over the Trust's insistence on a large endowment. Finally, in 1981, a new and independent body of trustees agreed to take over the Garden, and in return was promised grants totalling £200,000 to meet the estimated running costs over the next four years. A new scheme was published, and the formal transfer took place on 1 April 1983 when the Foundation's scheme grant came to an end. In the following year a garden party was held (at the

Foundation's expense) to mark the transfer of the trusteeship and was attended by the Prince of Wales.[17]

The small Devas Institute in Battersea was considered to have the potential to develop into a junior polytechnic when it was taken over by the Foundation in 1901, but it continued to function as a youth club and social institute. As such, of course, it was certainly looked upon as serving a useful social purpose, and the annual grant of £250 which the Foundation was obliged to pay under the Charity Commissioners' scheme of 1901 was supplemented by extra amounts, ranging from £500 per annum immediately after the war to £800 by the early 1970s. Additional sums were also given from time to time to meet the cost of repairs to the club premises and other expenses.

In the mid-1960s the site of the Institute was required for the new fruit and vegetable market at Nine Elms. Compensation of £75,000 was payable, and the Foundation agreed to top this up to nearly £100,000 to pay for the acquisition of an alternative site in Stormont Road, Battersea, and the erection of a new building. Officially opened on 6 October 1970, this provided improved facilities, which in turn led to increased activities and, paradoxically, created a financial problem. The committee of management thought that its own fund-raising activities were hampered by the association with the Foundation, which tended to be looked upon as the main provider, and it was mutually agreed that the Institute should become an independent charity with its own trustees. The Foundation handed over the freehold of the building, and, after discussions with the Charity Commissioners, gave a grant of £2,500 in redemption of the scheme grant at ten years' purchase.[18]

The grant paid to the Whitechapel Art Gallery was not obligatory, but the promise to provide an annual sum of £500, which had been an important element in helping to found the gallery in the first place, was regarded as binding. In 1947 an additional grant of £1,000 was made to assist in revitalizing the gallery, which had fallen into a state of torpor in the inter-war years, and other sums were given on occasion for repairs or alterations to comply with building regulations. However, in 1975 an appeal for an increase in the annual grant and a contribution to the cost of urgent repairs was rejected, and in the following year the gallery's trustees applied for a new scheme which *inter alia* would reduce the number of nominees appointed by the Foundation to the gallery's governing body from three to one. By that time the Foundation's grant (which had not risen in line with inflation) made up a very small proportion of the gallery's income, most of which came from the Arts Council and the Greater London Council. The Charity Commissioners approved a new scheme and ruled that the gallery had no legal right to expect an annual grant from the

Foundation. Payment of this was accordingly stopped, but in 1984 a grant of £50,000 was approved for a development scheme which would enhance the educational and community use of the gallery.[19]

The very last of the obligatory or semi-obligatory grants to be withdrawn (at least from the Central Fund) was not one to any institution, but a sum of £150 paid annually for the upkeep of the open space next to St Botolph, Aldersgate, usually referred to as Postman's Park. The origins of this payment lay in complex nego-tiations during the 1890s over the laying out of the open space which resulted in the payment of a 'rent' by the Post Office for rights of light. The grant was increased to £250 between 1920 and 1960, but reduced again when the City Corporation undertook to meet most of the costs of maintenance. By 1985 the rationale behind the continuance of the grant seemed increasingly obscure, and the trustees asked for an enquiry to be made into the circumstances. When it was pointed out that the payment from the Post Office for rights of light went into the City Church Fund, they decided that in future the grant should come out of the income of the City Churches Grants Committee set up under a scheme of 1980 (see page 329).[20]

The ending of all of the former scheme, supplementary and special grants which were made on an annual basis did not mean that the institutions concerned were cut off from all grant aid, as the substantial assistance subsequently given to the Whitechapel Art Gallery indicates. Several of the institutes which had long associations with the Foun-dation, such as Bishopsgate and St Bride, were helped with abnormal expenditure, and Sadler's Wells was given a grant of £7,000 in 1975 so that the upper circle could be renovated without increasing the price of the cheaper seats. Even when the most concerted efforts were being made to remove the mandatory grants to the polytechnics, they were still assisted with expenditure on the playing fields, and it was made clear that they would be eligible for grants for any projects which fitted in with the Foundation's objectives. The grants made in 1986, of £10,000 to the Polytechnic of North London to provide a lift for the disabled, and £30,000 over two years to the Polytechnic of the South Bank to employ a tutor for a diploma course for district nurses, come into this category.[21]

The last remnant of the support for the polytechnics disappeared when the sub-committee appointed to determine policy for the quin-quennium 1987–91 recommended that the Education Fund which had been set up under the revision of Clause 44 of the Central Scheme in 1962 should no longer be accounted for separately, and that Clause 44 itself should be deleted. The committee's reasoning was cogent enough; far more was, in fact, spent every year on educational purposes than the £18,600 specified in the amended Clause 44, and the continuance of the fund seemed particularly pointless.[22] The Charity Commissioners agreed, and the new Central Scheme of April 1989 makes no specific mention of education. Henceforth, all requests for aid by any institution, educational and otherwise, would be measured against the Foundation's wider aims in the various fields of social welfare.

NOTES

1. Minutes, L. 89, 160; LI, 142–3; LII, 13–14.
2. Ibid., LIV, 110; LV, 13, 77–8.
3. Ibid., LIV, 13–14; LVI, 115–16; LVII, 104; LVIII, 54, 162; LIX, 60–1.
4. Ibid., LVIII, 67.
5. PRO, CAB 124/141, q. 5358; 142, qq. 5985–6, 5991–2, 6985; 143, qq. 7294–7, 8th meeting of sub-committee, pp. 2–3: *Report of the Committee on the Law and Practice relating to Charitable Trusts* [Nathan Report] (1952), paras. 299–365.
6. CPF, file 1789/2.
7. CPF, *Report on Policy relating to the Allocation of Surplus Income of the Central Fund 1951 to 1955* (1951), 1–2.
8. PRO, CAB 124/143, 8th meeting of sub-committee, pp. 2–3.
9. Minutes, LXII, 65: file 1789/2, letter of 30 July 1953.
10. Minutes, LXIV, 200; LXV, 115–16: file 1789/2.
11. Minutes, LXV, 115–16; *Report on Policy . . . 1956 to 1960* (1956), 1–2.
12. *Report on Policy . . . 1961 to 1965* (1961), 1–4; Minutes, LXXII, 109–11, 138–9: file 1789/4.
13. Minutes, LXXII, 139, 157; LXXIII, 147–8.
14. Ibid., LXVIII, 136–7; LXXII, 141–3; LXXIV, 95–6; LXXVII, 49–50; LXXX, 10; XCII, 124–6; *Report on Policy . . . 1967 to 1971* (1967), 8; *Report on Policy . . . 1972 to 1976* (1971), 5: Denis Richards, *Offspring of the Vic: A History of Morley College* (1958), 276–306.
15. Minutes, LXIII, 137–9, 171–2; LXIV, 17, 90–1, 128.
16. Ibid., LVI, 67–8; LX, 21–2, 76–7, 135–6, 159; LXXIII, 110–11, 141–2; LXXXVIII, 78–9; XC, 22, 229; XCI, 62–3; XCII, 24, 88, 280; XCIV, 12.
17. Ibid., LI, 86; LXVI, 45, 87; LXVII, 46; LXVIII, 43; LXXIV, 53; LXXV, 57; LXXXVI, 22, 44–5, 62–3, 106–7; LXXXVIII, 51, 121, 172–3; LXXXIX, 19–21, 186–8; XC, 218–19, 230–1; XCI, 235–7; XCIII, 82–3, 90, 310; XCIV, 219.
18. Ibid., LVI, 113–14; LXIII, 59–60; LXVII, 134; LXXIV, 150–1; LXXVI, 122–3; LXXVII, 191–2; LXXVIII, 143; LXXX, 69; LXXXIII, 20–1, 173.
19. Ibid., LVII, 128–9; LXIII, 88; LXIV, 141–2; LXV, 122–3; LXXXV, 145–6; LXXXVII, 53–5, 146; XCIII, 142–5.
20. Ibid., XCV, 348.
21. Ibid., LXIV, 75; LXIX, 79–83; LXXIV, 91; LXXXV, 143–5; XCVI, 256, 294–6.
22. Ibid., XCVI, 453–4.

13 Grants 1940–1965

The year 1965 is a convenient point at which to divide the history of the Foundation's general grant-making policies over the second half of its first century. Not only was it the middle point chronologically, but it also marked the retirement of Sir Donald Allen, whose influence had been so considerable over the previous period. Nevertheless, one of the most important characteristics of the Foundation's history is continuity over time, and there was no sharp break or major change of direction after 1965.

Immediately on the outbreak of war in 1939, the trustees were warned that it was likely to prove very difficult to maintain the existing structure of the voluntary social services. A report, presumably prepared by Allen, suggested, with remarkable foresight, that the government might step in with emergency help 'without permanently impairing the character of voluntary enterprise in social service'.[1] In fact, one of the effects of total war was to produce a far greater degree of intervention by the state into the social lives of its citizens. Some needs diminished, while certain new ones were created by the war situation, but there was also a rapid recognition on the part of the government that the universalization of provision was a key factor in sustaining civilian morale. The sense of shared deprivation which was produced by rationing and the community spirit generated by common hardships also helped to create social cohesion.[2]

The effect on the Foundation was, ironically, that although its income fell, slowly at first as rents were reduced, and then sharply as the result of the destruction caused by the Blitz, the demands on that income which were regarded as legitimate declined even more. This was not at all apparent at first, and applications for grants were carefully scrutinized to see whether they were likely to lead to increasing demands on diminishing resources, but by the beginning of 1942 it could be predicted that the sums available would 'far exceed' the total amount which the trustees would wish to allocate in grants. Other factors which cushioned the effect of the fall in gross income were that several grants which had been made a short time before the war for building projects in connection with community centres or youth clubs had to be returned because the projects had had to be abandoned, and the gradual phasing out of the non-mandatory grants to the polytechnics and similar institutions also released money for general purposes. The net result, however, was the building up of a healthy reserve, which amounted to about £50,000 by the end of the war. That the trustees and their Clerk, who were keen to undertake 'experiments in the social service field' as soon as the war was over, regarded this as a highly desirable state of affairs cannot be doubted, and they were not about to let the fact that the nation was at war lessen the rigour with which they assessed the suitability of applicants for grants.[3]

Of course, voluntary organizations had a very imporant part to play in the war effort, and it was part of government policy to seek to work through them whenever possible. The very first grant that the trustees approved after war had been declared was £1,000 to the London Council of Social Service to assist with the cost of running citizens' advice bureaux, one of the earliest and most important innovations of wartime.[4] Another, made shortly afterwards, was £500 for the youth centres which had been set up in the metropolitan boroughs at the beginning of the war as a result of a government initiative to ensure that adequate provision was being made for adolescents and that existing youth work was properly organized.[5]

Some initiatives were taken directly by the trustees themselves. In September 1940, after a series of heavy air raids on London, Donald Allen toured the halls and other buildings in the suburbs to which those rendered homeless had been evacuated and found that there was a shortage of blankets and clothing. After consulting with the chairman of the Emergency Sub-Committee, Sir William Collins, he authorized immediate expenditure on blankets and footwear for children. By early 1941, well over 2,000 blankets had been ordered at a cost of nearly £2,000, and proved to be a great boon. Additional help was also given to the Dockland Settlement for its work in connection with the evacuation of the homeless, and in 1941 £1,000 was set aside to provide a home to which people could go for a short respite from the bombing. A suitably large house was found at Buckhurst Hill, and the Pilgrim

Trust and several of the City livery companies also agreed to make grants so that it could be adapted for the purpose. Further grants were given to assist with running costs and the home continued to function throughout the war. Similar help was given in 1942 to the Servers of the Blind League so that a home could be established for elderly people who had been rendered homeless through bombing, and grants were also made to Nazeing Camp, which had formerly catered to the unemployed but which was used to rehouse refugees from the severe bombing of Silvertown.[6]

One of the problems in London was the feeding of the dispossessed populace. In 1940 £500 was given to the London Council of Social Service for communal feeding, and in the following year a report commented on how well the service was being conducted by volunteers, with 37 centres feeding 7,500 people daily. Grants were also given on several occasions to the Invalid Kitchens of London which provided food for people suffering from conditions requiring special diets. Sir William Collins, whose own particular expertise was in the field of medicine, paid a surprise visit to one of the centres and was much impressed by the quality of the diet and the manner in which the service was appreciated by the sick poor.[7]

Several organizations which had been aided on a regular basis before the war continued to receive support. These included, in descending order of the average size of grants, the Central Council for District Nursing in London; National Council (later Association) and London Union of Girls' Clubs; National Association of Boys' Clubs; London Council of Social Service; YMCA (Metropolitan Union); YWCA (London branch); Central Council for the Social Welfare of Girls and Women in London; Invalid Children's Aid Association; National Council for the Unmarried Mother and her Child; and Homes for Working Boys in London. Annual grants were also made for the costs of running the camps on the Foundation-owned camping grounds at Chigwell Row and Cudham, and the expense of maintaining Grange Farm.

Some old favourites failed to outlast the war; the Factory Girls' Country Holiday Fund was wound up in 1943 following the death of its founder and secretary, and later in the year the same fate befell the MABYS Association for the Care of Young Girls after the death of its secretary, its work being taken over by the London County Council. The Greater London Fund for the Blind and the National Library for the Blind received grants in the early part of the war, but didn't apply in 1944 because of the satisfactory state of their finances. The Children's Central Rescue Fund was not given a grant in 1941 because mass evacuation appeared to have removed the need, but, significantly, the grant was restored in 1942 and subsequent years, when, with the return of children from the countryside, the problem reappeared. Intermittent grants, although sometimes large ones, were also given to some of the settlement houses, especially Toynbee Hall and University House, Bethnal Green.[8]

As always, there was a special relationship with the Charity Organisation Society. The COS took over the running of citizens' advice bureaux in London and was given an annual grant towards the cost. The Society was also called in to assist with one of those experiments in social service favoured by Donald Allen. This was the provision of spectacles to the elderly poor, a need to which attention had been drawn by Jimmy Mallon of Toynbee Hall. He pointed out that as pensioners could not recover the cost of spectacles from the Assistance Board, of which he was a member, and were reluctant to apply to the Relieving Officer because of a dread of the poor law, they bought them second-hand or from cheap stores. The trustees agreed to give grants to supply them free of charge, and the COS undertook to administer the scheme. By 1945 grants totalling £1,500 had been made for this purpose, and the Assistance Board 'expressed their immense gratitude for the work which the Foundation had been able to carry out' when asking for it to be continued until the need could be covered by legislation.[9]

One reason why the trustees readily embraced this cause was that the need for their own pensions had been substantially reduced by the Pensions Act of 1940, which made provision for the granting of supplementary pensions on proof of need. Most pensions under the amending scheme of 1935 were not renewed when they expired, apart from a few cases in which there was 'exceptional hardship', and by the end of 1945 there were only 28 pensioners of all kinds left on the Foundation's books.[10]

Early in 1945, even before the war had ended, a sub-committee was appointed to review the policy on the allocation of grants in the quinquennium 1946–51. It was the fourth such policy committee, the last having met in 1937. The committee was fully aware that there were likely to be considerable changes in the provision of social services following the publication of the Beveridge Report in 1942. The Education Act of 1944 was already on the statute book and other legislation was impending. The Welfare State was about to be created. To some extent the committee's deliberations had already been pre-empted by meetings which their Clerk, Donald Allen, had held with other people who were prominent in the social service field, to consider what the role of the voluntary sector should be in the new circumstances and what particular needs were likely to remain unsatisfied.[11]

The sub-committee's report strongly reiterated the view expressed by its predecessor in 1935 that grants should not be given for projects which could be financed out of local or national taxes, except to encourage official bodies to undertake new areas of work. The polytechnics almost certainly came into the former category, but the report considered that the future of the scheme grants was a matter to be dealt with separately. One area where it thought that statutory provision was now quite sufficient was the acquisition and preservation of open spaces, and it advocated that, in future, support should be restricted to organizations whose function was to protect the public interest in such matters. In the case of those voluntary organizations whose activities were likely to be taken over by statutory bodies under new legislation, however, it considered that care should be taken to give adequate support during a period of transition so that continuity would be maintained.[12]

As far as new policies were concerned, an important recommendation was that an estimate should be made of the surplus which would be available for grants over the quinquennium. It was possible to provide such an estimate with a reasonable degree of accuracy because the Foundation's income was predominantly based on rents. It was only later in the 1970s, at a time of high inflation and frequent rent reviews, that it became more difficult to predict income over a five-year period. Once the surplus had been calculated, the report recommended that it should be divided between the continued support of approved organizations and 'experiments in the social service field', the main objects of which should be 'to endeavour to indicate the direction which future development should follow to ameliorate the lot of the poorer inhabitants of the country'. Acting on this suggestion, the calculation was made that the total surplus over the next five years for general grants (once the mandatory grants to the polytechnics and other bodies had been paid) was likely to be about £220,000.[13] In addition a sizeable reserve had been built up during the war years. With this in mind, the report recommended the promotion by the trustees of two new enterprises, both of which would involve a considerable outlay of funds. One was the building on its Packington Estate of a block of flats which would include accommodation for the aged poor, and the other was the development of Grange Farm as a holiday centre.

The shortage of suitable accommodation for the elderly was one of the anticipated post-war needs which had emerged out of Donald Allen's round of discussions towards the end of the war. He thought that this was basically the kind of problem which could only be resolved by local authorities or the government, but considered that there was a role for charitable bodies in pointing the way forward, in this case by constructing model dwellings. He consulted widely with other interested bodies, the trustees gave their approval, and Campbell Jones & Sons were asked to prepare a scheme. The site chosen was a triangular one, bounded by Prebend Street, Coleman Fields and Bishop Street, which had suffered bombing. It was near to shops and other facilities in the centre of Islington.

The development was to be a mixed one, with flats for families on the upper floors, partly because it was considered to be important not to segregate the elderly from normal community life, but also because the income from rents (including any government subsidies) was expected to cover management costs. In addition, an administration block was to contain a communal dining room for the elderly, laundry and sick bay, with accommodation for a resident matron or nurse. The costs were initially estimated to be about £70,000, but on completion of the architects' elaborate plans, which provided for 42 family flats and 31 old people's flats and single-storey dwellings, they had risen to £200,000. The trustees were still prepared to proceed, and approved the allocation of £100,000 out of capital (to be replaced out of income over 30 years by a sinking fund) and £100,000 out of income (£50,000 from reserve and £50,000 from the anticipated surplus in the quinquennium). Tenders were approved in October 1946, and the name Isleden House was chosen. In December, in a rare bout of publicity, a booklet was published giving details of the scheme.[14]

Construction began early in 1947, priority having been given to the development despite the shortage of building materials, and at about the same time the Nuffield Foundation produced a report on the care of the elderly which was eagerly welcomed by Allen because it appeared to endorse pioneering work of the kind being undertaken by the Foundation. Lord Beveridge's *Voluntary Action*, which was published in 1948, also specifically praised the concept of the scheme. Building was completed in 1949 and Queen Mary opened the complex in May of that year. The total cost amounted to £275,000, of which some £18,000 was met by war damage compensation and payments by the LCC for materials from demolished houses. Of the remainder, the contribution from income was kept to £100,000, but £157,000 was now to be provided out of capital and replaced over 60 years.[15]

Isleden House was publicized in *The Builder*, and Allen reported that it had been visited by experts from Northern Ireland, Holland, France and Australia. But, even though he was later to complain that the publicity had led to more applications for grants and increased work for his staff, there is no indication that the scheme had much influence on the type of housing which was provided for the elderly by public authorities. It was, for one thing, almost certainly too ambitious, with features such as a sick bay and a resident matron, and appears not to have been cited subsequently as an exemplar. When, two years after its completion, government guidelines were issued on the provision of housing for the aged, they stated, quite specifically, that 'In our view, and in the opinion of those who have submitted evidence to us, it is not necessary to have a resident nurse among the old people; nursing is a service which is best organized for the community as a whole.' The conventional architecture of Isleden House, with its brick facades and tiled roofs, may also have militated against it, for at this time most of the housing schemes which tended to attract attention were those which stylistically belonged to the Modern Movement.[16]

Allen thought that the Foundation's task was to build and equip the flats, but that it should not be involved in managing them for an indefinite period. The first occupants were suggested by Islington Borough Council and the LCC, but it was to the City that he turned when looking for a statutory authority to take over the block. There was a certain logic in this in view of the Foundation's close historical links with the City, and the fact that T. C. Harrowing, who chaired the Corporation's Public Health Committee, was a trustee helped to smooth the path. The City offered £100,000, which, although well below the cost of building, was considered to be an equitable sum for taking on the responsibility of management, and Isleden House was formally conveyed to the Corporation of London in February 1953 with a covenant that the accommodation intended for the elderly should be retained for that purpose. The building is still owned and managed by the Corporation and, unfashionable as its architecture may have been at the time it was finished, it has stood the test of time rather better than some of its more avant-garde contemporaries. For several years it was the practice of the Foundation to give a small grant at Christmas to pay the cost of festivities for the residents.[17]

The development of Grange Farm as a camping and recreation centre was another venture to which Allen was strongly committed. It was situated just within the bounds of the Metropolitan Police District, in a part of Essex with which he was very familiar, and he had doubtless played a part in its acquisition in 1938. Plans for the utilization of the large site, which covered over one hundred acres, had been drawn up before the war but had had to be shelved. They were quickly revived when the war ended. Once more, an ambitious scheme was proposed, with a large swimming pool and other buildings designed by the architect Kenneth Lindy. Before building began, the cost was estimated to be about £130,000, but the Ministry of Education, which was now empowered to give grants for facilities for physical training and recreation, agreed to contribute £80,000. Work proceeded gradually, as permits had to be obtained and materials were in short supply, but was speeded up to allow for completion in time for 2,000 foreign students to be accommodated there during the Festival of

Britain in 1951. The centre was officially opened by Princess Elizabeth on 12 July 1951.[18]

A management committee was formed consisting of four members appointed by the Foundation (one of whom was Allen), three each by the London Council of Social Service and Chigwell Urban District Council, and two each by Essex County Council and the LCC, and was granted a 60-year lease of the centre at the nominal rent of £25 per annum.[19] Initially the centre was very popular. In 1953 over 8,000 people camped there, and it was visited by nearly 200,000; it was described as 'on a fine day, one of the main attractions for East Londoners'.[20] An additional £30,000 to meet the capital cost of providing more facilities was voted in the quinquennium 1951–6, and an annual grant was given for running costs, usually £1,000 but sometimes more. In 1962 it was said to have been used by 250,000 people, but by 1964 the question was being asked whether the time had not come to hand over its management to a local authority, and in the following year the lease was assigned to Chigwell UDC, which was also given a grant of £2,000 to cover the existing deficit.[21]

To complete the Grange Farm story, additional funds were given to the centre until 1969, when a decision was taken to make no further grants in view of the implied subsidy represented by the low rent. Several overtures to purchase the freehold were made by Chigwell Council, and one was finally accepted in 1973. By then doubts were being entertained whether the original purpose was still being fulfilled, as poor Londoners now appeared to constitute a distinct minority of users, and there was no longer 'evidence of charitable need'. Over £300,000 had been spent on the centre, £214,000 of it by the Foundation, and although the Council only offered £125,000 this was thought to be a reasonable sum in view of the length of time left on the lease at a very low rent and plans for the M11 motorway which would cut a swathe through the centre.[22]

Three acres of the original site of Grange Farm had been let to Essex County Council for the building of Chigwell House, a home and occupational centre for the disabled, which had been completed in 1966, and towards which the Foundation had provided half the cost of £140,000.[23] Two other small areas were also excepted from the sale, one let to the Pony Riding for the Disabled Trust, and the other to the Winged Fellowship Trust for the site of a holiday home for the disabled.[24]

Isleden House and Grange Farm Centre were by far the biggest projects of the immediate post-war period (and featured extensively in Donald Allen's history of the Foundation which was published in 1951[25]), but other important decisions on grants were also taken in the late 1940s.

In 1948, with the introduction of the National Health Service, the long series of annual grants to the Central Council of District Nursing (which were invariably the biggest of the year-on-year grants) came to an end. The Council continued to function, but responsibility for it devolved on the LCC as the local health authority.[26] Its place as the recipient of the largest grant was quite soon taken by the Family Welfare Association (as the Charity Organisation Society had been renamed in 1945). Most of the other organizations which were supported throughout the war continued to be aided, and some whose grants had been suspended for one reason or another were picked up again. Among these were the hostels for disabled and invalid women workers in Camberwell, which taught fine needlework to women who were incapacitated. The hostels had suffered serious damage during the war and were struggling to re-establish themselves. They were given additional funds in 1948, partly to help them in this task and partly because the spread of infantile paralysis was creating an increased demand for their services.[27]

In 1945 a grant of £300 had been made to the London Council of Social Service for the establishment of a legal aid centre in West Ham, and after the war, grants for other centres were made to the Family Welfare Association, which took over this work in addition to the running of citizens' advice bureaux. In 1950, £1,250 was given through the FWA to the Mary Ward Settlement in Bloomsbury and Cambridge House in Camberwell for centres there, a matching sum having been provided by the Pilgrim Trust and a larger amount by the LCC. A Legal Aid and Advice Act had been passed, but its implementation had been largely delayed as an economy measure, and in the following year the trustees decided not to give any more grants for legal aid centres on the grounds that 'they could not continue indefinitely to pay for the failure of a government to give effect to legislation which had been approved by Parliament'. Similarly, three years earlier, they had taken the view that 'no part of the burden of financing Citizens' Advice Bureaux should now be borne by charitable bodies'.[28]

Another innovatory series of grants, commencing in 1948, were those given to the LCC, initially at the rate of £1,000 per annum, to assist pupils or students who might otherwise be prevented from continuing their studies or playing a full part in school or college life. This aid would be over and above that allowed by statute, for, in the words of the Council, 'the necessary limitations of a general scheme governed by Act of Parliament must press hardly on individual students whose circumstances are exceptional.' Donald Allen fostered close links with the LCC and continually sought ways in which the Foundation could help where the Council's powers were limited by law. A scheme to provide aid to pay the travelling costs of parents visiting children who were in special boarding schools was introduced in 1950 with the explanation that, 'From time to time the Trustees have given favourable consideration to applications made by the London County Council to fill gaps in the social services.'[29]

Indeed, even after the introduction of the Welfare State there was a general awareness among philanthropic bodies that serious gaps in provision still existed, and that the voluntary sector had a very important role to play in trying to fill these gaps. This was a consideration that was at the forefront of the minds of the trustees and the applicants for grants. The Invalid Children's Aid Association, for instance, when applying for its usual grant in 1948 felt constrained to comment that it had 'always undertaken pioneer work' and added that 'even when there is a complete National Health Service, there will still be scope and need for voluntary effort'. An example of support for just such effort occurred three years later when £1,000 was given to the Association for the adaptation of a home at Worthing as a recuperative centre for chronically sick children, because although fees covering the costs of maintenance would be met from public funds, capital expenditure fell outside the scope of the relevant Acts.[30]

New areas of need were brought to the trustees' attention as conceptions of poverty changed. One was the plight of middle-class women who had to rely on limited means at a time of inflation, a concern which had indeed been singled out by the trustees' solicitor, Howard Bradshaw, when he left a bequest to the Foundation in his will (see page 220). It was the reason why a grant of £1,500 was given in 1949 to the Florence Nightingale Hospital for Gentlewomen, which was outside the National Health Service, even though there was a general presumption against giving grants in the medical field. Two years later £500 was given to the Westminster Homes in Streatham whose clientele were men and women from a similar background.[31]

The organizations which accounted for the biggest share of the funds available to the trustees for non-mandatory annual grants in the immediate post-war years, however, were those which catered to the needs of youth. As we have seen, considerable importance was attached to this area of work in the 1930s, leading at the official level to the inauguration of a national youth service in 1939. After the war, apprehension on the one hand that there might be an explosion of juvenile delinquency and the belief on the other that profitable and socially useful activities should be found to occupy the ample spare time and boundless energies of the young kept the issue in the forefront of social concerns. Moreover, it was one in which the state looked to the voluntary sector to take the lead. As Beveridge put it, 'To promote the right use of adolescent leisure is perhaps the greatest of all tasks for Voluntary Action to-day.'[32] The Foundation certainly took him at his word and devoted a remarkably large proportion of its available funds, both at this time and in succeeding years, to this one area of social welfare. The annual grants made to the associations of boys', girls' and mixed clubs, and to the YMCA, the YWCA, the Boy Scouts, the Boys Brigade, the Girl Guides (for camping), and other relevant bodies, rarely added up to less than £10,000 and frequently amounted to much more out of a total available of some £35,000.

The policy report for the 1951–5 quinquennium could cover a much broader spectrum of needs as no large-scale projects like Isleden House or Grange Farm were contemplated. The anticipated surplus for the quinquennium after the mandatory grants had been paid was £285,000, of which £30,000 was to be set aside for further work at Grange Farm and £95,000 for 'miscellaneous grants', meaning the general run of annual grants, leaving £160,000 for new initiatives.[33]

The most important of these initiatives, for which £50,000 was earmarked, was the utilization of the River Thames for recreation, and arose directly from that concern to promote healthy and purposeful leisure-time activities for young people to which the trustees were already devoting much of their resources. In 1948 a grant of £2,000 had been made to the London Federation of Boys' Clubs for an experiment in establishing a new type of club for the 'unclubbable boy' on a barge, and the resulting Barge Boys' Club had been relatively successful. Two years later, the City of London Sea Cadets applied for a grant, and this prompted the Grants Sub-Committee to consider whether a more concerted attempt should be made to provide a range of water-borne pursuits on the Thames and its tributaries.[34]

Donald Allen consulted widely with a number of organizations including the Sea Scouts, the Navy League and the Sea Cadet Corps, as well as the mainstream associations of youth clubs, and the result was the establishment in 1951 of a new co-ordinating body, the Thames Youth Venture Advisory Council. The Council was independent of the Foundation, but very much its progeny, and existed mainly to suggest specific schemes which were worthy of the trustees' support. The Council lasted for 25 years, and over that time the Foundation spent £240,000 (the equivalent at 1990 values of some £1.75 million) on activities which it had recommended. These consisted mainly of sailing, rowing and canoeing from a number of major bases which were established at Barn Elms, Putney, Ham Dock, Richmond, Raven's Ait, Surbiton, the River Lea at Cheshunt, and the Welsh Harp at Hendon, and smaller ones elsewhere.

One rationale behind such a level of support, as expressed at the beginning of the 1956–60 quinquennium, was that these activities instilled into those who participated in them 'the need for discipline

and self-reliance which are the ultimate goals of character training,'
and 'obedience to leaders which cannot but be for the general good
of young persons who will so order their lives that in future, as parents,
they will discipline themselves.' Such views were as much a reflection
of the social make-up of the Central Governing Body as they were an
indication of perceived social need, and by 1976, when the Council
was wound up, not only had the 'explosive development in water
activities', as it was then described, rather overtaken the Council's
efforts, but also sentiments like those expressed in 1956 were by no
means so fashionable.[35]

To return to the 1951–6 quinquennium, another need of young
people was for accommodation at reasonable prices; as the report
stated, 'there are thousands of youths struggling to exist in London
upon inadequate incomes.' Indeed, in 1948 a grant had been given to
the Fellowship of St Christopher to tackle the problem of homeless
boys sleeping on the Embankment.[36] One response, as it had been in
the 1930s, was the provision of hostels by various voluntary bodies,
and the organization singled out for initial support with an allocation
of £30,000 was HYELM (Hostels for Youthful Employees of Limited
Means) which was struggling to keep its hostels functioning in a group
of run-down leasehold houses in Camden Town. For the trustees, this
was no more than an interim measure, and assistance for hostels was
stepped up in succeeding years.

The same amount, £30,000, was set aside for a proposal to establish
a home for the severely handicapped in connection with Queen Elizabeth's Training College for the Disabled at Leatherhead. The needs
of the physically handicapped had indeed been singled out by Beveridge in his analysis of the role left for voluntary action in a social
service state.[37] In 1949 a grant of £2,000 had been given to Queen
Elizabeth's College, which was establishing a women's section, to be
used specifically for the benefit of poor women who came from the
metropolitan area. The project to be aided in the quinquennium,
however, was for new facilities where treatment, nursing, physio-
therapy, occupational therapy and training could be provided for severely handicapped people of young and early middle age. Eventually
administered as a separate body with the name Dorincourt Estates,
the facilities consisted of a residential rehabilitation centre at Banstead,
a residential sheltered workshop at Dorincourt near Leatherhead, and,
later, a holiday and convalescent home at Westcliff-on-Sea. Other
grants were given by the Pilgrim and Dulverton Trusts, and the
Foundation's support, which was continued into the 1960s and amounted in all to a little under £70,000, was related to the extent which
the units were used by people from the metropolis.[38]

Two relatively new concerns which had been brought to the attention of the trustees in the late 1940s, the problem of genteel poverty and the need for additional help for schoolchildren and college students from poor backgrounds, were also singled out for further support in the quinquennium. A sum of £5,000 was set aside to make annual grants of £1,000 to the Friends of the Poor to assist 'ladies whose present circumstances are distressing', and £15,000 was earmarked for allocation to all the education authorities in the metropolis for supplementary aid to pupils and students, rather than just to the LCC as before.

Other sums which were earmarked for specific purposes were £8,000 for the establishment of additional Family Service Units, which undertook intensive case work with problem families, a grant of £500 having already been made on the founding of the first unit in 1947; £6,000 to the National Institute for the Deaf towards the cost of providing a hostel for young deaf working men; £5,000 to provide additional children's playgrounds in the overcrowded inner boroughs; and £5,000 to the Hostels for Crippled and Invalid Women Workers in Camberwell, where a new hostel was being erected.

Of course, the sum which had been reserved for miscellaneous grants could always be used to help new applicants, particularly as the surplus which had been calculated for the quinquennium proved to be an underestimate in the event. In 1953 a grant of £1,000 was given for a scheme to provide accommodation for discharged prisoners which was the first step towards the establishment of the highly influential Norman House (see page 288), and this was supplemented by a further £6,000 in the following year. Also in 1954, £1,000 was given to the Holloway Discharged Prisoners Aid Society to enable a social worker to be employed, and this was followed up with further grants in subsequent years. These were not quite the first interventions by the trustees in the field of the after-care of offenders, but earlier efforts were chiefly concentrated on rescue work for girls and women who were considered to be in moral danger, whereas these grants marked the beginning of a systematic and continuous recognition of a different kind of need.[39] It was, of course, not a concern that was new to philanthropy in general; the origins of the various prisoners aid societies alone stretched well back into the nineteenth century. What was signified, as far as the Foundation was concerned, however, was a willingness to devote an increasing amount of attention to people who might be classed as social misfits and who, a few decades earlier, might have been thought to fall outside the category of the deserving poor.

At almost the opposite end of the spectrum, the concept of providing support to students from poor families was extended in 1953 when £250 was given to the Oxford Society to assist needy undergraduates from London with small disbursements. Other organizations including the Pilgrim Trust backed the scheme, but the trustees thought long and hard before agreeing to contribute. In the following year they gave £350 to the Vice-Chancellor's Discretionary Fund of the University of London for similar purposes, and later gave funds to Cambridge University 'to meet the needs of London undergraduates who encounter genuine hardship which is in no way due to improvidence on their part'.[40] One thought in the trustees' minds, and that of their Clerk, in making these grants may have been that they would have a better chance of succeeding in their attempt to rid themselves of their remaining obligations to the polytechnics and related institutions if they could be shown to be aiding other educational causes.

Other grants whose relevance to the foremost needs of the poorer classes might be questioned include the £1,000 which was given in 1953 (and repeated in 1956) to King Edward VII's Hospital for Officers, but memories of the Second World War and the Korean War were still very fresh. More understandable, perhaps, was the series of grants made from 1953 to the Royal Hospital and Home for the Incurables at Putney.[41] The advent of the National Health Service had, in fact, brought into focus the role that the voluntary sector could play in hospital care, a field which had previously seemed beyond the slender resources of the Foundation.

Not surprisingly, given the Foundation's current preoccupations, particular interest was shown in new ventures connected with youth. In 1954 a grant of £1,000 was given for the establishment of a club for 'Edwardian' youth, a somewhat stilted term for the Teddy Boys who were thought to constitute a menace to society. Of more long-term significance, however, were the grants made from 1953 onwards to the Outward Bound Trust, including £5,000 in 1955 to assist with the purchase of 'Halsteads' in the Lake District (for which the King George VI Foundation and the Dulverton Trust also gave grants) and other sums throughout the 1950s and 1960s amounting in total to over £20,000. Additionally, in 1955 a decision was taken to give £4,000 per annum for five years to the as yet to be publicly announced and therefore still 'highly confidential' Duke of Edinburgh's Awards Scheme.[42]

An important new initiative was taken in 1954 when the Clerk was asked to report on the problems which were arising as a result of the influx of immigrants from the New Commonwealth. The occasion was the receipt of an application for a grant from the Stepney Coloured People's Association, which was considered to be too vague in its aims for the trustees to support, but they recognized that there was a problem which they shouldn't ignore. In what seems to be a remarkably far-sighted recommendation, Allen suggested that, as an experiment, three black social workers should be engaged to undertake case-work in various parts of London and run an advice centre in Brixton, utilizing the facilities of the Family Welfare Association. He estimated that the cost, with clerical support, would be £4,500 per annum and the trustees agreed to make grants of this amount for three years. The FWA submitted a comprehensive report on the project, which was published in 1960 with the title *The West Indian Comes to England*, and the Dulverton Trust, in providing funds to finance a similar scheme in Bristol, said that it had been inspired 'by the fine example which your Trustees have set'.[43]

In 1955 the Grants Sub-Committee once more divided grants into categories, a practice which had been abandoned in the war. They were welfare of the aged; education; welfare of the handicapped; open spaces, camps, etc.; settlements and social centres; welfare of women and children; youth work; and unclassified. The last category included grants to the various Councils of Social Service and the sums, by now amounting to at least £3,000 per annum, which were given to the Family Welfare Association.

The Quinquennial Policy Sub-Committee for 1956–60 adhered to these basic groupings. It calculated that once the compulsory grants had been paid, some £625,000 would be available over the five years, ranging from a little over £100,000 in the first year to about £140,000 in 1960, but proposed remarkably few new ventures. Partly in consequence of this it advocated that after all other allocations had been made a reserve of £50,000 should be left to cater for any unforeseen eventualities in the period.[44].

The only substantial new scheme that was contemplated was the provision of hostels for educationally sub-normal school-leavers who, while employable, were thought to need residential care. The National Association of Mental Health was given £55,000 for the purpose and successfully carried out the project. An even larger sum, £112,000, was earmarked for distribution to various branches of the YMCA for the establishment of hostels of a more usual kind for boys. As we have seen, this was by no means a new problem, but it seemed to be one that was becoming increasingly acute as more and more young men flocked to London to take advantage of the employment opportunities offered there. A proposal was drawn up for a ring of hostels that would cost some £600,000 in all, of which £450,000 remained to be found. The Foundation's grant was intended to be a quarter of this sum.

Besides the continuing support for the work of the Thames Youth Venture Advisory Council, Grange Farm Centre, and Dorincourt Estates, a further £20,000 at £4,000 per annum was set aside for local education authorities, to continue to provide additional help to pupils and students from poor backgrounds. A further £7,500 was also assigned to the London and Greater London Playing Fields Association to open more children's playgrounds.

The needs of the new elderly poor, namely 'members of the professional classes who have been nurses, school teachers, army officers, their wives, widows and the like', for whom the rapid fall in the value of the pound had led to privation, still occupied the trustees' minds. They allocated £20,000 to the Friends of the Poor and Gentlefolk's Aid, £15,000 of it for the construction of an annexe to Stuart House, the society's home in Hampstead (to which the Foundation had given grants in the past), and £5,000 for grants to assist the residents to pay their living costs in the home.

Grants totalling £20,000 were also made to the Women's Voluntary Service (later the Women's Royal Voluntary Service) for help to the aged. Of this sum, £5,000 was to be spent in buying new vans for the 'meals on wheels' service which was run by the WVS in several areas of London, essentially on behalf of the local authorities under the terms of the National Assistance Act of 1948. The remaining £15,000 was to be used to erect, as an experiment, a building on a housing estate at Stepney which would provide a dining room, kitchen and recreation room for elderly people. Also coming within the category of the welfare of the aged was a proposal to make a special grant of £5,000 to the Family Welfare Association for its work in arranging holidays for the elderly.

Of the remaining projected surplus, £10,000 was apportioned for the rebuilding of the Dockland Settlement at Canning Town, which had been affected by bombing in the war. Grants to the Settlement, or the Mayflower Family Centre, as it was subsequently renamed, totalled over £20,000 between 1955 and 1964. One other scheme, for the expenditure of £25,000 in turning Walthamstow Marshes into a public open space, proved impossible to implement. After the setting aside of £50,000 as a reserve, this left £200,000 for miscellaneous grants over the five years.

The problem of members of the professional classes who had fallen on hard times was one that still clearly troubled the trustees. Of the organizations established to meet their needs, the Delves House Trust, which provided accommodation and care for elderly people from this background in seven houses in Kensington, received generous support from 1956 onwards, totalling over £12,000 by 1965. In 1956 a grant was given to the Officers' Association, on the grounds that it could be held 'to assist the aged and needy of today's poor class', and in the following year an application from the Ladies' Home for Gentlewomen of Small Means in St John's Wood, which would celebrate its centenary in 1959, was also accepted. The Elderly Invalids' Fund, which aimed to assist old people who did not fit easily into the kind of provision offered by the National Health Service, by offering relief for home carers or helping to meet the costs of placements in private nursing homes, first received a grant in 1955 and was, thereafter, given an increasing level of aid. Further resources for the care of the elderly were allocated in 1960 when a grant of £10,000 out of the quinquennial reserve was made to the WVS to establish a home for those suffering from senility.[45]

The welfare of the aged was, of course, one of the categories into which the Foundation divided its grants. Another was the welfare of the handicapped, and considerable resources were directed into this area. Support for organizations for the blind had again been spasmodic after the war, but the formation of the Greater London Fund for the Blind was welcomed as 'complete unification' and it was given £2,000 in 1956, and successive amounts in following years totalling £15,000 by 1965. Meanwhile, in 1958 a grant of £15,000 out of the quinquennial reserve was made to the Royal School for the Blind, Leatherhead, for the establishment of an occupational therapy unit, would would *inter alia* benefit poorer inhabitants of the metropolis.[46]

Annual grants were also given to the National Institute for the Deaf, including an additional £2,000 in 1959 to conduct the London part of a nationwide survey into the extent of the problem of deafness. Although, on the whole, the Foundation did not give grants for medical purposes, it was always prepared to support organizations which dealt with the social consequences of medical problems. The Multiple Sclerosis Society, which had been founded in 1953, the British Epilepsy Association and the British Rheumatic Association all received small grants to provide holidays for sufferers, and £1,000 was given to the WVS in 1960 to organize holidays for the disabled at Grange Farm Centre, as the trustees began to focus on this type of service as one for which the voluntary sector was particularly suited. The Western Cerebral Palsy Centre, which had been founded in 1951, received over £6,000 in the course of the decade, and the Cheshire Foundation Homes were given a grant of £10,000 out of the reserve to establish a new home at Dulwich.[47]

One field of voluntary endeavour which was not mentioned in the policy review but was singled out for assistance through the miscellaneous grants was the welfare of the ex-prisoner. In particular, Norman House in Highbury, which had been established in the mid-1950s with the assistance of the Foundation to provide after-care for homeless offenders, exercised a strong pull on the trustees. Norman House had proved to be a very successful experiment, and in 1959 a grant of £7,500 was made to enable a second house to be opened which would be a half-way house for offenders before full rehabilitation in the community. An additional £1,500 per annum for two years was promised so that the services of Merfyn Turner, who had been the inspiration behind the project and a source of much useful advice to the Foundation for many years, could be retained as director. As might be expected, this was by no means the end of the Foundation's support, which continued on a long-term basis. Other organizations which provided various forms of after-care also received grants on a smaller scale, including the London Police Court Mission, the London Sessions Probationers' Fund and the New Bridge.[48]

The quinquennial policy review for 1961–5 contained a long disquisition on the changes which had been brought about by statutory intervention in the field of welfare, but concluded that 'even though destitution has disappeared and no reason exists for extreme poverty amongst the able-bodied, relative poverty and in all too many cases real hardship are found amongst "handicapped" persons of all ages'. The term 'handicapped' as adopted in the report was intended to have a wide meaning, including not only physical disability, but also old age and 'inadequacy'. The use of this concept, and the connotations it carried in terms of the needs which remained to be addressed, marked another decisive step away from the notion that the Foundation's help should be directed primarily towards the deserving poor.[49]

Several of the special grants which were recommended for the quinquennium reflected these changing attitudes. In all, it was estimated that the sum available for grants over the five years would amount on average to about £200,000 per annum, or £1 million in all. Of this, £250,000 was to be earmarked for miscellaneous grants and £65,000 as a reserve. Apart from £120,000, which had to be set aside in case mandatory grants still had to be paid to the polytechnics and kindred institutions throughout the quinquennium, the remainder was divided between about 15 projects. Some of these were merely extensions of earlier schemes, including the Thames Youth Venture Advisory Council, children's playgrounds, aid to pupils and students, and a further grant to Stuart House in Hampstead. The largest single allocation of £75,000 for a proposed hostel in the Barbican complex, which would probably be managed by the YMCA, can also be construed as continuing support for the establishment of hostels, although it was justified as 'preventive' work in that it would cater 'for boys and young men who are away from home or living in undesirable surroundings'. After several delays, the hostel was completed in 1971 and the Foundation was invited to nominate two members of the committee of management.[50]

One major new initiative eventually had to be abandoned. This was a scheme to create a model common lodging hostel, for which £50,000 was reserved. The aim was to provide an environment in which 'the forgotten men of the Welfare State', as the report described them, who habitually resorted to common lodging houses, might be offered the chance of rehabilitation. Toynbee Hall was interested in hosting the project, but local opposition prevented the granting of planning permission. Another proposal, to establish an old people's unit containing a sick-bay, dining-room and common-rooms on the lines of that at Isleden House, on a site in Brixton owned by the Corporation of London which was adjacent to some almshouses, also proved abortive when the Corporation lost interest.

Other schemes for the aged and the physically handicapped proved more successful. The Elderly Invalids' Fund was given £30,000 to continue the work for which it had previously been supported out of the general grant fund. Another grant of £30,000 helped to finance the Larchmoor School for Maladjusted Deaf Children, which was opened in 1966, and £40,000, which was earmarked for permanent accommodation for the physically handicapped, was used for the building of Chigwell House on a site taken out of the Grange Farm Centre. Another £20,000 enabled the Pony Riding for the Disabled Trust to establish a riding centre, also at Grange Farm.[51]

A pioneering venture which proved of immense value was the building of St Christopher's Hospice for the dying, the inspiration of Dr Cicely Saunders, who had devoted her professional career to the care of dying patients. The hospice, which opened in 1967, eventually cost some £450,000, and towards this the Foundation contributed £50,000 in 1961–5 and a further £50,000 in the succeeding quinquennium.[52]

Another project which essentially broke new ground was an experiment to establish a combined family casework unit, for which £60,000 was set aside. A building to house the unit in Stoke Newington was purchased by the Foundation, and it was opened in 1963 and staffed by social workers who were seconded from the Family Welfare Association, Family Service Units and the Invalid Children's Aid Association. The unit, which was known as the Hackney Family Centre, was extensively used and was taken over by the Family Welfare Association when the experimental period came to an end.[53]

Other large sums which were earmarked for specific purposes in the quinquennium were £50,000 for the training of youth leaders in connection with the proposed National Recreation Centre at Crystal Palace, and £25,000 for general support to the Family Welfare Association. From the reserve, the largest sum, £25,000, was committed to a scheme which was to be operated by the National Association for Mental Health for maintaining a list of landladies in London who would be prepared to provide lodgings for difficult adolescent girls from Borstals, approved schools and other institutions. In 1964 £15,000 was promised to the National Institute for Social Work Training to enable a social worker to be attached to a group medical practice for a trial period of five years. A practice in Kentish Town was chosen and the experiment was later said to be 'arousing so much interest as to suggest that in future it might be necessary to protect it from the hazards of excessive limelight'. Open spaces were not at the forefront of the trustees' priorities at this time, but a contribution of £10,000 from the reserve was made to the cost of building changing rooms at Hackney Marshes, which were used for football and other sports. The idea behind this was to galvanize the LCC into spending the additional sums that were needed to provide these much-needed facilities, apparently with 'unqualified success'.[54]

Of the general grants that were made during the first half of the 1960s, a substantial proportion, as before, went to youth organizations. There were indications that the trustees were becoming concerned at the extent to which this work, important as they deemed it to be, was swallowing up their resources. In 1960 their attention was drawn to the Albemarle Report on the youth service which recommended increased financial assistance from statutory sources, and a number of organizations were informed that they should not expect future grants to be on as generous a scale as those at present. Calculations were made of the total sums spent on these grants, although exactly how the category was defined is not clear, and there was a decrease, from £86,000 in 1959 (nearly 50 per cent of the total sum spent on grants) to £66,000 in 1963. At the same time, according to figures which were given to the trustees, annual grants from the LCC to voluntary youth organizations increased from £55,000 to £335,000.[55]

Nevertheless, large grants continued to be made for youth work. Some had to be increased, such as those to the Girl Guides for the Chigwell Row and Cudham camps, and the National Association of Boys' Clubs for the Bellingham playing fields (subsequently transferred to the London Federation of Boys' Clubs), as it had been agreed to meet the extra costs which fell on those bodies as a result of the trustees' decision to charge economic rents for the grounds (see page 241). Some were special grants for capital expenditure, such as £10,000 to the Boy Scouts for work at a number of sites, and £10,000 to the YWCA, both in 1963. Some went to new organizations undertaking valuable pioneering work, such as Task Force, which was founded to harness the energies of youth for service to the old and lonely, and which received £8,500 in 1964–6 to establish area offices in Camden and Wandsworth.[56]

The trustees had previously considered that any contribution they could make to the problem of homelessness lay chiefly in supporting the establishment of hostels, but in the 1960s they began to look more broadly at the whole question of the shortage of housing. A number of the new housing associations and housing societies which were founded at about this time were given grants, generally for housing for special needs such as those of the elderly. In 1962 £2,000 was made available to the National Federation of Housing Societies, and this was followed up three years later with an even bigger grant of £5,500, on condition that most of it was used for schemes for housing the aged and handicapped. In 1964, however, more general help for the homeless was given when grants totalling £3,500 were made to the British Council of Churches Housing Project, the Housing the Homeless Central Fund and the LCC Welfare Fund for Homeless Families.[57]

From 1962 the earlier groupings of grants were, if not quite abandoned, at least vastly simplified into welfare of the handicapped (which included the aged), youth and open spaces, and unclassified. One trend that can be discerned in the increasing number and variety of miscellaneous grants that were made each year was a growing concern for those who had fallen by the wayside of society in various ways. Support for bodies which specialized in the after-care of offenders, including Norman House, the New Bridge, the Circle Trust and Apex, was maintained and in some cases stepped up, while the Griffins (formerly the Holloway Discharged Prisoners Aid Society) was given a grant of £5,000 per annum for three years, part of which was to be used to pay the salary of a psychiatric social worker.[58]

In addition, the trustees began to give help to organizations that dealt solely or primarily with the problem of addiction. In 1961 a grant of £1,200 was made to the St Botolph, Aldgate, Rehabilitation Centre, which catered for alcoholics, and this and other centres were given small grants in subsequent years. In 1964 a contribution of £100 was made towards the costs of a conference on the use and misuse of drugs which was organized by the Howard League, and grants in 1965 included £2,500 for the conversion of the crypt of Christ Church, Spitalfields, into a centre for vagrants and alcoholics, £1,000 to the Helping Hand Organization for residential therapeutic accommodation for alcoholics, and £500 to the Golborne Rehabilitation Centre for alcoholics and drug addicts.[59] These were small beginnings in what was to become a major area of concern for the Foundation.

Other grants of an innovatory nature included £3,000 per annum in 1961 and 1962 to the London Council of Social Service to run what was called a day sitter-in service for the elderly, providing relief for the carers, and £2,000 per annum for five years to the Invalid Children's Aid Association to study dyslexia, or as they termed it, 'word-blind' children. Among new organizations which were aided were the Samaritans with £1,000 in 1964 and £2,000 in 1965.[60] One of the most significant projects to be assisted in the period was what came to be known as the North Kensington Family Study. This began as a fact-finding survey of Notting Hill after the race riots of 1958, for which the Foundation gave grants of £1,700 in 1961 and £1,500 in 1963. This resulted in the publication in 1964 of *A Troubled Area* by Pearl Jephcott, which created quite a stir by revealing the appalling living conditions of the area. The trustees at once followed this up with a commitment to provide grants of £5,000 per annum for five years for the second stage of the project, which was basically an experiment in community development involving a number of voluntary agencies and the participation of local people.[61] This forward-looking decision, which was taken in 1964, exemplified the manner in which the Foundation's work now covered a broad spectrum of social endeavour, and pointed the way to future developments.

NOTES

1. Minutes, XLIX, 210.
2. Richard M. Titmuss, *Essays on 'The Welfare State'* (1958), 81–5.
3. Minutes, XLIX, 248–52; L, 29–31; LI, 141; LII, 16.
4. Ibid., XLIX, 211: A. F. C. Bourdillon, 'Voluntary Organizations in War-Time – Citizens' Advice Bureaux' in *Voluntary Social Services: Their Place in the Modern State*, ed. A. F. C. Bourdillon (1945), 194–205.
5. Minutes, XLIX, 251: P. F. Beard, 'Voluntary Youth Organizations', loc. cit., 141–9: Pearl Jephcott, 'Work among Boys and Girls' in *Voluntary Social Services Since 1918*, ed. Henry Mess and Gertrude Williams (1948), 137–143.
6. Minutes, L, 105–6, 171–2, 190–1; LI, 41, 51, 57, 104; LII, 31, 32, 98; LV, 43–4; LVI, 15.
7. Ibid., L, 189; LI, 104–5; LIII, 32; LV, 35.
8. Ibid., LIII, 12–14, 93; LIV, 28–37, 42.
9. Ibid., LI, 124–5; LIII, 35–6, 78; LV, 116–17.
10. Ibid., L. 132–3; LI, 117, 134; LII, 69, 73; LVI, 2.
11. PRO, CAB 124/142, q. 6018.
12. CPF, *Report on Policy Relating to the Allocation of Surplus Income of the Central Fund. 1946 to 1950* (1945).
13. Minutes, LVI, 88–9.
14. Ibid., LV, 105; LVI, 147–8: CPF, *Isleden House, Islington, London, N.1: Proposed Building to be erected to accommodate Aged Poor and others* (1946).
15. Minutes, LVII, 20–1, 28–9; LIX, 109–11, 124; LX, 95: Lord Beveridge, *Voluntary Action: A Report on Methods of Social Advance* (1948), 228, 230–1.
16. Minutes, LIX, 112: *The Builder*, 10 June 1949, 713–18: PRO, CAB 124/142, q. 6036: Ministry of Local Government and Planning, *Housing for Special Purposes. Supplement to the Housing Manual 1949* (1951), 12.
17. PRO, CAB 124/142, qq. 6025–9: Minutes, LXII, 66–8; LXIII, 17, 97, 197–8; LXIV, 198.
18. Minutes, LVII, 19; LVIII, 21–2; LIX, 140; LXI, 105.

19. Ibid., LVII, 63.
20. Ibid., LXIII, 170.
21. Ibid., LXXII, 37; LXXIV, 33; LXXV, 160, 174.
22. Ibid., LXXVI, 121-2, 140-2; LXXVII, 228; LXXIX, 117; LXXXIII, 37-40; LXXXIV, 19, 32-3.
23. Ibid., LXXI, 204; LXXIII, 156-7; LXXVI, 13; LXXVII, 33.
24. Ibid., LXXXIV, 32-3.
25. *A History of the City Parochial Foundation* (1951), 46-50, 66-71.
26. Minutes, LVII, 125: Mary Stocks, *A Hundred Years of District Nursing* (1960), 173-4: *History of the Central Council for District Nursing in London 1914-1966* [1966], 11.
27. Minutes, LVII, 49; LVIII, 47-8.
28. Ibid., LV, 14; LVI, 48-9; LVIII, 44-5; LX, 20-1; LXI, 72-3.
29. Ibid., LVIII, 135-7; LIX, 58, 162; LX, 114.
30. Ibid., LVIII, 48; LXI, 16-17.
31. Ibid., LIX, 54-5; LXI, 147.
32. Beveridge, *Voluntary Action*, 274.
33. CPF, *Report on Policy Relating to the Allocation of Surplus Income of the Central Fund. 1951 to 1955* (1951): Minutes, LXI, 170-9.
34. Minutes, LVIII, 104-5; LIX, 160; LX, 161; LXI, 165-6.
35. Ibid., LXXVII, 54-5; LXXXIV, 158; LXXXVII, 13, 21: CPF, *Report on Policy Relating to the Allocation of Surplus Income 1956 to 1960* (1956), 11.
36. Minutes, LVIII, 46.
37. Beveridge, op. cit., 243-59.
38. Minutes, LIX, 64; LXXVII, 32-3.
39. Ibid., LIV, 77-8; LVII, 24; LXIII, 198-9; LXIV, 56-7, 134-5; LXVI, 124-5.
40. Ibid., LXIII, 79-80; LXIV, 140-1; LXVII, 71.
41. Ibid., LXIII, 70, 81-2; LXIV, 73; LXV, 56; LXVI, 47-8, 74-5.
42. Ibid., LXIII, 77-8; LXIV, 70, 132-3; LXV, 21-3, 76, 190-1.
43. Ibid., LXIV, 177, 193-5; LXV, 81-2, 192: *The West Indian Comes to England. A Report prepared for the Trustees of the London Parochial Charities by the Family Welfare Association*, ed. S. K. Ruck (1960).
44. *Report on Policy . . . 1956 to 1960.*
45. Minutes, LXV, 164-5; LXVI, 115-16, 156-7; LXVII, 124, 171; LXX, 159.
46. Ibid., LXVI, 160; LXVII, 171-2; LXVIII, 23-5.
47. Ibid., LXV, 51-2; LXVII, 74-5; LXVIII, 76-7, 81, 139; LXIX, 66-7, 71, 73-5, 77, 168-9.
48. Ibid., LXIX, 99-101.
49. CPF, *Report on Policy Relating to the Allocation of Surplus Income of the Central Fund. 1961 to 1965* (1961).
50. Minutes, LXXXI, 9; LXXXII, 8.
51. CPF, *Report on Policy Relating to Grants in the Quinquennium 1967 to 1971* (1967), 2.
52. Minutes, LXXVII, 63.
53. Ibid., LXXIII, 13; LXXIV, 12; LXXIX, 12.
54. Ibid., LXXII, 117-18, 143-4: LXXIV, 154; LXXV, 10; LXXVI, 14-16.
55. Ibid., LXX, 56-8; LXXIII, 74; LXXIV, 72.
56. Ibid., LXXIII, 76-7, 90; LXXIV, 160-1; LXXV, 153-4.
57. Ibid., LXX, 116; LXXII, 15-16; LXXIII, 74; LXXIV, 56-7, 62, 63-4; LXXV, 96-7.
58. Ibid., LXXIV, 118-19; LXXV, 65.
59. Ibid., LXXI, 72-3, 198-9; LXX, 11, 113; LXXIV, 62-3; LXXV, 16-17, 62, 64.

60. Ibid., LXXI, 95–7; LXXII, 67; LXXIII, 117–18; LXXIV, 70; LXXV, 72–3.
61. Ibid., LXXI, 20–1; LXXIII, 18–19; LXXIV, 96: Pearl Jephcott, *A Troubled Area. Notes on Notting Hill* (1964).

14 Grants 1966–1990

A policy sub-committee was appointed in December 1965 to formulate proposals for grants in the quinquennium 1967–71. If a strict chronological sequence had been followed, the next quinquennium should have begun in 1966, but the last committee had reported late in 1961 and the policy it recommended was essentially carried out in the years 1962–6.

One result of this slight time lag, however, was that the committee could spend longer over its deliberations, which lasted for the whole of 1966, and as a result it produced a long, reflective report.[1] This contained a summary of the past history of grant-making by the Foundation, which drew out those characteristics with most relevance to future policy. It focused on two particular aspects of past practice, the 'emphasis on the importance of pioneering' and the attempts 'to repair the unavoidable gaps and inadequacies in the statutory social services'. To these principles which were to act as a guide to future action it added a third, the continued support of established charitable organizations and institutions.

Reviewing the contemporary scene, the report acknowledged 'the slow retreat of the great tide of poverty that once covered half or more of London', but concluded that 'though poverty is no longer a blight that affects whole classes of the population, it has by no means completely disappeared for the receding flood has left behind it many lakes and pools.' The most important of these it identified as 'those comprising the handicapped, the inadequate, the old who lack private means and family support, and families having large numbers of young children'. They comprised 'the core of the contemporary poor'. There was, additionally, one new problem which it considered to be potentially very worrying, namely 'how quickly new, hydra-headed evils – such as boredom, drink, drugs, promiscuity, hooliganism and violence – have sprung from the half-severed neck of the old enemy, poverty'. What effect this would have on the nature and incidence of poverty in the future it found impossible to predict, but believed that the existence of such influences was a sound reason for continuing to support organizations catering for the young and adolescent.

With these needs in mind, the committee advocated that a more detailed classification of grants should be adopted. The new headings were to be the disabled and handicapped; the inadequate or delinquent; the old; the young; education and training; open spaces and recreation; miscellaneous social services; and support of established charitable bodies.

It predicted that the annual surplus available for grants would rise from £258,000 in 1967 to £272,000 in 1971, and that, deducting some small sums already committed, the total for the quinquennium would be £1,275,000. Of this, it recommended that £375,000 (£75,000 a year) should be set aside for the miscellaneous annual grants not specified at the beginning of the quinquennium and £150,000 as a reserve. The remainder was to be divided between some 35 schemes grouped according to the above categories. Even allowing for inflation, the sum available represented a twofold increase over the immediate post-war period, and this is reflected in the increasing number and amounts of the grants.

Of the major grants for the disabled and handicapped, the largest was £37,500 to the Westminster Society for Mentally Handicapped Children, which was formed in 1962. The society proposed to erect a residential home for older children who would otherwise be confined to mental hospitals, and the Foundation's grant was intended to cover 50 per cent of the capital cost. Chigwell House, the home and occupational centre for the disabled erected by Essex County Council on land leased from the Foundation at Grange Farm, which was held up to be an excellent example of co-operation between the statutory and voluntary sectors, was given a further £30,000, making £70,000 in all, or, again, half of the capital cost. Other grants included £25,000 for Dorincourt Estates and £10,000 for a Cheshire Foundation Home at Tulse Hill which was experimental in combining a block of flats where families could live together with a nursing wing.

In the category of the inadequate and delinquent, Norman House was once more singled out for support to the extent of £14,000, in part to pay for the retention of the services of Merfyn Turner and to make a contribution to the cost of a third house which would represent a further stage in the rehabilitation of the offender. Assistance towards both of these ends was also provided by the Gulbenkian Foundation. The biggest grant, indeed at £45,000 one of the largest in the quinquennium, was reserved, however, for a pioneering project to set up a half-way house for drug addicts, which was eventually opened at Suffolk House, Iver Heath, in Buckinghamshire, under the management of the Helping Hand Organization.[2]

The old were assisted through block grants of £50,000 to the National Federation of Housing Societies and £25,000 to the Abbeyfield Society. The Federation had been chosen as the main channel for aid to housing societies which provided accommodation for the elderly. Of the £50,000, half was to be used for outright grants to affiliated societies in Greater London, and half for a revolving fund to give interest-free loans. Abbeyfield had been founded in 1955 to provide homes for the elderly who lived alone, and worked similarly through local societies. It had been given the occasional annual grant since 1960 but this was the first large allocation.

The young, as usual, received a large slice of the cake. The largest sums, £30,000 each, were reserved for new hostels planned by Toynbee Hall and the Fellowship of St Christopher. The former hostel for young people who needed a supportive environment was intended to replace the proposed common lodging hostel, which had been refused planning permission because of local opposition (see page 290), and the trustees, having persuaded Toynbee Hall to undertake the original scheme, felt honour bound to support its replacement. The accommodation was incorporated in Attlee House, which was opened in 1971.[3] The Fellowship of St Christopher had been founded in the depression of the 1930s to cater for homeless young men and boys, and the grant was to pay for the cost of converting a house it had just acquired in Putney. Other grants included £20,000 to the London Federation of Boys' Clubs for accommodation for youth leaders, £15,000 for new premises for the PM Boys' Club, for boys working in the catering trades, and £15,000 to the YWCA for pilot projects among unattached youth.

Most of the grants for education and training, as might be expected, also basically helped the young. Apart from continued supplementary aid for pupils and students to the extent of £20,000, a capital grant of £15,000 was made to the Peredur Trust to establish a residential training scheme in connection with the Peredur School for maladjusted children, and £6,000 was allocated to the London Union of Youth Clubs for a project to organize sandwich courses for young workers. The circumstances surrounding the largest grant in this category, £25,000 to Morley College, are described in Chapter 12.

Grants for open spaces and recreation mostly consisted of continued support for organizations which had been receiving grants for some time, and again naturally mainly benefited the young. The Thames Youth Venture Advisory Council was allocated £40,000, Grange Farm Centre received £30,000 and the London and Middlesex Playing Fields Association £7,500 for playgrounds, especially the new form of adventure playgrounds. The remaining grant, £15,000 to the City Corporation for work in connection with the playing fields it had created on part of the vast Wanstead Flats, also represented additional aid to a scheme which the Foundation had supported in the past.

Of the many grants in the somewhat catch-all grouping of miscellaneous social services, the largest were £50,000 to St Christopher's Hospice (see page 290), and £40,000 to the London Council of Social Service. The purpose of the latter grant was to enable the Council to establish or strengthen local councils of social service in the new boroughs which had been created as a result of the reorganization of local government in London, and is an illustration of the trustees' awareness of the need to support the infrastructure of the voluntary sector as well as direct services. A block grant of £24,000 to the London Housing Trust to launch local trusts to provide better housing for large families reflected the concern of the trustees at the findings of the Milner Holland Committee on housing in Greater London. Other recently founded organizations which were given grants included Task Force (£20,000 for central and local headquarters), The Richmond Fellowship for the rehabilitation of the mentally and emotionally disturbed (£18,000) and Kingsmoor House near Harlow for young unmarried mothers (£15,000).

The support of established charitable bodies consisted of £15,000 each to the Family Welfare Association and the Elderly Invalids' Fund, and £10,000 and £9,000 respectively for new headquarters for the National Association and London Union of Youth Clubs and the London District of the Boys' Brigade. The last two grants might, of course, just as easily have been classified as grants for youth.

From 1966 the annual grants were divided into the categories which had been recommended by the Quinquennial Policy Sub-Committee, but otherwise most of them followed a familiar pattern. The umbrella organizations which distributed grants to youth clubs, and bodies like the YMCA and YWCA still continued to receive substantial sums, amounting to more than £100,000 over the quinquennium, despite earlier indications that such aid was going to be reduced.

One problem to which the trustees gave increasing attention was that of addiction. Among several institutions which were assisted for the first time, Rathcoole House for vagrant alcoholics in Clapham (subsequently the Alcoholics Recovery Project) received a grant of £24,000 over three years in 1969, and this was supplemented by a further £15,000 in 1971–2. The Helping Hand Organization, which catered for both alcoholics and drug addicts, was given an additional £15,000 from the reserve over three years in grants tapering from £6,000 to £4,000. (The concept of the tapering grant appears to have been first introduced at about this time.) Other drug dependency units, such as Avenues Unlimited, which by their nature were bound to be experimental, were also supported, and a grant was made to the National Addiction and Research Institute to establish a day centre for addicts in Chelsea, while the Elizabeth House Association in Redcliffe Gardens, a residential community care centre for drug addicts, was given £7,500 in 1971.[4]

The needs of the ex-offender, too, remained at the forefront of concerns. The Griffins (formerly the Holloway Discharged Prisoners Aid Society) received £9,000 over three years in tapering grants in a continuing measure of support. One problem was that a number of organizations working in the field submitted competing applications, and when they co-operated in forming a joint appeal committee called National Lifeline in 1969, it was readily given a grant of £2,000 per annum for three years. Grants of a like amount were given in 1970–2 to the National Association for the Care and Resettlement of Offenders (NACRO), which had been formed in 1966 as the successor to the National Association of Discharged Prisoners Aid Societies, to appoint a regional co-ordinator for South-East England including London.[5]

A new sphere of activity to which the Foundation gave assistance was community development, following the recommendations of the Seebohm Report. A pilot scheme in Southwark run by the National Institute for Social Work Training received the largest grant from reserve – £30,000 – and a similar project on the Barnfield Estate in Greenwich (subsequently called the Greenwich Community Project) was given £15,000 over five years. An ambitious exercise in public participation was taking place in an area of planned redevelopment at Telegraph Hill in New Cross, and grants of £2,500 per annum were made, initially for two years, to the Telegraph Hill Neighbourhood Council towards the cost of appointing two community development workers and one social survey worker. And when the London Council of Social Service established a community development unit in 1970, it was given a grant of £7,500 for the purpose.[6]

Of the many other miscellaneous grants it is only possible to mention a few. Among those for the disabled and handicapped, the Elfrida Rathbone Association, which co-ordinated work on behalf of the educationally subnormal, began to receive a regular series of annual grants, usually of £2,000, while the Central Council for the Disabled was given £1,250 for four years to run a much-needed campaign to improve access facilities in public buildings. At virtually the opposite end of the spectrum, what was considered to be a continuing need for healthy recreational opportunities for the young accounts for the grant of £10,000 to the Poplar, Blackwall and District Rowing Club for a clubhouse that would include a gym and other amenities for the young men and boys of the district. More in the mainstream, and of greater significance for future developments, was the promise in 1970 of grants of £2,500 in the first year and £1,000 per annum for the next two years to the proposed North Kensington Law Centre, which was the first neighbourhood law centre to be opened.[7]

The policy review for the 1972–6 quinquennium produced few changes. Basically, the trustees were content to continue the policies mapped out in the preceding quinquennium. They remained convinced that, despite what they termed 'the social revolution which had taken place since the end of the Second World War', there was a substantial role for charity in the Welfare State. Some problems were old ones for which the state had not made adequate provision or were ones best tackled by other agencies, and some were new 'because the meaning of poverty has been widened to include many other things besides a lack of material means'. Two of the new social ills which were singled out, although the trustees acknowledged that they were new only in the sense that they had become more aware of them, were the housing problem and the corollary of homelessness, and the problem of race relations and the absorption of immigrants from the New Commonwealth. Nevertheless, they saw no reason to change the categories of grants which had recently been used, apart from dropping the final, somewhat superfluous, heading of grants to established charitable bodies.[8]

The policy committee calculated that the surplus of the Central Fund which would be available for all grants would rise from about £319,000 in 1972 to £387,000 in 1976, providing a total for the five years of some £1.78 million. This was a remarkably accurate estimate in the event, even though these were steeply inflationary times. The committee recommended that of the total a higher proportion than usual, about 40 per cent, or an average of £150,000 per annum, should be allocated to the general run of annual grants, but that a reserve should be maintained which would be boosted to £50,000 at the start of each year in case there was need for any large grants of an emergency nature. This left slightly over £1 million for major grants in the quinquennium, which was divided between 30 applicants out of 33 who appealed for large-scale support.

Some of the grants in various categories went to organizations which by now had been supported for many years. The Elderly Invalids' Fund received £30,000, Toynbee Hall £25,000 for yet another redevelopment scheme, the London and Middlesex Playing Fields Association £15,000 for playgrounds, the Thames Youth Venture Advisory Council £50,000, the YMCA a similar amount, and the YWCA £27,000, while a further £25,000 was given to local education authorities for supplementary aid to pupils and students. As before, many of these grants either contributed directly to youth work, or chiefly benefited the young, and the way in which the sub-committee introduced its recommendations for grants for youth to the Central Governing Body is perhaps indicative of the trustees' general attitude to such grants. 'Much of the time of the Trustees', the committee's report stated, 'is taken up in considering appeals on behalf of less fortunate members of Society and rightly so. It is, however, a great encouragement to have been called upon to make recommendations on six appeals only a part of one of which is concerned with other than average, healthy, run-of-the-mill, young people.'

Some relatively new bodies, to which the Foundation had just begun to give support, continued to receive assistance. Task Force was given a grant of £30,000, the Richmond Fellowship £30,000, NACRO £45,000, which was allocated to various projects, Norman Houses (as they had now become) £15,000, and Helping Hand £50,000 to be divided between shelter-type accommodation for drug addicts, longer-term accommodation for drug addicts and a house to be converted into bed-sitting-rooms for rehabilitated alcoholics.

The largest individual grant, as befitted one of the trustees' new found preoccupations, was £100,000 to the Housing Societies (later Housing Associations) Charitable Trust which had been set up by the National Federation of Housing Societies (later the National Federation of Housing Associations) to administer funds from the Foundation and other philanthropic bodies. Although some of the money was intended to be spent on schemes to house the old and infirm, most of it was to be used in more general ways to alleviate the housing shortage. Grants of £25,000 to the Boys' and Girls' Brigade for a hostel project, and a similar amount to the National Association of Voluntary Hostels for its work in finding accommodation for the single homeless in London, were of a broadly similar nature. Additionally some of the grant to the YMCA was for development projects in connection with its own hostels, and part of that to the YWCA was for an accommodation and advisory service for girls.

Another substantial grant of £75,000 went to London Council of Social Service for continuing work in establishing local councils of social service in the London boroughs and for its community development unit. The National Institute for Social Work Training at Mary Ward House in Bloomsbury, which had been established in 1961 to promote advanced training and research, received £50,000, to be spread over the five years. The Institute had been involved in community development projects for which grants had been given but this was the first time that it had been assisted directly; it was also supported by the Nuffield Foundation and the Joseph Rowntree Memorial Trust.

New organizations which were aided for the first time included the North Kensington Amenity Trust, which was formed in 1971 to assist in the development of some 23 acres of land under Westway in the interests of the local community. The Royal Borough of Kensington and Chelsea sought to work through the Trust and had given it an initial grant, and the Foundation agreed to provide £10,000 a year for five years, basically to cover administrative costs, with the strong intimation that individual projects would also receive favourable consideration, as indeed happened.

The Institute of Race Relations was allocated £45,000 to distribute among eight multi-racial projects and to help pay for a liaison worker. To the trustees this initiative was 'of an importance as great as any other of our recommendations', even though in their minds there was the risk of a high failure rate among the projects. Another large grant of £40,000 was given to the Navy League Sea Cadet Corps for the capital costs of redeveloping Ravens Ait, as the Thames continued to exercise its peculiar pull on the trustees. Grants of £25,000 were given to the National Council for the Single Woman and her Dependants, which catered for those women who stayed at home to care for parents or relatives, or in other words, which cared for the carers; to the Diamond Riding Group for Handicapped Children in Carshalton, which had been inspired by the success of the Pony Riding for the Disabled Trust at Grange Farm Centre; and to the Greater London Association for the Disabled.

One other unusual project for which a grant of £25,000 was made was the establishment of a loan fund to assist in the recruitment of Londoners from poor backgrounds to the Bar, and especially to assist them in their period of pupillage when they were not allowed to earn fees but were not eligible for grants from the education authorities. Finally, another new venture as far as the Foundation was concerned was its support for the Inter-Action Trust which aimed at integrating the arts, especially drama, into community life. As community work of all kinds was now highly fashionable the Trust was able to embark on a number of projects, and the policy committee recommended that it should be given £20,000 towards the capital costs of establishing a playhouse in Camden.

One decision of long-term significance was that the report of the policy sub-committee, without the appendices which gave details about the applicants for grants, should be sent to other grant-making trusts and foundations and to government departments concerned with the work of the Foundation. This represented a compromise over the issue of publicizing the Foundation's activities more widely. The matter had been raised early in 1971, but the Clerk, Bryan Woods, reminded the trustees that their predecessors had not favoured greater exposure for the activities of the Foundation, and concluded that 'there is no evidence, on the basis of the number of enquiries now received, that there is a number of people lacking information and who, if informed of the Foundation, would bring fresh and worthwhile projects to the notice of the Trustees.' Nevertheless he suggested that the trustees might like to consider distributing the quinquennial policy reports along the lines subsequently adopted.[9]

There was no great change in the pattern of annual grants throughout the 1972–6 quinquennium and there was as yet no substantial increase in the number of applicants. The size of grants was increasing, the average now being approximately £2,000, but the effect of inflation was such that £2,000 was only equivalent to about £150 in 1900. New organizations were appearing but at this stage they merely tended to replace others.

Some of the biggest grants still went to organizations which had come to expect support year after year. The London Federation of Boys' Clubs and the National Association of Boys' Clubs, which covered different parts of the metropolis, the London Union of Youth Clubs, the Girl Guides, the Boys' Brigade, and the YMCA and YWCA for youth work, accounted between them for well over £20,000 per annum. Nevertheless, there does seem to have been a concerted attempt in some categories of grant to avoid constant support for what were termed 'pensioner' applicants, and to favour instead intermittent aid, though sometimes on a large scale. The National Council for the Unmarried Mother and her Child, for instance, had last received an annual grant in 1968, but in 1976, shortly after it had changed its name to the National Council for One-Parent Families and broadened its scope, it was given a grant of £4,000 per annum for three years to employ a welfare rights officer for London.[10]

Several of the institutions which had been first grant-aided in the recent past received additional substantial support, such as the Alcoholics Recovery Project, the Delves House Trust, St Christopher's Hospice and the Richmond Fellowship.[11] Some organizations which were given grants for the first time in these years went on to become major pressure groups on the national scene, including Age Concern, which was awarded a grant of £2,500 per annum for three years in 1974, and the Child Poverty Action Group, which received £5,000 in 1976.[12] Applications from Family Service Units continued to be treated sympathetically, and Community Service Volunteers, another general social work service which utilized the energies and altruism of youth for the benefit of the disadvantaged, received generous support from 1969 onwards.[13]

Many of the new projects of the early 1970s which sought assistance were community-based, and several had a cultural or arts component. Centerprise, which aimed to combine a bookshop with a centre for cultural and educational activities and some forms of social work in Hackney, was given grants totalling over £15,000 between 1971 and 1975, despite an increasing concern that support from the London Borough of Hackney was woefully inadequate.[14] Another project to receive grant-aid of over £13,000 was one combining action and research in a run-down area of Hammersmith, which was instituted by the Community Urban Renewal Trust under the auspices of the Committee for City Poverty,[15] while the North Kensington Amenity Trust received a further £10,000, on top of its quinquennial grant of £50,000, towards the capital costs of building Acklam Road Hall.[16]

A number of grants went to organizations which catered for ethnic minorities in one way or another. Neighbourhood English Classes, a voluntary educational body, which was formed in 1970 to teach everyday English to adult immigrants, was given a grant of £3,500 per annum for three years. The Melting Pot Foundation, a centre for young blacks in Brixton, received £3,000 in 1974 and a further £2,500 in 1976, and the National Association for Indian Youth was given a capital sum of £1,450 and a grant of £750 per annum for three years for a project in Southall. The Keskidee Trust, which ran a centre for a primarily West Indian population in a part of Islington, received £5,000 in two grants in 1972 and 1974.[17]

The Foundation had strong historical links with Islington, and a number of other Islington-based organizations received grants. These included the Islington Society for Mentally Handicapped Children and the First London Free School (later the White Lion Street Free School) which was an educational experiment to try to reach out to children who could not cope with the normal school system.[18] Two other educational grants which were made at the same meeting in 1976 illustrate vividly how widely the trustees were now prepared to interpret the existence of need. One was to the National Association for Gifted Children and the other to the National Gypsy Education Council, for metropolitan aspects of their work.[19]

The next policy review took place in 1976, and the sub-committee's report was full of gloom and foreboding. The previous quinquennial report had warned of the problems which voluntary bodies would face in dealing with economic uncertainty and inflation, but the present one contained dire predictions of the effects of what it described as 'economic decline, rabid inflation and increasing unemployment'. One consequence it foresaw was a decrease in the real income of voluntary bodies as subscriptions and donations declined at the very time that cuts in public expenditure were taking place. It warned that in the present economic climate, grant-making foundations and trusts would be seen as alternative rather than complementary sources of finance, and recognized that, even though the main burden of dealing with the current crisis would fall on the government, the Foundation would have a crucial role 'in encouraging new initiatives and in helping to maintain existing work so that slowly but inexorably the conditions of poorer Londoners may be improved'.[20]

Reviewing the past quinquennium, the committee was basically satisfied with the work that had been undertaken but questioned the value of supporting national organizations 'on the somewhat flimsy grounds that they also work on behalf of poor Londoners'. It redefined current policy, beginning with a reaffirmation of the principle that support should not generally be given for schemes that could be financed out of public funds. Additionally, it summarized the trustees' aims as trying to make good deficiencies in the social, educational, recreational and environmental services; giving first priority to schemes which broke new ground; assisting voluntary organizations which had proved the value of their work; and working through eligible voluntary organizations registered as charities, approved institutions and statutory authorities, who should be stimulated to extend or improve their own services. The committee's wide-ranging review also embraced the question whether there should be a more precise definition of 'the poorer classes of the metropolis' but concluded that to attempt such a definition, or, more to the point, to risk involving the Charity Commissioners in such an exercise, might unduly restrict the trustees' discretion.

The committee estimated that the surplus income would be subject to considerable annual variation during the quinquennium, ranging from approximately £375,000 in 1977 to £675,000 in 1981, or some £2.73 million in total. Because of the volatility of the general situation and the unpredictable effects of inflation it recommended that only 40 per cent of income should be allocated to long-term projects and that 60 per cent should be made available for shorter-term applications and for the maintenance of a reserve which would be increased in proportion to the rise in income. Its caution about forecasting was indeed borne out as, for the first time, the estimates of future income proved to be inaccurate. A steeper than anticipated rise in the Foundation's income meant that by 1981 over £1 million was available for grants.

On the matter of grants, the committee saw no reason to change the previous classification, but recommended that further consideration should be given to making loans at low interest or interest free when appropriate, a practice which had been reintroduced in about 1973. More significantly, it thought that under present circumstances applications for major grants should no longer be reserved for the start of each quinquennium, but should be submitted more frequently. Consequently, in a surprising move, it decided not to make any recommendations itself but to turn the whole business of grant-making, both for long- and short-term grants, back over to the Grants Sub-Committee.

The Grants Sub-Committee considered 27 applications for large grants for the 1977–81 quinquennium and decided to accept 22 of them. Some were for the whole five years, but most were either one-off capital grants or for three years, sometimes with a recommendation for further grants in 1980 and 1981 but no firm commitment. They were divided almost equally between grants for capital sums or new projects and for recurrent costs, and a few were made for the establishment of specific posts in organizations.[21]

Apart from £117,000 which was reserved for a possible modernization programme at the Chelsea Physic Garden under circumstances which are described in Chapter 12, the largest grant was £75,000 (over the years 1977–9) to the London Council of Social Service and the Councils for Voluntary Service (the new name for local Councils of Social Service). Twenty-one councils, which acted as co-ordinating and information gathering and disseminating bodies, had now been established in the London boroughs, in part with the aid of earlier grants from the Foundation although all were now supported additionally by the borough councils. Eleven boroughs were still without councils, however, and others were contemplating cut-backs in aid.

Grants of £50,000 or more were approved for the Keskidee Trust (although in the event £25,000 was written back when an intended development scheme ran into difficulties[22]), Age Concern for a number of projects, and the Winged Fellowship Trust towards the capital costs of a new holiday home for the elderly severely handicapped at Grange Farm. The North Kensington Amenity Trust, whose Westway project was proceeding satisfactorily, was given £47,000 over three years, to which £53,000 was added in 1980–2, bringing the Foundation's total contribution since the establishment of the Trust to over £150,000.[23] The Metropolitan Region of the YMCA received £45,500 over five years for its Y-care service, which was concerned with community relations and sought to extend the resources of the YMCA to local communities, and £40,000 was made available to the Housing Associations Charitable Trust for allocation to individual housing associations in the metropolis.

Other grants included £37,000 to the Greater London Association for the Disabled for additional named staff, £36,000 to the Blackfriars Settlement for the renovation of its headquarters buildings in Nelson Square, £35,000 for supplementary aid to pupils and students, £30,000 to the Child Poverty Action Group towards the cost of its citizens' rights office and legal department, and £30,000 to the Greater London Citizens' Advice Bureaux Limited for the salaries of a training officer and a course organizer. The Shelter Housing Aid Centre received £24,000 to pay for staff to tackle the housing problems of unsupported mothers, and grants of the same amount were made to the Helping Hand Organization for a day centre for alcoholics in Ealing, and to the ROMA (Rehabilitation of Metropolitan Addicts) Housing Association, which catered for drug addicts. The Greater London Playing Fields Association was given £23,500 for various playground and holiday schemes, and the Invalid Children's Aid Association received £20,000 for a centre in south London.

As a result of a decision taken in 1974 to provide more information about the Foundation's grants to outside bodies, a digest of the quinquennial report together with details of the long-term and short-term grants was printed and circulated in 1977. Thereafter, summaries of the grants approved were printed and made available each year.[24]

Over the five years 1977–81, as a result of the decisions taken by the Quinquennial Policy Sub-Committee, a mixture of small and large grants were awarded each year for terms varying between one and three years, and very occasionally for longer. Grants like the £350 given in 1977 to the ILEA for its Holiday Fund for Handicapped Children, or £600 made in 1981 to the London Schools' Cricket Association to enable two 'poorer boys' to go on a cricket tour of Barbados, were at one end of the scale. At the other was the £281,350 approved in 1981 for payment in 1982–4 to the London Voluntary Service Council (formerly the London Council of Social Service) to set up a Neighbourhood Care Resource Unit as a pioneering initiative in promoting the concept of community care, which was increasingly coming to be seen as both a desirable policy in itself and one means of alleviating the pressure on scarce resources for the social services.[25]

With the number of organizations being grant-aided rising to over 120 by 1980, it is only possible here to single out the most important grants and to note some trends in grant-making. There was an increase in the number of applications, although still not a spectacular one. In 1980, for instance, there were 111 new applications, while another forty or so organizations had previously been promised annual grants for a period of years which included 1980 and therefore did not need to apply; the equivalent figures in 1970 had been 85 and about thirty-five. Four out of five applicants were given a grant, although by no means always as high a one as they had requested, a proportion which had remained roughly constant for some time. The remainder were turned down for a variety of reasons, some of which were that their objects did not fall within the Foundation's terms of reference or were of only marginal benefit to poor Londoners, that their current financial position was basically healthy, or that they did not inspire confidence in their stability or show evidence of the requisite degree of financial control. There was also a desire to avoid over-dependence on the Foundation's support by not automatically renewing grants every year.

The increase in applications, which was a trend that would continue throughout the 1980s, can doubtless in part be accounted for by the increased publicity for the Foundation's activities, but it was also the result of a growing fragmentation and specialization in the voluntary sector, as more bodies were created which dealt with very specific needs or covered individual localities. Many of the new organizations for which grants were approved exemplified this trend, such as the Cheyne Centre for Spastic Children, the Tower Hamlets Women's Aid Centre, the Simba Project for unemployed black youth in Woolwich, or the Hoxton Hall Friends Neighbourhood Centre and Theatre.[26]

Some trends that were noticeable among the organizations supported, partly reflecting tendencies in the voluntary sector itself and partly the trustees' own predilections, were that a number were community and neighbourhood based, several sought to apply the arts to social needs, and more of them catered for ethnic minorities. Sometimes all three characteristics were combined. The Laban Centre for Movement and Dance in New Cross was given £20,000 in 1978 towards the conversion of a church into a multiracial teaching centre and theatre, and grants totalling £25,000 in 1978–80 and £37,000 in 1981–3 were made to the Contemporary Dance Trust in King's Cross which ran a dance school and promoted multiethnic social and community activities in 'one of London's lesser privileged neighbourhoods'. Similarly, the L'Ouverture Theatre Trust Limited, named after Toussaint L'Ouverture, which was establishing an arts and community centre in Brixton, was given a grant of £7,500 per annum for 1981–3 to employ a workshop director and co-ordinator.[27]

This last grant illustrates the trustees' desire that their support should be directed towards definite ends rather than be swallowed up in general expenses. Occasionally, grants were given towards running costs, but most were for specific projects or aspects of work, including the establishment or continuance of staff posts. Sometimes, indeed, where administrative competence was lacking, it was possible to seek to tackle the problem by paying the salary of a suitable person.

Apart from the large sums to the London Voluntary Service Council (which had also received £85,000 in 1980–1 for its general work with local voluntary service councils), the biggest grant to be approved in the quinquennium was £172,000 over the years 1981–4 to pay for five places at the Dartmouth House Centre in Blackheath, a new experimental residential college for the rehabilitation of unsupported and inexperienced young mothers and their training in the care of children and home management. The centre ran into difficulties, but the trustees were reluctant to withdraw support, although the grant was eventually reduced to £135,000, of which the last instalment was not paid until 1987.[28]

Substantial grants were also made to some of the general organizations on which support had been focused in the recent past, because paradoxically the proliferation of smaller bodies made the need for co-ordination all the greater. Age Concern Greater London was given £93,000 over three years, partly towards the costs of its information service and to employ a field officer, and the Greater London Association for the Disabled received £69,000, also over three years, to maintain its information service at full strength. The Housing Associations Charitable Trust was allocated £60,000 to be paid in 1982–4, and the Child Poverty Action Group £35,000 towards the continuing costs of its citizens' rights office and legal department. One of the more unusual of the larger grants was £30,000 to the Metropolitan Police towards the cost of a study being undertaken by the Policy Studies Institute into the relationship between the police and the community. In this case the police had been advised that the worth of the study might be enhanced if it was known that it was in part independently funded, and in return the trustees insisted that they should be consulted and have the opportunity to see the final draft.[29]

In 1977 the Clerk had been asked to provide a return showing the amounts spent on grants and loans (of which they were very few) in the previous three years by categories. Subsequently, the figures were given annually, but one problem was that by far the largest category, accounting for about a third of the total, was the rather nebulous one of miscellaneous social services. In the remaining categories, however, some interesting trends can be discerned. In 1975 the next largest sum (about 25 per cent) was spent on the young, followed by education and training (15 per cent). This remained the pattern for the next two years, although the share of the young fell to about 15 per cent. By the beginning of the 1980s, apart from miscellaneous social services there was a much more even spread with some annual variations, except for open spaces and recreation which consistently came bottom by a long way.[30]

In 1980 the Grants Sub-Committee had recommended that in the light of the continuing high level of inflation no division of income should be maintained between longer- and short-term grants and that no further sums should be paid into a reserve.[31] This was a logical extension of the policy adopted at the beginning of the quinquennium that the amount spent on long-term commitments, certainly for more than three years, should be limited to 40 per cent of the available funds, as there was no reason to suppose that either the trustees or applicants were that prescient at a time of such rapid change. Moreover, it allowed current income to be used with maximum flexibility.

The next Quinquennial Policy Sub-Committee which met in 1981, therefore, was precisely that, a committee to review policy rather than to allocate grants. Looking back over the previous five years from the standpoint of yet another recession, the committee saw no reason to doubt that its predecessor had been correct in taking a pessimistic view and in anticipating a period of severe strain across the whole field of social services. Indeed, it regarded the position as one that was essentially worsening. In a rare incursion into the political arena, it referred to the success of the Conservative Party at both the local and national level in the past few years, and while not wishing to discuss 'the pros and cons of the policies of the principal political parties' felt obliged to comment on the effects of the reduction in public expenditure which was a necessary part of the government's declared policy of reducing inflation. It took the view that:

> since 1980 the financial position of all fundraising and of all operational charities has deteriorated sharply, and particularly of those which are almost wholly dependent upon statutory funds. At a time when the statutory services providing health, education, housing and personal social services have all of necessity been reduced, and when the numbers of unemployed have reached an unprecedentedly high level, there is all too little public money to spare for the work of charities.

Put in another way, 'the Welfare State system, which in almost every year since 1945 had advanced to offer more services to meet an ever-increasing and varied demand, has suddenly stopped in its tracks, even retreated in some quarters. No-one is quite certain of the outcome.'[32]

As well as these more general concerns, the committee noted some worrying tendencies. One was the way in which the traditional roles of the statutory and voluntary sectors were being changed and in some cases reversed. Whereas in the past charitable trusts and foundations had supported pioneering efforts on the general understanding that if their worth was proved they would be taken over by the statutory services, now both central government and local authorities were providing initial grants either on condition or in the expectation that continuing support would come from non-statutory sources. In addition, some statutory institutions were being encouraged to set up charitable arms in order to raise funds from trusts and foundations for equipment or capital projects that would previously have been paid for out of central or local government finance. The committee's report quoted with obvious disapprobation an extract from one recent application which had stated that, 'In general the aim will be to use public funds to "lever" contributions from the private and voluntary sectors', remarking that such an attitude meant that there would be increasing competition with voluntary bodies for already scarce sources of funds. There was also disquiet that the government had been disinclined to hold consultations even though its own encouragement of the use of the voluntary sector had helped to create the confusion of responsibilities. These were to be concerns that troubled the world of philanthropy throughout the 1980s and it is interesting that the trustees articulated them so early in the decade.

Nevertheless, the picture was not all dark. The government's very emphasis on the part to be played by voluntary organizations had led to a 'buoyant' attitude, but there was an increasing need for professionally trained workers, and here the trustees doubtless thought that the Foundation could be of help. According to the committee, there was also better co-operation between grant-making trusts and foundations and more approaches to joint funding, although it must be said that there were many prior examples of such arrangements.

Looking ahead, the committee foresaw a number of problems which would have an effect on social policy. The age composition of London's population was changing, with an increase in the number of people over retirement age, and the concomitant demands on services; ethnic minorities, who had particular needs, now accounted for some 14 per cent of the population; the proportion of single-person households was increasing, especially in some inner boroughs; there was a serious housing deficit, and a growing problem of homelessness; the health services were under strain; and, despite falling rolls, the number of pupils with social needs or for whom English was a second language was placing a stress on the education service. As if this was not enough, the social consequences of high and continuous unemployment were sufficient by themselves to take up all the funds, and more, that charitable trusts could direct to them. It is small wonder that the committee concluded that 'we do not foresee the conditions of the poorer people living in the Metropolis improving over the next five years.'

In terms of policies to guide grant-making, the committee anticipated that there would be an increasing demand for the neighbourhood community style of provision. While recognizing that certain services were best provided by voluntary organizations working as agents of the statutory authorities with funding from both sources, it counselled caution about accepting new commitments on this basis because the indications were that statutory authorities would be reluctant to pick up responsibilities for longer-term funding and that the burden would continue to fall on the Foundation. In particular, it thought that care should be taken in giving capital grants for new buildings because of future revenue implications. Apart from these strictures, however, the committee was basically content to endorse the policies delineated by the last committee with a few changes in wording and some minor additions, and to adhere to the same classification of grants. It did recommend that there should no longer be a quinquennial reserve, and left it to the good sense of the Grants Sub-Committee to make sure that there were sufficient funds unallocated to meet any new exceptionally worthy application. Otherwise it believed that no detailed plan for the quinquennium should be adopted at this juncture.

There was no significant change in the overall pattern of grants in the first half of the 1980s. In 1985 there were some 120 applications leading to the award of 95 grants, and another 40 grants had already been approved in previous years for payment in 1985, figures which were only marginally higher than those five years earlier. Statistics issued at the time of the next quinquennial review showed that, by categories, 32 per cent of grants had been made for miscellaneous social services, 16 per cent for the disabled and handicapped, 16 per cent for education and training, 15 per cent for the young, 11 per cent for the inadequate and delinquent, 7 per cent for the old, and 3 per cent for open spaces and recreation. Once more, there was nothing particularly novel in such a breakdown.

This statistical conformity, however, hid some new trends. There was an increasing concern that over the whole spectrum of social services, organizations receiving grants should, wherever possible, demonstrate that they paid due attention to the needs of ethnic minorities. This could apply equally to housing associations, or to bodies which catered for the elderly or the young, or to those which provided education and training, for instance. As new groups run by and for ethnic minorities began to emerge, every effort was made to support them. More than once the trustees questioned whether in such cases the criteria for accepting applications for grants should be relaxed, but resolved to adhere to the policies laid down while seeking to discuss with the applicants ways in which they could comply with the criteria.[33] Nevertheless, the Foundation bent over backwards to give aid, even in cases where projects ran into difficulties, and would sometimes make grants to organizations that were not registered charities on condition that they were successful in applying for such status. One other attribute which the trustees were eager to see adopted by organizations to which they gave grants was a willingness to encourage the participation of the local community, and especially those for whom their services were intended.

There was still a mixture of large and small grants, as the trustees acknowledged that a modest grant to a local group could have a beneficial effect out of all proportion to the amount spent, but with the income available for grants reaching about £1.5 million by the middle of the 1980s, the average size of annual grant was now nearly £10,000. As before, it is only possible to mention a few of the many individual grants that were made. Several of the organizations supported were the, by now, very familiar ones which had received considerable assistance in the past. The largest single grant, £357,000 over three years, went once more to the London Voluntary Service Council in continuation of the earlier grants given for its Neighbourhood Care Action Programme, which was shortly to be constituted as a separate body under the name Advance (which stood for Advice and Development for Volunteering and Neighbourhood Care in London). The increasing emphasis being placed on the policy of 'care in the community' meant that the demand for such a service was likely to be very considerable. Another big grant of £166,500 over three years was made to Age Concern Greater London, and one of £90,000 over the same time span to the Greater London Association for the Disabled for a resource centre.[34]

Toynbee Hall, which had been one of the earliest institutions to call on the Foundation for assistance, celebrated its centenary in 1984 and embarked on a major fundraising exercise for a number of new initiatives, but its administrative machinery needed strengthening and, somewhat exceptionally, it was given grants of £90,000 over the years 1982–4 for core costs, and then a further £90,000 payable in 1985–7 for an education project which was intended to be of particular benefit to the Bangladeshi and other immigrant communities of Tower Hamlets.[35] Of other long-term 'clients' of the Foundation, the main youth organizations continued to be well supported, the London Federation of Boys' Clubs and the London Union of Youth Clubs being allocated grants totalling £95,000 in 1985 for payment in 1985–7 as well as annual grants of upwards of £10,000 per annum each earlier in the decade, for instance.[36] Of newer organizations, the Richmond Fellowship received further grants which brought its total funding from the Foundation to over £100,000 by 1985, and St Christopher's Hospice was given another £35,000 in 1982–4.[37]

Some of the grants which were made for the first time illustrate the trustees' involvement with some of the particular concerns of the age. The Royal Jubilee Trusts and the Prince's Trust Youth Business Initiative, which was launched in 1982 to try to combat youth unemployment by providing grants to young people who wanted to set themselves up in business, were given annual grants totalling £200,000 in the years 1983–7 for bursaries for 'poorer young unemployed Londoners'.[38] No Fixed Abode, which was also established as a charity in 1982 to co-ordinate the activities of numerous organizations dealing with the problem of the single homeless in the East End, received a grant of £30,000 over three years towards the cost of employing a fieldworker, and grants were also given for the first time to the St Mungo Community Housing Association which provided premises for homeless single men.[39]

The problems of addiction still ranked high among the Foundation's priorities; in 1984, for instance, grants of £30,000 were made to the Greater London Alcohol Advisory Service and £50,000 to Turning Point Limited (formerly the Helping Hand Organization).[40] Several substantial grants went to arts organizations, including the Contemporary Dance Trust for bursaries for poor Londoners, the Almeida Theatre Company (in Islington), the London Festival Ballet Trust for its education and community programme, and Shape, which had begun by using dance to help the handicapped but now sought to employ a wide range of performing arts to assist the socially disadvantaged in general.[41] Finally, grants to the Immigrants' Aid Trust towards the additional expenses incurred by the Joint Council for the Welfare of Immigrants as a result of the British Nationality Act, and to the British Refugee Council illustrate new anxieties.[42]

The next policy review took place in 1986 to determine priorities for the quinquennium 1987–91, which would neatly carry the Foundation up to its centennial. The sub-committee met against the background of considerable uncertainty created by the abolition of the Greater London Council, which, in addition to the sheer volume of its funding capacity, had, in the committee's view, changed the shape of voluntary organizations in London by fostering initiatives of self-help and community participation. Reviewing the somewhat gloomy prognostications of the last sub-committee, the trustees thought that little had happened to change their earlier pessimistic view, and that 'The social problems have in many respects intensified, and the funding crises for voluntary bodies have been an ever-increasing feature of their lives.'[43]

In addition to the concerns already voiced about the social consequences of unemployment, the housing crisis, the shift in the age balance of the population, and the number of one-parent families, the committee thought that there were a number of other issues which had to be faced, many of them stemming from or connected with the larger problems. Among these were the effects of the 'care in the community' programme and the decanting of people from institutions which were likely to place considerable demands on voluntary services; partly in consequence of this, the emphasis on informal caring and the strain this could place on the carers, especially women; the issue of race and the alienation of black communities, brought into sharp focus by urban riots, so that 'the ethnic dimension in every service field is a critical issue that has continually to be addressed'; the effects of the changes in social security under the Social Security Act of 1986, which many feared would lead to 'a significant worsening of some claimants' financial positions'; and the need for legal and other advice and a well-resourced welfare rights service. On top of these, changes in the emphasis of statutory funding to pump-priming with no guarantee of continuing assistance, and the shift of the Urban Aid Programme to initiatives fostering economic regeneration rather than welfare service provision, had significant implications for the voluntary sector. And if, in addition, the appearance of new phenomena like 'cardboard city' and vast new problems like AIDS were taken into account, it was difficult to avoid a 'catalogue of woe'.

In determining how to address these problems through the Foundation's grant-making policies, the committee decided not to single out priorities at this stage and to develop a funding strategy in the course of the quinquennium rather than at the beginning of it. Nevertheless, it made a number of recommendations as the start of such an exercise. For one, it advocated that the categories of grants should be updated in view of the fact that 'miscellaneous social services' accounted for about a third of grants. The new groupings were to be physical and mental handicap; mental illness; addictions; penal matters; family and social welfare; youth; elderly; community work; race relations; education and training; arts, open spaces and recreation; and miscellaneous. The point was made that such categories were not solely determined by social concerns, but also covered the responses such as education and training, and the need to take into account 'the quality of life' through the category of arts, open spaces and recreation.

The committee was very concerned that the Foundation should be as accessible as possible to all groups, including those in the outer boroughs and ethnic minority and women's groups concerned with helping the poor. In furtherance of this, it proposed that the geographical spread of grants should be monitored, and that the nature and extent of support for ethnic minority organizations should be kept under review to ensure that there was sufficient awareness of the Foundation's existence among such bodies. As a practical measure, the committee advocated the printing of a leaflet about the Foundation and the wide distribution of its own report. It also asked that policy papers should be prepared twice a year for consideration by the Grants Sub-Committee.

In terms of the general attitude to funding, the committee urged the trustees to be wary of the danger of organizations becoming too dependent on the Foundation, and noted that of those applicants which had been regularly funded since 1960 most worked in the field of youth. It recommended, therefore, that a review should be undertaken of the nature and extent of youth provision supported by the Foundation. In general, however, it thought that it was right to ensure that resources were adequate for the continuation of existing work as well as encouraging new projects, and that a balance had to be struck between the two. Indeed, under present circumstances, there was a limit to the amount of responsible new work that could be generated, and it was critical of the government's tendency to fund pilot projects with the assumption that trusts would subsequently take over the funding. It went so far as to urge resistance to such a policy, and asked that discussions should take place with both central and local government to make this position clear.

It asked the Clerk and the Grants Sub-Committee to pay particular attention to three areas of concern which had already become apparent to trustees. These were whether applicants paid sufficient attention to the needs of ethnic minorities; whether they encouraged their client groups to be actively involved in the running of the organization; and whether they were able to evaluate the effectiveness of posts whose salaries were being paid for by the Foundation, recognizing that in some cases extra funds might be needed for such an evaluation. Finally, despite its earlier cautions, it thought that one of the most important roles of the Foundation was still to fund innovative and experimental work.

The committee recommended some technical changes to the grant-making procedures and the abolition of Clause 47 (the denominational clause) of the Central Scheme, both of which are discussed on page 226. Suffice it to say here that the effect of the latter was very considerable, and demonstrated how right the trustees had been to regard it as an unnecessary barrier to giving assistance for the excellent work in social welfare being undertaken by a wide variety of religious bodies and groups with a common religious identity. The move should particularly be seen in the light of the trustees' concern that all ethnic minority groups which provided services for poorer Londoners should be eligible for aid.

Finally, the committee thought that it was worthwhile to reaffirm that it was the trustees' policy not to consider applications in certain categories. Those they singled out, because they were ones in which the number of applications was increasing, were research, and especially medical research, and fee-paying schools. In the former case, however, they were careful to draw a distinction between formal research and monitoring and evaluation, which they thought to be essential in determining whether the organizations they funded were fulfilling the basic purpose of assisting the poor. As far as fee-paying schools were concerned, there was a state education system available to all, most of their pupils manifestly did not belong to the poorer classes, and to provide bursaries for individuals was contrary to the Foundation's general policy of not assisting individuals, even if this had not always been scrupulously adhered to in the past.

The twelfth Quinquennial Policy Sub-Committee, despite its claims that it was not establishing priorities or determining a funding strategy for the next five years, provided one of the most comprehensive and far-reaching reviews of the Foundation's work. One of its recommendations had immediate effect when a much fuller version than usual of the committee's report, with basically only the internal procedural matters left out, was printed for public circulation.[44] Other initiatives were taken to try to ensure wide accessibility, and in 1987 a grant was made to the Directory of Social Change towards the costs of publishing a directory of grant-making bodies in London.[45]

The period since the last quinquennial review has been one of great volatility as far as the work of the Foundation is concerned. The most striking feature is the steep rise that has taken place in the number of applications for grants. In 1990 there were 289 applicants, of whom 245 were given grants, but even this is not a full indication of the number of organizations to which the Foundation was now offering support, for a further 125 were still receiving grants which had been awarded in previous years. This was a threefold increase over 1985. Probably the most important single reason for this prodigious leap in the volume of applications was the removal of the denominational clause which opened up the Foundation to a whole new constituency of applicants, but the increased publicity which had led to one source describing the Foundation as a trust that set 'a standard of approachability and openness to potential applicants which is a model for other trusts'[46] was also a factor. Additionally, the Trust for London, although in general it gave more modest grants to smaller groups, by its active field-worker approach produced a greater awareness of the Foundation among bodies which might be eligible for its assistance.

It must also be said that the voluntary sector itself was displaying considerable dynamism as it sought to respond to the new responsibilities which were being placed on it. Long gone was the period of the heyday of the Welfare State when doubts were being voiced over whether there was a continuing role for voluntary organizations. Now there were no such questions, as the government's declared reliance on voluntary bodies and its exhortations to the 'active citizen' had given them a new lease of life, even if the problems seemed vast and the resources woefully inadequate. The Quinquennial Policy Sub-Committee had indeed seen one chink of light in an otherwise sombre scene in the 'energy, imagination and number of voluntary organisations that have emerged in recent years'.

Fortunately, the rise in the Foundation's income kept pace with the increase in the number of applications and meant that almost exactly £4 million per annum was available for grants by the end of the decade. Faced with a fundamentally more complex situation in assessing the demands placed on it than even five years earlier, the Foundation responded by developing its own internal procedures for providing a strategic assessment of needs. Papers were prepared on a number of topics, as the policy committee had recommended, with the assistance of an experienced social policy research worker, and other studies were commissioned from outside experts. Additionally, despite the large rise in the number of applications, it was still considered to be very important to see all applicants, even if this meant an increase in staff. Finally, new procedures were devised for monitoring the effects of grants and a decision was also taken to appoint a monitoring officer.

A year-by-year analysis of grants by the new categories was prepared, and although this showed wide annual variations, in general most grants (about a third) were made for community work and family and social welfare. Of course, it was frequently difficult to determine the category to which a grant should be allocated and such divisions were only vaguely indicative. For instance, the category of race relations was soon abandoned as not particularly meaningful, but a record was kept of the grants made to ethnic minority groups, and these doubled in 1987.[47] The policy committee had clearly regarded the needs of ethnic minorities as a pressing priority and several grants made over the past few years give an indication of how this was translated into action. For instance, when the London Voluntary Service Council was given another large grant of £275,000 over three years in 1987, it was specifically earmarked for the Council's African-- Caribbean Community Development Unit. Similarly, a grant to the Tower Hamlets Law Centre in 1988 was for the appointment of a Bengali woman worker. Another grant made in 1988 of £45,000 over three years to MIND in Tower Hamlets was to be used to employ two black and ethnic minorities liaison workers.[48]

Such examples could be repeated many times. Of the many ethnic minority organizations which were directly aided, several were women's groups, such as the African Women's Welfare Association (Ayoka Project) in Tower Hamlets, or the Nari Samity (Women's Association) in the same borough, or Appna (the Greenwich Muslim Women's Project).[49] One particular set of needs which had emerged over the past few years were those of the many refugee groups which had migrated to the capital, and several grants were directed to bodies like the Lewisham Indo-Chinese Refugee Group, the Sudan Relief and Rehabilitation Association, the Kurdish Workers' Association, the Tamil Refugee Action Group, or the Vietnamese Refugee Community in Southwark.[50] Another trend which is certainly discernible in recent years has been the number of women's groups which have applied and been given grants. To take just a sample, in 1988–9 these included the Women's Liaison Group of Barking and Dagenham, the Enfield Women's Centre, Hammersmith Women's Aid, the Women's Therapy Centre and the Women's Legal Defence Fund.[51] That is not to say that older needs were being sacrificed as new ones came to the fore. Appendix D contains a list of all the organizations which were given fresh grants in 1990 and indicates the very broad range of overall assistance.

The Foundation thus reached the end of its first century in a positive mood. Its income had risen dramatically over the previous few years, although no more than was necessary to meet the vastly expanded demands on its resources. There was a new Central Scheme with a much more straightforward definition of how the Foundation's income was to be applied which left much to the discretion of a knowledgeable and enthusiastic body of trustees. There was a consciousness, however, that much remained to be done. A century of experience had demonstrated that, though definitions of poor Londoners might greatly change over time, their needful presence remained. The Trustees had no grounds for believing that the future would be otherwise.

NOTES

1. CPF, *Report on Policy Relating to Grants in the Quinquennium 1967 to 1971* (1967); Minutes, LXXVII, 17–69.
2. Minutes, LXXX, 9.
3. Ibid., LXXVII, 44–5; LXXVIII, 19: Asa Briggs and Anne Macartney, *Toynbee Hall: The First Hundred Years* (1984), 170.
4. Minutes, LXXIX, 18–20, 127–8, 171; LXXXI, 16–17; LXXXII, 15–16.
5. Ibid., LXXVIII, 165–6; LXXIX, 70–1; LXXX, 111–12; LXXXI, 68–9.
6. Ibid., LXXVII, 156–7; LXXVIII, 185–6; LXXX, 78–9, 83.
7. Ibid., LXXVI, 144–5, 161–2; LXXVII, 211–12; LXXX, 80–1.
8. CPF, *Report on Policy Relating to Grants in the Quinquennium 1972 to 1976* (1971); Minutes, LXXXI, 177–238.
9. Minutes, LXXXI, 103–4, 186.
10. Ibid., LXXXVI, 199–200.
11. Ibid., LXXXII, 15–16, 168–9, 173; LXXXIV, 167; LXXXV, 76, 202.
12. Ibid., LXXXIV, 78; LXXXV, 211–14.
13. Ibid., LXXIX, 20–1; LXXXI, 129–30; LXXXII, 125; LXXXIII, 143; LXXXIV, 174–5; LXXXV, 154–5.
14. Ibid., LXXXI, 84–5; LXXXIV, 131; LXXXV, 149.
15. Ibid., LXXXII, 183; LXXXV, 149–50.
16. Ibid., LXXXIV, 160; LXXXVI, 202–3.

17. Ibid., LXXXII, 94–5; LXXXIV, 91–2, 181–2, 186–7; LXXXV, 93–5; LXXXVI, 96–7.
18. Ibid., LXXXII, 179–80; LXXXIII, 76; LXXXV, 209–10.
19. Ibid., LXXXVI, 194–6.
20. Ibid., LXXXVI, 101–11.
21. Ibid., LXXXVI, 209–64.
22. Ibid., XCII, 11–12.
23. Ibid., XC, 184–6.
24. Ibid., LXXXIV, 16–17, 94; CPF, *Report on Current Policy Relating to Grants and Loans 1977 to 1981* (1977).
25. Minutes, LXXXVII, 82; XCI, 89–90, 297–9.
26. Ibid., LXXXIX, 59–60, 83, 91, 221.
27. Ibid., LXXXVIII, 74, 194–5; XC, 178–9; XCI, 114–15, 198–9.
28. Ibid., XCVII, 153–4.
29. Ibid., LXXXIX, 153–4, 195–7; XCI, 107–8, 260–3, 292–4.
30. Ibid., LXXXVII, 72; LXXXVIII, 49; LXXXIX, 50; XC, 52; XCI, 56; XCII, 83.
31. Ibid., XC, 57.
32. Ibid., XCII, 33–47.
33. Ibid., XC, 53; XCII, 285.
34. Ibid., XCII, 292–4; XCIV, 331–4, 388–90.
35. Ibid., XCII, 329–31; XCV, 150–3.
36. Ibid., XCV, 271–5.
37. Ibid., XCII, 96–7, 216–17; XCV, 110–11.
38. Ibid., XCIII, 264–7; XCIV, 358–9; XCVI, 285–7.
39. Ibid., XCII, 105–6; XCIV, 152–4; XCV, 380–2.
40. Ibid., XCIV, 325–6, 329–31.
41. Ibid., XCII, 98–9; XCIV, 350–1; XCV, 392–4, 402–4.
42. Ibid., XCIV, 266–7, 384–6.
43. Ibid., XCVI, 443–62.
44. CPF, *Policy for 1987–1991* (1986).
45. Minutes, XCVII, 457–8.
46. Directory of Social Change, *A Guide to the Major Trusts* (1989), 50–2.
47. Minutes, XCVIII, 19; XCIX, 24.
48. Ibid., XCVII, 403–6; XCVIII, 41–4, 520–1.
49. Ibid., XCVIII, 376–7, 396–7; XCIX, 614–15.
50. Ibid., XCVI, 15–16; XCVIII, 51–2, 247–8; XCIX, 457–8, 623–4.
51. Ibid., XCVIII, 374–5, 512–13; XCIX, 123–4, 466–7, 474–6.

15 The City Church Fund

St Paul's Cathedral may have miraculously escaped the worst attentions of the Luftwaffe, but many of the City churches were by no means so fortunate. When the trustees began to take stock after the nightmare events of 1940–1, they found that of the 39 churches which received grants from the City Church Fund, only 12 had remained undamaged. Eighteen had been either destroyed or suffered such serious damage that special arrangements had to be made for the conduct of services, where this proved at all possible. Under the terms of the amending scheme of 1899, the Charity Commissioners could, with the consent of the Bishop and Archdeacon of London, suspend or reduce the payments specified in the Central Scheme if there had been any changes in circumstances affecting the maintenance of a church or the arrangements for public worship.

The trustees, after consulting with a committee which had been set up by the Bishop of London to review the situation, took the view that in the case of damaged churches it was necessary to continue to pay the grants so that the remaining fabric could be adequately protected, and as most churches were attempting to make some provision for services caution should be exercised in stopping grants for such purposes. In the end, they considered that only one grant should definitely cease, namely that paid for repairs to the fabric of St Mildred, Bread Street, which had been totally destroyed. Of the grants for everyday maintenance and services, they recommended that one, to St Mary Aldermanbury, should be suspended, while those to three other churches should be reduced, and a further half-dozen paid in full for the present but reconsidered later. The Bishop and Archdeacon agreed to the changes and the Charity Commissioners issued the necessary order.[1] In 1942, on the recommendation of the Bishop's committee, the grants to five of the six churches which had been kept under review were also reduced.

In the meantime, however, several of the discretionary grants to ministers which had been discontinued in the past were resumed temporarily because the incomes of several incumbents were dependent on rents from property which had been destroyed by bombing. Thus, the overall grants to the City churches and clergy decreased only marginally during the war, from about £15,000 to £14,000, but the surplus paid to the Ecclesiastical Commissioners suffered a steep decline from nearly £50,000 in 1939 to £34,000 in 1945, as a result of the effect of the war on the overall income of the City Church Fund.[2]

Not surprisingly, it took some time after the war to decide on the fate of all of the churches which had been seriously damaged, but in the event the recommendations of the Bishop of London's Commission which reported in 1946 were followed remarkably closely. These were that nine churches should not be rebuilt, of which, in fact, the only one that was eventually restored was St Andrew-by-the-Wardrobe. The trustees immediately asked that the question of the remaining grants to those churches should be examined, but, because of the uncertainties of the situation, only some of the maintenance grants, amounting in fact to very little money, were immediately withdrawn. The Reverend Allan John Macdonald, the rector of St Dunstan-in-the-West and Rural Dean of the East and West City since 1943, who had been appointed as a trustee by the Ecclesiastical Commissioners in 1944, pressed the claim of the remaining City churches to any money that was saved. He was concerned that there was no provision for increasing grants for repair and maintenance which had been fixed over fifty years ago.[3]

The Church Commissioners (as the Ecclesiastical Commissioners were renamed in 1948) were not averse to the redistribution of any savings from the grants withdrawn from war-damaged churches to other benefices in the City on the recommendation of the Bishop of London. They could afford to take a relaxed view, as their income from the surplus of the City Church Fund had risen above the level of 1939 by 1948 when it passed £50,000, while grants to the City churches remained static at a little over £14,000.[4]

Little actually happened, however, until 1954 (apart from the rise in the surplus received by the Church Commissioners to £68,500) when a reorganization of the City churches took place as the result of the report of yet another commission under the chairmanship of Sir Frederick Tidbury-Beer and the passing of the City of London (Guild

Churches) Act of 1952. Under the Act 15 churches were relieved of their parochial responsibilities and were designated 'guild' churches with the freedom to pursue their ministry in various ways. As far as the Foundation was concerned, the status of the church did not matter and grants were paid equally to parish and guild churches. Under the new arrangements, however, a number of the incumbents whose salaries had been supplemented as an interim measure received secured stipends and their grants were withdrawn.

The trustees, at the prompting of the Bishop and Archdeacon, decided to apply to the Charity Commissioners for a new scheme in which there would be a revised schedule of grants. They wanted the sums for the maintenance of the fabric and services to be merged and a fifth of the grants to be reserved for repairs to the fabric. The Charity Commissioners went a step further by asking in addition for a separate fund to be set up for the maintenance and restoration of any churches within the City of architectural or historic interest, but the Church Commissioners objected on the grounds that payments into such a fund would diminish the surplus received by them. The Charity Commissioners had their way, however, and in a new scheme which came into operation in January 1956 £5,000 per annum was to be set aside in the years 1956 to 1965 inclusive for a City Churches (Extraordinary Repair) Fund. Sums from this fund could be used, on the direction of the Bishop of London, for the extraordinary repair, restoration or rebuilding of the churches named in the scheme and any others in the City which the Charity Commissioners and the Church Commissioners between them agreed should benefit.

Under the revised scheme, annual fixed grants totalling £14,852 were paid to 34 churches, excluding seven of the churches which had been so badly damaged in the war that rebuilding was no longer contemplated (although one, St Anne and St Agnes, was eventually restored for a Lutheran congregation), but including for the first time All Hallows, London Wall, and St Benet, Paul's Wharf, which had been designated guild churches. In the case of ten of the churches which had not yet been restored, the sums for the maintenance of the fabric were paid into a suspended grants fund.[5]

Almost immediately there was a dispute about the use of the repair fund when the Archdeacon of London wanted the first £5,000 to be allocated for the restoration of St James, Garlickhythe. The trustees considered that this was contrary to the original intention which had been to establish a long-term reserve earning interest, and the application was withdrawn.[6] The last payment to supplement the stipends of ministers ceased in 1958, and thereafter, the grants to the City churches remained static at just under £15,000 with a further £5,000 for the repair fund until 1964, when the total of the latter, with interest, stood at over £60,000 (which was equivalent to about £500,000 at 1990 values).[7]

After discussions involving the Clerk of the Foundation, the Archdeacon of London and the Church Commissioners, it was agreed that the repair fund should be closed and drawn on as needed. In its place, £1,500 per annum would be paid into a new fund called the City Churches Reserve Fund which could be used as the Bishop of London directed for the repair, restoration and maintenance of the buildings, fittings or furnishings of the churches. In addition the fund into which the suspended grants had been paid was also to be wound up, as it was by now reasonably certain which churches were not going to be restored, and the annual fixed grants to the parish and guild churches were to be increased by the £3,500 which would be saved by stopping payments to the repair fund after the payments to the new reserve fund had been taken into account.[8]

All of these changes necessitated a new scheme which was duly implemented by the Charity Commissioners on 20 June 1968. Under this, grants totalling £2,308 for the repair and restoration of the fabric and £15,251 towards the maintenance of the services were paid to 31 churches, three having been removed from the list. These were St Dunstan-in-the-East and St Mary Aldermanbury, which were not being rebuilt, at least in London (St Mary Aldermanbury being re-erected in Fulton, Missouri, USA), and St Michael Paternoster Royal, which was restored for use as the headquarters of the Missions to Seamen. With the £1,500 paid into the reserve fund, this meant that some £19,000 out of the income of the City Church Fund was now being spent annually on the City churches; in comparison, the amount payable to the Church Commissioners stood at £135,000 in 1968.[9]

Sums from the Extraordinary Repair Fund were used for major works at six churches between 1966 and 1972, when the small balance remaining was transferred to the reserve fund and the repair fund was wound up.[10] In the meantime, yet another commission on the City churches under the chairmanship of Sir Denys Buckley (later Lord Justice Buckley) had reported in 1971. Like the Phillimore Report just over 50 years ago, the recommendations of the Buckley Report were too radical for the City and its clergy to accept. It expressed the view that there were too many churches holding services and too many clergy in the City, but not enough halls and other buildings for pastoral work. While recognizing that the City churches were among the nation's outstanding architectural treasures and setting its face adamantly against the demolition of any of them, it none the less advocated that nine should be made pastorally redundant and adapted for other uses. Of the remainder, 20 should be grouped together into seven unions served by team ministries. As far as the grants from the

Foundation were concerned, it thought that those for the fabric of the churches had so far been adequate but would need to be increased, whereas those for what it slightly puzzlingly termed the 'living agents' had failed to keep pace with inflation and were now 'totally inadequate'.[11]

The City Deanery Synod rejected the Buckley Report virtually out of hand. Several observers at the time, and subsequently, felt that this was a lost opportunity to rationalize the provision of churches for worship in the City. But others besides the City establishment and clergy felt uneasy about the recommendations for the redundancy of so many of the churches and the effect this would have on their fabric. Thus followed an uneasy alliance between the conservationists and the City clergy which has helped to preserve the status quo.[12] At the Foundation, the Clerk reported that the report had been rejected, but urged that its strictures about the inadequacy of the sums paid to the City churches should not be ignored, and suggested that the appropriate authorities should be informed that the trustees favoured a review, especially in view of the decline of the share of the income of the City Church Fund which went to the City churches, from 22 per cent to 10 per cent between 1956 and 1971.[13]

Perhaps unfortunately, however, nothing was done immediately, and shortly after Gerald Ellison became Bishop of London in 1973 he appointed a commission under Lord Carr of Hadley to advise whether any alteration in the allocation of the City Church Fund was desirable in view of the considerable rise in its income. Indeed, the disparity in 1976, when the Carr Commission met, was only too striking. The City churches still received a little over £19,000 per annum in total, whereas the surplus which was paid to the Church Commissioners for distribution to the various dioceses in the Metropolitan Police District now amounted to £356,000.

John Smallwood, who was both a trustee and the Chairman of the Southwark Diocesan Board of Finance, submitted a memorandum to the Carr Commission suggesting that payments to the City churches might be made out of the allocation to the Diocese of London, which could be augmented for the purpose. Bryan Woods advised that such a proposal could only be made in his capacity as a representative of the Southwark Diocese. The trustees as a whole, on the firm recommendation of their Clerk, had taken the view that the distribution of the income was a matter for the church authorities, but a little anticipation might have saved a great deal of later grief.

Almost immediately the Carr Commission produced an interim report recommending that the grants to the City churches should be doubled pending the publication of its final report, and the trustees asked the Charity Commissioners to make an amending scheme. Such was the slowness of the Commissioners, however, and so many complications did they find in the way of preparing the scheme, that it was not issued until 23 September 1977, after the commission had produced its report.[14]

The Carr Report, which was submitted in the first place to the Bishop of London, recommended that £88,000 per annum should for the present be allocated to the City churches, calculated as £70,000 for the maintenance of services, £13,000 for ordinary repairs and the restoration of the fabric and £5,000 for extraordinary repairs. It advocated that, in order to simplify matters, one sum should be paid to each church council as a fixed grant, and that the apportionment of the money between the upkeep of the fabric and the costs of services could be left to the good sense of the councils. The actual amounts specified as fixed grants to the 31 churches took into account their needs and any other sources of regular income, and ranged from £1,620 for St Michael, Cornhill, to £764 for St Helen, Bishopsgate, adding up to a total of £32,865.

The remaining £55,135 was to be paid into a pool and distributed annually by a grants committee chaired by the Archdeacon of London with the Rural Dean of the City, the lay chairman of the City Deanery Synod and the General Secretary of the Diocese of London as its other members. The report further recommended that the overall sum spent on grants to the City churches should be adjusted every three years to take account of any rise or fall in the value of money, provided that the total of the fixed and variable grants should not amount to a higher proportion of the income of the City Church Fund than that applying when the recommendations were first put into effect (which, in 1977, would have been about 16 per cent). If any participating church was subsequently declared redundant, its grant was to lapse and the amount transferred to the residue paid to the Church Commissioners, while the pool for distribution by the grants committee was also to be reduced by an amount equivalent to the average grant paid to that church over the past three years.[15]

As soon as he had received the report, the Bishop came under a great deal of pressure. The City clergy decided that they would hold out for more, doubtless encouraged by a rather perfunctory and one-sided history of the Foundation in the report, which had included the statement that, 'The income under discussion is entirely derived from the charitable endowments of the churches listed, whose needs therefore have a prior claim.' The Rural Dean, the Reverend Basil Watson, who was vicar of St Lawrence Jewry, acted as the spokesman of the City interest, and he wrote to the Bishop on 27 September 1977 expressing concern and suggesting that legal advice might be sought.

'We shall feel very aggrieved,' he wrote, 'if ways are not found of treating us very differently out of the Fund.'[16]

What followed could have come straight from the pages of Trollope, with an increasingly intemperate correspondence ensuing between the Rural Dean and his Bishop, and other actors engaged in various machinations flitting in and out of the scene. It took the Bishop until early in 1978 to announce his response to the report, but he accepted most of its findings, differing only on two points. He added the chairman of the London Diocesan Finance Committee to the membership of the City Churches Grants Committee, as it was to be known, and, more significantly, proposed the substitution of a percentage of the income of the City Church Fund for the sum total of all grants to be paid to the City churches instead of the set amount, reviewable triennially, which had been favoured by the Carr Commission. He fixed the proportion at 20 per cent of the disposable income of the Fund, which was slightly more generous to the City churches than the formula in the Carr Report.[17]

At once the City clergy, through the Rural Dean, returned to the warpath. They objected in principle to the adoption of a percentage division of the funds, claiming that the needs of the City churches should be regarded as a first charge on the income 'and it is only after these needs have been satisfied that it is proper to consider diverting any surplus to other purposes'. Once more there was a vague threat of legal action, and a suggestion that the Charity Commissioners should be asked to adjudicate. The Bishop, becoming increasingly exasperated at this continuing objection to a settlement which, in his view, was eminently reasonable and in which he had striven hard to accommodate the wishes of the City party, was determined to stick to his percentage and asked the trustees to request a new scheme from the Charity Commissioners on the lines he had proposed.[18]

Bryan Woods cautioned the trustees against becoming involved in the dispute, but took the legalistic view that he was bound to act on the request of the Bishop and ask the Charity Commissioners to prepare a new scheme. The Commission issued a draft scheme in November 1978, but the City Deanery Synod objected to it in principle, and the staff of the Commission were loathe to proceed further in the face of an objection which they regarded as a fundamental one without first seeing if there was some common ground. In the meantime the Bishop and the Rural Dean, who admittedly was merely acting as the spokesman for his fellow clerics, seemed to be locked into an adversarial position. Early in February 1979 Watson wrote, 'We do oppose the Scheme root and branch. We hope that it will not be implemented. It is not that we think that your Scheme does not go far enough, but that it should never have started where it did.'

Ellison replied by expressing his 'great disappointment that the City should prove so intransigent in meeting the efforts which I have made to help them', to which Watson responded, 'our divergence is initial and basic'.[19]

Woods was determined that the trustees should remain aloof, at least officially, which doubtless helps to explain why the role played by the successive Archdeacons of London, Sam Woodhouse up till his retirement in 1978 and then Frank Harvey, does not appear in the records. In any case, it was left to the staff of the Charity Commission to act as honest brokers, a task to which they seem to have warmed. Meetings were held with the Bishop and Archdeacon of London, at which, after a long discussion, the Bishop agreed if necessary to raise the proportion which went to the City churches, and subsequently with the City Synod which was prepared to accept a third share. This solution was put to the Bishop in July 1979 and he agreed, commenting that 'I hope it will be made clear to other interested parties that it is not I who have pressed for this amendment but it is one which has been proposed by the Charity Commissioners and accepted by the City churches.' He also stated that as far as he was concerned he was content that the largest possible amount should be made available to the City churches, but doubted whether the other benefiting dioceses would be prepared to accept such a modification. The metropolitan dioceses were unhappy but did not object formally, probably reasoning that even though their share was reduced the funds from the Foundation were increasing rapidly and enough blood had already been spilt, and the Charity Commissioners duly amended the draft scheme.[20]

One other change from the recommendations of the Carr Commission was that in the case of redundancy, the overall proportion to be allotted to the City churches was not to be reduced. This had been proposed by the Charity Commissioners, ostensibly to avoid complex calculations in the case of such an event, and accepted by the Bishop despite considerable misgivings on the part of all parties outside the City. At one time, the Commissioners had also proposed that all of the parish and guild churches in the City should benefit from the one-third share of the City Church Fund, but although the Bishop was agreeable, there was by no means unanimous agreement to such a change within the City Chapter and the proposal was withdrawn. The revised scheme also stipulated that any money unspent by the grants committee after three years should be added to the residue payable to the Church Commissioners, and made provision for the Bishop of London to review every five years the allocation to the named churches from the overall proportion allotted to them.

The new scheme became operative on 1 January 1980. In that year a little over £600,000 was available to be divided, one third to the City churches (£32,865 in fixed grants and the remainder for distribution by the City Churches Grants Committee) and the remainder to the Church Commissioners. In 1986, by when the net income of the City Church Fund had risen to over £1 million, the Bishop of London decided that the parish and guild churches which had been previously excluded should now become eligible to receive grants from the City Churches Grants Committee. The number of churches benefiting had been reduced to 30 since 1982, when St Nicholas Cole Abbey became a Presbyterian church for the London congregation of the Free Church of Scotland (the total of the fixed grants being adjusted to £31,852, at which sum it has remained up to the time of writing).[21]

In 1988 the trustees received for the first time a schedule showing the grants that had been made by the City Churches Grants Committee over the previous seven years. For some time the Church Commissioners had supplied a general breakdown of the way in which their share of the income of the City Church Fund had been spent. This had shown the amounts received by each of the six dioceses which covered parts of the Metropolitan Police District (generally in proportion to the population of each within the District), and the totals spent on grants and loans, together with some indication of the uses to which the money was put. At this time, nearly all of the grants and loans were in fact spent on the maintenance of churches, church halls, parsonages and other buildings. Under the new Central Scheme of 1989 the sums allocated were paid directly to the various Diocesan Boards of Finance, with only a small residual amount going to the Church Commissioners. The trustees were concerned that in contrast they had received so little information about how the, by now, very considerable amount available to the City churches had been used. The Archdeacon of London had had some difficulty in obtaining audited accounts from some of the parish and guild councils applying for grants, and the trustees put on record their support for such a requirement.[22]

Virtually all of the grants which were made by the City Churches Grants Committee were for works to the fabric of the churches and there was no question of the money being misspent. But behind the request for more information was a deep disquiet on the part of many of the trustees that so much money, estimated to be about £1 million by the end of the decade, was now going to City churches, few of which had significant weekday or weekend congregations. They raised the 'moral dimension' of the amount of funds made available to the few City churches, as against the needs of the many parish churches in the more deprived areas of London. Gone were the days of a non-interventionist Central Governing Body. Now discussions were sought with the Bishop of London with a view to seeking a major review of the financial arrangements, and the issue was not going to be allowed to die down.[23]

Once more there were two seemingly diametrically opposed viewpoints. One stressed the origins of the City Church Fund in bequests to the City parishes for ecclesiastical purposes and the difficulties in meeting the expense of maintaining architectural masterpieces which were national assets. Indeed, such had been the fall in the value of money that the seemingly very large sum which was available to the City churches out of the City Church Fund at the beginning of the 1990s represented little more in real terms than the total amount which had been set aside for the upkeep of their fabric and the costs of services under the Central Scheme of 1891 (see page 193). At that time, however, 48 churches benefited, whereas in 1991 the number was 36, of which six had only recently become eligible. There were also many in the 1890s who thought that in drawing up the Central Scheme the Charity Commissioners had been too generous to the City churches.

The other view was that it was morally wrong that 36 churches in an area of enormous wealth should claim a third share of the income of the City Church Fund while the remaining two-thirds had to be distributed between some 700 or so churches, many of them facing desperate problems in impoverished areas. Moreover, there was a feeling that the very existence of such a bonanza from the City Parochial Foundation cocooned the City churches from the harsh realities of a world of falling congregations and declining endowments, and delayed some hard decisions which would have to be taken in the end. In the late nineteenth century there had been an outcry about the extent of the charitable endowments of City parishes with a negligible population and churches whose congregations consisted of little more than church officials, while there was overwhelming evidence of manifest need in the wider metropolis. Some of the critics of the ecclesiastical provisions of the Central Scheme of 1891 also claimed that they merely served to delay much needed reforms in the organization of the City churches. If history never quite repeats itself, it sometimes seems to try very hard.

NOTES

1. Minutes, L, 98–9, 118–19; 135–6; LII, 70.
2. Ibid., LI, 136–7; LVI, 74–5, 84.
3. Ibid., LVI, 156–7; LVII, 5–6; LVIII, 6–7.
4. Ibid., LVIII, 125; LIX, 80, 90.
5. Ibid., LXIV, 6, 40–3, 120–1, 136–7, 188; LXV, 3–4, 158; LXVI, 4: Amending Scheme of 2 Dec. 1955.

6. Minutes, LXVII, 160, 190–1.
7. Ibid., LXXVI, 4–6.
8. Ibid., LXXVI, 4–6, 132.
9. Ibid., LXXIX, 64; LXXX, 4.
10. Ibid., LXXXII, 41.
11. *The Report of the Commission on the Churches in the City of London* (1971).
12. See, for instance, Peter Burman, 'City churches' in *Save the City: A Conservation Study of the City of London*, ed. David Lloyd (1976), 142–4.
13. Minutes, LXXXII, 41–2.
14. Ibid., LXXXVI, 174; LXXXVII, 204–5.
15. CPF, file 1418/7, 'Report of the Commission appointed by the Bishop of London to make recommendations concerning the grants from the City Church Fund to certain churches in the City of London', May 1977.
16. File 1418/7, letter of 27 Sept. 1977.
17. Minutes, LXXXVIII, 42–3; file 1418/7, letter of 17 Feb. 1978.
18. File 1418/7, esp. letters of 28 March, 15 May and 5 June 1978.
19. Ibid., letters of 3 Jan., 6 Feb., 12 Feb. and 20 Feb. 1979.
20. Ibid., esp. letter of 18 July 1979.
21. Minutes, XCVI, 83–5.
22. Ibid., XCVIII, 166–7.
23. Ibid., XCVIII, 166; XCIX, 21.

Retrospect and prospect

It is always tempting for the historian of an organization to claim that the period in which he is writing is one of particular complexity and change for that organization. To some extent this is because he is aware of all the confusing detail and lacks the perspective (and, it must be said, selectivity) which frequently makes the past seem so much clearer than the present. Nevertheless, in the case of the City Parochial Foundation there does seem to be more than usual substance for the claim. Over the period 1985–90 its income has well nigh trebled, only to be matched by a threefold increase in applications for grants; a new Clerk has been appointed, with, inevitably, different ideas from his predecessors; a new Central Scheme has been drawn up to replace that, which, with amendments, had governed proceedings for 98 years; there has been a significant increase in staff and a move to a new office, which is also the first to be actually owned by the Foundation; the management of the Trust for London has been taken on, with the reciprocal effect that the subtly different ways of working demanded of the Trust have communicated themselves powerfully to the Foundation; and, over all, there has been a perceptible change in attitudes and conceptions on the part of a body of trustees which in itself has undergone a significant transformation, no fewer than two-thirds of its members at the beginning of the Centenary year having been appointed in the past four years. From the first fruits of policy-making for the quinquennium 1992–6 which is even now underway, that process of change looks set to continue.

And yet, the historian above all people should be conscious of the fact that changes rarely occur overnight. Organizations are not generally prone to revolutions. In focusing on the salient features of a hundred years of history, therefore, it is important to notice not merely the signposts on the road to change, but equally those factors which may have inhibited change, for good or ill, and which may, consciously or unconsciously, still be at work. Certainly, if one of the characteristics of the Foundation at the time of its Centenary appears to be a culture of change, two of its dominant hallmarks over the past 100 years have been continuity and adaptability.

An overview of the trustees of the Foundation during its first 100 years reveals certain characteristics. If at the very end of that long period there has been a high turnover of members of the Central Governing Body, this was certainly not the case for most of the Foundation's history to date. The average length of service of a trustee was about 11 years. Some served for very long periods – over 40 years in one or two cases – while the tenure of some others was brief, but the average probably accurately reflects the degree of experience and continuity which the trustees as a whole were able to bring to the Foundation's deliberations. It must also be said, however, that some trustees continued to a very ripe old age, even into their nineties in two instances, and that the Central Governing Body as a whole sometimes took on a rather elderly complexion. Of course, until very recently, the Foundation has had virtually no say in whoever was appointed by the nominating bodies, nor how often they were reappointed, but the standing orders adopted under the Central Scheme of 1989 have now imposed an upper age limit of 60 for new nominees and 70 for reappointees. Not surprisingly, the majority of trustees were men. In fact, only two women trustees were appointed up to the Second World War, and in total only 17 (out of 176). Eight of those have been nominated in the past 20 years, and seven are members of the Central Governing Body in 1991.

At the beginning there was a preponderance of men who were involved with technical education and of City fathers; as far as possible, indeed, the nominating bodies selected men who combined both characteristics. There was also nearly always a strong contingent of professional men, especially barristers and solicitors, although most of them had used their professional qualifications as a springboard to other careers and had been chosen as trustees in other capacities. The high representation accorded the City Corporation and the London County Council (and subsequently the GLC) meant that local politicians were always present in numbers, and, especially in the early years, some of the LCC's nominees were extremely influential. The body of trustees usually included one or two Members of Parliament at any one time, but few were prominent in national politics. While it is always risky to generalize in the case of such a large and regularly changing group of people, the dominant impression for much of the period is that the governing body consisted principally of men with strong professional roots who belonged to some of the major institutions of power in London, and who had a deep sense of public duty but little direct connection with the poor and, with one or two notable exceptions, limited experience of the voluntary sector.

In terms of the overall influence of the trustees, it is possible to trace three distinct phases. At first and for many years, the Central Governing Body contained a large number of dominant personalities who had a very considerable say in the conduct of the Foundation's business. For a long period on each side of the Second World War, however, and especially when Donald Allen was Clerk, only a handful of trustees appear to have been involved in much more than a peripheral manner. When Allen remarked to the Nathan Committee in 1951 that it was an 'extraordinary thing' that trustees who initially represented their nominating body rapidly came to represent the Foundation on that body,[1] he may unconsciously have been saying something about his own dominant influence on the policies and attitudes which they came to represent. In contrast, over the past few years in particular, but in origins perhaps traceable back for a decade or more, there has been a tendency towards an increased participation in decision making and a much greater contribution to policy making on the part of a younger, very knowledgeable body of trustees, several of whom have had a close involvement with the work of the voluntary sector.

As indicated in Appendix B, there have been only eight Chairmen of the Foundation in a hundred years, and one of those was Chairman for less than a year. If such a record can be taken as a measure of stability and continuity, even more can such a criterion be said to apply in the case of the Clerks, of whom there have only been six, one of whom held the office for less than three years. The successive Clerks have exercised a very great influence over the Foundation, and if this seems more evident in recent years, during the tenure of Sir Donald Allen, Bryan Woods and Timothy Cook, it may be because the records of the time of Howard Batten and Ernald Warre are less expansive. In the discussion of the Foundation's policies which follows below, their presence in the background, and frequently the foreground, should be assumed. Their contributions to the seminal reports of the Quinquennial Policy Sub-Committees, for instance, were invariably highly significant.

The 'small, selective and well qualified' staff, as Allen described them, many of whom were exceptionally long serving, provided year-by-year consistency in the administration of the Foundation at remarkably low cost. The Foundation has also been fortunate in its professional advisers. It is, perhaps, not surprising that only two firms of solicitors advised the trustees on legal matters, but more noteworthy that only four named partners were officially appointed to the role – Robert Pearce, Howard Bradshaw, J. W. French and Mark Farrer – although they were assisted by other members of their firms. There have been five principal surveyors, namely Herbert Winstanley, William Campbell Jones, Mervyn Campbell Jones, Frank Hewitt and Bill Killick.

The continuity which these surveyors brought to the conduct of estate business has been extremely valuable. One of the undoubted successes of the Foundation has been the management of its endowment, and in this it is certainly possible to see a logical progression from the beginning to the present day, although not without the high degree of flexibility which was necessary to respond to changing conditions. To give credit to the Charity Commissioners, after some initial reluctance to hand over the assets of the Foundation, and while maintaining watchful oversight, they allowed considerable freedom to the trustees and their advisers to negotiate property transactions. In recent years, indeed, even the measure of control which the Commissioners used to exercise has in large measure been removed in a resounding vote of confidence in the way in which the Foundation has carried out this aspect of its work.

Most of the Foundation's endowment consisted of property. This has been true of all periods, even though a readiness to move in or out of various forms of investment as circumstances dictated has always characterized the Foundation's management of its assets, and in recent years the importance of the non-property portfolio has led to the appointment of professional investment managers. The Foundation's estate was never treated as a fixed and immutable body of property, and the policy of rationalization and consolidation which has been such a marked feature of the management of the estate in recent years has, in fact, been consistently followed throughout the whole period.

Another cardinal principle which has always been borne in mind is that long-term interests should never be sacrificed for short-term gain. The Foundation could, of course, afford to think in decades and wait for the patient maturing of plans laid a long time in advance. It has always eschewed the quick fix in the property market which might present a seductive vision of present gain but carried with it uncertain prospects for the future.

The advantage to the Foundation of having an income based primarily on rents was demonstrated particularly in its grants policy after the Second World War, when estimates of the likely surplus which would be available for grants over the next five years could be made

with a reasonable degree of certainty at the beginning of each quinquennium because the rental income was for the most part predictable.
Thus, although it has never been the practice to assign budgets to
specific categories of need, it was possible to plan rationally in the
knowledge that there would be an assured level of funds. Grants could
be made for a period of years – usually two or three but sometimes
up to five – to the undoubted advantage of applicant bodies. To some
extent the degree of predictability has diminished in recent years with
more regular rent reviews and arrangements for sharing in occupational rents, but a base level of income can virtually be guaranteed.
It also helped in matching the available funds to the applications
received that after 1908 the discretionary grants were always made
out of the previous year's income, which was therefore known in
advance.

Appendix C gives the income of the Foundation at regular intervals.
It shows the slow and fluctuating growth in the period up to the First
World War, much of which coincided with the long Edwardian property depression; the steady increase in the inter-war years; the shatter-
ing effect of the Second World War, and in particular the London
Blitz; and the post-war recovery, gradually gathering pace as, with
the aid of astute management, backed up by professional advice of
the highest calibre, the Foundation was able to profit from the development booms and ride over the slumps. The overall effect has been
quite dramatic, with a substantial growth in real income taking place
in the 1980s. The figures for 1989 and 1990 to some extent reflect the
very large sum which was received in 1988 from the sale of playing
fields at Mitcham which had been bought in 1920 for social reasons
alone, but even before that, and independently of it, the rate of increase
was already moving sharply upwards.

The net result of virtually continuous activity in the property market
over many years is that the Foundation's holdings in 1991 principally
consist of about 1.7 million square feet of offices in the City of London,
concentrated on a select number of prime sites, many of them in new
buildings and the vast majority let to first-class tenants with regular
rent reviews. In addition, as a result of the policy of diversification
which was adopted in 1980 and which seems more prudent in 1991
than it did as late as 1989, four substantial office developments in
outer London and the south-east region have also been acquired, and
part of the proceeds of the Mitcham sale have been invested in a
sizeable portfolio of stocks and shares. Future predictions are that the
rise in income will continue, but the rate of increase will largely
depend on extraneous factors and, in particular, on the general economic situation. Nevertheless, it looks very much as if it would take
a catastrophe of the proportions of the Second World War to halt the

upward progress of the Foundation's income. And if that occurred it would be very much more than the Foundation which would suffer.

In examining the overall rise in the Foundation's income, however, it is all too easy to forget the effects of inflation. The long-term indicator of the prices of consumer goods and services which provides the basis of the retail price index shown in Appendix C is a salutary reminder that the difference between a gross income of over £9 million in 1991 and one of £90,000 in 1892 is far less than it seems when the purchasing power of the pound is taken into consideration. What it does bring home is that the Foundation had extensive funds at its disposal from the beginning, and that if it made few grants to a very limited number of organizations, this is because such a large proportion of its funds were dedicated to one particular purpose, namely the polytechnics.

As part of the process of policy making which takes place every five years, the trustees look back with a critical eye at their own work in the period just ending. In the Foundation's Centenary year, it is understandable that they would wish that reflective approach, which has become such an important element in their deliberations, to be extended back further in time, to embrace not only the work of the past five or ten years but also that of their remote predecessors from the very beginnings of the Foundation. As such, some searching questions are being asked about whether and to what extent the Foundation has fulfilled its trust to the poor of London. One view, which has been expressed with some incredulity, is that it took the Foundation nearly half a century to begin to deal with the needs of the poor. There is, of course, a deliberate element of exaggeration in such a view, but it nevertheless contains enough substance to cause one to pause and take stock.

And yet it is important to keep a sense of perspective, and to realize that the range of options open to individuals at any one time are always limited by constraints, and that it is invariably easier to identify these from a distance of several years than at the time. Certainly, there have been a number of constraints affecting the work of the trustees, many of them external and some of their own making. To some extent, however, they all reflect prevalent attitudes in society in general, for perhaps the greatest constraint of all is the ethos of the time. If in one respect the history of the Foundation can be seen as a progression towards the adoption of new and more varied ways of assisting the poor (as indicated by the growth in the number of organizations given grants shown in Appendix D), this is at least in part a reflection of changing concepts of poverty and the needs of the poor.

One of the most important factors affecting the work of the Foundation – not perhaps, strictly speaking, a constraint and in some ways a source of strength – is its nature as a corporate body established by Act of Parliament. This immediately puts it in a different category from most of the other foundations and large trusts established by individuals. They can, and to a varying degree have to, carry out the aims of their founders, whereas the City Parochial Foundation's remit tends to be both broader and more difficult to define. In addition, well and conscientiously as the trustees of the other foundations carry out their trusts, there is perhaps a greater degree of public accountability in the case of the City Parochial Foundation. This thought has certainly exercised its trustees of late and may have been to the forefront of the minds of the Charity Commissioners when they so comprehensively directed the way in which the income of the Foundation was originally to be spent.

The way in which the Commissioners interpreted the duty placed on them in Bryce's Act to draw up a scheme to govern the Foundation's operations, and their particular concentration on the need for open spaces and, especially, technical education, placed the greatest possible restriction on the trustees' freedom of action. The complex reasons are adduced elsewhere, but behind them all appears to be their insistence, almost amounting to an obsession, that philanthropic assistance should only be given to the deserving poor. In this, of course, they were merely reflecting the views of society at large. Bryce saw the danger, remarking how there was 'a tendency for benefactions intended for the very poor to fall into the hands of a somewhat higher class',[2] a stricture to which the trustees themselves were to return time and again. He appealed for greater flexibility in the use of the endowments and for greater responsibility to be given to the trustees. The situation whereby 80 per cent of the capital of its secular Central Fund and about 60 per cent of its disposable income was already committed even before its trustees met for the first time, was clearly not to the liking of the one man who had done more than any other individual to bring the Foundation into being.

The nature of the trustees and of the bodies which appointed them not only tended to reinforce the attitudes of the Charity Commissioners, who had indeed been allowed to choose most of the nominating bodies, but also acted as a continuing constraint. It was the trustees who, of their own volition, decided at once to supplement the mandatory grants to the polytechnics with additional funds. They could, indeed, hardly have done otherwise at the time if those fledgling institutions for which they considered they had been given responsibility were to flourish. It is also fair to say that they themselves on more than one occasion questioned whether such support was a rightful use of the Foundation's funds.

The importance of the funds which were available from the City parochial charities, both capital and revenue, to the polytechnics can hardly be overstressed. Nor should their immense educational contribution be underestimated. Education has, of course, always been regarded as one of the most important means of combating poverty and the Foundation's trustees have consistently adopted education and training as one of the categories for grants. But even if the polytechnics, especially in the early years, satisfied the Charity Commissioners' very wide brief that the Foundation's funds should be used to assist the 'poorer classes', what increasingly came to be a matter of concern to the trustees was that such a very large percentage of the income should be spent in this one cause, and whether, as Bryce put it, such a use really met the needs of the very poorest.

We have seen how the process of disengagement was slow and painful, despite the single-minded determination of Allen to carry it through, resulting, after due consideration and debate, firstly in the withdrawal of the discretionary grants, and subsequently, after a very long interval, in an agreement on the part of the Charity Commissioners as late as 1962 that the mandatory grants should be terminated. That the whole episode took most of the long Clerkship of Allen before the matter was finally resolved says much about the infuriatingly legalistic and obfuscating attitudes that could at times be adopted by the Charity Commissioners at this particular time in their history.

The perceived need to distinguish between the deserving and undeserving poor was a powerful determinant of social action in the late nineteenth century, which lingered on for a long time; indeed, it has never entirely disappeared. It would be unrealistic to expect that it would not permeate the Foundation in its early years. That it did is shown by the way in which, under the scheme of 1895 for giving pensions to 'deserving poor persons' in the metropolis, applicants were rigorously scrutinized to make sure that they had shown the requisite degree of providence and thrift and were of sufficiently good character. In contrast, however, by 1935 when the scheme was revived, although nominally applicants still had to show evidence of thrift and good character, the only criterion on which they were in fact judged appears to have been need.

Because so little money was left over for other purposes after the needs of the polytechnics had been satisfied until at least the 1920s, a certain initial caution in advertising the Foundation's existence is understandable. What is less explicable is the persistence of that attitude for so long, essentially until the 1970s. One reason was the understandable anxiety that the Foundation should not simply be responding to demand, but the accompanying notion that in formulating policy the trustees could be confident that there was no great body of needs waiting to be addressed of which they were unaware begs the question of how they could have known if they did not provide the necessary publicity. An analysis of organizations which received grants in the years 1987–9 demonstrates that two-thirds of them had not previously applied to the Foundation. Even though there has undoubtedly been a prodigious growth in the number of voluntary bodies in recent years (as evidenced by the considerable increase in the number of registered charities), such a high proportion of new applicants suggests that not all of those who could have benefited knew of the Foundation, and indeed that this may still be the case.

An external constraint which came to seem particularly irksome and has now been removed was the clause in the original Central Scheme which prevented assistance being given to any organization which could be construed as in any way denominational in its composition. The attention which the churches and institutions of other faiths have given to social problems in recent years made its removal imperative, but it is interesting to note that Donald Allen remarked on the difficulties created by the clause in his evidence to the Nathan Committee in 1951.

An internal constraint to which all trusts are somewhat prone is the tendency to feel obligated to certain causes, from which it is difficult to become extricated, because an expectation of continuing assistance is created. The polytechnics, of course, fall into such a category, but in this case the trustees had very little room for manoeuvre. Their continuing support for the youth movement, however, was a matter of choice. In the years just before and after the Second World War youth work was regarded as a service of the utmost importance by virtually all the authorities on social policy, with Beveridge to the fore, and the trustees' concentration on it is perfectly explicable, but the extent to which in its institutional form of youth clubs and similar organizations it came to command an increasing share of resources eventually became a matter of concern to subsequent trustees.

If there were a number of factors which inhibited the Foundation in the degree to which it could provide help to the poor of London, there were others which were positively beneficial. One such, predating the Foundation itself, was the definition of the area of benefit in the Act of 1883 as the Metropolitan Police District and the City and Liberties of London. It is to the very great credit of Bryce and those who helped him to frame the Act that they should envisage the metropolis in such broad terms. There was then no administrative county of London, but the area covered by the Metropolitan Board of Works, the predecessor of the London County Council, was very much smaller. The Metropolitan Police District was sometimes adopted as a measure of greater London for statistical purposes and it may have been this which gave Bryce the idea of using it.

Despite the relative lack of opportunity because such a large proportion of the Foundation's resources was absorbed by the polytechnics, a great deal was achieved, even in the early years. What has generally been recognized as one of the most important aspects of the work of voluntary bodies has been their pioneering spirit, by which they have demonstrated the value of welfare services and paved the way for their subsequent adoption by the state or local authorities. Several of those areas of provision which were supported by the Foundation fall into this category. One of these was the feeding of schoolchildren, where a relatively modest expenditure could make a very significant contribution. Another was the support for the evening play-centre movement which was eventually taken over by the LCC.

Another service which was frequently cited as an excellent example of co-operation between the statutory and voluntary sectors was district nursing. For years, until indeed the entire responsibility for its financing devolved on the LCC as the local health authority with the introduction of the National Health Service in 1948, it received the largest of the Foundation's non-educational grants. Health services in general ranked high on the trustees' agenda. A case in point is infant welfare, which for many years was a paramount concern of the trustees. While not ignoring the strictures of latter-day critics that infant welfare centres concentrated rather too much on the failings of the mother, they did provide a service which appears to have been much appreciated by the poor and which may have contributed to a significant decline in infant mortality.

Even here, however, in areas where the Foundation's intervention seems to have been far-sighted and entirely beneficial, there were external factors at work. For society in general, the concern at the scandal of hungry schoolchildren and high infant mortality, and the preoccupation with the health of the populace in general, were aspects of the drive for 'national efficiency'. Revelations about the poor physical condition of recruits for the Boer War, and subsequently for the First World War, had aroused apprehensions about the fitness of those on whom the nation's future depended. The need to take positive steps to remedy this state of affairs, especially when Britain's main European rival, Germany, began to make such a fetish of physical fitness, was consciously or unconsciously a wellspring of much social action in the inter-war years. It was one of the motivations behind the preoccupation with the youth service, for instance.

It also helps to explain why the Foundation placed so much emphasis on supporting the social and recreational side of the work of the polytechnics, and why, in particular, it was concerned to ensure that each and every one of the institutions it grant-aided had adequate playing fields, even if this meant purchasing the sites, laying out the facilities and letting them to the institutions at nominal rents. Thus, the direct purchase of the playing fields which now form an important part of the Foundation's overall estate was undertaken for overwhelmingly social reasons, to aid the polytechnics to which the trustees felt obligated and to assist in the general drive towards physical well-being. In 1990 the trustees reiterated their desire to see open spaces retained, but utilized in a variety of ways for the benefit of the wider community.

There are many other examples of the pioneering spirit at work. In the 1930s, for instance, considerable support was given for services, including community centres, on the vast new LCC out-of-centre estates in places like Dagenham or Watling, as the social problems which accompanied the uprooting of people on such a large scale began to manifest themselves. Such assistance was, of course, only possible because the Foundation's area of benefit had been drawn so widely. Ways of helping the unemployed were sought, grants were given for the building of hostels – a need which recurred at regular intervals after the Second World War and has once more reasserted itself at the beginning of the 1990s – and the Foundation played a major part in founding the London Council of Social Service.

During the Second World War, the initiatives were of a more unusual kind and savoured more of the direct relief work which was as a rule eschewed. The distribution of blankets to those bombed out of their homes, the supply of spectacles to old-age pensioners, and communal feeding schemes all suggest a willingness to respond to emergencies in an imaginative way.

As more funds became available after the war, in part it must be said because of the vast extension of what Beveridge called the 'social service state' during wartime, it was possible to embark on some bold, imaginative ventures, like Isleden House, which, if it was not entirely successful as an exemplar, was a laudable attempt to make a contribution to the resolution of the problem of housing the elderly. Indeed, the propensity to take risks appears, not surprisingly, to have risen in proportion to the rise in income.

There are numerous examples of far-sighted projects and innovative work in the post-war period. One such, undertaken on Donald Allen's own initiative in the 1950s, was the experiment of appointing black social workers to work with immigrants, which was described in *The West Indian Comes to London*. A similar kind of project was the study of Notting Hill by Pearl Jephcott which resulted in the publication of *A Troubled Area*. Other pioneering work for which grants were given included Family Service Units, the setting up of a family casework unit in Hackney and the placing of a social worker in a group medical practice. An experiment that did not in the end succeed, but was important in conception, was the attempt to build a model common-lodging hostel for the 'forgotten men of the Welfare State'.

The support from the early 1950s of work with ex-offenders, and in particular the help given towards the establishment of Norman House when this was by no means a fashionable activity in the social service field, was another attempt to break new ground. From the early 1960s, indeed, whole new concepts began to colour the Foundation's thinking, as the needs of the 'inadequate' came to assume an increasing import-ance, and problems such as addiction were addressed for the first time.

The pattern of seeking out new avenues for assisting the poor was by then firmly established. Social ills which were singled out in the 1970s and 1980s, for instance, were the housing problem and associ-ated homelessness, and race relations. Here, grants for organizations which catered for ethnic minorities increasingly gave way to grants for organizations run by ethnic minorities, as participation was encour-aged in virtually every sphere. The needs of the various and growing refugee groups have, in particular, been singled out because they frequently represent, however temporarily, pockets of extreme poverty, and because, as newcomers, they find it difficult to obtain assistance through regular channels. The sheer diversity of applications for grants since the mid-1980s has ensured the continuance of an exploratory, risk-taking approach.

Underlying the inquiring attitude that marks the work of the trustees is the vehicle of the quinquennial policy review. This process, itself an innovation of the 1930s when a far more positive attitude towards grant making developed as the Foundation's income rose and the demands of the polytechnics receded, has been an enormously ben-eficial influence. The second policy report of 1935 set the tone by its comprehensiveness, and included lengthy quotations from Bryce's observations on the Central Scheme. Those after the war reflect in a vivid manner contemporary attitudes towards the Welfare State, buoy-antly optimistic about tackling the problems of the poor up to about the middle of the 1970s, and consistently pessimistic from that time onwards as confidence evaporated in the face of successive recessions and the political triumph in the 1980s of a radically different social philosophy. These remarkable documents, often written with great panache, provide an extraordinarily striking record of the ethos of an age.

The overall impression, at the end of the Foundation's first century, is that after a slow and somewhat unpromising start, the trustees sought diligently and on the whole successfully to help the poor of London. They were assisted by those among themselves who were individuals of outstanding ability and dedication, and by the high calibre of their Clerks, staff and professional advisers. They nurtured the Foundation's endowment with immense care and thoughtfulness, bringing it to a very sound position for future growth as the second century commences, and approached the business of utilizing the resources thereby created with the same scrupulous attention to detail and perceptive vision. Perhaps the outstanding feature of the way they conducted themselves was that they were never satisfied that they were taking the right decisions, but were always seeking to reflect on the effects of their work. They were constantly questioning whether there might not be other and better ways of assisting the poor.

The need, however, to refine these processes and develop mechanisms for the monitoring and evaluation of not only the effectiveness of the Foundation's grants to organizations but also the effectiveness of those organizations in benefiting the poor of London, has emerged as a key element in current policy making. Already it has been recognized that to do this well, with the aim of both assisting the beneficiaries and informing future policy making on the part of the Foundation, is a task of no small dimension and that considerable resources will need to be devoted to it. As a corollary, it has been the practice, since at least the 1930s, to see all the applicants for grants as part of the careful process of assessment which has always characterized the Foundation's grant making. An important aspect of this has always been the wish to identify and encourage applicants with potential, and much thought has likewise been given of late to ways in which this element of the Foundation's work can be expanded, with the aid of active field workers, to seek out new services worth supporting. However, the large increase in the number of applicants poses severe problems in this respect which also have to be addressed.

The signals about the state of the nation which the trustees are receiving while formulating their policy for 1992–6 are indeed confusing ones. On the one hand, the threats to the Welfare State have been loudly trumpeted and its decline bewailed, but, on the other, recent studies have indicated that it has proved remarkably resilient even if there has been some redistribution of resources within it. There has undoubtedly been a significant increase in average earnings over the past decade, but the proportion of the population living on less than half of the average income in the same period has doubled, and, according to one source, the gap between the highest paid manual workers and the lowest paid is higher than at any time since the 1880s. And, in yet another echo of the late nineteenth century, there is talk once more of a dangerous underclass, feeding off crime, which is beyond assistance.[3]

In terms of the Foundation's policy making, it is clear that there will be no decrease in the demands on its resources, and some manifestations of present need which demand early attention, such as the plight of the homeless living in 'cardboard cities' and bed and breakfast accommodation. The increase in the Foundation's income over the 1987–91 quinquennium has indeed been impressive and the predictions are of a continuing rise. That there is an ample power for good in resources for grants which are confidently expected to exceed £5 million a year cannot be doubted, but this amount must be kept in perspective. The annual budget of the social services department of a London borough in 1989–90 was on average £26 million and the total for all 33 boroughs over £850 million. This was just for local services, and does not include those provided by the state.

Already the requests for funds from the Foundation exceed those available by about three to one, and the paradoxical situation has arisen that despite having far more money at their disposal than even a few years ago, the trustees are in danger of being overwhelmed by an increase in demand which has partly been created by their own insistence on greater accessibility. In addition, there is continuing concern at the fall off in statutory funding and the inability, or unwillingness, of both the central government and local authorities to take over the funding of pilot projects started by the voluntary sector, and indeed to look to the voluntary sector to take over the funding of initiatives begun by themselves. One effect has been a reluctance on the Foundation's part to fund capital projects with future revenue implications which the statutory authorities are unlikely to meet, and it is noticeable that over the years 1987–9 the overwhelming preponderance of grants have been made for revenue purposes.

It is already abundantly clear that the challenges over the next quinquennium are likely to be as great, if not greater than those of previous ones, and that the responses will demand the same care, thought and imagination on the part of the trustees. Concepts of poverty may change, but the needs of the poor remain. As *The Times* expressed it, in its long leading article on the charities of London in 1885, 'Civilization does not tend to dispense with the occasion for charity. Rather it seems to extend the need. It is continually producing tremendous inequalities, and charity is impelled to strive to level them.'[4]

NOTES

1. PRO, CAB 124/142, q. 6011.
2. *PP*, 1890, LV, *Return of . . . certain Objections and Suggestions received by the Charity Commissioners . . .* , 5.
3. *The Independent*, 21 May 1990, 21: *The Guardian*, 5 Dec. 1990, 23; 21 Dec. 1990, 6.
4. *The Times*, 9 Jan. 1885, 9.

Appendix A Trustees of the City Parochial Foundation listed in chronological order

Name	Term of office
W. H. Dickinson	1891–1892
H. J. Felton	1891–1907
W. H. Fisher, MP	1891–1920
E. Freshfield	1891–1902
Gen. Lynedoch Gardiner	1891–1895
Dean Gregory	1891–1903
C. T. Harris	1891–1913
A. B. Hopkins	1891–1895
W. J. Orsman	1891–1899
Lord Reay	1891–1894
Sir Owen Roberts	1891–1915
Rev. W. Rogers	1891–1896
Rt. Hon. J. Savory	1891–1920
J. E. Sly	1891–1892
Evan Spicer	1891–1937
John Thomas Bedford	1891–1897
C. J. Drummond	1891–1929
Sir P. Magnus	1891–1894
	1899–1933
H. C. Saunders	1891–1893
J. Beck	1891
H. H. Gibbs	1891–1893
Quintin Hogg	1891–1901

347

Samuel Price	1892–1897
Charles Hallyburton Campbell	1892–1897
Richard Buckley Litchfield	1893–1899
Lewis Boyd Sebastian	1893–1926
Sir Albert Kaye Rollit, MP	1894–1899
Prof. (Sir) W. Ramsay	1895–1905
Rev. R. H. Hadden	1895–1909
Edward Bond	1895–1907
	1909–1920
George N. Johnson	1896–1904
Charles John Todd	1897–1908
Sidney Webb	1897–1909
T. H. Ellis	1897–1932
T. A. Organ	1899–1904
C. A. Whitmore, MP	1899–1908
Edric Bayley	1901–1920
Rev. H. C. Beeching	1903–1904
Sir Lees Knowles, MP	1903–1906
Earl of Lytton	1904–1911
Sir William Collins, MD	1904–1945
Rev. Thomas Grear	1904–1922
Sir Richard Farrant	1905–1906
Arthur Henry Aylmer Morton	1906–1911
Sir Felix Schuster	1907–1917
E. J. Horniman	1907–1932
J. J. Baddeley	1907–1926
Arthur Holt Barber	1908–1911
Rev. E. H. Pearce	1908–1919
W. Whitaker Thompson	1909–1917
Dr C. Addison	1911–1917
Sir Robert Carr Selfe	1911–1926
J. Douglass Mathews	1911–1921
Francis Farnan	1913–1932
P. M. Evans	1915–1944
Sir Edward H. Busk	1917–1925
H. W. Liversidge	1917–1921
Rev. J. H. Ellison	1919–1944
Hon. F. N. Curzon	1920–1941
Sir Wm Purdie Treloar	1920–1922
Lady Cooper	1920–1932
W. Edgar Horne, MP	1921–1941
Sir Henry P. Harris, MP	1921–1941
Sir William Phene Neal	1921–1942
(Dame Jessie) Mrs Wilton Phipps	1921–1934

Col. Sir Louis Arthur Newton	1922–1943
John Farquharson	1922–1931
Sir Andrew T. Taylor	1925–1937
Ald. Sir John Wm Baddeley	1926–1938
Walter T. Prideaux	1926–1957
Charles Hogg	1927–1935
Sir Reginald J. Neville, MP	1929–1946
David Anidjar Romain	1932–1936
Helbert A. Game	1932–1949
Sir Herbert James Read	1932–1946
John Stopher	1932–1941
Bertrand Johnson	1933–1944
Prof. L. N. G. Filon	1933–1937
Charles Robertson	1934–1965
Francis Allen	1935–1945
Richard Clewin Griffith	1936–1947
Rev. E. G. Turner	1938–1941
	1956–1970
Sir Robert H. Pickard	1938–1941
H. Arthur Baker	1938–1947
J. P. Blake	1938–1951
Sir Ernest H. Pooley	1941–1948
Cyril Turner	1941–1967
E. D. Alley	1941–1956
Lord Hambleden	1941–1947
Major Edward Chadwyck-Healey	1942–1972
Hon. Arthur Howard	1942–1971
Edgar Sefton Underwood	1942–1949
William Charles Brett	1943–1963
Rev. A. J. M. Macdonald	1944–1959
Henry Maguire	1944–1946
S. T. Shovelton	1944–1958
Colonel John Digby Mills	1945–1951
Dame Barrie Lambert	1945–1947
Lady Deller	1946–1957
Sir George Sampson Elliston	1946–1952
Sir Cosmo Parkinson	1946–1966
Seymour Howard	1947–1949
W. H. Green	1947–1953
A. S. Holness	1947–1959
T. C. Harrowing	1947–1981
Prof. D. Hughes Parry	1948–1953
J. K. Newson-Smith	1949–1961
Lewis F. Sturge	1950–1973

Sir John W. Russell	1950–1977
Mrs L'Estrange Malone	1951
Lord Burden	1951–1963
Mrs Irene Chaplin	1951–1969
J. Lionel P. Denny	1952–1977
Dr D. W. Logan	1953–1967
Hon. John Fremantle (later Lord Cottesloe)	1953–1977
Walter A. Prideaux	1957–1984
Lady Walton	1957–1967
I. P. Shaw	1958–1987
R. D. McLellan	1959–1968
Ven. O. H. Gibbs-Smith	1959–1961
Roland Francis Champness	1961–1969
Ven. G. Appleton	1962–1963
Ven. Martin Sullivan	1963–1977
Sir James Brown	1963–1969
R. W. Skinner	1963–1970
Sir George Haynes	1966–1975
Alfred F. J. Chorley	1966–1969
Baroness Phillips	1967–1973
Dr L. L. Pownall	1967–1974
E. T. Floyd Ewin	1967–1987
Professor Denys C. Holland	1968–1972
Lady Donaldson	1969–1975
Sir Graham Rowlandson	1969–1975
	1977–1983
Rev. Canon H. W. Hinds	1969–1986
J. F. M. Smallwood	1969–
James Mansfield Keith	1970–1984
E. A. Parker	1970–1979
Earl of Limerick	1971–
Angus F. Murray	1972–1975
Dr C. J. Holdsworth	1972–1977
John Udal	1973–
Lord Henniker	1973–1990
Dr R. C. Tress	1974–1977
	1979–1989
Sir Ashley Bramall	1975–1987
Lady Marre	1975–
J. N. Butterwick	1975–1987
Henry W. S. Horlock	1975–1979
Leslie Freeman	1977–1983
Prof. J. P. Quilliam	1977–1989

Lady Melchett	1977–1978
Ven. Sam Woodhouse	1977–1979
Prof. Gerald Manners	1977–
Ven. Frank Harvey	1978–1986
Harold B. Titchener	1979–1986
P. H. Champness	1979–1983
R. L. Payton	1981–
Dr David Avery	1983–1989
Brigadier J. J. Packard	1983–1989
J. L. Reed	1983–1989
P. B. Burke	1984–
Mrs Rosemary Humphrays	1984–
P. E. Haynes	1986–
David Brown	1987
Prof. Julian Franks	1987–
Rabbi Julia Neuberger	1987–
Mrs Ros Howells	1987–
Ven. George Cassidy	1987–
Prof. Stewart R. Sutherland	1988–1990
Lady Ponsonby	1988–1991
Mrs Winifred Tumim	1989–
Ian D. Gainsford	1989–
Ms Maggie Baxter	1989–
John Alfred Barker	1989–
Richard Martin	1989–
Lord Elton	1990–
John Muir	1990–

Appendix B   Chairmen and Clerks of the Foundation

Chairmen	Term of office
Rt Hon. Joseph Savory	1891–1920
Sir Evan Spicer	1920–1933
P. M. Evans	1934–1944
Walter T. Prideaux	1944–1956
Sir Arthur Howard	1957–1971
Sir Edward R. Chadwyck-Healey	1971
Walter A. Prideaux	1972–1980
John Smallwood	1981–

Clerks	Term of office
Howard Batten	1891–1907
Ernald R. Warre	1907–1929
Donald Allen	1930–1965
H. A. S. 'Tim' Johnston	1965–1967
Bryan H. Woods	1968–1986
Timothy Cook	1986–

Appendix C   Gross income of the Foundation

Year	Central Fund £'000s	City Church Fund £'000s	Total £'000s	Retail Price Index* Jan. 1987=100
1892	57	34	91	2.5
1897	61	37	98	2.5
1902	66	45	111	2.6
1907	56	45	101	2.7
1912	58	46	104	2.8
1917	60	55	115	5.0
1922	67	66	133	5.2
1927	74	69	143	4.7
1932	89	76	165	4.1
1937	105	71	176	4.4
1942	70	60	130	—
1947	92	71	163	7.9
1952	138	98	236	10.3
1957	205	106	311	12.0
1962	275	134	409	13.4
1967	353	177	530	15.8

Year	Central Fund £'000s	City Church Fund £'000s	Total £'000s	Retail Price Index* Jan. 1987=100
1972	408	241	649	21.7
1977	718	715	1,433	46.1
1982	1,502	821	2,323	81.2
1987	2,459	1,680	4,139	101.9
1988	3,480	2,509	5,989	106.9
1989	6,473	3,057	9,530	115.2
1990	6,137	3,869	10,006	126.1

*The retail price index is based on the long-term index of consumer goods and services issued by the Central Statistical Office back to 1914, and before that on figures given in C. H. Feinstein, *National Income, Expenditure and Output of the United Kingdom, 1855–1965*. There are no figures available for 1942.

Appendix D Organizations receiving fresh grants in 1910, 1938, 1970 and 1990

ORGANIZATIONS RECEIVING FRESH GRANTS IN 1910

After-care Association for Blind, Deaf and Crippled Children
Bermondsey Medical Mission
Homes for Mothers and Babies, Woolwich
London Playing Fields Society
Metropolitan Association for the Befriending of Young Servants
Metropolitan Provident Medical Association
Queen Victoria Jubilee Institute for Nurses
Ragged School Union and Shaftesbury Society
University of London, University Extension

In addition, grants were made both under the Scheme and as supplementary or special grants to 17 polytechnics and kindred institutes.

ORGANIZATIONS RECEIVING FRESH GRANTS IN 1938

Ashton Playing Fields
Central Council for District Nursing in London
Central Council for the Social Welfare of Girls and Women in London
Charity Organisation Society

Chigwell Row Camp
Children's Central Rescue Fund
Children's Fresh Air Mission
Children's Play Centres
Children's Playroom, W2
Christ Church United Clubs, Kennington
City of London – Luncheon Club – London Federation of Boys' Clubs
Cudham Camping Site
Factory Girls' Country Holiday Fund
Foundling Hospital Site, Dinner Club for Children
Greater London Fund for the Blind
Highway Clubs in East London
Hostels for Crippled and Invalid Women Workers, Camberwell
Inns of Court Mission
Invalid Children's Aid Association
John Woolman Settlement, EC1
King's Roll Clerks Association
Kingsley Hall, Bow
Kingsley Hall, Dagenham
Knebworth Memorial Camps
London Children's Gardens Fund
London Council of Social Service
London County Council – Purchase of Gymnastic kit
London County Council Evening Institutes, Sports Association
London Gardens Society
London Schools Cricket Association
London Union of Girls Clubs
London YMCA
MABYS Association for the Care of Young Girls
National Association of Boys' Clubs
National Council of Girls' Clubs
National Library for the Blind
Nazeing Camp
Over Thirty Association
Oxford House
Packington Estate, Islington
Proposed Observation Centre for Juvenile Delinquents
Provision of Occupational Industries for the Physically Handicapped
Seaside Camps for London Boys
South London Family Camp, Deal
Stanhope Institute
Toynbee Hall
Wallingford Farm Training Colony
Women's Employment Federation

Women's Holiday Fund
YMCA (Metropolitan Union)

In addition, grants were made to 18 polytechnics and kindred institutions.

ORGANIZATIONS RECEIVING FRESH GRANTS IN 1970

Boys' Brigade – London District
Carter Foundation
Centre '70, West Norwood
Community Settlement, W11
Delves House Trust
Dockland Settlements
Dunoran House, Bickley
Eliot Housing Association
Employment Fellowship
Ex-Service Fellowship Centres
Family Service Units – Haringey
Family Service Units – Islington
Family Welfare Association
Frimhurst Recuperative House
Girl Guides Association – Chigwell Row and Cudham Camps
Greater London Association for the Disabled
Greater London Federation of Samaritans
Greater London Fund for the Blind
Havens Guild
Inner London Education Authority – School Health Service
Inner London Sessions Probationers Fund
International Social Service of Great Britain
Kitchen
Lady Margaret Hall Settlement
Lingfield Hospital School
London and Middlesex Playing Fields Association
London Council of Social Service
London Council of Social Service – Community Development in London
London Federation of Boys' Clubs
London Marriage Guidance Council
London Union of Youth Clubs
Love Walk Hostel for Disabled Women Workers
National Association of Boys' Clubs

National Association for the Care and Resettlement of Offenders
National Federation of Housing Societies
Navy League – Sen. Cadet Corps
North Kensington Neighbourhood Law Centre
Notting Hill Ecumenical Centre
Outward Bound Trust
Over Forty Association for Women Workers
Poplar, Blackwall and District Rowing Club
Prisoners' Wives Service
Royal Hospital and Home for Incurables
Royal London Prisoners Aid Society
Scout Association
Seafarers Education Service and College of the Sea
St. Anne's Trust for the Blind-Deaf
St. Christopher's Hospice
St. Raphael Association
Tavistock Institute of Human Relations
Telegraph Hill Neighbourhood Council
Third Feathers Club
Three-in-One Club
Upward Bound Trust
Wellclose Square Fund
Wellgarth Nursery Training College
Western Cerebral Palsy Centre
Winant and Clayton Volunteers
Winged Fellowship Trust
Women's Royal Voluntary Service
YMCA
YWCA
Youth and Music Limited

In addition, grants were made to about 55 other organizations as a result of commitments made in previous years.

ORGANIZATIONS RECEIVING FRESH GRANTS IN 1990

Abbeyfield Mangrove Society
Action for Disability, Tower Hamlets
African Women's Association, Ealing
African Women's Support Group, Southwark
Afro-Caribbean Education Resource Project
Age Concern, Ealing

Age Concern, Waltham Forest
All Saints Church – Youth Project
Alone in London Service
Apex Trust
Apple Theatre, Lewisham
APPNA – Greenwich Muslim Women's Project
Archbishop Sumner's C.E. Primary School, Lambeth
Association to Combat Huntington's Chorea
Barking and Dagenham Bereavement Service
Barking and Dagenham Voluntary Services Association
Barnet Care Attendant Scheme
Bede House Association, Southwark
Birkbeck College – Project to Extend Educational Opportunities to
    the Asian Adult Unemployed
Black Mental Health Project, Lewisham
Blenheim Project, W10
Body Positive
Bondway Housing Association
Bootstrap Company Limited – Bootstrap Enterprises, Hackney
Borough Recreation and Arts Group
Bow Nursery Centre
Bradians Trust – Skeet House, Orpington
Bridge Project Trust, Bethnal Green
British Association of Cancer United Patients
British Refugee Council
Brixton Against Robbery Project
Calthorpe Project, Camden
The Cambodian Society in the United Kingdom
Camden One Parent Respite Service
Canonbury Playground, Islington
Carers National Association, Contact-a-Family and the Association of
    Crossroads Care Scheme
CASH – Community Accountancy Self Help
Charlton Park School, Greenwich
Charterhouse Mission – Charterhouse-in-Southwark
Chelsea Hospice Trust
Christ Church (Oxford) United Clubs – Oval House, SE11
City Roads (Crisis Intervention), EC1
Civil Liberties Trust
Community Concern for Substance Abuse, Barking and Dagenham
Community Drug Project, Southwark
Community Economy Limited – Pier Training Shop, Newham
Community Language Centre, Kensington and Chelsea
Conservation of Manpower Unit – Hornsey YMCA Drug Clinic

The CORE Trust, Westminster
Creative and Supportive Trust
Crossroads Care Attendant Scheme, Hillingdon
Croydon Disablement Association
Croydon Opportunity Group for Children with Special Needs
Croydon Pastoral Foundation
Cuckoo Estate Tenants and Residents Association, Ealing
Cultural Partnership Limited, Hackney
Dale Youth Club, W11
Dame Colet House, Tower Hamlets
Dance for Everyone
Davenant Centre – Jagonari Women's Educational Resource Centre
The Daycare Trust
Deptford Mission – Disabled People's Contact
Disability Action Sutton
Disability Alliance Educational and Research Association
Drake Research Project, Greenwich
Drink Crisis Centre
Ealing Family Housing Association – Southall Day Centre
East of London Handicapped Adventure Playground
Edgecombe Community Centre Association, Croydon
Elfrida Rathbone (Camden) – Special Education Advice and Support
    Service
Eltham United Reformed Church, Greenwich
Enfield Crossroads Care Scheme
Enfield Disablement Association
Equal Play Adventure Park, Hackney
The Factory Community Project and Youth Centre, Islington
Family Link, Greenwich
Family Rights Group
Family Welfare Association – Islington City Choice Centre
Filipino Migrant Centre, Kensington and Chelsea
Finsbury Park Methodist Church – Homeless Families Project
Friends of Battersea Churches Housing Trust
Friends of Cheviots – Cheviots Children's Centre, Enfield
Friends of Park Avenue Day Centre, Enfield
The Gillespie Early Years Centre Association, Islington
Goldcrest Youth Centre, Croydon
Good Shepherd & St. Peter, Lewisham
Greenwich Association of Disabled People
Greenwich Theatre Limited
Hackney Marsh Team Parish Church Council – Homerton Youth
    Project
Hackney Quest

Hammersmith and Fulham Association for Mental Health
The Hampden Community Association
Hampstead Community Action, Camden
Handicapped Adventure Playground Association
Handicapped Adventure Playground Association for Ealing – The Log
  Cabin
Hanley Crouch Community Group
Haringey Action Group on Alcohol
Haringey Women and Health Centre
Harlington Hospice Association (Hillingdon)
Harrow Home Start
Hi-Pact
Highbury Roundhouse Association, Islington
Hillingdon Legal Resources Centre
Holloway Neighbourhood Group
Home Farm Development Trust
Homeless Action & Accommodation
Homerton Community Centre, E9 – Chats Palace
Hornsey Lane Tenants Association
Hospital Radio Hillingdon
Hounslow Association of Disabled People
Hoxton Health Group, Hackney
Immigrants' Aid Trust
InterChange Trust, Camden
International Educational and Cultural Movement (London UK),
  Lewisham
Islington Boys' Club
Islington Mental Health Forum
Islington Voluntary Action Council
Islington Women and Mental Health Centre
Jackson's Lane Community Centre Association, Haringey
Jardin Infantil Latino Americano Mafalda
Kensington and Chelsea Talking Newspaper Association
Kings Corner Project, EC1
Kingsgate Community Association, Camden
Kingston and Richmond Furniture Project
L'Arche Limited – L'Arche in Lambeth
Laburnum Boat Club, Hackney
Lady Margaret Hall Settlement
Lambeth Wel-Care
League of British Muslims UK, Redbridge
Lewisham African Organisation
Lewisham Indo-Chinese Refugee Group
Lewisham Women's Aid

London Borough of Hackney Education Department – Parental Involvement in Primary Education Project
London Playing Fields Society – Douglas Eyre Playing Field
London School of Economics and Political Science (University of London) – Short Course Diploma: Mental Health Work with the Continued Care Client
London Tamil Sangam, Newham
London Voluntary Service Council
Maharashtra Mandal London
Mansfield House University Settlement, E13, Lambourne End Outdoor Centre
Mary Ward Settlement – Mary Ward Centre, WC1
Marylands Community Association, W9 – Yaa Asantewaa Arts Centre
Melting Pot Foundation, Lambeth
Merton Afro-Caribbean Organisation
Merton Voluntary Service Council
Migrants Resource Centre
Milton House Trust, Islington
Mission Dine Club for the Elderly, Brent
Morley College
Mount Bethel Senior Citizens Club, Brent
Music Works, Lambeth
The National Gypsy Council
Neighbourhood Care Project, Newham
The New Assembly of Churches – Social Rehabilitation and Aftercare Project
New Horizon Youth Centre, Camden
Newham Shortstop
No Fixed Abode, Tower Hamlets
North East London Autistic Society
North Lambeth Day Centre Limited
North London College, Islington – The Mentor Programme
Nucleus (Earls Court Community Action Limited)
One-to-One – Enfield Scheme
Orange Tree Theatre Limited
Outdoor Activities Initiative
The Oxford Boys' Club Trust, NW6
Oxford House in Bethnal Green
Pakamani, Wandsworth
Pepperpot Club, Kensington and Chelsea
The Polytechnic of North London
The Project for Advice, Counselling and Education
Pumphouse Educational Trust, Southwark
Putney Vale Youth Group, Wandsworth

Pyramid Arts Development Company Limited
Queen Mary College – Access Course in Science, Engineering and
   Medicine
Redbridge Citizens Advice Bureau
Redbridge Voluntary Services Association
Release Legal Emergency and Drugs Service
Riverpoint (Single Homeless) Limited, Hammersmith
The Runnymede Trust
Sea Cadet Association, Hendon Unit
Shades Project, Redbridge
Shaftesbury Park Primary School, Wandsworth
Shalom Justice and Peace Centre, Newham
Shelter Westminster Action Team
Shepherds Bush Families Project
Shobujshati, Tower Hamlets
Short Stay Young Homeless Project
Silwood Family Centre, Lewisham
Silwood Youth Centre, Southwark
Soho Community Centre Trust – Family Centre
Somali Counselling Project
South Islington Law Centre
Southside Rehabilitation Association, Lambeth
Southwark Diocesan Board of Education – Access Course
Southwark Diocesan Housing Association
Specialist Information Training Resource Agency
Springboard Islington Trust
St. Alfege with St. Peter's Primary School, Greenwich
St. Andrew's United Reformed Church, Ealing
St. Angela's Centre for Deaf People, Redbridge
St. Hilda's East Community Centre, E2
St. John's Church, Southall
St. Luke Great Ilford, Redbridge – Community Project
St. Margaret's House, Bethnal Green
St. Mary's Church, Woolwich
St. Mary's Family Centre, Croydon
St. Pancras Housing Association – St. Pancras Care and Repair
St. Peter's Church, Norbiton – The Parish Rooms
The Standing Conference of Ethnic Minority Senior Citizens
Stillbirth and Neonatal Death Society
Stonham Housing Association – Orwell House, Lewisham
Strathcona Theatre Company
Strutton Housing Association
Studio 3, Barking and Dagenham
Sudan Relief and Rehabilitation Association

The Sundial Project, Tower Hamlets
Surrey Docks Farm, Southwark
Tabernacle Community Association, W11
Tachbrook Family Centre, Pimlico
Tadworth Playgroup, Southwark
Theatro Technis, Camden
Threshold Centre
Toffee Park Playground and Club Association, Islington
Tower Hamlets Mission
The Uganda Asylum Seekers Association
Unity Centre of South London
University of London (Institute of Education), HIV/AIDS Young
    People's Project
Victim Support, Lambeth
Vine United Reformed Church, Redbridge
Wakefield Tricycle Company Limited
Waltham Forest Young People's Housing Project – Ashiana Project
Wandsworth Housing Support Project
Wellgate Community Farm, Barking and Dagenham
Wendlesworth Drop-In Centre, Wandsworth
West London Committee for the Protection of Children
West London Tamil School – Computer Centre, Brent
Westminster Community Initiative
Westminster Play Association – Lisson Green Play Project
Westminster Women's Aid
Westway Nursery Association
Women Against Sexual Harassment
Women's Liaison Group, Barking and Dagenham
Woodgrange Park Village Co-op Limited, Newham
Workers' Educational Association – London District
Working for Children in Wandsworth – Parents Information Centre
YWCA London and Southern England Region – Avenues Unlimited

In addition, grants were made to about 125 other organizations as a
result of commitments made in previous years.

Index